TO

BLANCHE

who knows what it meant

if not what it means

PREFACE

The problems with which this book is mainly concerned may appear to be technical, narrow, and limited. Technical they may be, but narrow and limited they are not, for they have ramifications extending over the whole area of moral philosophy, and consequently over the whole of life. The book begins with the problem whether a certain line of argument, of frequent occurrence in moral contexts, is valid—that is, can ever be used to establish a moral judgment—and if so, under what conditions. It ends with an attempt to determine the basis of morality, and to solve the problem of the justification of moral principles. Thus it deals with the basic problems of moral philosophy. It aims to establish a rational basis for distinguishing between right and wrong, and thus to lay the groundwork for a rational and normative system of ethics. These are high aims, and it is not for me to say whether I have accomplished them. But this at least is what I have attempted.

The consideration central to the book is the argument that underlies the very common question: "What would happen if everyone did that?": "If everyone did that, the consequences would be terrible; therefore you ought not to do that." This sort of argument is sometimes called the argument from universalization. Here it is called the generalization argument; hence we have the topic of generalization in ethics. And on the problems connected with generalization in ethics the book aims at comprehensiveness and completeness of treatment: on this matter it is intended to be a treatise.

Since the pivotal problem of the book is one concerning the validity of a certain type of argument, the book is also an essay in logic, specifically in the logic of ethics, although on this matter it does not aim at comprehensiveness or completeness of treatment. The thesis put forward is that the procedure of generalization in ethics is perfectly valid, when properly used and qualified, that it is central and decisive in moral reasoning, and that it is fundamental in any adequate moral philosophy. It is, I claim, the fundamental principle of morality. But it is not the only principle, and its proper understanding requires that it be taken together with a number of others, which are formulated and elaborated in the course of this book. These various principles, taken together, form a system. So the book contains also at least the rudiments of a system of moral philosophy.

But I have not aimed at presenting a complete system of moral philosophy. No moral philosophy can be complete unless it is applied to the actual institutions and practices of society. To do this it must be supplemented by a philosophy of politics, economics, and law, as well as a theory of value, which, together with ethics, logic, and aesthetics, make up the basic normative sciences. Needless to say, I have not attempted this. Moreover, in addition to not dealing with the morality of institutions, I have not dealt with questions of international or group morality, with the morality of laws, evaluations, moral psychology, or problems of character. Nor will the reader find in the book any recipes for the conduct of life. This is a book on the theory of morals, and though it is intended to be normative and not merely speculative, it does not contain a set of nostrums or admonitions.

A preface is, in practice, the appropriate place for the expression of a more personal note. This book grew out of my doctoral dissertation, presented to Cornell University in 1952. Although I have been working on this subject, off and on, for several years now, I am even now only too aware of several serious deficiencies, and since there are some of which I am aware, there must be at least as many of which I am not aware. Yet the book would be more defective than it is if it were not for the help, encouragement, and stimulation I received from my teachers at Cornell: Max Black, Stuart Brown, Arthur

PREFACE

Murphy, and Gregory Vlastos; and which I have continued to
receive, at various stages, from William Hay and Julius Wein-
berg and my other colleagues in the Philosophy Department of
the University of Wisconsin. To Atwell Turquette and Fred-
erick Will, my teachers at the University of Illinois, I owe a
debt of great magnitude: they generated my enthusiasm for
philosophy. The book assumed its present shape in 1956-57, as
a result of a year's leisure in which to work on it, received
through the generosity of the Committee to Advance Original
Work in Philosophy of the Western Division of the American
Philosophical Association. I am also grateful to the Research
Committee of the Graduate School of the University of Wisconsin for research support in the summer of 1955 and the year
1956-57; and to Dean Mark Ingraham of the College of Letters
and Science for support of various kinds. To William Marshall
and Paul Ziff I owe a debt for obstinate opposition and vigorous
criticism. Abraham Melden of the University of Washington
and Israel Scheffler of Harvard University read the manuscript
as a whole, and I am grateful to them for their kind and helpful remarks. I must also express my appreciation for the help
and enthusiasm of my editor at Knopf, Gerard McCauley.
Lastly, my debt to my wife is incalculable, and is not really
fittingly expressed in the dedication. One cannot even begin
to repay devotion.

                                                    M. G. S.

Madison, Wisconsin
September 15, 1960

PREFACE 1971

Since it was first published, in 1961, this book has enjoyed an
unusual amount of discussion, criticism, and commentary. It
has been enshrined, or perhaps embalmed, in a number of doctoral dissertations. And there has been a veritable carnage of
opinions. Thus one reviewer, who thought the book was easy
reading, regarded it as a collection of errors; another, who regarded it as difficult reading, thought it might well be right;
and so on. This has, on the whole, been fun, and it has certainly
been enlightening, but it has not been a wholly unmixed bless-
ing. For now some commentators have suggested that it be
revised, to take account of the various criticisms that have been
made, so that I could make it clear just where I now stand on
the points that have proved to be the most controversial. I feel
that at least this idea deserves some sort of reply from me.

I feel the force of this demand, and am even somewhat sym-
pathetic to it. But I am not convinced that basic revision is
needed, and I actually doubt whether it would be desirable. I
have had little inclination to undertake any work of revision,
and I cannot regard a matter of this kind as a matter of duty or
even of professional obligation. Certainly none of the principles
set forth in this work would show it to be.

Consequently, in the present impression the text of this book
has been reprinted unaltered, except for the correction of a
number of typographical errors. I am grateful to the various
critics and correspondents who have brought these to my attention. I am also grateful to those critics and correspondents who
have pointed out, often in very subtle and sophisticated ways,
other errors, as they take them to be, of a philosophically more
fundamental nature.

The inevitable dialectical process, in which the criticisms of the critics have themselves been criticized, can easily leave one with a somewhat confused impression. So let it be said, here and now, that I am by no means convinced that all of the errors that have been charged against this book have been proved, or that very many of them are as serious as they have been alleged to be. This is not to claim that it does not contain some serious mistakes. But I do not at all agree that its main thesis (see, for example, p. vi) has been vitiated. Nor do I at all agree that its main argument (since there is no such thing) is fallacious in a way that is quite easily shown. But I cannot deal with these matters here. I intend to return to this subject at some later time, after the dust raised by some of the most minute philosophers has settled, after I have acquired still greater perspective, and after some other work, not altogether unconnected with the theme of this volume, has been completed.

I would not leave the impression that I do not appreciate and have not learned from the various discussions and commentaries I have been enabled to see. It has, on the whole, been an interesting experience, and I have learned a great deal, even if I have not always learned the lesson some critic was attempting to impart. A number of notices, incidentally, have come to my attention only by accident, so I must assume that there are others of which I am unaware. So I should appreciate it if copies, or else notices, be sent to me of discussions that have so far appeared or that might appear in future. Perhaps some day the subject can again be put in some semblance of order, philosophical as well as bibliographical.

M.G.S.

Madison, Wisconsin
February 16, 1971

ACKNOWLEDGMENTS

Parts of Chapters II, V, and VIII, as well as sections 2 and 4 of Chapter X, have been previously published, as specified in the Bibliographical Notes. I am grateful to the editors of *Mind* and *The Philosophical Review*, the University of Chicago Press, publishers of *Ethics* (copyright 1959 by the University of Chicago), and the University of Washington Press, publishers of *Essays in Moral Philosophy* (1958), for permission to use this previously published material.

I am also grateful to the following publishers or editors of periodicals for permission to quote passages from material published or copyrighted by them.

George Allen & Unwin Ltd., for permission to quote from *Equality*, by R. H. Tawney, and *The Phenomenology of Mind*, by Hegel, translated by J. B. Baillie.

Appleton-Century-Crofts, Inc., for permission to quote from *Ethics*, by Frank Chapman Sharp, copyright 1928 by The Century Company.

J. W. Arrowsmith Ltd., for permission to quote from *Studies in Philosophy*, by G. C. Field, copyright 1935 by the University of Bristol.

Cambridge University Press, for permission to use the excerpts from *Principia Ethica*, by G. E. Moore, and *The Uses of Argument*, by Stephen Toulmin.

Jonathan Cape Limited, for permission to quote from *The Logic of Personality*, by Bernard Mayo.

The Clarendon Press for permission to use quotations from *Kant's Ethical Theory*, by Sir David Ross; *Kantian Ethics*, by A. E. Teale; and Hegel's *Philosophy of Right*, translated by T. M. Knox.

Houghton Mifflin Company, for permission to quote from *A Modern Introduction to Ethics*, by Lucius Garvin.

Hutchinson's University Library, for permission to use quotations from *The Moral Law*, by H. J. Paton.

Jackson, Son & Co. Ltd., for permission to quote from *The Critical Philosophy of Immanuel Kant*, by Edward Caird, published by James MacLehose & Sons.

Longmans, Green & Co. Ltd., for permission to use passages from Kant's *Critique of Practical Reason and Other Works on the Theory of Ethics*, translated by T. K. Abbott.

Macmillan & Co. Ltd., London, and St. Martin's Press, Inc., New York, for permission to quote from *Space, Time, and Deity*, by S. Alexander; and *Experiments in Living*, by A. Macbeath.

Methuen & Co. Ltd., for permission to use quotations from Kant's *Lectures on Ethics*, translated by Louis Infield.

The New York Times, for permission to quote from an article by Hanson W. Baldwin.

The New Yorker, for permission to use various quotations.

Penguin Books Ltd., for permission to quote a passage from *Ethics*, by P. H. Nowell-Smith.

Prentice-Hall, Inc., for permission to quote from *Critical Thinking*, 2nd ed., by Max Black, © 1952 by Prentice-Hall, Inc., Englewood Cliffs, N. J.; and from *Ethical Theory*, by Richard B. Brandt, © 1959 by Prentice-Hall, Inc.

The Ronald Press Company, for permission to quote from *Ethics: A Critical Introduction*, by A. Campbell Garnett, copyright 1960 by The Ronald Press Company.

The University of Chicago Press, for permission to quote from *The Categorical Imperative* (1948), by H. J. Paton, copyright 1948 by the University of Chicago; and from an article by C. D. Broad, in *The International Journal of Ethics*, vol. XXVI, copyright 1916 by the University of Chicago.

Yale University Press, for permission to quote from *The Growth of the Law*, by Benjamin N. Cardozo, and *Ethics and Language*, by Charles L. Stevenson.

Full references will be found in the appropriate footnotes.

A number of other publishers, periodicals, and authors were kind enough not to require special acknowledgment, aside from the footnote citation.

CONTENTS

ANALYSIS

GENERALIZATION

IN ETHICS

❀

CHAPTER I

INTRODUCTORY

§ 1 §

The question "What would happen if everyone did that?" is one with which we are all familiar. We have heard it asked, and perhaps have asked it ourselves. We have some familiarity with the sort of context in which it would be appropriate to ask it. Thus we understand that it is either elliptical for or a prelude to saying, "If everyone did that, the consequences would be disastrous," and that this is often considered a good reason for concluding that one ought not to do that. The situations in which this sort of consideration might be advanced are of course exceedingly diverse. One who announces his intention of not voting in some election might be met by the question, "What would happen if no one voted?" If no one voted, the government would collapse, or the democratic system would be repudiated, and this is deemed by many to indicate decisively that everyone should vote. Again, one who disapproves of another's attempts to avoid military service might point out: "If everyone refused to serve, we would lose the war." The members of a discussion group, which meets to discuss papers presented by members, presumably all realize that each should take a turn in reading a paper, even one who may not want to and prefers to take part in the discussions only, because if everyone refused the club would dissolve, and there would be no discussions. This sort of consideration would not be decisive to one who did not care whether the club dissolved. But it undoubtedly would be decisive to one who enjoys the meetings and wishes them to continue.

Each of these cases provides an example of the use or application of a type of argument which I propose to call *the generalization argument*: "If everyone were to do that, the consequences would be disastrous (or undesirable); therefore, no one ought to do that." Any argument of the form "The consequences of no one's doing that would be undesirable; therefore everyone ought to do that" is also, obviously, an instance of the generalization argument. It is this line of argument, and considerations resembling it, that will be at the very center of this inquiry.

The basic problem about the generalization argument (which can be thought of indifferently as either an argument or a moral principle) is to determine the conditions under which it is a good or valid one, that is to say, the conditions under which the fact that the consequences of *everyone's* acting in a certain way would be undesirable, provides a good reason for concluding that it is wrong for *anyone* to act in that way. For there are conditions under which the generalization argument is obviously not applicable, and it is necessary to determine just what they are. The instances presented above are ones in which the consideration of the consequences of everyone's acting in a certain way seems clearly relevant to a moral judgment about that way of acting. But there are others in which this sort of consideration is just as clearly irrelevant. For instance, while "humanity would probably perish from cold if everyone produced food, and would certainly starve if everyone made clothes or built houses," [1] it would be absurd to infer from this that no one ought to produce food or to build houses.

It might be thought that this is a counterexample, which proves the generalization argument to be invalid or fallacious generally. To argue that you ought not to do something be-

[1] Morris R. Cohen, *The Faith of a Liberal* (New York: Henry Holt and Company, 1946), p. 86.

cause of what would happen if *everyone* did, though it is somewhat like arguing that you ought not to do something because of what would happen if *you* do, is also quite different. On the pattern of, "If you were to do that the consequences would be disastrous, therefore you ought not to do that," we can argue, "If everyone were to do that the consequences would be disastrous, therefore not everyone ought to do that." But the transition from "not everyone ought to do that" to "no one ought to do that," from "not everyone has the right" to "no one has the right," seems surely fallacious. It is like saying that no one has red hair because not everyone does. Yet this transition, or something very much like it, is essential to the generalization argument.

But there is actually no fallacy involved in the generalization argument, though there may be in particular applications of it. For it is not always a fallacy to argue from "some" to "all," and the belief that it is always fallacious is merely a prejudice arising out of a preoccupation with certain types of statements. It is a fact of logic that if any one argument of a certain form is invalid then all arguments of that form are invalid, and this is the principle underlying the use of counter-examples. Yet it involves an inference from "some" to "all." It is true that the generalization argument involves an inference from "not everyone has the right" to "no one has the right," from "it would not be right for everyone" to "it would not be right for anyone." This inference, however, is mediated, and therefore qualified, by the principle that *what is right (or wrong) for one person must be right (or wrong) for any similar person in similar circumstances.* For obvious reasons I shall refer to this principle as "the generalization *principle*," even though it has traditionally been known as the principle of fairness or justice or impartiality.

The generalization principle is not likely to be regarded as fallacious. Yet it has frequently been regarded as vacuous and hence devoid of significant application. This also is not so, and the best way of showing this is by showing how it can be significantly and usefully applied. The generalization argument presupposes and consequently depends upon the gener-

alization principle, and the generalization principle is certainly
of considerable interest in its own right. So the next chapter
will be devoted to determining the meaning and importance of
this principle. This will involve a consideration of the meaning and function of the qualification "similar persons in similar circumstances," and this in turn will provide us with the
basis for determining its connections with moral judgment and
moral reasoning.

My examination of the generalization *argument* will follow
this, and my method here, for the most part, will be to consider a number of fairly plausible objections to it and to show
that they are not decisive. This will take us some distance towards the formulation of the conditions under which the
generalization argument is valid.

§ 2 §

The pivotal problem of this book is the examination of these
two principles. But it is not an end in itself. My ultimate aim
is to determine, through the examination of these principles,
how moral judgments can rationally be supported, how moral
perplexities can rationally be resolved, and how moral disputes can rationally be settled. Some moral arguments are
good ones; some are not. Some facts have moral relevance;
some do not. What is the basis for this distinction, and how
can it be made out in particular cases? These are some of the
questions that I shall attempt to answer, though I shall not in
all cases attempt to deal with them directly, in their full generality. What I hope to do is to lay the groundwork for a rational and normative system of ethics. And in doing this I
hope to exhibit, if only incidentally, the "genuine interplay of
practical issues and theoretic philosophy." [2]

In this process some recognition must be given to the claims
of moral skepticism. There are many varieties of this. Yet they
all agree in maintaining, in one way or another, that there
can be no such thing as a good reason for a moral judgment,

[2] Morris R. Cohen, *Reason and Nature* (New York: Harcourt, Brace
and Company, 1931), p. xv.

that there are no valid moral arguments, that morality has no rational basis, and that the difference between right and wrong is merely a matter of taste, opinion, or convention. Such skepticism, of course, is not new. What is new is the extent of its influence. This is an age of dogmatic moral judgment and skeptical moral philosophy, and that the two go hand in hand is not just a coincidence.

I shall have something to say about some varieties of moral skepticism as we go along, though I shall not engage in a full-dress treatment of the subject. Yet I should like to mention here that, even though such skeptical theories have had some value as a stimulus to more accurate thought about the matter, there is an important sense in which all such theories are morally irrelevant. They have no relevance to the problems of *morality* (and at the same time they are productive of moral confusion). Hence they can be no substitute for a theory that does. To one who is trying to decide whether something ought or ought not to be done, it is no help to be told that moral judgments are all subjective, or merely expressive of attitudes. And to claim that therefore one ought not to have some moral problem, because moral ideas have no objective or rational basis, is to depart from the moral neutrality that is now so widely regarded as the paragon of philosophic virtue.

In saying that an ethical theory should be relevant to the solution of moral problems, I do not mean that it must provide automatic solutions to them. This is out of the question, in any case, for in morality the factor of judgment can never be totally eliminated, and the problems of morality often depend upon determinations of fact for which no theory can provide a guarantee. What I mean is that an ethical theory should help to clarify the situations in which moral problems arise, and throw some light on the factors that are relevant to and the conditions to be met by a satisfactory solution. It should, in other words, help to bring order out of confusion. The problems of ethics, even those at the highest levels of abstraction, arise, and have in fact arisen, out of the attempt to solve practical and concrete moral problems. Hence one of the tests of an ethical theory—and for practical purposes the most important test—is its relevance to these very problems.

It is not, of course, the only test. We all have moral beliefs, beliefs about what is right and what is wrong. If we did not we should not have any moral problems. For moral problems arise out of the moral beliefs we have—from the fact that they are sometimes inadequate, often vague, and frequently in conflict. These beliefs provide the data and the starting point for ethical theory, which never arises in a vacuum. Ethical theory, which is simply systematized reflection about morality, arises out of the attempt to coordinate these beliefs, to systematize them, to make them coherent, and to make sense out of them. An ethical theory, therefore, may be defined as "a theory about the nature and basis of morality and the standards for moral judgment, which arises out of the moral perplexities of everyday life." [3] Its first task, consequently, is to explain—make clear the reasons—why certain kinds of acts are right and others wrong (what makes right actions right and wrong actions wrong). This obviously presupposes that some actions are right and others wrong, and this is a supposition that must be defended in the development of the theory. But the first test of an ethical theory is how well it performs this task of *explanation*.

Secondly, an ethical theory should be *coherent*, both with itself and with other widely accepted ideas (what on other grounds is known to be true), and should help to make our moral ideas and beliefs coherent. Thirdly, such a theory should *enlighten*, in the sense of being relevant, in the way explained, to moral problems.

So there are at least three tests of an ethical theory—explanation, coherence, and enlightenment—and the theory to be developed in this book is intended to be submitted to these tests.

[3] Cf. Arthur E. Murphy, *The Uses of Reason* (New York: The Macmillan Company, 1943), p. 141: An ethical theory is "a theory about the nature of moral conduct and the validity of moral judgment which has (or is supposed to have) an important bearing on the further direction of such conduct. . . ."

An ethical theory always consists, among other things, in the elaboration and defense, and even the application, of one or more moral principles. Now both the generalization principle and the generalization argument are moral principles. But they are not the only ones. There are others that I shall defend, and others that I shall attack. Yet the generalization argument has a central role to play. What I shall attempt to show about it is not simply that it is valid, when properly qualified, but that it serves as a test or criterion of the morality of conduct, and provides the basis for moral rules.

Moral rules, such as the rule that it is wrong to steal, are distinct from moral principles. The full meaning of this distinction will be developed later. I shall only mention here that, whereas rules are more specific and concrete, principles are more general and abstract. Principles are involved in the justification and clarification of rules, and both are involved in determining the morality of conduct. So both are required for the distinction between right and wrong. As we shall see, to establish an adequate, coherent, and consistent set of moral principles is to establish the rational basis of morality.

§ 3 §

I see no real need for any further summary of the contents of this book. If it is not clear enough as we go along, then it is defective in a way that cannot be alleviated by preliminary summaries. Yet there is one further matter that should be mentioned.

There are some obvious resemblances between the generalization argument and Kant's categorical imperative: "Act only on that maxim whereby thou canst at the same time will that it should become a universal law." One similarity is that they both involve generalization, the consideration of what would happen if everyone acted in a certain way. Another is that they both involve the generalization principle and provide criteria for its application. But, even though the generalization argument and the categorical imperative are in this way

quite similar, they are also quite different. For the categorical
imperative involves a reference to *willing*, and to the *maxim*
of an action, while the generalization argument does not.
Kant's criterion is, "We must *be able to will* that a maxim of
our action should become a universal law—this is the general
canon for all moral judgment of action." The "general canon"
provided by the generalization argument can perhaps be expressed as, "The consequences of everyone's acting in a certain way must not be undesirable."

Of course, it may be that these differences are only on the
surface, and not of fundamental significance. The following
scene from Lewis Carroll's *Through the Looking Glass* is
worth recalling here:

> "Please, would you tell me——" she began, looking timidly
> at the Red Queen.
> "Speak when you're spoken to!" the Queen sharply inter-
> rupted her.
> "But if everybody obeyed that rule," said Alice, who was
> always ready for a little argument, "and if you only spoke
> when you were spoken to, and the other person always waited
> for *you* to begin, you see nobody would ever say anything, so
> that——"
> "Ridiculous!" cried the Queen. "Why, don't you see,
> child——" here she broke off with a frown, and, after think-
> ing for a minute, suddenly changed the topic of the conversa-
> tion (Chap. 9).

There would appear to be no essential difference between
saying "if everyone were to do that," "if everyone were to act
in that way," "if everyone obeyed that rule," or "if everyone
acted on that maxim." In fact, any of these locutions may be
used in an application of the generalization argument.

What is more, it seems significant that the categorical imperative (or, as I shall also call it, the principle of universality)
has rarely, if ever, been thought of as distinct from what I
have called the generalization argument. One writer, for example, in the course of criticizing Kant's ethics, claims that
"in general the attempt to determine whether this is right
conduct for me here and now, by considering the conse-

quences of everyone acting in the same way always, is futile," [4] and assumes that he has thereby said all there is to be said about the matter. This is no isolated incident. Note how the two principles are apparently identified in the following passage from an outstanding commentary on Kant's ethics:

> The best, if not the only, way to make such a law [the categorical imperative] vivid in our imagination is to picture to ourselves a world in which everybody in fact acted in accordance with it. This is the eminently sensible procedure which Kant now commends to us. It is one which is commonly followed by ordinary men. The duty of fire-watching, for example, was sometimes pressed home by the question "What would happen if everybody refused to do it?" To ask questions of this kind is to consider a maxim as if it were to become through our will a universal law of nature.[5]

These facts provide good reason for considering the categorical imperative, both in its own right and in its relation to the generalization argument, and this will be done in Chapters VIII and IX of this book. These chapters are probably those that presuppose the most knowledge, in the sense of some prior familiarity with Kant's moral philosophy, and may therefore seem the most specialized and technical. This is no doubt the case. Yet they are essential to my argument, and my purpose in them is not primarily historical or antiquarian. I am not out to determine what Kant really meant, or actually intended to say. My aim, rather, is to establish the soundness of a moral principle.

One more point should be made clear at the outset. The application of the generalization argument presupposes, and does not by itself determine, that the consequences of everyone's acting in a certain way would be undesirable. Where this point is problematic, so is the application of the generalization argument, and where it does not hold, the argument will have no force. This was already illustrated by the example

[4] E. F. Carritt, *The Theory of Morals* (London: Oxford University Press, 1930), p. 80.

[5] H. J. Paton, *The Categorical Imperative* (Chicago: University of Chicago Press, 1948), p. 146.

given above about a discussion group. For one who does not care whether the club dissolves, the argument "What would happen if no one read a paper?" would have no force or relevance. Still another example is provided by the following bit of dialogue: "There is no point in my buying a war bond; the money I can spend will make no difference to the winning of the war. . . . But if everyone were to think that way, no one would buy any bonds." We have here a clear case of the application of the generalization argument, which is almost typical in its abbreviated and elliptical character. A consequence of "everyone's thinking that way," it is stated, would be that no one would buy any bonds, and the consequence of this, it is implied, would be that the war would be lost, or perhaps that taxes would be sharply increased. The argument presupposes that such consequences would be undesirable. But for one who does not care whether the war is lost, or whether taxes would be increased (if there is such a one), they would not be undesirable (or would not be regarded as undesirable), and the conclusion cannot be brought home.

There may be cases in which this sort of relativity is unavoidable. But this matter need not be left here. There are many cases in which this sort of relativity is not unavoidable, in which it does not even arise. I shall say more about this later. I mention it here merely to indicate that our examination of the categorical imperative will enable us in many cases to by-pass, or even to settle, this sort of question.

❦

CHAPTER II

THE GENERALIZATION
PRINCIPLE

It is almost axiomatic that "the character of every act depends
upon the circumstances in which it is done." [1] As we may
otherwise put it: whether an act is right or wrong depends on
the circumstances or context in which it is done, or on the conditions or circumstances under which it is done. (Indeed, the
actual nature of an act, what the act is, is indeterminate when
it is taken apart from its context.) Although such a general
statement may raise some doubts, this is recognized implicitly
in practice, much more extensively than is indicated by such
phrases as "extenuating circumstances." It is recognized, for
example, that under certain circumstances one may be justified in breaking a promise, telling a lie, taking a life, or taking
something that belongs to another without first obtaining his
permission. (Compare the commonplace, "Circumstances
alter cases.") Accordingly, the assertion that an act cannot be
right for one person unless it is right for everyone would be
patently absurd, unless some such qualification as "in the
same or similar circumstances" is implicitly understood. If an
act can be right in one context and wrong in another, *a for-*

[1] J. Holmes, *Schenck* v. *U.S.*, 249 U. S. (Supreme Court Reports) 47
(1919).

tiori it can be right for one person and wrong for another, provided they do it in different contexts. However, if an act is right for A it *must* be right for B, if the circumstances are the same, or sufficiently similar, just as it must be right for A on any other occasion if there is no significant difference in the circumstances. The generalization principle could therefore be stated in the form: What is right for one person must be right for anyone in the same or similar circumstances.

The trouble with stating it in this form, however, is that a further necessary qualification is left inexplicit, with the consequence that in this form the principle is ambiguous. It could properly be stated in this form provided it is implicitly understood that the nature, characteristics, relationships, or abilities of the agent who is considered as being in certain circumstances can often make for a significant difference in those circumstances. It would not be a duty of a blind man, or one without legs, to jump into the water to save someone from drowning, while it might be the duty of a good swimmer to do so. If the principle, that what is right or a duty for one person is right or a duty for anyone in similar circumstances, is to be maintained in spite of this, it must be on the ground that one's ability to swim is a factor to be considered, in this context, in determining whether or not something is his duty; and that consequently the circumstances of an act can vary with the characteristics of the agent. The term "circumstances" is to some extent ambiguous. In one sense the circumstances of an act can be determined without any reference to the agent. In another sense they cannot. In this sense in order to specify adequately the circumstances in or under which someone acted, we must take account of *his* characteristics or nature. If the term is used in the first sense then it is false that what is right for one person must be right for anyone in similar circumstances. For what is right for a certain person can depend on his personal characteristics as well as on what might be called his "external circumstances." Stating the generalization principle in the form, "What is right for one person must be right for any *similar person* in similar circumstances," instead of in the form, "What is right for one person must be right for anyone in similar circumstances," is merely a way of making this point explicit.

This qualification, however, merely makes explicit what would ordinarily be understood by the assertion that what is right for one person in certain circumstances would be right for anyone in those circumstances. It is ordinarily recognized that while it may be right for an expert surgeon to undertake a delicate operation under trying circumstances, it might very well be wrong for a medical student or a manifest incompetent, no matter how good his intentions. Thus Samuel Alexander says, "The good act . . . may vary according to the nature of the individual and the place he holds in the society. Still, so far as it is allowed, it is approved for any one in those circumstances and of that nature or temperament, and the approbation of the commonalty belongs to it not as a favour to this individual but to any such person under such conditions." [2]

It should be noted that such expressions as "right for" and "wrong for" are ambiguous. Something may be right for someone in the sense (1) that it is right for him to *do* it, or in the sense (2) that it is right for him to *be treated* in that way. It is fairly obvious that it may be wrong for one person to be treated in the same way as another, even in the same sort of situation, if they are not sufficiently similar in character, background, personality, or ability. The way in which the generalization principle has been stated abstracts from this difference in the meaning of "right for," or, in other words, from the difference between considering someone as an "agent" and considering him as a "patient." It is a generalization of, and consequently entails, the following two propositions: (1) It is right for A to act in a certain way if and only if it is right for anyone similar to A to act in that way in similar circumstances; (2) It is right for A to be treated in a certain way if and only if it would be right for anyone similar to A to be treated in that way in similar circumstances.

There is an obvious resemblance between the generaliza-

[2] S. Alexander, *Space, Time, and Deity* (London: Macmillan & Co., Ltd., 1920), vol. II, p. 275.

tion principle and what is known as the Golden Rule, which
in one of its formulations reads, "Do unto others as you
would have them do unto you." The exact nature of this resemblance, however, may not be so obvious. In any of its
traditional formulations this rule is not only imprecise, but if
taken literally would be an abomination. "One might wish for
another's co-operation in sin, and be willing to reciprocate it,"
as Sidgwick points out. Understood literally this rule invites,
even enjoins, a masochist to become a sadist: one who would
have others torture him is enjoined to torture others. Furthermore, as Kant notices, "on this basis the criminal would be
able to dispute with the judges who punish him," and "many
a man would readily agree that others should not help him
if only he could be dispensed from affording help to them." [3]
Such literal interpretations of the rule are undoubtedly mis-
interpretations of what is intended by it. But what this shows
is that as it stands the rule is imprecise and needs qualification.
It neither says what it means nor means what it says. Stated
precisely, the Golden Rule would be an immediate consequence of the generalization principle. Sidgwick remarks that
Samuel Clarke's "rule of equity" ("Whatever I judge reasonable or unreasonable that another should do for me; that by
the same judgment I declare reasonable or unreasonable that
I should *in the like case* do for him") is "the 'Golden
Rule' precisely stated." He also claims that the "principle
strictly stated must take some such negative form as this: 'it
cannot be right for A to treat B in a manner in which it would
be wrong for B to treat A, merely on the ground that they are
two different individuals, and without there being any difference between the natures or circumstances of the two which
can be stated as a reasonable ground for difference of treatment,'" and adds that "such a principle manifestly does not
give complete guidance—indeed its effect, strictly speaking, is
merely to throw a definite *onus probandi* on the man who ap-

---

[3] Henry Sidgwick, *The Methods of Ethics* (7th ed.; London: Mac-
millan & Co., Ltd., 1907), p. 380; Immanuel Kant, *Groundwork of the
Metaphysic of Morals*, in *The Moral Law*, transl. by H. J. Paton (London:
Hutchinson's University Library, 1948), p. 97 note.

plies to another a treatment of which he would complain if applied to himself." [4] This last statement can be taken as applying not only to "the Golden Rule precisely stated" but, as I shall point out later on, to the generalization principle itself.

§ 1 §

The remarks so far are no more than preliminary. They are intended to show why such a qualification as "similar persons in similar circumstances" is needed in the statement of the generalization principle. But they do not so much as begin to raise the basic question about this principle, which concerns the import of this very qualification. For this purpose it will be useful to consider some further statements of Sidgwick's about this principle:

> We cannot judge an action to be right for A and wrong for B, unless we can find in the natures or circumstances of the two some difference which we can regard as a reasonable ground for difference in their duties. If therefore I judge any action to be right for myself, I implicitly judge it to be right for any other person whose nature and circumstances do not differ from my own in certain important respects. . . .
>
> If a kind of conduct that is right (or wrong) for me is not right (or wrong) for some one else, it must be on the ground of some difference between the two cases, other than the fact that I and he are different persons.[5]

It should be clear that these last statements are perfectly general ones. They do not apply just to me, but to everyone. Anyone who judges an action to be right for himself implicitly judges it to be right for anyone else whose nature and circumstances do not differ from his own in certain important respects (that is, for any similar person in similar circumstances). If a kind of conduct that is right (or wrong) for one person is not right (or wrong) for someone else, it must be on the

---

[4] Sidgwick, *op. cit.*, pp. 384-5, quoting from Clarke's *Boyle Lectures* (1705), pp. 86-7; *ibid.*, p. 380.
[5] Sidgwick, *op. cit.*, pp. 209, 379.

ground of some difference between the two cases, other than the (tautological) fact that the individuals involved are distinct individuals.

This, however, does not go very far towards meeting the basic objection that might be made against this principle, which might be put in this manner: "It is all very well to insist that what is right for one person must be right for any similar person in similar circumstances. But what does this mean? How can you tell in any particular case whether the natures or circumstances of the people involved are similar or not? Indeed, under what conditions could two people not be said to be similar? You can always find some similarities, and since this is the case, this principle is so vague as to be useless. And it will not help matters to say that 'similar persons in similar circumstances' are those persons 'whose natures and circumstances do not differ in certain important respects.' For which respects are important ones? Obviously there will always be some differences. How can you tell in any particular case which differences are important and which are not?"

Though I think this objection rests on a confusion, it is an important one and must be met. (It was on this ground that C. D. Broad asserted that Sidgwick's principle, while "not absolutely verbal," is "extraordinarily trivial," while Bradley claimed that it is a "bare tautology." [6]) The questions it sets forth, so far as they are sensible, can be given satisfactory answers. These questions, however, are not altogether legitimate, as they stand. They arise, to some extent, out of a confusion.

For this sort of objection to the generalization principle assumes that it pretends or is supposed to contain within itself the criteria for "similar persons in similar circumstances," while it most emphatically does not. And the fact that it does

---

[6] C. D. Broad, *Five Types of Ethical Theory* (London: Kegan Paul, Trench, Trubner & Co., Ltd., 1930), p. 223; F. H. Bradley, "Mr. Sidgwick's Hedonism," in *Collected Essays* (Oxford: The Clarendon Press, 1935), vol. I, p. 100.

not is not a defect in it. The occurrences of the term "similar" in the statement of this principle do not make it vague or inapplicable. They ensure its generality. The expression "similar persons in similar circumstances" is to be construed as a "place holder," to be filled in different ways in different contexts. In other words, the occurrences of the term "similar" in the statement of this principle are to be regarded as *blanks, to be filled in* in different ways depending on the context. Different applications of the principle, in which this term does not occur, will result from different ways of filling in these blanks, or in other words, of specifying the circumstances. Each of these applications may be regarded as a rule or principle on a lower level of generality than the generalization principle itself, or simply as a particular application of the general principle.

I realize that these brief remarks are in need of illustration. But I propose postponing for a moment giving illustrations of the application of this principle. It is necessary first to answer the legitimate questions involved in the foregoing objection. While it is not a legitimate criticism of the generalization principle that it cannot by itself determine the concrete meaning of the phrase "similar persons in similar circumstances," it would be a legitimate criticism of it if there were no way at all of determining this. For if such were the case, the principle would be inapplicable. It is therefore necessary to show that this is not the case.

One thing that gives rise to this sort of objection is the fact that things may be similar in different ways. A and B may be similar in one respect and not in another. And it holds trivially that given any two things it is possible to specify some respect in which they are alike as well as some respect in which they are different. But this does not prove that the principle is vacuous and trivial. For while some similarities, and differences, can always be specified, not all of them will be relevant ones. The generalization principle must be understood in the sense that what is right for one person must be right for every *relevantly* similar person in *relevantly* similar circumstances. An important or relevant difference is one that "can be stated as a *reasonable ground* for difference of treatment." [7]

While it is true that two things may be similar in one respect and not in another, it is also true that two things may be similar for one purpose and not for another. Whether A and B are to be regarded as similar in any nontrivial sense is thus dependent on the purpose or context. If we think of relevant and irrelevant similarities, this should be obvious. For the notion of relevance has no meaning apart from some determinate context. A statement of the form "A is relevant" is, as it stands, incomplete. It is either elliptical for a statement of the form "A is relevant to B," where this further reference is determined from the context, or else it is nonsense. Now just as what is relevant to one thing may not be relevant to another, what is relevant in one context may not be relevant in another. Thus the phrase "(relevantly) similar persons in (relevantly) similar circumstances" cannot be translated or defined or made more specific in abstraction from any definite context. If a more definite term were substituted for it, we should have a particular application of the generalization principle, and not the principle itself. However, it is not impossible to formulate criteria or a general set of directions for determining whether or not certain persons or their circumstances are to be regarded as similar in various contexts; that is, whether or not the similarities between them are relevant in the context. This I shall now proceed to do, constructing for this purpose some model cases which can appropriately serve as paradigms of the application of this principle.

§ 2 §

Consider the following case presented by Sidgwick, in which he mentions certain conditions under which lying might be justified.

> Suppose . . . A Utilitarian thinks it on general grounds right to answer falsely a question as to the manner in which

[7] Sidgwick, *op. cit.*, p. 380 (italics added).

he has voted at a political election where the voting is by secret ballot. His reasons will probably be that the Utilitarian prohibition of falsehood is based on (1) the harm done by misleading particular individuals, and (2) the tendency of false statements to diminish the mutual confidence that men ought to have in each other's assertions: and that in this exceptional case it is (1) expedient that the questioner should be misled; while (2) in so far as the falsehood tends to produce a general distrust of all assertions as to the manner in which a man has voted, it only furthers the end for which voting has been made secret. It is evident, that if these reasons are valid for any person, they are valid for all persons. . . .[8]

The particular reasons Sidgwick gives are not very important in this context. Neither is his reference to utilitarianism. What is important is his statement that *if these reasons are valid for any person, they are valid for all persons.*[9] Sidgwick goes on to say (p. 486) that the principle of justice means "that an act, if right for any individual, must be right on general grounds, and therefore for some *class* of persons." Now the importance of these two statements is that they provide the clue to the proper interpretation of "similar" as it appears in this principle. The criteria for "all similar cases" are contained in the "general grounds" or reasons on the basis of which an act is, or is said to be, right or wrong. These reasons determine who are similar and who are not in a certain context. All those to whom the reasons apply are similar to

[8] Sidgwick, *op. cit.*, p. 485. Cf. p. 318: "It is not necessarily an evil that men's confidence in each other's assertions should, *under certain peculiar circumstances*, be impaired or destroyed; it may even be the very result which we should most desire to produce: e.g., it is obviously a most effective protection for legitimate secrets that it should be universally understood and expected that those who ask questions which they have no right to ask will have lies told them. . . ."

[9] Sidgwick adds that "they establish the expediency of a new general rule in respect of truth and falsehood, more complicated than the old one. . . ." This is in line with his earlier statement on the same page: "The admission of an exception on general grounds is merely the establishment of a more complex and delicate rule, instead of one that is broader and simpler; for if it is conducive to the general good that such an exception be admitted in one case, it will be equally so in all similar cases."

each other and relevantly different from those to whom the reasons do not apply.

The following remarks may help to bring this out:

> Although I may feel the force of my own rights as a passionate demand, and still decline to entertain those of others, I cannot make of them a *social concept*, cannot argue about them and present them to others for their recognition, without generalizing them, and so implicitly granting to the other man the right to use the same words with reference to himself. . . . Argument implies general principles as its basis; a rational right is therefore by definition something that can be made general. . . . What you claim for yourself, every man whatsoever has the right to claim for himself, *unless* you can show definite reasons, that a reasonable being is bound to admit, why the principle applies in the one instance and not in the other. And the reasons must be themselves general ones; it is not enough to make the difference consist merely in the fact that I am I, and that you are someone else.[1]

This last statement, of course, is essentially the same as one of Sidgwick's presented above: a difference in what is right for two individuals cannot be justified on the ground that they are *two* individuals, that A is A and B is B. The fact that I am I, or the person I am, cannot justify my claim that my case is exceptional, that I have the right to do something others do not have the right to do. But this is not because this purported reason is not a general one, or does not have a general application. It actually has *too general* an application. If I can say "I am I, and you are someone else," *everyone* can say "I am I, and you are someone else." Thus this cannot show that one case is different from another. The attempt to use the fact that I am I to justify the claim that my case is exceptional actually involves a contradiction. For since it is true of everyone that he is he, since everyone can say "I am I," it would follow that every case is exceptional, and this is self-contradictory.

The claim that "I am John Smith, while you are not,"

[1] Arthur Kenyon Rogers, *The Theory of Ethics* (New York: The Macmillan Company, 1922), pp. 191-2.

which is not tautological, still could not justify one in holding that he is an exception. Everyone can make a similar claim: "I am John Jones, while you are not," or "I am Stan Spatz III, while you are not." If the fact that someone has a certain name could be used to show that his case is an exception, it could be used to show that every case is an exception, which is, again, self-contradictory. Nor can the attempt to justify oneself by reference to a "rule" that refers to oneself by name (and which of course would not be a general rule at all) work any better. If John Smith can say "Everyone whose name is John Smith has the right to act in such and such a way," Stan Spatz III can say "Everyone whose name is Stan Spatz III has the right to act in such and such a way," and everyone else can invoke a similar "rule." If one could invoke the fact that he has a certain name or is a certain person—is "someone special"—to justify his acting in a certain way, he could invoke the same consideration to justify his acting in any way he pleases under any circumstances whatsoever. But so could everyone else. It would follow that everyone has the right to act in whatever way he pleases. Now this is not just false—it is self-contradictory.

The fact that one has a certain name or is a certain person may be relevant to the claim that one has the right to do something or is an exception to some rule. But the point is that one has to show how it is relevant. To do this is to show how one is genuinely different from others in the situation in question. It is to show that one is an exception on the basis of considerations that would not show everyone to be an exception. Though not everyone has the same name, everyone has some name, or can easily assume one. Thus it is not sufficient merely to specify the respects in which one differs from everyone else. For everyone else can do the same. What is important is the principle on which the circumstances are specified. Suppose one claims to be an exception to some rule, or to be justified in some action, on the ground that he lives in a red house, with purple shutters and a green roof, situated on the corner of Cheshire Street and Kickaboo Lane. Suppose he even goes so far as to specify the exact geographic coordinates of the house in which he lives. This still will not do. Nor will it do to say that *"everyone* who lives in such a house has the right to act in such and such a way." For every house, just like every person, has some features that distinguish it from every other. If nothing else, every house has a location that no other house has. What is important is not so much the specification of these details, as the principle on which the specification is made. And in practice this principle is not really so difficult to discover. In this last case the principle is the specification of the peculiarities, the distinguishing features, of one's house; in the former the principle is the specification of one's name. But the same criticism applies to both.

The statement of a reason certainly need not be given in general or abstract terms. Nevertheless it must be *generalizable.* The statement of a reason, that is to say, must imply a rule or general proposition. The reason given must be capable of applying beyond the particular person in the particular situation to a class of persons in a certain type of situation. Hence to give a reason in support of the judgment that a certain individual, A, ought or has the right to do some act, presupposes that anyone with the characteristics specified in the statement of the reason ought or has the right to do the same kind of act in a situation of the kind specified. If the statement of a reason does not imply this, then it is not the statement of a reason at all, but merely the reiteration of the assertion. Now anyone, and everyone, who has these characteristics is *similar* to A in this context. Any set of circumstances with the characteristics described by the reasons offered is in this context similar to the circumstances in which it is right for A to do the act in question. If B meets these conditions, then in this context B is similar to A. If C does not then there is an important difference in this context between C and A. This is quite consistent with the fact that A and B may be similar in one context and not in another. On the basis of the reasons justifying an act of some other kind, or the same sort of act in different circumstances (or for someone with different characteristics), A and B may be dissimilar, and if

so it will be right for one of them to act in this way and wrong
for the other.

§ 3 §

In a speech in Parliament, Macaulay once said, "Official ap-
pointments ought not to be subject to regulations purely arbitrary, to regulations for which no reason can be given but
mere caprice, . . . those who would exclude any class from
public employment are bound to show some special reason for
the exclusion." [2] This is an obvious though implicit appeal to
the generalization principle, and this should serve to provide
us with our second model.

What sort of consideration could serve as a "reason for the
exclusion"? What would justify excluding some class of persons from public employment, or more generally, from appoint-
ment to any sort of position? "Purely arbitrary" regulations
would be those "for which no reason can be given but mere
caprice," or simply those for which no genuine reason can be
given. It is relatively easy to see what would fall into this class.
The fact that someone does not like people of a certain type
would not, by itself, justify him in claiming that they ought to
be excluded from some position. The fact that he does not
like them would not be a reason, though he might think that
it is. For suppose that it were. Then the argument would be
that people of type T ought not to be allowed to hold a certain type of position because A does not like people of type T.
But this presupposes that anyone A does not like ought not to
be allowed to obtain that sort of position. This involves us in
the situation discussed above. Anyone can argue in the same
way. If there is anyone who does not like the people A does
like (himself included), then these people ought to be excluded also. It is possible to maintain on these grounds that no
one ought to hold any position, and this is absurd. How does
A justify his claim to a privileged status for his likes and dis-

[2] Thomas Babington Macaulay, speech on "Jewish Disabilities" (April
17, 1833), in *Speeches and Legal Studies* (New York: Sully & Kleinteich,
1900), p. 116.

likes? It is possible for him to do so, but not on the ground that he is he, or is a person of "special importance." Nor could people of type T justifiably be excluded simply on the ground that they are people of type T. This (or the principle underlying it) also would apply to everybody: people of type U ought to be excluded because they are of type U, and so on. Perhaps no one would be persuaded by this sort of reasoning when it is set out in this abstract form. It does not follow that no one has ever argued this way. I should say that this sort of "reasoning" is fairly common. If it were not there would have been no point to Macaulay's statement, and no one familiar with the context in which his speech was made could maintain this.

It might be alleged that, though an instance of the sort of thing I have just been considering may not be a *good* reason, it is nevertheless a reason, simply because it is advanced as such. People do give this sort of thing as their reason; they say this is their reason. This signifies nothing. There are certainly some contexts in which it is important to distinguish among reasons, good reasons, bad reasons, and nonreasons. But this is not one of them. What I am claiming is that this sort of consideration is not a reason at all, and therefore certainly not a good reason. The fact that it is advanced as a reason, or is thought to be one, is totally irrelevant. I should not deny that someone may give this sort of invocation ("I do not like people of type T," or "because they are T's") as his reason for claiming that something ought or ought not to be done. There is even a sense in which we can say that this is his reason. But this would be *his* reason, not *a* reason, and it would be a reason in the sense of an explanation, not in the sense of a justification. Someone may have a reason for committing murder, he may have a very strong motive for doing so, and this can be used to explain why he did it; but one cannot have a justification for committing murder. Corresponding points apply to the notion of evidence. Someone's reason for believing that the earth is round (or that the earth is flat) may be that he has tingles in his left ear. Not only is this not a good reason for so believing, it is not a reason at all.

Now what would count as a reason for excluding a class of people from a certain type of employment? In order to justify the claim that a certain class or group of people ought to be excluded from a certain type of position, it would have to be shown that the members of that class have certain characteristics, *in virtue of their membership in that class*, which are such as to unfit them or make them incompetent to perform the duties of that position. But then this class of people must be defined by these characteristics. Identification of them in terms of some popular category, as say Negroes, or Poles, or Jews, will not be sufficient. It would have to be shown that because someone is a Negro, or has certain characteristics commonly associated with Negroes, he is incapable of carrying out the requirements of the position in question. Obviously the relevance of this consideration will vary with different offices or positions. The fact that a man has red hair may of course be sufficient to exclude him from being sent as an emissary to a land or region where red-headed people are regarded with ill will. It is not sufficient to exclude him from being sent as an emissary to some other place. If the Erewhonians liked and respected only fair-haired people, and had a horror of physical weakness, then the fact that someone has dark hair or is sickly may be a good reason for excluding him from the class of those who are acceptable as emissaries to Erewhon. But the fact that someone has dark hair would be irrelevant in a situation in which someone has to be picked as an emissary to a place where people do not care about the color of one's hair. Furthermore, the fact that someone has dark hair would not justify excluding him from the class of possible emissaries to Erewhon unless *all* people with dark hair were thereby excluded. It is not simply that it would be unfair to exclude someone from the position on the ground that he has dark hair, while some other dark-haired person is not excluded. It *would* be unfair. But the reason why it is unfair is that in such a case the color of one's hair would not, and could not possibly, be the reason or ground for the exclusion. This is obvious from the form of argument involved: A would not be a good ambassador to Erewhon (and therefore ought not to

be sent there) *because* he has dark hair and *because* the Erewhonians do not like people with dark hair. This statement
would be senseless unless it were applicable not only to A but
to B, C, . . . in short, to everyone. It presupposes the proposition that no one with dark hair would make a good ambassador to Erewhon; or, more generally, that no one with dark hair
should be sent as ambassador to a place where dark-haired people are not liked. To paraphrase a statement from Sidgwick
quoted previously, a reason in one case is a reason in all cases
—or else it is not a reason at all. (This is not to say that a
motive in one case is a motive in all cases.) This should make
fairly obvious the connection between impartiality, generality,
and consistency or rationality.

The relation of the generalization principle to this sort of
case should be apparent. Let us state the application of the
principle to it in easy stages. The principle is: what is right for
one person must be right for every similar person in similar
circumstances. In the first stage of its application to this case
we have the proposition (a) it is right for A to be prevented
from being an emissary to Erewhon if and only if it is right to
prevent everyone similar to A from being sent. (It is not
really necessary to add here the qualification "in similar circumstances." For we can consider the circumstances as already specified.) Now the class of persons similar to A in this
context is determined by the reasons that justify, or are said to
justify, this exclusion of A. It is right to prevent A from being
sent as an emissary to Erewhon because A has dark hair and
because the Erewhonians have a great distaste for dark-haired
people. This consideration, to be a genuine reason, must apply to all people with dark hair. It thus defines the class of people who are similar to A in this context. Hence we have (b) it
is right to prevent A from being sent as an emissary to Erewhon, because he has dark hair and the Erewhonians do not
like dark-haired people, if, and only if, it would be right to
prevent any dark-haired person from being sent as an emissary
to Erewhon. Or more simply, it is right to prevent one dark-
haired person from being sent as an emissary to Erewhon (on
the ground that he has dark hair) if, and only if, it would be

right to prevent any dark-haired person from being sent. The term "similar" does not occur here at all. But this is obviously an application of the more general principle in which it does occur.

It should be noticed that the fact that someone has dark hair, though it is a good reason for excluding him, is not a logically conclusive reason. Even this may be overridden in some cases. Hence a case may arise in which a dark-haired person may justifiably be sent, because *on other grounds* he is likely to make a good ambassador. "He has certain qualities to make up for the deficiency." But then, if so, having dark hair is not, by itself, *the* reason for exclusion. A cannot be excluded *simply because* he has dark hair. And if everyone in the country had dark hair, having dark hair clearly could not at all be a ground of exclusion; one would have to be disqualified on some other ground. The ground for excluding A must be that he has dark hair and does not have other qualities to make up for this. Having dark hair is then one reason, or a presumptive reason, for exclusion; it is not a conclusive reason.

The present discussion can be summed up in more general terms. Any office, job, or position involves certain duties and requires certain abilities and characteristics for the performance of these duties. Thus, given any office or position, it is possible to draw up a list of conditions stating the requirements of that position, so that anyone satisfying these conditions is capable of fulfilling these requirements. These conditions define a class, the class of those who are eligible for that position. With respect to these conditions, or with respect to the position in question, all those with the specified characteristics are similar to each other. Now A can rightfully be excluded from this position only on the ground that he does not satisfy the specified conditions. But these grounds that justify excluding A are general grounds: they exclude anyone who does not satisfy the conditions for the position. Thus it is right to exclude A from some position only if it is right to exclude all persons who are similar to A in this respect. If A does not meet the conditions for the position p, then with respect to p anyone who does not meet these conditions is similar to A, and anyone who does meet these conditions is dissimilar to A. If B satisfies the requirements for the position while A does not, then there is a relevant difference between them, one that justifies giving the position to B and not to A. The term "similar circumstances" may be explained in a parallel manner. Any position the requirements of which are the same as, or similar to, those of p, is similar to p. Consequently, if there is a reasonable presumption that A satisfies the conditions for a position of the kind p, then the attempt to exclude him from it must be justified; for there is *a fortiori* a reasonable presumption that the attempt to exclude him from it is unjustified. In order for this to be justified it would have to be shown either that A does not really satisfy these conditions, although he appears to; or that the position from which it is desired to exclude him is not actually a position of the kind p, although it appears to be; or that the list of conditions for p needs revision. The list of conditions may need revision if the requirements for the position have changed (the Erewhonians now decide that they do not like short people either), or if it can be shown that a mistake has been made about these requirements (the Erewhonians disliked short people all the time only we were unaware of this).[3]

[3] Cf. R. H. Tawney, *Equality* (4th ed.; London: George Allen & Unwin Ltd., 1952), pp. 40-41: "Everyone realizes that, in order to justify inequalities of circumstance or opportunity by reference to differences of personal quality, it is necessary . . . to show that the differences in question are relevant to the inequalities. Everyone now sees, for example, that it is not a valid argument against women's suffrage to urge, as used to be urged not so long ago, that women are physically weaker than men, since physical strength is not relevant to the question of the ability to exercise the franchise, or a valid argument in favour of slavery that some men are less intelligent than others, since it is not certain that slavery is the most suitable penalty for lack of intelligence. Not everyone, however, is so quick to detect the fallacy when it is expressed in general terms. It is still possible, for example, for one eminent statesman to ridicule the demand for a diminution of economic inequalities on the ground that every mother knows that her children are not equal, without reflecting whether it is the habit of mothers to lavish care on the strong and neglect the delicate; and for another to dismiss the suggestion that greater economic equality is desirable, for the reason, apparently, that men are naturally unequal. It is probable, however, that the first does not think that the fact that some children are born with good digestions, and others with bad, is a

This brings us to one further fact about the generalization principle that must be elaborated. Sidgwick remarked about this principle that its effect is to "throw a definite *onus probandi* on the man who applies to another a treatment of which he would complain if applied to himself" (p. 380). This is in line with his statement (p. 209) that "we cannot judge an action to be right for A and wrong for B, unless we can find in the natures or circumstances of the two some difference which we can regard as a reasonable ground for difference in their duties." The generalization principle can be regarded as specifying the conditions under which an act must be justified, and as specifying abstractly the conditions that must be met by a justification. Thus the generalization principle can be formulated in any of the following ways. What is right for one person cannot be wrong for another, unless there is some relevant difference in their natures or circumstances. Or, what is right (or wrong) for one person must be right (or wrong) for everyone, if there is no reason to the contrary. This is obviously equivalent to saying that what is right for one person must be right for every similar person in similar circumstances. Thus the claim that something that would not be right for everyone is right for a given person is one that must be justified. In the form especially appropriate to the generalization argument, the principle may be stated: *If not everyone ought to act or be treated in a certain way, then no one ought to act or be treated in that way without a reason.*

When it is formulated in some such way as this, it is clear that when Macaulay said that "those who would exclude any class from public employment are bound to show some special reason for the exclusion," he was appealing to the generalization principle.

---

reason for supplying good food to the former and bad food to the latter, rather than for giving to both food which is equal in quality but different in kind, and that the second does not suppose that the natural inequality of men makes legal equality a contemptible principle. . . ."

§ 4 §

I have said that the generalization principle implies that an act that is right or wrong is right or wrong on "general grounds" and is therefore right or wrong for a class of persons. This class of persons is determined by the reasons in terms of which the act is right or wrong. This may appear to conflict with the fact that there are some acts that would be right for only one person. But there is really no conflict here. An act of this sort is still right for a class of persons in the sense that it would be right for anyone who meets certain conditions, even though these conditions may be such that just one person can meet them. The act is still right as an act of a certain kind, or as an instance of a certain class of acts. It may be right for A and for no one else to do act d in certain circumstances. Yet if B were similar to A in certain respects then it would be right for B to do d. (The act may be described in such a way that this last statement may seem absurd. It would amount to saying "if B were A then. . . ." But this can be met by redescribing the act.) Furthermore, since d must be an act of a certain kind (if it were not it could not be described at all), it must be the case that it would be right for everyone similar to A to do an act of the same kind (to act in the same way) in similar circumstances.

The following example should make this clear. While it would not be wrong for Mr. Jones to have sexual relations with Mrs. Jones, it would (generally) be wrong for anyone else to do so, and it would certainly be wrong for everyone else to do so. Here we have an act that is right for just one person. But there is no conflict with the generalization principle. This principle does not say that no one ought to do anything that not everyone ought to do. It says that no one ought to do anything that not everyone ought to do, without a reason or justification. Mr. Jones is justified in having sexual relations with Mrs. Jones by the fact that he is married to her. If he were not he could (presumably) not be justified in this, and anyone else who was married to Mrs. Jones could be justified in having sexual relations with her. Furthermore, this act is an act of a certain kind, and can be described in a more general way so as to bring this out. Instead of describing Mr. Jones' act as one of "having sexual relations with Mrs. Jones," it can be referred to as "having sexual relations with one's own wife." Everyone is justified in doing an act of this kind in similar circumstances—everyone has the right to have sexual relations with his own wife, though not with anyone else's. (This rule as just stated necessarily does not apply to women. This does not make it unfair or unjust. It can obviously be restated to cover this.) Mr. Jones is justified in having sexual relations with Mrs. Jones because she is his wife. This last statement, it should be evident, is perfectly general. It has no peculiar application to Mr. Jones. It can thus be seen to be a further application of the more general generalization principle.

CHAPTER · III

❧

MORAL JUDGMENTS, MORAL REASONS, AND GENERALITY

What has now been shown about the generalization principle is that it is not vague or useless or inapplicable. What remains to be shown about it is that it is at the heart of moral reasoning. The generalization principle, I shall argue, is involved in or presupposed by every genuine moral judgment, for it is an essential part of the meaning of such distinctively moral terms as "right," "wrong," and "ought," in their distinctively moral senses. It is also an essential feature of moral reasoning, for it is presupposed in every attempt to give a reason for a moral judgment. It thus determines what can count as a moral reason. At the same time, it is the reasons that are given in any particular case that determine the application of the principle, for they determine the scope of the qualification "similar persons in similar circumstances."

It follows from this that there can be no genuine moral judgment apart from reasons, and no moral reasons apart from the generalization principle. This, incidentally, provides all the proof or justification this principle requires, supposing, what is not obvious, that it requires any. If the generalization principle is presupposed in every moral judgment and in all moral reasoning, there is no sense in demanding any further proof of it. For not only is this a demand that cannot possibly be satisfied, it is not even relevant to the subject.

If these contentions are correct, then those theories must be wrong which assert, in any of the variety of ways in which it is asserted, that moral judgments cannot be supported by reasons, or that there is no such thing as a valid moral argument. There is a distinction, which many regard as important, between what have come to be known as emotive and subjective ethical theories. On both these views moral judgments are regarded as having no objective significance. The distinction between them is that while on the subjective theory a moral judgment states that the speaker (or someone else) has a certain attitude, on the emotive theory a moral judgment does not state anything at all, but merely gives expression to an attitude. However, it is not the case that moral judgments are merely vehicles for the expression of emotion, or merely state that someone or other likes or approves or has some other sort of feeling or attitude toward something. An alleged moral judgment that one is unable to support by reasons is not a genuine moral judgment at all, but merely an indication of what someone likes or dislikes, and whether it is taken as a description or as an expression of these feelings or attitudes is of no great import. This will be seen to have some relevance to the ill-defined question whether moral judgments are subjective or objective.

Moral judgments, of course, are of many different kinds, and can be about many different kinds of things. Thus it is necessary to specify that I am dealing here only with moral judgments about actions, such as can be expressed by saying that some act (or kind of act) is right or wrong, ought or ought not to be done, or is just or unjust. I am not dealing with judgments of motives or character. Nor am I dealing with evaluations of or judgments about the quality, worth, or desirability of activities, situations, consequences, or institutions, such as can be expressed by saying that something is or is not valuable, desirable, or good. I am distinguishing, it will be seen, between moral judgments and evaluations (value judgments). Some evaluations, to be sure, are indistinguishable from moral judgments. But not all of them involve moral considerations, and the distinction is important. This is not to deny that we can often say that some course of *action* is good, is the best one to adopt, or is better than another. But such a statement is either equivalent to the statement that the act is right, or else it is a mixed judgment and evaluation, in which the evaluation of the consequences enters into and modifies the moral judgment of the action. Some wrong acts are worse than others, just as some crimes are worse than others. It is worse to torture a man than it is to steal five dollars from him. Since the terms "right" and "wrong" have no corresponding comparative or superlative forms, as do "good" and "bad," where we think that an act is not so much wrong as just not the best thing to do, or, though wrong, yet "not so terrible" (perhaps because the consequences are not so bad), we tend to use locutions of the latter sort. But the generalization principle governs judgments of this kind as well.

§ 1 §

The generalization principle has so far been stated in such a way as to refer more explicitly to actions than to moral judgments. But it can easily be restated so as to make its application to moral judgments more explicit. One of the ways in which Sidgwick stated the principle was this: "Whatever action any of us judges to be right for himself, he *implicitly* judges to be right for all similar persons in similar circumstances." Sidgwick also pointed out that "even when a moral judgment relates primarily to some particular action we commonly regard it as applicable to any other action belonging to a certain definable class; so that the moral truth apprehended is implicitly conceived to be intrinsically universal, though particular in our first apprehension of it." [1] This point may be summarized by the statement that every moral judgment is intrinsically universal, and if not explicitly so, then implicitly. Every moral judgment, in other words, involves a generaliza-

[1] Henry Sidgwick, *The Methods of Ethics* (7th ed.; London: Macmillan & Co., Ltd., 1907), p. 379 (italics added), p. 34.

tion. Moral judgments thus possess what may be called the characteristic of implicit generality.

This point is not really a new one, different from what has been said before. It is just a consequence of the generalization principle itself. For the principle, that what is right for one person must be right for every similar person in similar circumstances, implies that if it is right for A to do x then it is right for anyone similar to A to do x (or an act of the same kind as x) in similar circumstances. To put it another way, the judgment that A ought to do x implies that everyone similar to A ought to do x (or an act of the same kind as x) in similar circumstances. Thus the particular judgment that A ought to do x can be said to imply a general rule, though just what the rule is that it implies cannot be stated with any definiteness apart from the reasons adduced for the claim that A ought to do x, since apart from these reasons it cannot be determined what persons or circumstances are to be regarded as similar. This is what is meant by saying that moral judgments are governed by the generalization principle.

This characteristic of moral judgments, that of implicit generality, is by no means a trivial one. Not every particular judgment or statement implies a generalization. That it is fallacious to infer from "some" to "all," or from "this case" to "all cases," is well-established logical doctrine, and with regard to most kinds of statements it certainly holds. But it is simply false that no particular statement whatever implies a generalization. Not only do moral judgments have this characteristic, they are not unique in this respect. The particular (or specific) statement "The plane crashed because its wings fell off" implies, or presupposes, the generalization "Whenever a plane's wings fall off it will crash." One who says "This book must be good because it was written by Thomas Mann" is implying that every book written by Thomas Mann is good. In general, this characteristic of implicit generality is possessed by any statement that is used as an explanation, or to give evidence or a reason for something. Explanations, evidence, and reasons are governed by general rules or laws, which establish a connection between the fact to be explained or established and the fact used to explain or establish it. It is possessed not only by particular "because" statements, where "because" indicates a reason, but by particular causal statements. This characteristic of causal propositions is brought out very well in the following passage:

> In all such statements to the effect that something is a cause, there is involved a generalization. When we say that the decay in our molar is the cause of the toothache, we imply that *if these conditions were repeated* (the same state of decay in the tooth, the same condition of our nerves, and so on for all the other factors concerned)—toothache would result. . . . When we say that C is the cause of E, therefore, we are not only making a statement about two particular happenings; we are also implying a generalization about *any* happenings of the same kind.[2]

Moral judgments are thus analogous to causal judgments and "because" statements generally in possessing this characteristic of implicit generality. An assertion to the effect that some particular event C caused some other event E presupposes that whenever any event of the *kind* C occurs an event of the *kind* E occurs. In a brief formula: "causes in this case" implies "causes always." The assertion "The car stopped because it ran out of gas" implies or presupposes the general statement "Whenever a car runs out of gas it stops," or "Any car that runs out of gas stops." It also implies the general statement "*This* car will always stop whenever it runs out of gas." But there is nothing peculiar or special about *this* car, assuming it has a gasoline engine and can sensibly be said to have "run out of gas." This car is in this respect like any other car. If someone were to maintain that sometimes when his car runs out of gas the engine does not stop running, he could hardly maintain that the cause of its stopping on some other occasion was that it ran out of gas. To do so would be self-contradictory. An event of the kind C cannot cause an event of the kind E on one occasion and fail to cause it on another, unless its operation is counteracted by other causes,

[2] Max Black, *Critical Thinking* (2nd ed.; New York: Prentice-Hall Inc., 1952), p. 324.

in which case the conditions are different, and consequently
the events are different.

The generalization implied by a particular causal statement
cannot always, of course, be definitely and precisely formulated. "The generalizations indicated by the common-sense
use of words such as 'cause' and 'effect' are inaccurate and inexplicit. They hold only within ranges whose limits are not
stated, and require other factors that are often not even
mentioned to be held constant." [3] Thus an event of the kind
C *can* cause an event of the kind E on one occasion and fail
to cause it on another, if these other factors do not remain
constant, that is to say, *if there is some other difference in the
circumstances to account for the discrepancy*. And thus the
formula—"causes in this case" implies "causes in all cases"—
like any such formula, requires some qualification. It holds
only if "other factors remain the same." However, if C is not
always followed by E, but only under certain conditions, then
there are other factors, factors other than C, relevant to the
occurrence of E, and C is not *the* cause, or the only cause, of
E. The particular causal statement is subject to the same restrictions or understood limitations as the generalization it
implies, and the one is no more inaccurate or inexplicit than
the other. This same general point applies in the case of
moral judgments.

The importance of this characteristic of generality possessed by moral judgments lies in the way they may be justified or substantiated. One such way is the appeal to analogy.
When one of our moral judgments is challenged we may try
to support it by invoking an analogy, by citing an analogous
case, that is to say, a case that is, or is supposed to be, analogous in all relevant respects. "It was right for me to do it because it was right for you." The appeal to precedent is but a
form of the appeal to analogy, and the point of it is that one
who claims that an act is right for one person and not right
for another, is involved in a logical difficulty, unless he can
cite a relevant difference between the two cases. Where this is
not felt as a difficulty, it is because the two cases are ante-

[3] Black, *op. cit.*, p. 326.

cedently regarded as obviously different, and thus as not analogous. Now this procedure of citing analogies may in a specific instance be no more than an *argumentum ad hominem*—it may show no more than that someone is involved in an inconsistency. Yet to be inconsistent, in such contexts, is to be unfair; and the extent to which all moral arguments are *ad hominem*—ultimately, if pushed far enough—should not be overlooked. And of course the analogy invoked in a specific instance may not be justified. Nevertheless to invoke an analogy is to appeal to a general rule, to the generalization implicit in the judgment: it would be right for anyone in such a situation. "Consider the ethical atomists who think that life breaks itself up into a number of separate autonomous situations, each immediately revealing its own good or proper solution to our conscience, intuition, or intuitive reason, intelligence or common sense. When these moralists are confronted by a challenge to any of their particular judgments, they generally adduce some reason or at least cite an analogous case, thus involving explicitly or implicitly an appeal to some determining principle more abstract and wider than the specific case before them." [4]

Essentially the same sort of procedure may be used to substantiate or refute causal judgments, or "because" statements. To show that a reason is valid we can cite an analogous case in which it is admitted to be valid; to refute an argument we can give a counterexample, an analogous argument that is obviously invalid. The appeal to a counterexample or a supporting analogy is the appeal to a general rule, in accordance with which any argument of the form in question is valid or invalid, as the case may be.

Now a little reflection suffices to show that the appeal to analogy is always relevant in the consideration of a moral judgment. It is explicitly or implicitly a part of the procedure that must be followed in the justification of any claim that a certain act is right or wrong. In many cases merely to invoke an analogy will not be sufficient to demonstrate the judg-

[4] Morris Raphael Cohen, *Reason and Law* (Glencoe, Ill.: The Free Press, 1950), p. 15.

ment in question—establish it beyond any reasonable doubt. In many cases it may not even provide a very strong reason. For not only can one often find competing analogies, but it may be that the act was wrong (or right) in the cited case as well. Yet neither will it be sufficient merely to show that the act in question will, in the particular instance, have desirable consequences. For it may be that it would not be right for everyone to act in that way, and if this is so it is immaterial whether the consequences of a given person's doing the act would be desirable, unless a relevant difference can be established showing him to be an exception. The appeal to analogy is always *relevant*, however, and this shows conclusively that the generalization principle is involved in every moral judgment. To invoke an analogy is always, both in moral and nonmoral contexts, to appeal to the generalization principle —the principle of justice: it would be right for any similar person in similar circumstances. Indeed, this principle is presupposed even in cases in which some particular analogy is rejected, and certainly in cases in which competing analogies are offered. To show that there is a relevant difference in the circumstances of the two cases is to show that the analogy cited does not hold in all relevant respects and hence does not establish the judgment in question. There would be no sense in this apart from the generalization principle.

Although the appeal to analogy is always relevant in the consideration of a moral judgment, it has in many instances relatively little force. This is particularly so where competing analogies are readily available. And it is by no means the only kind of reason that can be given for a moral judgment, even though, as I have just been urging, it is implicit in these others. Thus it may be useful to reinforce the point I am trying to make by a brief consideration of these other kinds of reasons. There are at least five, and in each case the generalization principle is presupposed.

In the first place, one can describe the facts of the case, and thus offer as reasons particular statements of fact about the situation, such as "You promised," or "You owe it to him," or "That would be dishonest," or "But he is your brother."

But to do this is to presuppose a general rule, such as "One ought to keep one's promises," or "One ought to pay one's debts," in virtue of which there is a connection between the facts of the case and the judgment to which they are claimed to be relevant. It may not always be clear just what the rule is; nevertheless, there is one, for otherwise there would be no such connection. It is only in virtue of moral rules and principles that facts have moral relevance or implications, just as it is only on the basis of legal rules and principles that facts have legal consequences. And notice, incidentally, that there are cases in which it is just a plain matter of fact that one has made a promise, or owes someone some money. Secondly, one can appeal explicitly to a rule ("It is wrong to break a promise"), and either go on to show, by describing the facts of the case, that the rule actually applies, or take this as understood. It should be clear that in both these types of moral argument the generalization principle is presupposed. If the fact that one has promised is relevant in one case it is relevant in all cases; all cases, that is, in which it is a fact that one has promised. It may not be conclusive in all cases, but where it is not it is because it is outweighed by some other reason, in which event the situations are not similar in all relevant respects. The same point applies to the appeal to a rule; if it is relevant in one case it is relevant in all similar cases.

Thirdly, one can consider or point out the consequences the act can reasonably be expected to have, its effects on others, and whether they will be desirable or undesirable (in the case of a past act, the consequences it actually did have, so far as they can be determined). This is perhaps just a form of the appeal to fact. But it is worth distinguishing, in so far as it is worth distinguishing the circumstances of an action from its consequences, and also because in this case a question may arise about the evaluation of the consequences. Even so, the generalization principle is involved here also, for if the fact that the consequences of an action will be undesirable is relevant in one case it is relevant in all similar cases, that is to say, all cases in which the act will have the same or similar consequences or in which the consequences will be undesirable.

Fourthly, one can appeal explicitly to the generalization principle. But I mention this only for the sake of completeness, since it is merely a generalized form of the appeal to analogy. Finally, one can appeal explicitly to the generalization argument, by raising the question, "What would happen if everyone acted in that way?" That this also involves the generalization principle I hope to show in the next chapter.

In distinguishing these different kinds of moral reasons (appeal to analogy, appeal to fact, appeal to a rule, appeal to consequences, and appeal to principle), which I claim to be exhaustive, I by no means wish to imply that they are mutually exclusive. All of them are relevant in the consideration of a moral judgment, and in the more complicated cases all of them may in fact be used. This is particularly so in cases in which a question is raised, not about the applicability, but about the validity of some rule. But there is no different kind of reasoning involved in the justification of a rule, and the generalization principle is involved here also (as I shall show in Chapter V).

The fact that the generalization principle is an essential feature of moral reasoning removes the ground from the claim that the characteristic of implicit generality is a trivial one. It might be alleged that every particular statement (meaning every statement about a particular person or thing) involves a generalization in this way. For example, the statement "This table is sixty-three inches long" would imply the generalization, not that every table is 63 inches long, but that every table similar to this one would be 63 inches long; and the statement "Napoleon lost the battle of Waterloo" would involve the generalization "Anyone similar to Napoleon would have lost the battle of Waterloo" (or perhaps "Anyone similar to Napoleon would lose any battle similar to Waterloo"). But characterizing such statements as these as implicitly general is surely vacuous. The statement that this table is 63 inches long cannot be substantiated by citing an analogous case: "that table is sixty-three inches long, therefore this one must be." The way to verify it is to measure the length of the table; in other words, by performing an operation upon the object about which the assertion is made. It can be substantiated, to be sure, by comparing the length of the table with an object known to be 63 inches long, or by measuring the length of some other table known to have the same length as this one, but this is still not to invoke an analogy. No generalization supposedly involved in the statement will serve as evidence for it, nor has it any connection with the evidence for it. What is more, in any ordinary use of "similar" an object can be similar to the given table, even in length or dimension, without being 63 inches long or having the same length. In the stated generalization the term "similar" is actually used in such a way that whatever is not 63 inches long would *a fortiori* not be similar to the given table. Fully stated, therefore, it would take the form, "Any table similar in length to a table sixty-three inches long is sixty-three inches long," and this is clearly trivial.

In connection with moral and causal judgments the characteristic of implicit generality is far from trivial, owing to its connection with the procedures through which such judgments are substantiated. Indeed, this characteristic of involving a generalization is an essential part of the meaning of such terms as "cause" and "because" and related inferential terms, and of such distinctively moral terms as "right" and "wrong." "There would be no significance in the assertion of causation unless we at least meant to assert that *whenever* a given occurrence happens, then some other given occurrence happens." [5] Similarly, there would be no significance in the assertion that it was right (or wrong) for someone to do something unless we at least meant to assert that it would have been right (or wrong) for any similar person in similar circumstances. No such point applies to any of the terms involved in statements of the type just presented.

The statement about Napoleon is a more complicated one, though similar considerations apply. One could not prove

<hr />

[5] L. S. Stebbing, *A Modern Introduction to Logic* (2nd. ed.; London: Methuen & Co., Ltd., 1933), p. 276.

that Napoleon lost the battle of Waterloo by the generalization stated, nor by any supposedly analogous cases. No generalization supposedly involved in the statement could serve as evidence for its truth, nor would it be in any way connected with the evidence for it. Yet the generalization mentioned is the sort of statement one might make in trying to explain why Napoleon lost at Waterloo. One might claim that Napoleon lost because he had certain personal traits, and hence that anyone with the same traits would have lost in such a case. But then the generalization is not implied by the simple particular statement about Napoleon. It is implied by a "because" statement having this statement as a component part.

The difference is this. An ordinary narrative or descriptive statement, such as the ones just presented, is not an *instance* or an *application* of a generalization. Arguments, causal assertions, and "because" statements generally, however, are instances or applications of generalizations.[6] They are what can be called *inferential statements*. (This is, incidentally, also characteristic of statements to the effect that something *must be* the case. The occurrence of the term "must" is a sign of an inference. If we see or otherwise observe the thing in question, we do not say that it must be, but that it *is*.) It is characteristic of inferential statements that they are the results of inference, in the sense that inference is essential to their establishment. They cannot be established merely by observation. This is not the case with noninferential statements. In some cases, of course, we are not in a position to observe the thing in question. It happened too far away, perhaps, or too long ago. But we recognize that we could have observed it, under appropriate conditions, and the case in

6 Cf. Irving M. Copi, *Introduction to Logic* (New York: The Macmillan Company, 1953), p. 330: "Part of the very meaning of the word 'cause' . . . is that every occurrence of a cause producing an effect is an *instance* or *example* of the general causal law that such circumstances are *always* accompanied by such phenomena." See also p. 332: "Since a general causal law is implied by every assertion that a particular circumstance was the cause of a particular phenomenon, there is an element of generality in every such assertion."

question is one of a type other members of which can be established by observation. What I am saying about moral judgments, then, is that they are inferential judgments. They are necessarily the conclusions of inference. But this is, indeed, already implied by the term "judgment."

§ 2 §

That moral judgments are implicitly general, or are governed by what I have called the generalization principle, is coming to be pointed out with increasing frequency in the literature of the subject. It has, indeed, been given at least implicit acknowledgment by the vast majority of moral philosophers, and this is a good thing, for were a point of this nature to be absolutely novel, this in itself would be something of an argument against it. It has, however, in recent discussions of the subject, come to be regarded as a matter of only linguistic importance, and thus not as a point that has any moral relevance. It is now widely regarded as merely a matter of how we use the term "moral judgment," as simply a fact of usage. Thus, on this view, a judgment about what ought to be done that one is not prepared to generalize or apply universally would simply not be *called* a "moral judgment," but, since this is merely a fact about the use of language, no moral judgments can be based on this. It should be clear that this is not at all my view of the matter. I have agreed that this characteristic is part of the meaning of what I have called distinctively moral terms, and that one who says that a certain act is right for some given person and not right for any similar person in similar circumstances would be involved in a contradiction. But I do not at all agree that this is merely a fact of language, that it is trivial, or that it is morally neutral. (It should be remembered that the traditional name for what I have been calling the generalization principle is the principle of justice.) The analysis I have already given of this principle is in itself an argument against this view, and the discussions in the chapters to follow will provide further evidence against it. For the best way to show that the generalization principle has moral consequences is actually to trace out these consequences. Yet this particular point is so important as to be worth explicit consideration, and for this purpose I should like to examine some actual samples of the view I have just mentioned.

Consider first the following passage:

> Whenever I think that I ought to do something, it is essential to the moral nature of the case that I think that anybody else, in the same circumstances, would be under the same obligation. . . .
> It is important to notice that I am only analyzing our actual behaviour, not recommending anything. I am not saying that we *ought* to generalize our actions when we are faced with a moral problem; I am not saying that we shall best solve our moral problems by considering how we would wish other people to behave in similar circumstances. All I am saying is that, whenever we reflect morally on our proposed actions, we actually do extend the class of actions to include every possible agent. If we didn't, our reflections wouldn't be moral reflections. . . . I say, not that we ought to act in this way, but that, when we act morally, we cannot help acting in this way.[7]

This last statement is a very curious one. It is, in fact, self-contradictory. For it is a sheer tautology that *one ought to act morally*. Given that when we act morally we necessarily act in this way, then, since we ought to act morally, it follows that we ought to act in this way. I must admit that I had not before supposed that this tautology had any practical use, but it has one in this case, probably because, like all tautologies, it does have a use in inference.

There is no need to consider in detail all the other statements in the passage just quoted, for the same job can be done by considering, instead, another sample of this same view, one which is stated somewhat differently and in a somewhat more forceful way. Although the passage to follow refers to moral principles, rather than to moral judgments, this

[7] Bernard Mayo, *The Logic of Personality* (London: Jonathan Cape, Ltd., 1952), pp. 147-8.

does not affect the point at issue, and essentially the same sort of criticism will apply.

A principle is not usually called a moral one unless the person who adopts it is prepared to apply it universally. If a man says that he does something as a matter of principle, he cannot (logically) make exceptions unless another moral principle is involved. . . . He is *abusing language* if he says that it is a matter of moral principle with him to pay his debts and he pays Jones, while refusing to pay Smith, without being able to give any reason for the discrepancy.

The logical fact that a pro-attitude is not called a "moral principle" unless a man is prepared to universalize it has led some philosophers to suppose that it can be proved that we ought to be impartial. But this is to commit the fallacy of deducing a moral injunction from a feature of moral language. A man who has no principles that he is prepared to apply impartially has no moral principles; but we cannot prove that he ought to have any moral principles by pointing out how the phrase "moral principles" is used.[8]

This, it may readily be admitted, is an impressive and powerful argument. Yet I do not think it is sound, and in fact I think it wrong almost from beginning to end. Note, in the first place, that one who says that "it is a matter of moral principle with him to pay his debts and . . . pays Jones, while refusing to pay Smith, without being able to give any reason for the discrepancy," is not just abusing language. He is being immoral. It does not matter in the least whether or not he *says* "that it is a matter of moral principle with him to pay his debts." For if it is not, it ought to be, and whether he says this or not his act is still wrong. For it is of the sort that requires justification, and is wrong without it. To treat Jones in one way and Smith in another, without there being any relevant difference between them to justify this difference in treatment, is wrong; and if one is unable "to give any reason for the discrepancy" it may be presumed that there is none.

---

[8] P. H. Nowell-Smith, *Ethics* (London: Penguin Books, 1954), p. 309 (italics added). See also p. 177.

It is curious that this violation of a moral principle should be regarded as merely an abuse of language.

Notice, in the second place, the rather blithe reference to "the fallacy of deducing a moral injunction from a feature of moral language." This has the nature of an invocation. But the question to be asked about it is, what is this fallacy? Is there such a fallacy? And is it committed in the instance before us? My answer, at least to this last question, is "No." For there is really no question about proving that we ought to be impartial. If a proof is wanted, nothing is easier than to give one. Thus: "To be partial is to be unfair, to be unfair is to be unjust, to be unjust is to be immoral. But it is morally wrong to be immoral. Therefore we ought not to be immoral, therefore we ought not to be unjust, therefore we ought not to be unfair, and therefore we ought not to be partial. It follows that we ought to be impartial. Q.E.D." The only question that can sensibly be raised in this connection, and the only one that actually is raised, is, What does being impartial consist in, in concrete cases, in this case or in that? Similarly, there is no question of proving that we ought to be moral. The only question that can be raised about it is, What in particular is it to be moral in this or that situation? Of course, to prove that we ought to be impartial is not to prove it *to* the man in question. It does not mean that he can be convinced of it or brought to admit it. A proof is not a restraining force, and neither is a moral principle. One can continue to be unjust, no matter how many proofs are given. But it must also be recognized that there is no more difficulty in proving to someone that he ought to be impartial than there is in proving to him that he ought not to "abuse language," or that he actually is doing so. It *may* be a fallacy to deduce a moral injunction from a feature of moral language. But whether it is depends on the feature in question. What we have here is a deduction of a moral injunction from a moral principle, a principle so fundamental as to be a pervasive feature of moral language. And it is not a fallacy to deduce a moral injunction from *it*.

Consider, finally, the last statement in the passage we are

examining. It is said that "we cannot prove that [one] ought to have any moral principles by pointing out how the phrase 'moral principles' is used." This sounds sententious. But it is also seriously misleading. "Of course," we say, "by pointing out how some word is used, which is a matter of fact about usage, we cannot prove anything about what ought to be done. One can use words correctly and still be immoral." But it is not really a matter of how the phrase "moral principles" is used. It is rather a matter of what moral principles are. And from this it is not so hard to prove that. one "ought to have moral principles." If "having" moral principles means anything at all, it means acting in accordance with them. But to act in accordance with moral principles is to be moral. When we say of someone that he has no moral principles, we mean that he is immoral, that he does not act in accordance with moral principles. Hence to prove that one ought "to have" moral principles is to prove that one ought to be moral, and this has already been dealt with. Therefore the real meaning of the sentence, "A man who has no principles that he is prepared to apply impartially has no moral principles," is "A man who is not impartial in his treatment of others, who treats others unfairly, is not acting in accordance with moral principles, is violating the principle of justice, and is thus acting immorally." Any other meaning that might be given to the phrase "having moral principles" is irrelevant in this context.

I conclude from this that the generalization principle, and the associated generality of moral judgments, does have moral consequences. Moral judgments can be based on this characteristic of moral judgments. To claim that this is to confuse logical considerations with ethical ones (or language with morals), is to invoke a dogma, and one that has not been shown to have any relevant application in the present context. This illustrates something, I think, concerning the nature of facts about "moral language," and about the possibility of a "morally neutral" ethics.

Yet there is one thing that I have already said that I wish to re-emphasize. To ask whether one ought to be impartial is one question, and a senseless one. To ask what it is to be impartial in particular contexts is another question, and not at all a senseless one. Questions of this sort cannot be answered merely by facts about language, or, in actual situations, merely by reasoning about them, any more than they can be answered merely by a recital of facts. It is possible that these two sorts of questions have been confused.

§ 3 §

There is still another kind of statement or judgment to which moral judgments bear a significant analogy. Moral judgments are in an important way analogous to judgments of probability, to judgments of what it is reasonable to believe or expect. (I speak of a *judgment* of probability in order to emphasize that we have to judge, or assess, or evaluate, the probability of a proposition in the light of the available evidence for and against it. And I speak of the probability of a proposition, rather than of the probability of an event, because the probability of an event is the probability of the proposition that the event will occur.) The probability of a proposition not only depends on the evidence for it; it is inextricably connected with it. Whether it is reasonable to believe some proposition to be true depends on there being reasons for it, and on the extent to which the reasons for it outweigh the reasons against it. It can never be reasonable to believe something for which there are no reasons; it can never be reasonable for *me* to believe something for which *I* have no reasons. Now the same proposition can be probable in relation to certain evidence and improbable in relation to different, or conflicting, evidence. That is to say, it may be reasonable to believe some proposition on the basis of certain evidence, and unreasonable to believe it on the basis of different evidence. At one time it was perfectly reasonable for people to believe that the earth was flat, for this was supported by all the evidence then available; it would not be reasonable for anyone, in any civilized community, to believe this today, for the evidence on this matter is now of quite a different order. We can thus say that at one time the proposition that the earth is flat was probable (meaning that it was reasonable to believe it), and in saying this we are not saying something about the proposition by itself or in isolation, but about the proposition in relation to the evidence then available.

This point, which is often summed up by saying that "probability is relative to evidence," is by now almost canonical in discussions of the subject. Yet it has its difficulties, and it has in fact recently been disputed, in the following way:

> Certainly the most reasonable estimate a man can make of the probability of some hypothesis depends in every case on the evidence at his disposal—not just any batch he chooses to consider, but *all* the relevant evidence he has access to—but equally, it depends on the same body of evidence whether he can reasonably conclude that a given statement is *true*. To put the point in other words, it depends on the evidence a man has at his disposal which of the possibilities he considers are to be accepted with complete trust (accepted as true) and what weight he is entitled to put on the others (how probable he should consider them). In each case, the reasonable conclusion is that which is warranted by the evidence. . . . However, all that goes here for "probable" goes also for "true"; so if we accept "Probability is Relative to Evidence" as more than an epigram, then we are saddled with "Truth is Relative to Evidence" as well.[9]

I am not here seeking to establish something about probability, but about moral judgments, namely that they are inextricably tied to the reasons that support them, and simply in order to elucidate this point, I am claiming that they are in this respect analogous to judgments of probability. This purpose could equally well be accomplished by talking, not about judgments of probability, but about judgments of what it is reasonable to believe. For these are obviously relative to reasons. Nevertheless, the argument just presented, as ingenious as it is, is demonstrably unsound.

[9] Stephen Toulmin, *The Uses of Argument* (Cambridge: Cambridge University Press, 1958), p. 81.

The argument we are examining can be stated as follows: If probability is relative to evidence, then so is truth; but truth is not relative to evidence, therefore probability is not. The only point that can be questioned here is the conditional premise, and through it the conclusion. For truth is clearly not relative to evidence. Whether a proposition is true or not does not depend on the evidence for it. It is independent of evidence, just as it is independent of human wishes, desires, or thoughts. The probability of a proposition, however, is not similarly independent of evidence, though it is independent of human wishes or desires. To be sure, whether I have *a right* to conclude that a proposition is true, or to accept it as true, does depend on the evidence at my disposal. But the argument we are examining actually confuses *accepting* a proposition as true, or having a right to do so, with its *being* true. One can conclude that a proposition is true or accept it as true without its actually being so. (Just as one can accept it as true without any evidence. But in this case one has no right to do so, one cannot do so reasonably.) To be sure, one cannot *know* that it is true unless it is true; nevertheless to know that it is true one must have evidence or a way of knowing, so that it can be true without one's knowing it or indeed without anyone knowing it. Now what we know or judge when we know or judge that some proposition is probable is not something incompatible with its being true; what we know or judge is that it is *probably true*. These two terms, "probable" and "true," do not compete with each other, but play altogether different roles. (They do not play in the same league, because they do not play the same kind of game.) "Probable" is opposed, in one direction, to "certain," and in another to "improbable," but not at all to "true" or "false." Probability, like knowledge, but unlike truth, is an epistemic concept. It has the character of what I before called an inferential term.

Thus, granted that it depends on a body of evidence whether one "can reasonably conclude that a given statement is true," what depends on this evidence is whether *the conclusion drawn is reasonable*, and not whether the statement is true. Now to say that the conclusion drawn is reasonable, that is, to say that it is reasonable to draw that conclusion, is the same as saying that the conclusion drawn is probable. (To say that it is unreasonable to doubt it is the same as saying that it is certain.) Supposing two conclusions to be drawn from the same body of evidence, the more reasonable one is the more probable one, the one better supported by the evidence. Probability is related to evidence just as "reasonable" is related to reasons.

It follows that, like a statement of the form "A is relevant," a statement of the form "A is probable" is, as it stands, incomplete or elliptical. It is elliptical for a statement of the form "A is probable on the basis of such and such evidence." Thus judgments of probability involve an implicit reference to the evidence on which they are based, and cannot be understood, discussed, or rationally accepted apart from it. Of course the evidence on which such a judgment is based is often apparent from the context. I am not saying that it must necessarily be stated. It can often be taken as understood, and usually is. Yet if the judgment is questioned, then the evidence cannot be taken for granted but must be specified. If one is unable to specify the evidence for his statement that A is probable, then one's statement is merely subjective, and is thus in a sense not a genuine judgment of probability at all. In such a case the statement is not, as it appears to be, a statement about A; it is merely an indication of the beliefs of the speaker. It can be taken as a statement about these beliefs, or as just an expression of them (together perhaps with an incitement to others to believe the same), but it does not really matter which. Failure to make this distinction is at the roots of the dispute whether probability is objective or subjective. A statement of probability is subjective—is merely about someone's beliefs, perhaps a measure of them or an expression of them—if, and only if, the speaker is unable to specify the evidence on the basis of which it is made. (It should be obvious that if someone specifies as evidence for his statement that A is probable the fact that he believes it will happen, this in no way denies that his statement is about his beliefs.) But in such a case his statement that something is probable is not a genuine probability judgment at all, for no *judgment* enters into it. It merely appears to be, in virtue of its verbal or external form. On the other hand, one's statement is objective to the degree to which one is able to specify the evidence on which it is based. For this evidence makes, or purports to make, a claim on others; if they accept the evidence they ought to accept the judgment as well. Thus through the evidence the judgment is taken out of the personal, subjective realm into the impersonal, objective realm.

Now precisely analogous considerations apply to moral judgments. A genuine moral judgment involves implicit reference to the reasons upon which it is based, for a genuine moral judgment is governed by the generalization principle. Apart from this reference to the reasons supporting them, statements like "x is right" are indeterminate and merely subjective. Such a statement is merely subjective if the speaker is unable to specify reasons in support of it. (If he is able to, and at the same time refuses to, then from the point of view of the hearer his statement is still merely subjective.) In this case it is merely an indication of what the speaker likes or dislikes, approves of or disapproves of, and it can be taken either as a statement of these attitudes or preferences or as merely an expression of them. "An opinion on a point of conduct, not supported by reasons, can only count as one person's preference; and if the reasons, when given, are a mere appeal to a similar preference felt by other people, it is still only many people's liking instead of one." [1] This point can be extended further: if it can count only as a *preference*, then it cannot count as a *judgment*. Thus a statement of this form, unsupported by reasons, is not really a moral judgment at all. It appears to be one. It has the verbal form of a moral judgment. It is couched in the language in which moral judgments are normally expressed. It contains the term "right," or "wrong," or some synonymous or associated expression. But it is not a statement about what it appears or is supposed to be about.

[1] John Stuart Mill, *On Liberty* (Everyman's Library ed.; New York: E. P. Dutton and Company, 1910), chap. I, par. 6, p. 69.

It is merely about the emotions or preferences or attitudes of the speaker.

This point, I think, had best be elaborated. What I am maintaining is that one who makes a moral judgment, or a statement having the verbal form of a moral judgment, but is unable to give reasons in support of it, has not really made a *judgment* about the action or whatever it is that is in question. Or, if we choose to call it so, his judgment is merely subjective—it is merely an indication of his attitudes (or desires or feelings). Now, whether it is taken as a statement that one has a certain attitude, or merely as an expression of this attitude, is of no great import, for it is one and the same thing for practical purposes. The judgment is still subjective in a perfectly proper sense: it tells us more about the speaker than about what he was ostensibly talking about, than the action referred to. On the other hand, if one is able to give reasons in support of the judgment then one's judgment is objective. This does not mean that it is necessarily correct or cannot reasonably be disputed. A judgment can be objective without being sound or true. For, even though reasons must be given, they may not be conclusive reasons or even especially good ones. They must be genuine reasons, but there may be better reasons against the judgment. The objectivity of a judgment would thus appear to be a matter of degree, some being more objective than others, and it may thus be better to say that one's judgment is objective to the extent to which one is able to give reasons in support of it. But if a "judgment" is merely subjective, there is a perfectly proper sense in which it is not a genuine moral judgment at all, for it is not about what it appears to be about. It is a spurious moral judgment, a disguised autobiographical statement.

There is a perfectly good reason why a reference to reasons is necessary for objectivity. In giving a reason, my reason, for believing something, I am attempting to give you a reason for believing likewise. A reason necessarily makes a claim to objectivity. My reason makes a claim to being *a* reason, that is, a reason independently of the person who so regards it. It is not a reason simply because I regard it as one. It may not in fact be anyone else's reason, but it must be such that it could be, and would be if he were aware of it.[2] To regard something as a reason for arriving at a certain conclusion is to assume that everyone who knows the fact or whatever it is that is regarded as a reason ought to arrive at the same conclusion, and will so far as he is rational. Of course, my reasons for believing something may not be the same as your reasons. There are all sorts of possibilities here. I might be aware of facts that you are not aware of, and vice versa. We might have different reasons for believing the same thing, or our different reasons may lead us to different conclusions. Again, we might weigh the reasons differently. Or something that is given as a reason may be one only under certain assumptions, which perhaps I do not accept, and so on. It still holds that if I claim that something is a reason I am claiming that anyone who accepts it as true ought also to accept it as a reason, and in the absence of conflicting considerations, as a good reason. Note that to give a reason is not necessarily to give a motive. I am talking here about conviction, not about persuasion. One can be persuaded by all sorts of means, ranging from clubs and social pressure to rhetorical devices and transparently fallacious arguments. Conviction requires rational grounds. I am also not talking about a reason for *doing* something, in the sense in which my reason for sitting in the

---

[2] Cf. Bernard Mayo, "Commitments and Reasons," *Mind*, vol. LXIV (July 1955), pp. 355-8, especially p. 355: "It is in the nature of a moral action or a moral judgment that it can be supported by reasons. But if I advance a reason for my action, then, although it would be correct idiom to speak of 'my' reason for my action, the relation denoted by 'my' is quite different from what it would be if I had spoken of my motives or my inclinations. . . . The difference is this. My having an inclination is logically (though not always causally) independent of other people having similar inclinations; but my having a reason, either for a theoretical conclusion or for a nontheoretical action, is not logically independent of other people having a reason. What counts for me as a reason counts for others, and if I could not regard it as counting for others also, it could not count for me. In other words, it is self-contradictory to say both that I have a reason for doing X and that no one else could have that reason for doing X."

sun may not be your reason, and may not impel you to do the same; there is no question here of objectivity, or of justification.

In saying that a moral judgment is not objective or genuine if not supported by reasons I do not intend to imply that the speaker must actually give his reasons. If I agree with you in thinking some act to be wrong I will be unlikely to ask for your reasons. Sometimes, indeed in a great many cases, one's reasons are obvious from the context, or simply from the way in which the judgment is formulated, and the fact that they are not actually stated would not make one's judgment subjective or any the less genuine. Yet in cases of doubt or disagreement, in cases where a question arises, then reasons must be given. For in such cases it is not obvious from the context what the reasons are, or, if it is, whether they are sufficient.

Again, in saying that one must be able to give reasons I am not implying that one must be able to *analyze* them. To be able to give an argument in support of one's view is not the same as being able to analyze one's argument. The latter is on a different level of activity. All that I am implying is that one must have a reason—a genuine reason, not "because I am I" or "because I like it that way" or anything of that sort. For if one is unable to give a reason then it may be presumed that he has none.

What I am saying, then, is that someone who says that a certain act is wrong, but is unable to say why it is wrong or what reason there is to believe that it is wrong, has said no more than that he does not approve of the act, or would prefer that it not be done. Note that it is quite possible for someone to approve of an act's being done by one person and to disapprove of its being done by another without being able to specify any relevant difference between the two cases. This should be obvious where one offers as his "reasons" the fact that he likes the one person and does not like the other. It has been said that "I cannot approve of an action of mine without approving of a possible similar action by someone else; likewise I cannot approve of someone else's action unless I am prepared to approve of myself doing it." [3] This is not so. To do this would no doubt involve me in a contradiction, but it is not impossible for me to contradict myself. What is impossible is for it to be right for A to do x and not right for anyone similar to A to do x in similar circumstances. But it is not impossible for me to *regard it as right* for A to do x and as not right for anyone similar in similar circumstances. It is possible for me to believe that P is true and also that P is false. What is impossible is for P to *be* both true and false. This means that my beliefs would be inconsistent, but not that I cannot have them.

It follows that statements like "x is right" do not, necessarily or in general, mean "I approve of x," or anything along these lines. They do so in case, and only in case, the speaker is unable to provide reasons for his assertion. Of course, from the fact that someone asserts "x is right" it can be inferred, if his assertion was honest, that he approves of x, that is, that he regards x as right. But this holds for any assertion—from the fact that it is made one can infer, on the assumption that it is honestly made, that the speaker believes what he is saying.

It also follows, trivially, that moral judgments can be supported by reasons; a statement having the verbal form of a moral judgment for which one is unable to give reasons does not express a genuine moral judgment at all.[4] It appears that

[3] Bernard Mayo, *The Logic of Personality*, p. 152. It is interesting to note that an "emotive theory" of probability can be constructed by analogy to the emotive theory of ethics. "This is probable" can be analyzed as meaning "I have a strong determination to believe this; do so as well." We can also construct on these lines an emotive theory of truth, or epistemology: "This is true" means "I believe this; do so as well." Depending on which statement of the emotive theory, out of the many available, is taken as a model, one can construct analogous extensions to probability and truth. It is thus rather remarkable that the emotive analysis should be thought to apply peculiarly to moral judgments. Cf. H. J. Paton, "The Emotive Theory of Ethics," in *In Defence of Reason* (London: Hutchinson's University Library, 1951), pp. 205-6.

[4] Essentially this same view has been set forth by Stuart Hampshire in "Fallacies in Moral Philosophy," *Mind*, vol. LVIII (October 1949), p. 471: "If I am not prepared to produce such practical arguments, pointing to what ought to have been done, I shall admit that I am not making a

adherents of emotive or subjective ethical theories have not
been analyzing genuine moral judgments, but expressions
that are parasitic on them.

---

genuine moral judgment, but merely expressing or reporting my own
feelings; and I shall admit that it was misleading to use the form of sentence ordinarily associated with moral judgments, and not with expressions
of feeling. Doubtless many sentences containing moral terms are ambiguous, and may be normally used both as expressions of practical
judgments and as expressions of feeling; but the important point is that,
if challenged about our intentions, we are required to *distinguish* between
such uses. . . ." I am not prepared to go along with Mr. Hampshire's
wording of the point, which unduly assumes that people will admit, in the
sort of situation he describes, to using a misleading form of words, and
seems to imply that this is relevant. It is not.

❀

CHAPTER IV

THE GENERALIZATION
ARGUMENT

The generalization argument has the general form: "If everyone were to do x, the consequences would be disastrous (or undesirable); therefore no one ought to do x." It will be convenient to refer to any particular argument of this or some equivalent form as an instance, or application, of the generalization argument. Any actual instance of this argument may of course appear with many variations of wording. One might merely ask the question, "What would happen if everyone did that?" or "How would you like it if everyone did that?" This sort of argument, however, underlies the use of such questions. But there is actually no great difficulty in identifying instances of this argument. The major problem is that of determining its rational force, both in the general case and in particular applications.

As we have seen, there are certain conditions under which this argument is applicable, and certain conditions under which it is not. Some applications of this argument are fallacious, and some are not. Thus the basic problem about the generalization argument is to determine the conditions under which it is valid. To say that this argument is *valid* under certain conditions is to say that, under those conditions, the proposition that the consequences of everyone's acting in a certain way would be undesirable provides good reason for concluding that it is wrong to act in that way.

The statement that an application of the argument must meet certain conditions in order to be valid presupposes that the form of the argument itself is not invalid, that the argument is not invalid altogether. If the form of the argument were itself fallacious, there could be no question of distinguishing valid applications from invalid ones, for it would be invalid in every instance. And if this were the case, then the fact that it would be disastrous if everyone acted in a certain way could have no bearing on the question whether it is wrong to act in that way. It would be a fact with no moral relevance.

When stated in this way, the idea that the generalization argument is invalid in every instance should sound somewhat less plausible. Nevertheless, it is supported by the fact that the argument certainly appears to involve a formal fallacy, that of arguing from "not everyone" to "no one," or from "some" to "all." If it does, then while it might still be an effective means for persuasion, it could have no claim on rational conviction.

But this is a case in which grammatical form is a misleading guide to logical form. It is true that the generalization argument involves an inference from a statement of the form "Not everyone ought to do that" to one of the form "No one ought to do that," and thus may be said to involve an inference from "some" to "all." This is precisely why I have called it the generalization argument. But, as should by now be clear, it is not true that this sort of inference is always fallacious. It would be fallacious to argue that, since not everyone loves music, no one loves music. It is not necessarily fallacious to argue that, since not everyone ought to act in a certain way, therefore no one ought to act in that way. The difference is that in the latter case we are dealing with moral judgments, and the inference from "not everyone ought" to "no one ought" is mediated, and hence qualified, by the generalization *principle*.

That the generalization principle is involved in the generalization argument is no doubt obscured by the fact that in applications of the argument the qualification "all similar persons in similar circumstances" is left inexplicit. But in valid applications of the argument this restriction is either implicitly understood from the context or is indicated by various linguistic devices. For example, the argument "everyone ought to vote because if no one voted the government would collapse" is evidently meant to apply only to those legally permitted to vote. This condition on the argument I shall call that of *restricted universality*, and I shall go on to discuss it presently. Before doing so, however, it will be useful to set forth with some precision the various steps involved in the generalization argument, in order to illustrate more clearly its logical structure. For the generalization principle is not the only principle involved in it. Let us consider, then, the anatomy of the generalization argument.

§ 1 §

The argument involves, in the first place, the principle, "If the consequences of A's doing x would be disastrous, then A ought not to do x." The term "disastrous" is a stronger term than is actually necessary for the statement of this principle, as are such roughly synonymous terms as "terrible" and "catastrophic." It can be replaced by the somewhat weaker and more general term "undesirable." The consequences of an act can be undesirable without being disastrous. But if they are disastrous then they are undesirable. Thus this principle, which I shall call the *principle of consequences*, can be stated as follows: (1) If the consequences of A's doing x would be undesirable, then A ought not to do x. This is, obviously, equivalent to "If the consequences of A's *not* doing x would be undesirable, then A ought to do x." It is not, however, equivalent to "If the consequences of A's doing x would be desirable, then A ought to do x." I doubt very much whether the latter proposition is true (and whether it is or not will be discussed in Chapter VII). At any rate, it is no part of the generalization argument.

The principle of consequences is a necessary ethical or moral principle. It is necessary not only in the sense that its denial involves self-contradiction. It is necessary also in the sense that like the generalization principle, it is a necessary presupposition or precondition of moral reasoning. There can be sensible and fruitful disagreement about matters within the field delimited by it, but there can be no sensible or fruitful disagreement about the principle itself. We might say that, like the generalization principle, it is both necessary and fundamental.

I do not wish to imply that anyone ever has seriously questioned or denied this principle. It may be that no one has done so, at least explicitly; though there are probably many instances in which it has been denied by implication, just as there are unquestionably many cases in which it has been violated or disregarded. Yet the principle can be misunderstood, especially if the term "undesirable" is not properly understood. This term may be interpreted in either of two senses, with the consequence that there are two ways of interpreting the principle. Though these two ways are consistent with each other, they should be kept distinct.

One sense of "undesirable" is that of "undesirable on the whole." On this interpretation, the principle does not mean that if *some* of the consequences of A's doing x would be undesirable then A ought not to do x. It is perfectly consistent with it for some of the consequences of an act to be desirable and others to be undesirable, or for them to be undesirable in some respects but not in others. And it may well be that while some of the consequences of an act are undesirable, it is not undesirable, on the whole, for the act to be done. For the desirable consequences may *outweigh* the undesirable ones. Or it may be that the consequences of A's not doing x would be worse (more undesirable) than the consequences of his doing it.

In the second sense of "undesirable" it does not have this proviso of "on the whole." On this interpretation, the fact that some of the consequences of A's doing x would be undesirable is a reason for asserting that A ought not to do x, but it is not a conclusive reason. On the basis of this fact one could reasonably presume that it would be wrong for A to do x.[1] This presumption can be rebutted by showing that not all the consequences are undesirable, and that the undesirable consequences are outweighed by (are less important than) the desirable ones; in other words, by showing that the consequences of A's doing x would not be undesirable on the whole. Thus a more adequate, because less elliptical, statement of the principle, on this interpretation, would be: If the consequences of A's doing x would be undesirable, then A ought not to do x *without a reason or justification*. Such statements as "A ought to do x" are usually elliptical in this way.

These brief remarks should make it clear that this principle assumes a good deal less than might at first glance be supposed. It does not by itself determine the meaning of the term "undesirable," or what is desirable or undesirable, or how the various consequences of an action are to be weighed against each other in order to determine whether they are undesirable on the whole. Agreement on the principle is quite consistent with disagreement on these latter questions. Indeed, without agreement on the principle, disagreement on these other matters would have no point.

Now this first step in the generalization argument is the basis for the second, which is a generalization from it: (2) If the consequences of everyone's doing x would be undesirable, then not everyone ought to do x.[2]

---

[1] I am using the expressions "A ought not to do x," "It would be wrong for A to do x," and "A has no right to do x," synonymously, and I should say that this is in general conformity with their ordinary use. Thus I am treating "A ought to do x" as equivalent to "It would be wrong for A not to do x" and "A has no right not to do x." Note that the contradictory of "A ought to do x" is not "A ought not to do x," which is rather its contrary (for neither may hold), but "A has the right not to do x" (or "A need not do x").

[2] Since expressions like "not everyone ought" and "no one ought" can be deceptive, perhaps it should be said here that I definitely do not mean by "not everyone ought" the same as "not everyone is *required*," but rather "not everyone has the right" or "it would not be right for everyone." Similarly, by "no one ought" I do not mean "no one is required, or has the duty," but rather "no one has the right," or "it would not be right for *anyone*." (If one prefers to translate "not everyone ought to do

It is in the third step of the argument that the generalization principle comes into play: (3) If not everyone ought to do x, then no one ought to do x. This can of course be stated in the alternative form: If it is wrong for everyone to do x, then it is wrong for anyone to do x. Note that I have left unstated the necessary qualifications.

All of these steps are actually telescoped in the generalization argument itself, which is obviously deducible from (2) and (3): If the consequences of everyone's doing x would be undesirable, then no one ought to do x.

It may be useful to display in one place, in slightly different language, this deduction of the generalization argument from the generalization principle and the principle of consequences. The principle of consequences (C) states that: If the consequences of A's doing x would be undesirable, then A does not have the right to do x. The following principle (GC) is what I called a generalization from C: If the consequences of everyone's doing x would be undesirable, then not everyone has the right to do x. Now the generalization principle (GP) may be stated as follows: If not everyone has the right to do x, then not anyone (no one) has the right to do x. The generalization argument (if the consequences of everyone's doing x would be undesirable, then no one has the right to do x) clearly follows from GP and GC.

Some remarks on this deduction are now in order. In the above generalization from the principle of consequences, (GC), "everyone" is treated collectively, not distributively. The hypothesis "If the consequences of everyone's acting in a certain way would be undesirable" differs from "If the consequences of *each and every act* of that kind would be undesirable." The latter implies that each and every act of that kind would be wrong. This is the true logical generalization of the principle of consequences, but it is not the one intended, nor is it particularly important.

Thus GC has as its consequent "not everyone ought to do

---

x" by "it ought not to be the case that everyone does x," I can see no objection to it, except that it is not very idiomatic, and I cannot see that it is helpful.)

x," instead of "everyone ought not to do *x*," because supposedly if not everyone does *x* the undesirable consequences that would result from everyone's doing it would be avoided. Hence the generalization argument does not imply that the consequences of each and every act of the kind mentioned would be undesirable. By reason of the generalization principle it implies that each and every act of that kind may be presumed to be wrong. Yet from the fact that an act is wrong it does not follow that its consequences would be undesirable.

The generalization argument is to be distinguished from what may be called the *generalized principle of consequences*: If the consequences of doing *x* would be undesirable (in general, or usually), then it is wrong (in general) to do *x*. Here "*x*" refers, not to a specific action, but to a kind of action. The consequences of lying are usually undesirable; hence lying is usually wrong. The generalized principle of consequences refers to the *individual consequences* of actions of a certain kind. The generalization argument refers to the *collective consequences* of everyone's acting in a certain way. These are not always the same.

From the fact that the generalization principle is involved in the generalization argument, in the way shown, it follows that all the qualifications required by the former are required by the latter. They are therefore necessary for any application of the argument to be valid. The first is that of restricted universality, the restriction to "every similar person in similar circumstances." The second is the elliptical nature of the conclusion that no one has the right to do *x*. As I mentioned once before, the form of the generalization principle especially appropriate for the proper understanding of the generalization argument is: If not everyone ought to act or be treated in a certain way, then no one ought to act or be treated in that way *without a reason or justification*. A more adequate statement of the generalization argument, therefore, is: If the consequences of everyone's acting or being treated in a certain way would be undesirable, then no one ought to act or be treated in that way *without a reason*. In other words, whoever acts in a way in which it would be undesirable for everyone to act must justify his conduct. The fact that it would be undesirable for everyone to act in that way provides a presumptive reason, and not a conclusive one, for the judgment that his conduct is wrong. One can justify oneself, or show that one is an exception, by showing that one's circumstances are relevantly different from those in which the act is wrong.

But the discussion of the procedures by which one can justify his (or someone else's) acting in a way in which it would be undesirable for everyone to act, or in which it would be generally wrong to act, may be left for later on. What I propose to do now is to consider in somewhat greater detail the condition of restricted universality.

§ 2 §

In actual applications of the generalization argument, the universal terms "everyone" and "no one" are not, as they may appear to be, unrestricted. They are rarely, if ever, meant to include each and every human being. Their scope is restricted to each and every member of a certain *class* of persons, to those who have certain characteristics or meet certain conditions. This restriction can easily be incorporated into the statement of the argument: "If the consequences of *every member of K's* doing x would be undesirable, then *no member of K* has the right to do x." But, as I said before, this sort of restriction is ordinarily understood from the context in which the argument is applied. In some instances, of course, the class involved may be explicitly mentioned, but it is not in all, and even where it is, it is unlikely to be specified completely, so that the context must still be relied on for its more precise determination. No one would interpret the term "everyone" as it is used in this argument as including cats and dogs, or mice and beetles. At the very most it is meant to include only human beings or rational agents. This is so obvious that it never needs to be mentioned. A similar point is true of the act in question, which may be referred to by a term like "that," or "in that way." Such a term makes no sense apart from a context. In order to know to what, in a particular context, a term like "that" is used to refer, one must know what the context is. Even when the act is referred to in some more definite manner, as by indicating the kind of act it is, it is always considered as taking place in a certain context, or under certain conditions, which may remain unstated.

This point is clearly illustrated by the two following examples of the application of the generalization argument, in which, though the argument is explicitly restricted to a certain class of persons, it is still necessary to know something of the context of application.

The first example is taken from Trollope's novel *Phineas Finn:*

> Early on the next morning he saw Mr. Bunce, and used all his eloquence to keep that respectable member of society at home;—but in vain. "What good do you expect to do, Mr. Bunce?" he said, with perhaps some little tone of authority in his voice.
>
> "To carry my point," said Bunce.
>
> "And what is your point?"
>
> "My present point is the ballot, as a part of the Government measure."
>
> "And you expect to carry that by going out into the streets with all the roughs of London, and putting yourself in direct opposition to the authority of the magistrates? Do you really believe that the ballot will become the law of the land any sooner because you incur this danger and inconvenience?"
>
> "Look here, Mr. Finn; I don't believe the sea will become any fuller because the Piddle runs into it out of the Dorsetshire fields; but I do believe that the waters from all the countries is what makes the ocean. I shall help; and it's my duty to help."
>
> "It's your duty as a respectable citizen, with a wife and family, to stay at home."
>
> "If everybody with a wife and family was to say so, there'd be none there but roughs, and then where should we be? What would the Government people say to us then? If everyman with a wife and family was to show hisself in the streets to-night, we should have the ballot before Parliament breaks

up, and if none of 'em don't do it, we shall never have the
ballot. Ain't that so?" Phineas, who intended to be honest,
was not prepared to dispute the assertion on the spur of the
moment. "If that's so," said Bunce, triumphantly, "a man's
duty's clear enough. He ought to go, though he'd two wives
and families." And he went. (Chap. xxv.)

The second example is taken from an article about a Miss
Vivien Kellems, a contemporary female tycoon who has become famous through her refusal to comply with the law requiring employers to withhold their employees' income taxes.
The editors of some three hundred and fifty newspapers, it is
reported, have devoted

> much of the space they expend on her . . . to spelling out
> for her some elementary facts of life—announcing that, in
> case she doesn't realize it, what she has really been practicing
> is anarchy, and warning her that if all employers followed her
> example and refused to withhold their employees' taxes, a
> vast amount of the money due the government would never
> be forked over at all, millions of people would wish they were
> dead on each March 15th, the present regiment of Internal
> Revenue men would have to be expanded many times over,
> and the net result would be that tax rates would almost
> certainly go up for people like Miss Kellems.[3]

These are certainly two clear cases of the application of the
generalization argument. In each instance it is certainly clear
that, although the class of persons to which the argument
is meant to be applicable is not specified completely, the
argument is not intended to apply to all human beings in all
possible circumstances. In the first case, for example, the
argument is applied to the class of men with wives and
families; and it is clear from the context that it is not meant
to apply to all such men, but is restricted at least to those who
are citizens of England. In the second case, not only is the
argument explicitly applied only to members of the class of
employers, but it would be senseless to suppose it applied to

[3] From a profile by Andy Logan, *The New Yorker*, Vol. XXVI, no. 51
(February 10, 1951), p. 50.

someone who has no employees. It makes no sense to ask whether someone who has no employees has the right to refuse to withhold his employees' taxes. There are further restrictions, clear from the context, that are not expressly mentioned. For one thing, the argument is meant to apply only to employers within the United States, and only to those in the United States who are required by law to withhold their employees' taxes. Thus what follows from the argument is that no employer in the United States covered by this law has the right to refuse to withhold his employees' taxes, and not that employers in Brazil, or some other place, do not have this right. The class of persons who are "similar" in this context is the class of persons satisfying these conditions.

It should accordingly be clear that the generalization argument, in typical applications, is not meant to apply to every person no matter what the circumstances, but to every similar person in similar circumstances. Note also how, in such applications, the consequences of everyone's acting in a certain way are described. It is not merely *stated* that they would be undesirable—frequently this is not *stated* at all; they are, rather, spelled out in some detail, with the effect (or at least the intent) of putting their undesirability beyond doubt.

§ 3 §

When people begin to admonish me that if everyone did as I did, etc., I answer that humanity would probably perish from cold if everyone produced food, and would certainly starve if everyone made clothes or built houses.[4]

[4] Morris R. Cohen, *The Faith of a Liberal* (New York: Henry Holt and Company, 1946), p. 86. Part of the sentence just prior to the one quoted in the text is: "It would be a poor world if there were no diversity of function to suit the diversity of natural aptitudes." This is true; it does not follow that we have here a valid counterexample to the generalization argument. Cf. Cohen's *Reason and Nature* (New York: Harcourt, Brace and Company, 1931), p. 433: "Nor is there any force in the argument that lying is morally bad because it cannot be made universal. The familiar argument, 'If everybody did so and so . . .' applies just as well to baking bread, building houses, and the like. It is just as impossible for everybody to tell lies all the time as to bake bread all the time or to build houses all the time."

This certainly has the appearance of a genuine counter-example to the generalization argument. Since the consequences of everyone's producing food would be undesirable, on the pattern of the generalization argument it would seem to follow that it is wrong for anyone to do so, and this, of course, is absurd.

But this actually does not follow, and the generalization argument does not at all have this consequence. For consider what would happen if no one produced food. If no one produced food, everyone would starve. Hence on the same line of reasoning it might be argued that everyone ought to produce food. The argument that no one ought to produce food because of what would happen if everyone did can thus be met by the counterargument that everyone ought to produce food because of what would happen if no one did. A valid application of the generalization argument, however, cannot be met by such a counterargument. The argument that everyone ought to vote because of what would happen if no one did cannot be rebutted in this way.

In a case in which the consequences of everyone's acting in a certain way would be undesirable, while the consequences of no one's acting in that way would also be undesirable, I shall say that the argument can be *inverted*. Thus the argument is invertible with respect to producing food, building houses, and making clothes. Now in order for the generalization argument to have a valid application with respect to some action it is necessary that it not be invertible with respect to that action. In other words, an argument of the form, "Since the consequences of everyone's doing x would be undesirable, no one ought to do x," is valid only if it is not the case that the consequences of no one's doing x would also be undesirable.

This condition on the validity of the generalization argument is not something *ad hoc*, devised just to meet this kind of case, though even if it were, this would be no objection to it. It is another of those conditions implicitly understood but not explicitly stated, and can readily be incorporated into the statement of the argument: "If the consequences of everyone's doing x would be undesirable, while the consequences of no one's doing x would not be undesirable, then no one has the right to do x." This of course also holds in the form: "If the consequences of no one's doing x would be undesirable, while the consequences of everyone's doing x would not be undesirable, then everyone ought to do x." It is important to remember that the restrictions already discussed apply here also. The conclusion that no one has the right to do x is elliptical for "no one has the right to do x *without a reason*. Furthermore, the terms "everyone" and "no one" involved here are restricted in their scope. Thus, fully stated, incorporating all the restrictions so far discussed, the generalization argument may be stated: "If the consequences of every member of K's doing x in certain circumstances would be undesirable, while the consequence of no member of K's doing x (in those circumstances) would not be undesirable, then no member of K has the right to do x (in such circumstances) without a special reason."

The condition of restricted universality deserves special mention in this context. The terms "everyone" and "no one" must have the same restrictions on their scope in any one application of the argument. For an application of the argument may be invertible, or may seem to be so, if the term "no one" is used with a wider extension than "everyone," or if "everyone" is used with a wider extension than "no one." Such a situation can arise in the following manner. Suppose (1) that if everyone were to act in a certain way the consequences would be undesirable, and (2) that if no one were to act in that way the consequences would be undesirable. Such a case so far conforms to the condition under which the argument is invertible, and hence invalid. However, it may be that in (1) "everyone" is restricted to the members of a certain class K, while in (2) "no one" is not restricted to the members of this class but has a wider range, so that it means, say, "no one at all." In such a case the argument is not really invertible. In order for it to be invertible it is necessary for the consequences of every member of K's acting in that way and the consequences of no member of K's acting in that way both to be undesirable. It may very well be true of some kind of action that the consequences of no one *at all* acting in that way would be undesirable while the consequences of no member of a certain class acting in that way would not be.

Consider a concrete case. Suppose an attempt is made to invert the argument, "Everyone ought to vote, since the consequences would be disastrous if no one voted." To attempt to invert this argument is to raise the question of what would happen if everyone voted. "If everyone were to vote, this would mean that idiots, imbeciles, infants, illiterates, incompetents, lunatics, and public enemies would vote. And it would be just as bad if all these people were to vote as it would be if no one were to vote at all." But this has not the slightest tendency to show that the original argument is invalid. One who claims that everyone ought to vote, because of what would happen if no one did, does not mean that everyone in the universe, including idiots, illiterates, lunatics, and Martians, ought to vote. The conclusion that everyone ought to vote is restricted to the same class or classes of persons to which the term "no one," in the premise, is restricted. This is obviously, or is obviously meant to be, the class of persons of which it is true that if none of them voted the consequences would be disastrous, and does not include imbeciles, infants, or lunatics. For of these people it is not true that if none of them voted the consequences would be disastrous; on the contrary, it would be disastrous if all such people did vote or attempt to vote. (It may be noted that this is normally the consideration invoked in order to justify legal restrictions on the right to vote.) Such people furthermore are not usually among those legally permitted to vote. Yet the argument is certainly restricted to those who are legally permitted to vote in the election in question, though it is hardly necessary for this condition to be made explicit in concrete applications. No one can justly be held responsible for not voting in an election in which he has no legal right to vote, even if there are good grounds for holding that he ought to have this right. (The question whether a law is just, is distinct from the question whether it ought to be broken; though the two are related, an answer to the one is not an automatic answer to the other.) This restriction would be even more obvious if the original premise were phrased "If everyone *refused* to vote . . ." instead of "If no one voted. . . ." For one who is not permitted or has no opportunity to do something cannot sensibly be said to have refused to do so. This argument is therefore not invertible.

It follows that not every application of the generalization argument is invertible, and therefore that this condition is not a trivial one.

§ 4 §

We have just seen that there are certain kinds of actions to which the argument cannot be applied. Specifically, with respect to such actions as producing food and making clothes, the argument is invertible and hence invalid. Yet it ought to be explained why this is the case. What is there about actions such as these that distinguishes them so markedly from other kinds of actions, apart from the fact that the generalization argument is not applicable to them? The explanation of this is to be found in the way such actions are described or conceived in the application of the argument.

There is certainly nothing strange in the fact that there are certain aspects of human behavior, certain kinds of events involving human beings, to which moral notions generally, and therefore the generalization argument in particular, cannot properly be applied. It would clearly be absurd to argue that someone has no right to be sick because of what would happen if everyone were. At the most this could only be a joke. Whether or not one is sick is not ordinarily the sort of thing over which one has any control or about which one has any choice, and we cannot therefore sensibly say that someone ought not to be sick. Being sick is properly not an *action* at all, but an event. It is not something we do, but something that happens to us, like coming-to-be and passing-away. But notice that there is nothing *grammatically* wrong with the sentence, "No one has the right to be sick, since if everyone

were sick the consequences would be disastrous." This by
itself is sufficient to show that certain conditions must be met
for the generalization argument to be applicable. Yet the explanation of why the generalization argument is not applicable to such acts as producing food is not to be found along
these lines. It is true that producing food and making clothes
are morally indifferent actions in a way in which stealing and
keeping one's word are not. Yet we cannot explain why the
generalization argument is inapplicable to such actions in
terms of their moral indifference. The proper explanation is
rather the other way around. The reason why such actions
are morally indifferent is that the generalization argument is
invertible with respect to them. (The point that producing
food is not so much an action as an occupation, while true,
is really irrelevant here.)

The reason the generalization argument is invertible with
respect to such actions as producing food is that the description "producing food," as well as "making clothes" and
"building houses," is indeterminate for moral purposes. The
action, whatever it is—and a whole host of quite different
actions can answer to this description—is described in too
general a way. To be morally determinate it would have to be
given a context. When described simply as "producing food"
it is taken apart from any context. The question, "Is it right or
wrong to produce food?" has no clear sense. (Of course, it
might be interpreted as meaning "Is it necessary or not for
food to be produced?", but this is really another question.) It
is too general to be answered. The most we can say is that it
depends on the circumstances—ordinarily it is neither, but in
some, peculiar, circumstances it may be right and in some it
may be wrong. This so far corresponds with the results obtained from the application of the generalization argument to
this case. Given that if everyone produced food the consequences would be disastrous, it follows that *not everyone*
ought to produce food; but, for reasons already elaborated, it
does not follow that no one ought to. For if no one did the
consequences would be equally disastrous. Given this it follows that some people ought to produce food, that food ought

to be produced, and also that not everyone ought to produce food. This is certainly indefinite enough—for how do we determine *who*, in particular, ought or ought not to produce it? But what this in effect amounts to is that food ought to be produced, and is not the only thing that ought to be produced. Thus we cannot assert either that everyone ought, or that no one ought. For this would be to assert either that nothing but food ought to be produced, or that food ought not to be produced. Now for an act to be right or wrong it must be right or wrong for everyone, in similar circumstances. This is a simple consequence of the generalization principle. Since producing food is neither right for everyone nor wrong for everyone, it cannot be said to be either right or wrong. *An act to which the generalization principle does not apply is not an act at all for the purposes of moral judgment.* This is not to say that it is not an act. It is not an act to which moral notions are applicable. Thus producing food is not an act for the purposes of moral judgment. An act describable as one of producing food *may* be right or wrong. But in terms of the description "producing food" it is impossible to say. This sort of description does not even warrant a presumption as to its rightness or wrongness. It is thus what may be called a *morally neutral description.* Such a description as "stealing," on the other hand, is not morally neutral. If an act is truly describable as one of stealing it may reasonably be presumed to be wrong—for stealing is generally wrong —and thus is the sort of act that must be justified.

Some examples of moral questions that are too general to be answered and are thus, as they stand, undecidable, are the questions "whether the requital of a benefit ought to be proportionate to what it cost the benefactor, or to what it is worth to the recipient," "how far the promise of aid to a friend ought to override the duty of giving one's children a good education," and "how far a promise is binding if any material concealment is shown to have been used to obtain it." [5] The answers to such questions depend on the circum-

[5] Henry Sidgwick, *The Methods of Ethics* (7th ed.; London: Macmillan & Co., Ltd., 1907), pp. 349, 305, and 306.

stances in which they arise, and as they stand they are
divorced from any context that would make them determinate. We cannot say that the promise of aid to a friend ought
always to override the duty of giving one's children a good
education, nor can we say that it ought *never* to do so. Numerous counterinstances could be found to each of these
claims. Neither can we say that it ought or ought not to do so
in general, or as a general rule. Whether or not it ought to do
so depends on the circumstances—in some cases it ought to
and in some cases it ought not to. Yet the answer in terms
of "always" or "never" is the sort of answer demanded by the
question. And since this sort of answer cannot be given, the
question is, as it stands, undecidable. It can be answered only
if given further qualification. In the form in which the question has here been raised, it is the common framework of a
whole series of different, more detailed, and less general questions, the answers to which will depend on the filled in details (the so far unstated circumstances or context).

Now what has just been said is actually what would follow
from an application of the generalization argument to any of
these questions. The argument is invertible with respect to
each of these actions, as they have been described in these
questions, such actions as "depriving one's children of a good
education in order to keep a promise to aid a friend" and
"breaking a promise to aid a friend in order to give one's
children a good education." The argument that no one ought
ever to break a promise to aid a friend in order to give one's
children a good education, because of what would happen if
everyone did, can be met by the counterargument that no one
ought ever to deprive his children of a good education in
order to keep a promise to aid a friend, because of what
would happen if everyone did. To put it another way, the
question "What would happen if everyone broke a promise
to aid a friend in order to give one's children a good education?" is invertible. For one can ask the counterquestion,
"What would happen if everyone deprived his children of a
good education in order to keep a promise to aid a friend?"
In each case the consequences would be undesirable. Now it

is part of the view being maintained here that when the question whether such actions are right or wrong is made determinate, by filling in the context, it can be answered by the application of the generalization argument (provided the question of relative desirability can be settled).

What was said about the examples just given equally applies to the sort of actions we were considering earlier, such as producing food and building houses. The description "producing food" must be filled in with further details, must be made less general, in order for it to be morally determinate. This can be done by providing it with a context, by specifying the circumstances in which the act is done. One can produce food in all sorts of ways, for all sorts of purposes, and under a variety of different conditions (just as one can produce food of different kinds). Each of these different ways, purposes, or conditions determines a different action, some of which will be right and some of which will be wrong, and most of which will still be indifferent. When the act is in this way made determinate or more specific, then the question whether it is right or wrong can be answered, and the generalization argument will be applicable to it. However, the test of whether an action is morally determinate *is* whether the generalization argument is applicable to it.

Just one example should be sufficient to illustrate what I mean. We have seen that the generalization argument is inapplicable to producing food, when the act is described in just this way, apart from any context. For we cannot say either that everyone ought to produce food, or that no one ought to produce food. But now consider the case of someone with a certain communicable disease who is engaged in producing food. Here the circumstances in which food is being produced are those in which the agent has a disease that he is likely to transmit to others through the food he produces. When specified as taking place under such circumstances the act of producing food is a morally determinate act. For consider what would happen if everyone with such a disease produced food, or was engaged in handling it or dispensing it. If every such person were to do so the consequences would be disastrous, while if every such person refrained from producing food (that is, if no such person engaged in this activity) the consequences would not be undesirable. Therefore no such person has the right to produce food—it is wrong to produce food under such conditions. This application of the argument of course presupposes that not everyone has such a disease. But if everyone (or everyone in a certain limited community) had the disease, it would make no difference who produced food, for then the consequences would not be disastrous, and the question whether such persons should produce food would not arise.

This example should make clear what I mean by "filling in the context" of an act, by making such descriptions as "producing food" less general. This is done by specifying the circumstances of the act to the point sufficient for the generalization argument to be applicable to it. Whether we are to say that someone with such a disease who produces food is doing the same thing as someone without the disease who produces food, only under different conditions or in different circumstances, or whether we are to say that they are doing essentially different things, is not a very important matter. In other words, it does not matter whether we say that the same act is being done under different circumstances, or rather that the acts are different. In this context, the difference between having such a disease and not having one is a difference that makes a difference. In this context, it is an important or relevant difference, although there are some contexts in which it would not be. But whether a difference is relevant is determined by the generalization argument.

§ 5 §

The generalization argument is invertible with respect to certain actions because there is something wrong in the way they are described. In the cases just considered the actions were described in too general a way. An opposite inadequacy is at the root of another class of invalid applications of the argument.

"If everyone ate at six o'clock there would be no one to perform certain essential functions, things that must be attended to at all times, and so on, with the net result that no one would be able to eat at six or any other time, and with various other undesirable consequences." Does it follow that no one has the right to eat at six o'clock? If it did, we should have a genuine counterexample to the generalization argument.

The important point to notice here is that this argument in no way depends on the exact time specified. If we could argue that no one has the right to eat at six, we could argue that no one has the right to eat at five, or at seven, or at three minutes past two, and so on. We could therefore argue that no one has the right to eat at any time, and this would mean that no one has the right to eat.

In such a case as this the argument may be said to be *reiterable*. Thus the argument is reiterable whenever it is applied to some action arbitrarily specified, as part of its description, as taking place at some particular time, or at some particular place, or by some particular person, or in relation to some particular person or thing. To take another example: "If everyone were to eat in this restaurant it would get so crowded that no one would be able to do so . . . ; therefore no one ought to eat in this restaurant." The reference to *this* restaurant is not essential here; the same argument would apply to *that* one, and to any other one. The argument can obviously be reiterated for every restaurant, and its consequence would be not just that no one ought to eat at this or that restaurant but that no one ought to eat at any restaurant. And the same argument would apply not only to restaurants but to any place or location whatsoever. Hence in this case also the implication would be that no one ought to eat. Furthermore, note that there is no need to restrict ourselves to eating in order to obtain examples of reiterable arguments. Any action, such as walking, talking, sleeping, or drinking—even doing nothing at all—when particularized in this way, will do as well.

This last point should have indicated that such examples as these can have no rational force as counterexamples. Any instance of the generalization argument that is reiterable is invalid. For any instance of the generalization argument that is reiterable is also invertible. Note that the instances just given, which are clearly representative ones, are just as clearly invertible. The argument from "not everyone has the right to eat at six o'clock" to "no one has the right to eat at six o'clock," since it can be reiterated for any time, implies "no one has the right to eat." But what would happen if no one ate? If no one were to eat the consequences would be just as undesirable, presumably, as if everyone were to eat at the same time.

Still there is a clear-cut difference between those instances of the argument that are reiterable, and therefore invertible, and those that are invertible without being reiterable. In the latter instances the actions are described in too general a way. In the former instances the descriptions of the actions are not general enough—the actions are described in too particularized a way. In these cases particular details of the action that are really arbitrary and inessential are treated as though they were essential. These specified details—in the cases considered, the specification of the exact time and place of an action —are shown to be arbitrary, and hence not essential, by the fact that the argument can be reiterated with respect to them. There may be cases in which the exact time or place of an action are morally relevant. In these cases the argument would not be reiterable with respect to time or place, and this is the test of whether such details are essential. In the instances presented above, these details are inessential (arbitrary, irrelevant) because the argument does not depend on them, and this is shown by the fact that it can be reiterated with respect to them. The same argument applies for any given selection of time or place, and hence for every time or place.

It should be evident that the instances of reiterable arguments just given are in all important respects representative of an indefinitely large class of similar instances that might be advanced as counterexamples to the generalization argument. A few further candidates would be the following: "What would happen if everyone tried to sit in the front row?" "What would happen if everyone went to the circus today?" "What would happen if everybody tried to crowd into Times Square on New Year's Eve?" and so on. Since these are all reiterable, in one way or another, they are all invalid applications of the generalization argument, and thus provide no reason to suppose that the actions referred to are wrong. Of course, though all of these instances are invertible, not all of them are invertible directly. Yet, since the reference to a particular type of action is no more essential in these instances than the reference to the particular time or place of the action, on the same line of reasoning we could argue with equal cogency that no one ought ever to do anything at all, and this is clearly invertible. This is further evidence that every application of the generalization argument that is reiterable is invertible and hence invalid.

§ 6 §

This last condition, that the argument not be reiterable, is closely tied up with the procedure by which one can justify acting in a way in which it would be undesirable for everyone to act. One can justify acting in such a way by showing that one is a member of a certain class of persons (has certain characteristics) such that if every member of that class (everyone with those characteristics) were to act in that way the consequences would not be undesirable, or by showing that the circumstances of one's action are such that the consequences of everyone's acting in that way in those circumstances would not be undesirable. This would be to show either that there is a relevant difference in the characteristics of the agents involved, or that there is a relevant difference in the circumstances. But the argument must not be reiterable with respect to the class of persons or circumstances selected. Otherwise, the class in question would be "distinguished" by a characteristic in terms of which everyone would be an exception, and hence not really distinguished at all.

It is possible to state this more precisely. It will be remem-

bered that the universal terms involved in an application of
the generalization argument ("everyone," "no one," the description of the kind of action referred to) have restrictions
on their scope, the precise nature of which must be determined from the context. Thus the argument really has the
form: "If every member of K (every person with the characteristics defining the class K) were to . . . ; therefore no
member of K ought to . . . ," instead of simply "If everyone
were to . . . ; therefore no one ought to. . . . " Now an act
of a kind shown to be generally wrong by the generalization
argument can be justified in any one of the four following
ways.

First of all, one can show that one is not a member of K,
and that if everyone who is not a member of K (every non-K)
were to do s (an act of a kind that is generally wrong or that
not everyone ought to do) the consequences would not be
undesirable. (One would, incidentally, have the duty to do s,
and not merely the right, if the consequences of no non-K's
doing s would be undesirable.) This case is really a trivial one,
because it is explicitly stated, or else readily apparent from the
context, that the argument applies only to members of K.
Thus the question whether some non-K is justified in doing
s would ordinarily not arise. In other words, this particular
argument requires only members of K to justify their doing
s; it does not require those who are not members of K to do
so, though some other argument might. However, the question can arise if there is reason to believe that someone is a
member of K. In this case the justification would consist
simply in showing that he is not.

Secondly, one can show that, although one is a member of
K and the consequences of every member of K's doing s
would be undesirable, the circumstances of one's action are
such that if everyone, or every member of K, were to do s in
those circumstances, the consequences would not be undesirable.

Thirdly, one can show that, although one is a member of
K and if every K were to do s, the consequences would be

undesirable, one is also a member of the class L, which is included in K, and if every L were to do s the consequences would not be undesirable. (The conditions that must be met by this subclass L will be discussed in a moment.)

It is not really necessary for L to be included in K. Thus there is a fourth case which should be considered for the sake of completeness. Even though L is not included in K, one may be a member of both L and K. In this case, it would have to be shown that, although the consequences of every K's doing s would be undesirable, the agent in question is also a member of L, and if every LK (everyone who is a member of both L and K) were to do s the consequences would not be undesirable. It would *not* be sufficient merely to show that the consequences of every L's doing s would not be undesirable. For it may be all right for the L's who are not K's, and not all right for the L's who are. Note that it is possible for an act to be wrong for the K's, wrong for the L's, and not wrong for the LK's.

To use again an example already developed, while it would be undesirable if no one (that is, no citizen) were to vote, it would not be undesirable if no one who had recently moved were to vote. It would, indeed, be undesirable (for reasons that should not need elaboration here) if everyone who had recently moved were to vote. This justifies a restriction on the right to vote, for the circumstances of one who has recently moved (depending on how far and how long ago) are, in this context, relevantly different from the circumstances of others. Of course, this argument presupposes that not everyone has recently moved. If everyone had recently moved there would be no distinction.[6] It should be noted, further, that it makes no difference here whether this condition of having recently

---

[6] In this connection, the following may be of interest: "Having been jailed as an enemy of the people did not mean that Miss Tolstoy had been deprived of her position as commissar of Yasnaya Polyana. (Conceivably, it was felt that if only persons without prison records were ruled eligible to be commissars, half the commissariats in the country would be vacant.)" (From a profile of Alexandra Lvovna Tolstoy, by Robert Rice, *The New Yorker*, vol. XXVII, no. 5 [March 22, 1952], p. 38.)

moved is regarded as defining a class of persons and hence as a characteristic of a person, or whether it is regarded as one of the circumstances of the action. In many other cases this sort of distinction is similarly immaterial.

It was just mentioned parenthetically that certain conditions must be met by the subclass L. Certain conditions must also be met for the claim to be justified that the circumstances of an action are relevantly different from the circumstances in which an action of that kind would be wrong. The circumstances must be genuinely different. There must be a reason for the distinction. For, given that there will always be some differences in circumstances, the specific difference cited must be one that is, in the context, morally relevant. In brief, the subclass L must be defined by a condition that does not apply to all or most members of K. The reason for the distinction in the circumstances must not be such that in its terms every possible variation of circumstances would be relevant. Otherwise it would not be a reason at all. It would show that everyone is an exception. Now the test for this is whether or not the argument to the effect that such and such a person is an exception to the rule (or that such and such circumstances are exceptional ones) is reiterable. If it is, then it applies to everyone, and cannot show that anyone is an exception.

The following example, in which the generalization argument is applied to the question whether one has the duty to pay taxes, should be useful in making this point clear.

Suppose a man to urge that he will miss the sum he has to pay much more than it would be missed by society. The absence of the few pounds which he has to pay will not, he may urge, make any perceptible difference whatever to the public funds, but it will make a very perceptible difference to himself, therefore to force him to pay it will do more harm than good; and it will be difficult to answer him if we consider the particular act by itself. But the real answer surely is that he still ought to pay it, because this argument, if admitted at all, would apply to practically everybody, and it would therefore be unfair of him to benefit by other people's taxes while

not paying his own share. (The unfairness would not arise if
he has strong special grounds for exemption which did not
apply to everybody.) [7]

This is certainly a valid application of the generalization
argument, and though it is not stated very elegantly, it is
presented in a way that is most effective for making clear not
only the rational force of the argument but also the conditions that must be met to justify the claim that a certain case
is a legitimate exception. It is clear that although, considered
by themselves, the consequences of A's not paying his taxes
may not, on balance, be undesirable, for he may miss the
money more than the government would, yet this cannot justify A in not paying his taxes. For exactly the same sort
of consideration would apply to everyone. Thus this sort of
consideration could not show anyone to be an exception to
the rule, simply because it would apply to everyone and
hence would imply that everyone is an exception, which is,
as I have already mentioned, self-contradictory.

It follows that the class of persons alleged to be an exception to the rule cannot be a unit class (a class of just one
member) determined simply by the fact that if no member of
this class paid his taxes the consequences would not be undesirable. Ignatz McGillicuddy cannot claim that he has the
right not to pay his taxes merely on the ground that if no
one named Ignatz McGillicuddy paid his taxes the consequences would not be undesirable. If Ignatz McGillicuddy
can argue in this way, then so can John Smith, and so can our
old friend, Stan Spatz III. The same argument is reiterable
with respect to everyone, or with respect to every such unit
class. It would apply also to people without a name.

Of course, the class of persons named Ignatz McGillicuddy
may not be a unit class. There may be more than one person
named Ignatz McGillicuddy. And, though there may be only
one Stan Spatz III, there is certainly more than one John

---

[7] A. C. Ewing, *The Definition of Good* (New York: The Macmillan
Company, 1947), pp. 88-9. Ewing adds that it "would be inconsistent
. . . for me to try to justify my action by any argument which, if valid
at all, would apply to everybody."

Smith. Thus it may well be false that if no one named Ignatz McGillicuddy (or John Smith) were to pay his taxes the consequences would not be undesirable. So let us suppose that Ignatz McGillicuddy refers to himself not simply by name, but as the possessor of certain characteristics that make him unique. In the abstract it is not easy to see what these could be. So let us imagine that Ignatz McGillicuddy is unique in having twelve toes on each foot. Given that if everyone with twelve toes on each foot fails to pay his taxes the consequences would not be undesirable, this is still not a justification. If Ignatz McGillicuddy can claim that he is unique in having twelve toes on each foot and is therefore entitled not to pay taxes, John Smith can claim that he is unique in being the only person named John Smith employed as a bookkeeper by the Underwater Pencil Company of Roaring Hide, South Dakota, that if every such person failed to pay taxes the consequences would not be undesirable, and that he is therefore entitled not to pay taxes. And everyone else can make a similar claim. For everyone is unique in some respect; everyone has some characteristics that no one else has. The argument is thus reiterable with respect to any characteristic selected as unique, and therefore applies to everyone.

Consider a somewhat more complicated case. Suppose someone claims, "If everyone who lives in this house were not to pay taxes, the consequences would not be undesirable. I live in this house, and therefore have the right not to pay taxes." This also will not do. For what distinguishes this house from any other house? Everyone, at least everyone who lives in a house, can argue in the same way. So this same argument is reiterable with respect to (may be applied to) every house, and the consequence would be that everyone has the right not to pay taxes. The test for whether the subclass L of persons claimed to be exceptions to the rule has been legitimately defined is not simply that the consequences of every such person's not conforming to the rule would not be undesirable. It must also be the case that the argument is not reiterable with respect to every such subclass. That is, the distinction must not be based on a consideration that implies that everyone to whom the rule applies is an exception to the rule, for this is simply a contradiction. Thus "this house" cannot be distinguished from others (in such a context as this) on the ground that it is painted red or is located on a hill or has fourteen windows, or has any combination of such features in virtue of which it is unique. For every house has features that distinguish it from every other, even if it is only its specific location or history, and it is true of a house with any other topographical or architectural features that if every one in such a house were exempt from paying taxes the consequences would not be undesirable. Such a characteristic as being thirty years old is also not a reasonable ground for exemption. For with respect to age the argument is also reiterable.

As I mentioned previously in dealing with this topic, in connection with the generalization principle, what is important in these cases is not so much the actual specification of the details of one's situation, as the principle on which the specification is made. Just as the argument from "not everyone has the right to eat at six o'clock" to "no one has the right to eat at six o'clock" does not depend on the exact time specified, such arguments as the ones we have just been considering do not depend on the specified respects in which one is different from others. Just as the former argument is reiterable with respect to any time, the latter arguments are reiterable with respect to any feature that differentiates one person's situation from that of others.

But now what would justify the claim to be an exception? It follows from what has been said that the test here is the nonreiterability of the argument with respect to the characteristic selected. One can justify the claim to be an exception only on the basis of some characteristic that would not show everyone to be an exception. In the case of paying taxes one such characteristic, presumably, is earning less than a certain amount of money. For if everyone earning less than a certain amount of money were allowed not to pay taxes the consequences would not be undesirable, but might be quite the contrary. And the distinction between those who earn more money than is necessary for existence and those who do not is, in this context, a relevant and justifiable one. (If there were no one earning an amount barely necessary for existence there would be no question about paying taxes.) Such a distinction is not arbitrary because the principle on which it is based does not imply that everyone is an exception. It is not the case that if everyone earning *more* than a certain amount of money failed to pay taxes the consequences would not be undesirable. This, incidentally, indicates how to answer the "Where do you draw the line?" argument. Ideally, the line is to be drawn at the point at which it is false that if everyone who earns less than this amount were not to pay taxes the consequences would not be undesirable. Of course, the actual tax laws of any one time or place, on even the most charitable estimate, only approximate to this. The fact that this line is a shifting one, varying with the needs of the time and with people's varying estimates of these needs, only makes it more difficult to determine. Who can deny that the tax laws actually in force at any one time are almost always inequitable?

§ 7 §

There is one other objection to the generalization argument, one which is, oddly enough, fairly popular, that must be disposed of. I shall only mention it here, and save extended discussion of it for the sequel (Chapter VI, section 4). It is simply irrelevant to reply, "Not everyone *will* do it." It is irrelevant because the argument does not imply or presuppose that everyone will. It may be the case, and in most cases almost certainly is, that not everyone will do the act in question; but the generalization argument in no way denies this. What the argument implies is that if A has the right to do something, then everyone else, or everyone similar to A in certain respects, has this same right in a similar situation; and therefore if it would be undesirable for everyone to have this right, then A cannot have such a right. Incidentally, this is not to say that if the consequences of everyone's acting in a certain way would be undesirable, then the consequences of some particular individual's acting in this way would be undesirable.

The consequences of any particular act of this kind, considered by themselves, may be beneficial. But this makes no difference. What has to be shown is how A is an exception. Now one is not shown to be an exception by the fact that the consequences of his acting in a certain way would not be the same as the consequences of everyone's acting in that way. Neither is one shown to be an exception by the fact that not everyone will act in that way. For, since everyone could argue in the same way, what such facts would show is that everyone is an exception, which is strictly nonsense.

Another curious misconception is one that has just been alluded to. This is to interpret the generalization argument as implying that if the consequences of everyone's doing some act would be undesirable, then the consequences of *anyone's* doing that act would be undesirable. This latter statement is so obviously false that it ought to be obvious that it is no part of the generalization argument. Yet apparently it is not. This misconception is actually the basis of a whole essay on the subject, which confidently claims that the argument "bristles with difficulties," that it has very "modest and doubtful functions," and that "most of its alleged uses . . . are sheerly fallacious . . . often where we cannot prove a fallacy we can see that there is very likely to be one and can produce no clear case where it is quite certain that no fallacy lurks." [8] These claims are not surprising, given the assumptions from which they start. They are nevertheless very wide of the mark, and that they do rest on the misinterpretation mentioned is clearly shown by such a passage as the following:

> The result of one man's action may be very small, and it may be impossible for him to see by contemplating it alone whether it be good, bad, or indifferent. But he may be able to see that a great number of such actions would produce a result

[8] C. D. Broad, "On the Function of False Hypotheses in Ethics," *The International Journal of Ethics*, vol. XXVI (April 1916), pp. 377-97 at 397. The generalization argument, ostensibly, is here called, variously, the "principle of false universalisation," the "principle of false generalisation," the "argument from false universalisation," and the "argument from false generalisation." Given the argument in the text, however, these names themselves are all false.

of the same kind as a single one but of much greater magnitude, and that this result would be unmistakably good or
bad. If he has reason to suppose that the goodness or badness
of the results of a large number of similar actions is the sum
of the goodness or badness of the results of the separate
actions, he will be able to conclude as to the moral quality
of his own proposed action though it was not obvious on mere
inspection.[9]

But the procedure here detailed, which is described as "the
use of the principle of false generalisation as a moral micro-
scope," is not at all an application of the generalization argument, and it is no function of the argument to determine
the consequences of a particular act of a certain kind. To ask
"What would happen if everyone did what you propose to
do?," though it implies that your doing it must be *wrong*, is
not to imply that the *consequences* of your doing it must be
bad. The consequences of your doing it may be good. Yet this
possibility is actually ruled out in advance by this interpretation of the argument, since what it presupposes is that an act
can be wrong only if *its* consequences would be undesirable.[1]
This assumption is certainly false.

The confusion involved here is aptly brought out in the
following passage:

> You cannot argue from the fact that the *coexistence* of this
> motive in a great many people would lead to bad results that
> its existence in any particular person will lead to bad results.
> . . . It is very easy to commit a gross fallacy here. This is to

[9] *Ibid.*, p. 382. Cf. pp. 385-6, where this same interpretation is again
very clearly brought out: "It may be said that the argument is to show
that A's abstention must be wrong though its badness is not obvious on
inspection, because a large number of precisely similar abstentions would
have admittedly bad results. But it is surely easy to see that this argument is here a very feeble one. It is quite true that A's abstention *would*
have bad consequences if it took place together with the abstention of a
great many other people. But it does not in the least follow that it *will*
have any bad consequences if it take place together with but few other
abstentions." The confusion between the morality of an act and the evaluation of its consequences is here self-evident.
[1] Cf. *ibid.*, p. 394, where it is stated unmistakably that "We have all
along assumed that the rightness or wrongness of an action depends wholly
on its actual or probable consequences."

confuse the two statements "the motive m frequently leads
to bad results" and "the frequency of the motive m would
lead to bad results." From the former we could conclude that
any particular instance of the motive is likely to lead to bad
results; from the latter we can conclude nothing of the
sort. . . .[2]

This is very true, and the distinction presented is a most useful one, most usefully put. But it is one that can also apply to
actions. Thus: (1) the action a frequently leads to bad results;
(2) the frequency of the action a would lead to bad results.
Now this first statement is connected with the principle of
consequences, in its generalized form—indeed, it is but another statement of it—and from it we can conclude that any
instance of the action a is likely to have bad results, and
hence that any instance of the action a is likely to be wrong.
The second statement, however, is connected, not with the
principle of consequences, but with the generalization argument, and is actually an alternative statement of its premise.
This gives us a good way of stating the confusion noted above.
For the generalization argument does not imply that if the
frequency of the action a would lead to bad results, then the
action a frequently leads to bad results. Neither does it imply that if the frequency of the action a would lead to bad
results, then any instance of the action a is likely to have bad
results. The second statement, as well as the generalization
argument, does imply that any instance of the action a may be
presumed to be wrong. But, to repeat, this is not to imply that
any instance of the action is likely to have bad consequences.

Finally, it should, perhaps, be reiterated that the application of the generalization argument presupposes, and does not
by itself determine, that the consequences of everyone's acting
in a certain way would be undesirable. Since the argument
cannot show an act to be wrong unless the consequences of
everyone's acting in that way would be undesirable, it can
have rational force only if they are, and if they are not it
would be inapplicable, or even irrelevant. The argument, incidentally, is *altogether inapplicable* in a case where both the

[2] *Ibid.*, p. 396.

consequences of everyone's doing some act and the consequences of no one's doing that act would *not* be undesirable. This is just the opposite of the situation in which the argument is invertible, though the effects are similar. Any action to which the argument is altogether inapplicable is morally indifferent. Thus the argument is altogether inapplicable to the action of signing one's name on the flyleaf of a book upon purchasing it, and such an action is neither right nor wrong.

It follows from the point just mentioned that an application of the argument cannot be expected to carry conviction for one who does not regard these consequences as undesirable, or who regards them as positively desirable.[3] For such a one the force of the argument could be only hypothetical, and this is as nothing in an actual case. But, though such situations will no doubt occur, they can affect only particular applications, and not the argument itself. And I have not been concerned with the question how to determine the undesirability of a certain set of consequences. It is sufficient to have shown the argument to be *valid*. The question of the *soundness* of any particular application of it, that is to say, the question whether its premises are true, is another matter.

But this is not all that can be said about it. As complex and difficult as questions of desirability frequently are, they are not so always, and they are not so in many of the cases that matter, so far as concerns the application of the generalization argument. There are many clear cases in which there is just no question that something is undesirable. For there are many clear cases in which there is just no question that something is disastrous. An earthquake is a disaster; so is a tornado, a shipwreck, or a plane crash, and so would be a nuclear war; and this does not depend on anyone's theory of value, or on anyone's interests or point of view, except in exceptional circumstances. To take an example more germane

---

[3] This is well illustrated by a cartoon, by Whitney Darrow, Jr. (*The New Yorker*, Vol. XXV, no. 17 [June 18, 1949], p. 31), in which an irate housewife says to a bill collector, "Has it occurred to you that if everybody paid their bills promptly, you'd be out of a job?"

to our topic, if everyone were to kill anyone he did not like, or to lie whenever he pleased, it is beyond doubt that the consequences would be disastrous. It is beyond doubt, therefore, that they would be undesirable, and the same holds for many other cases of importance, such as will be taken up in the next two chapters. I see no need for qualms, therefore, about the fact that many of my judgments or assumptions of desirability are unsupported. They need no support. Moreover, as we shall see when we come to consider the categorical imperative, with its criterion of "being able to will that the maxim of an action be a universal law," there are numerous instances in which the argument, or one closely resembling it, is sufficient by itself to settle, or to by-pass, the question whether the consequences would be undesirable. So this matter will not be left entirely in limbo.

❀

CHAPTER V

MORAL RULES AND PRINCIPLES

It has generally been recognized that there is a distinction, of some importance, between moral rules and moral principles. Yet it has not generally received explicit formulation, and there is no general agreement on just what it is. These terms tend to be used in different ways, and consequently the distinction between them has been drawn at different places. I shall make no attempt, however, to take account of all uses of these terms. Different purposes require different classifications and hence different distinctions. I shall use these terms in such a way that moral principles are more general, pervasive, and fundamental than moral rules, and serve as their sources or grounds. It is in accordance with this usage that we sometimes speak of the principle underlying a certain rule, determining its scope and justifying exceptions to it. And this usage certainly has respectable precedents. It is, for one thing, basic in the utilitarian tradition, which distinguishes the principle of utility from the moral rules that it sanctions or authorizes. A distinction along these lines is stated explicitly by Whewell, who speaks of moral principles as the "fundamental maxims or rules, the basis of other rules," and says that "in order . . . to establish and apply moral rules, we must state the moral principles which are the foundation of such rules." The sort of distinction I have in mind, furthermore, corresponds very closely to that between *legal* rules and *legal* principles which has been formulated by Roscoe Pound: "Legal principles . . . are made use of to supply new rules, to interpret old ones, to meet new situations, to measure the scope and application of rules and standards and to reconcile them when they conflict or overlap. . . ." The distinctions embodied in the traditions on which I have just reported, however, are not *exactly* like the one to be set forth here, and I am not prepared to accept, as *principles*, those laid down, for example, by Whewell, or even the principle of utility.[1]

But my object in this chapter is not simply to distinguish between moral rules and principles. What I hope to show is how moral principles—especially the generalization principle and the generalization argument—are involved in the justification or establishment of moral rules. This will lead us to a further distinction between different kinds of moral rules. About the generalization argument, in particular, I shall try to show that it serves to generate and establish moral rules and is also involved in determining the range of their application, and that, in cases in which rules conflict, it serves as the principle for deciding or mediating between them. It is therefore decisive in determining the moral relevance of the considerations that might be advanced, in various situations, as reasons for a moral judgment.

But first let us consider the nature of moral rules.

[1] William Whewell, *The Elements of Morality* (3rd ed.; London: John W. Parker & Son, 1854), Bk. II, ch. iv, p. 117. Roscoe Pound, *An Introduction to the Philosophy of Law* (New Haven: Yale University Press, 1922), p. 116. Cf. G. W. Paton, *A Textbook of Jurisprudence* (2nd ed.; Oxford: The Clarendon Press, 1951), p. 176; and John Dickinson, *Administrative Justice and the Supremacy of Law* (Cambridge, Mass.: Harvard University Press, 1927), pp. 128 ff.

§ 1 §

There are certain kinds of action or courses of conduct that
are generally prudent or generally imprudent. It is, for example, generally imprudent to climb very high on a rickety
ladder, or to invest all one's money in just one stock. It follows that there are certain rules, called rules (or maxims) of
prudence, to serve as guides to judgment, which state that
certain kinds of actions are generally prudent or generally imprudent. Similarly, there are certain kinds of actions that are
generally right or generally wrong, such as being kind to
people, or depriving them of their rightful possessions. If an
act is of a kind that is generally right or generally wrong, then
it is governed by a moral rule. For a moral rule, as I shall understand the term, is simply a proposition to the effect that a
certain kind of action is generally right or generally wrong.
Any action of a kind that is generally wrong may reasonably
be presumed to be wrong, and, in the absence of any evidence
to the contrary, is wrong. Thus, while it is merely foolish to
go against a rule of prudence without a good reason, it is
immoral to violate or act contrary to a moral rule without a
good reason. An act that violates a moral rule, or appears to
do so, requires justification.

The term "right" may be used in either a permissive (weak)
sense or a mandatory (strong) sense. In the mandatory sense,
to say that an act is right is to say that it is wrong not to do it,
and hence to say that it is a duty to do it or that it ought to
be done. In the permissive sense, to say that an act is right is
not to say that it is wrong not to do it. In this sense "a right
act" seems to mean no more than one that is not wrong, or
one that the agent has a right to do or not to do as he pleases;
in this sense, to say that an act is right is equivalent to saying
that it is "all right." Of course, "right act" may also be used in
the sense of a heroic deed, or one that goes beyond what is required. But this sense is not covered by rules. Now a moral rule
can prohibit, require, or permit a certain kind of action (either
directly or indirectly). If an act is right or wrong, *as a rule*,
then there is a moral rule requiring, prohibiting, or per-

mitting it. If a certain kind of action is prohibited by a moral
rule, then actions of that kind are generally wrong; if it is
required, then it is generally wrong not to do an act of that
kind; and if it is permitted, then actions of that kind are
generally not wrong. (This also holds if there is no rule prohibiting it.) This last point should take account of any objection that might be felt to speaking of a rule as a proposition. For I am speaking here of moral rules, not of the rules of
chess or baseball, which have quite a different character. Moral
rules do not define a game.

Moral rules state what is right or wrong *usually*, or *for the
most part*, though they need not be, and ordinarily are not,
stated with this qualification. As examples of moral rules we
may take the rules that stealing is wrong, that it is wrong to
deceive people, and that everyone ought to keep his promises.
The differences of verbal expression are irrelevant. These
rules must all be understood with the qualification "generally,"
or "usually." It is not *always* wrong to lie—it is generally
wrong. Similarly, it is not always right to keep a promise—it
is generally right; and there are cases in which it is not only
justifiable to break a promise, but wrong not to. To say that
some kind of action is generally wrong is equivalent to
saying that any action of that kind is wrong unless there is
a reason to the contrary. (This obviously provides another
way of defining moral rules.) To say that a certain kind of
action is always wrong, on the other hand, would be to say
that an action of that kind would be wrong under any and all
circumstances or conditions, and that there can be no reason
to the contrary. As Mill has pointed out, "It is not the fault
of any creed, but of the complicated nature of human affairs,
that rules of conduct cannot be so framed as to require no
exceptions, and that hardly any kind of action can safely be
laid down as either always obligatory or always condemnable." [2] That moral rules require the qualification "generally"
is shown by the fact of conflicting claims or obligations. Cases
arise in which rules conflict; even if they did not arise in

[2] John Stuart Mill, *Utilitarianism* (Everyman's Library ed.; New York:
E. P. Dutton and Company, 1910), chap. II, last paragraph, p. 23.

actuality, they could always be constructed.[3] An action of a kind that is generally wrong and also of a kind that is generally right would be a case of this sort. For actions can be described in different ways. Accordingly, under some circumstances it may be right, or even a duty, to break a promise, tell a lie, or take something that belongs to another without his permission.

There are, of course, other ways of defining moral rules, and it may be possible so to analyze them as to remove all possibility of a conflict between them. One could do this, perhaps, by incorporating explicitly into the statement of a given rule the conditions generally understood to govern its application, and by repeating this process for the rule that, apart from this procedure, would be taken as conflicting with it. This, at any rate, is a procedure that has actually been recommended, and it is certainly worth considering.

> Our moral rules . . . appear to conflict . . . only because we mistakenly try to analyze them in terms of unconditional rather than conditional statements. When they are regarded as concealed conditional statements, an adequate analysis of the conditions will always remove the possibility of conflict. . . . The rule that a person ought to speak the truth means, among other things, that if a person is asked a question about a matter of fact, if he knows the answer and can give an answer, and *if giving a correct answer would not cause pain or injury to another person*, then he ought to give a correct answer. On the other hand, the rule that a person ought not to cause pain or injury to anyone unnecessarily, means, among other things, that if a person is asked a question about a matter of fact, if he knows the answer and can give the answer, and *if giving a correct answer would cause pain or injury to another person or persons without bringing any benefit to*

[3] One famous attempt to deny the possibility of a conflict of rules, or, to use the traditional terminology, a conflict of duties, was made by Kant. But in this case the denial is more apparent than real. For, though Kant denied the possibility of a conflict of duties, he did not deny, but rather affirmed, the possibility of conflicting *grounds of obligation*. See the Introduction to *The Metaphysic of Morals*, in T. K. Abbott (trans.), *Kant's Theory of Ethics* (6th ed.; London: Longmans, Green and Company, 1909), p. 280.

anyone else, then he ought to give an incorrect answer. If these two rules are analyzed in this way, they do not conflict. . . .[4]

Now it may be granted that "if these two rules are analyzed in this way, they do not conflict," but then neither do they settle anything. For this sort of analysis removes the possibility of a conflict between these rules at the expense of creating a class of situations to which they are no longer applicable. Suppose A is asked a question about a matter of fact by B and that A knows the answer and can give the answer, and suppose further that if A gives a correct answer C will be injured but B, or perhaps D, will benefit. It is clear that to such a case neither of these rules, analyzed in this way, is applicable, whereas, on what I would regard as the ordinary understanding of them, they are applicable but conflicting. And this class of cases is not a small one. For it is usually the case that giving a correct answer to a question will bring *some* benefit to the person who asked the question—at least he will find out what he wants to know. Thus it is questionable whether this sort of analysis is advantageous, for the question of what ought to be done in such a situation remains. On the one analysis it arises out of a conflict of rules, on the other it arises because of the inapplicability of these rules.

But it is not just a matter of the relative advantages of two competing modes of analysis. For the procedure I am examining seems to me to be mainly *ad hoc*; once a conflict between two rules has been brought out, one can proceed to state them in such a way as to remove it, though with the consequence already mentioned. Though it has been shown that the two rules considered do not conflict, it has not been shown that it is impossible for these rules to conflict with *any other*. One difficulty here is whether it is possible to state explicitly *all* the conditions generally understood to govern the application of a rule. This is not just a pedantic objection.

[4] W. J. Rees, "Moral Rules and the Analysis of 'Ought,' " *The Philosophical Review*, vol. LXII (January 1953), p. 27 (italics added). Cf. the same author's "The General Nature of a Moral Duty," *Philosophy*, vol. XXVIII (January 1953), pp. 41-57.

For note the important proviso: "among other things." The statements given do not *exhaust* the meaning of these rules. Indeed, what would a full statement of their meaning look like? So consider the rule that promises óught to be kept, and suppose that A has promised B to keep a certain secret, that is to say, never to give the answer to a certain question. Suppose, futhermore, that C asks A the answer to this question. Giving the answer to this question may not cause pain or injury to another person, but it would be the breaking of a promise, and would thus conflict with another rule. Of course, that giving the answer to a certain question would break a promise creates the presumption that it would cause pain or injury to another person, namely the person to whom the promise was made. But then the important condition of the rule that a person ought to speak the truth, namely, "if giving a correct answer would not cause pain or injury to another person," really amounts to: "if giving a correct answer would not conflict with some other rule." A similar point applies to the second rule, the rule that a person ought not to cause pain or injury to anyone else unnecessarily. The important proviso in the analysis of this rule is "without bringing any benefit to anyone else." This seems to me to make the condition in which it occurs equivalent to: "if giving a correct answer would cause pain or injury to another person or persons *without conflicting with some other rule*"; or, to put it another way, "then he ought to give an incorrect answer, *unless giving an incorrect answer would conflict with some other rule.*" Thus not all possibilities of conflict have been eliminated.

It may be possible to analyze the rule to keep promises, along the lines indicated, in such a way as to eliminate the conflict between it and the rule to tell the truth. But, for reasons already given, this procedure would be *ad hoc*, and, after the analysis is given, another case can be constructed. Furthermore, if my first point is sound, this analysis would create a large class of situations to which the rule would be inapplicable. Yet the suggestion I have been considering is certainly illuminating for *some* purposes, and, if they do nothing else, my objections to it should help to clarify the conception of moral rules that I have been advocating. I take the existence of conflicting claims or obligations to be a fact of the moral life, as obvious as that there are conflicts of interests and desires. It is not something to be deduced, but something from which we start, for it is the main source of moral problems. Now any analysis that denies the existence of conflicting claims or obligations must be wrong, and the mode of analysis that I have been examining can avoid this consequence only at the expense of severing all connection between moral rules and moral obligations.

§ 2 §

So far I have been discussing moral rules, and have said little about how they differ from moral principles. A moral rule states that a certain kind of action is generally wrong (or obligatory), and leaves open the possibility that an act (or omission) of that kind may be justifiable. Thus moral rules do not hold in all circumstances; they are not invariant; in a useful legal phrase, they are "defeasible." Moral principles, however, hold in all circumstances and allow of no exceptions; they are invariant with respect to every moral judgment and every moral situation. They are thus "indefeasible." A further point of difference between rules and principles is that principles are always *relevant*, whereas rules are not. For example, the rule against lying is not relevant to a situation in which lying is not involved, and the rule against killing is not relevant where killing is not involved. Moral principles, however, are relevant in every moral situation, in every situation in which a moral question arises. It is evident that such principles, at least in most instances, are bound to be somewhat more abstract than moral rules, though they are not necessarily less definite.[5]

[5] Some other conceptions of moral principles that have recently been presented may be worth mentioning. K. Baier, for example, in "Decisions and Descriptions," *Mind*, vol. LX (April 1951), p. 199, says: "Moral principles and moral laws differ from moral rules in that the former need

The principle of a rule can be thought of as analogous to the intent of a piece of legislation, which is the purpose it was designed to achieve, and hence the reason for its existence. Situations are constantly arising in which the literal or strict interpretation of a rule would be contrary to its intent or purpose. This is, in fact, the basis of the distinction between the spirit and the letter of the law. In such situations the rule ought not to be applied. Thus, though one can have *some* understanding of a rule without understanding its intent, for an adequate understanding of the rule one should know the intent behind it. Only so can exceptions to it be made with justice and revisions of it be made with intelligence. For a perfect understanding of a rule, one should, ideally, understand how it fits into the system of rules and the system of purposes they are designed to further. Now a similar point applies to moral rules and principles. One can have some understanding of a moral rule without understanding how to apply moral principles. But for an adequate understanding of a rule one must know the principles on which it is based—to put it another way, the reasons on which it is established. This is one reason why reflection on morality is essential to morality.

Let us now consider some examples of moral principles. The generalization argument is one. The generalization prin-

---

not be recognized. . . . A moral law or principle becomes a moral rule by becoming recognized." This seems to me no more than verbal legislation, without much chance of passing. P. H. Nowell-Smith, *Ethics* (London: Penguin Books, 1954), regards a moral principle as a "disposition to choose," and speaks of adopting, changing and choosing to change one's moral principles (pp. 306-14). I know of no sense in which a principle can be adopted or chosen, and this is reinforced by the consideration that it is "logically odd" to speak of someone's adopting or choosing different motives or dispositions. (Notice that to "choose to change one's moral principles" would, on this view, be to "choose to change one's dispositions to choose.") So I regard this as just another instance of verbal legislation. This is not to imply that there is nothing to be said for these ways of defining moral principles; it implies that there is very little. The basic ambiguity in the term "principle," from which these varying views derive ("principle" is often used in the sense of "motive," and was originally used in the sense of "fundamental source" or "origin"), is well brought out by Whewell, *The Elements of Morality*, Bk. II, chap. IV, p. 117.

ciple is another. A third is what I have called the *principle of consequences:* "If the consequences of A's doing x would be undesirable, then A ought not to do x." A fourth principle, obviously similar to the third, is: "It is always wrong to cause unnecessary suffering." Let us call this the *principle of suffering.* A fifth principle concerns the character of moral rules and follows from what has already been said about them: "Any violation of a moral rule must be justified." This principle, which is an obvious and immediate consequence of the generalization argument, may be called the *principle of justification.*

A little reflection suffices to show that it is impossible for any of these principles to conflict, though they are all closely related, and this is a further important difference between moral rules and principles.

Yet it might be supposed that there is a possibility of a conflict between the generalization argument and the principle of consequences. For the consequences of an action in a particular case might be undesirable, while the consequences of the general performance of that sort of action might not be undesirable, and this would seem to give us incompatible results. So it is advisable to examine this possibility.

Suppose, then, that if A were to do x the consequences would be undesirable; it follows, on the principle of consequences, that A ought not to do x. Suppose, also, that if no one were to do x, the consequences would be undesirable; it would seem to follow, on the basis of the generalization argument, that everyone, including A, ought to do x. But there are two possibilities here: (1) if everyone were to do x, the consequences would also be undesirable; or (2) if everyone were to do x, the consequences would not be undesirable. In the first case, the generalization argument is invertible, and nothing follows from it. So in this case the conclusion from the principle of consequences prevails, and A ought not to do x. In the second case, there must be something distinctive about A, or the circumstances in which he is placed, to explain this difference between the consequences of his performing such an action and the consequences of everyone's performing it. If everyone similar to A did *x* in a similar situation, the consequences would be undesirable, and so in this case also it follows that A ought not to do *x*.

I conclude from this that there is no possibility of a conflict between these two principles, and hence that there is no possibility of a conflict between any of them. Since the appearance of conflict arises out of an insufficiently detailed specification of circumstances, it can always be dispelled, and this does not have the consequence of creating a class of situations to which they are inapplicable. But there are some important points to be noted about each of the last three principles I have listed, as well as about moral principles in general, and it is the intention of the following remarks to bring these out.

1. The principle of consequences states that, if the consequences of A's doing *x* would be undesirable, then A ought not to do *x*; and I have already pointed out that this is equivalent to, "If the consequences of A's *not* doing *x* would be undesirable, then A ought to *do x*." Now it might be supposed that a case can arise in which these two statements of the principle could come into conflict, in which, in other words, this principle can lead to conflicting results. Suppose that the consequences of A's doing *x* would be undesirable and also that the consequences of A's not doing *x* would be undesirable, and that these consequences would be *equally undesirable*. What follows then?

It should be noticed that in most cases where one might appear to be in such a situation as this the circumstances are not exactly the same—the circumstances under which the consequences of doing *x* would be undesirable will be different from the circumstances under which the consequences of not doing *x* would be undesirable—and hence the contradiction is easily avoided. So let us imagine that the circumstances are exactly the same, and that we are referring to one and the same occasion. The condition that leads to the difficulty, then, is the one that the consequences are *equally* undesirable. Apart from this condition, the situation described would correspond almost exactly with the situation that almost al-

ways exists when two rules conflict, and one has to choose
"the lesser of two evils." Apart from this condition, one's
action (either of doing x or of not doing x) could be justified,
on the ground that its consequences would not be undesirable
on the whole, given the relevant facts about the situation,
since the consequences of the alternative action would be
worse. In the situation described, however, this possibility is
closed. Since this is so, it is evident that these equally undesirable "consequences" are not actually the consequences of
A's action. By hypothesis, these "consequences" are *inevitable*,
no matter what A does. This does not mean that they will be
exactly the same, no matter what A does, though this is a distinct possibility. What it means is that, under these peculiar
circumstances, it does not matter what A does—these "consequences" are no more the consequences of A's action than
they are of what B does, of what C does, or of what anyone
does. Such a situation would be one beyond human control,
and questions of right and wrong are as out of place as they
would be in connection with an earthquake or a hurricane.
What A might justly be blamed for is for getting into such a
predicament in the first place. But this is something else
again, and it is clear that the supposition that we have just
examined constitutes no objection to this principle or to anything I have said about it.

2. In my previous discussion of the principle of consequences (pp. 63-65), I pointed out that this principle assumes
a good deal less than might at first glance be supposed, that
it does not by itself determine what is desirable or undesirable, and that agreement on the principle is perfectly consistent with disagreement on these other matters. A somewhat
similar point is relevant to the principle that it is always
wrong to cause unnecessary suffering. This principle does
not by itself determine whether the suffering caused by an
act is necessary or unavoidable. This is determined by other
factors, and varies with different conditions. Neither does this
principle by itself determine the extent or the amount of the
suffering caused by an act, nor whether this suffering is
genuine or adventitious, serious or trivial. (There are some

people who "suffer" whenever they hear an opinion expressed that is different from their own; this is a paradigm of adventitious suffering.) Yet the determination of such factors as these may well be essential for the judgment of an action. It should be noted that the term "cause" as it appears in this principle is almost as problematic as the terms "suffering" and "unnecessary." Practically every act of a legislature "causes" someone to suffer, even if it is only some vigorous partisan of an alternative measure. Does this imply that practically every act of a legislature must automatically be wrong? This would be absurd. The reasonable answer, surely, is that the suffering here is not really caused by the act in question, either because it is adventitious, or trivial in relation to the other interests involved, or because it is unavoidable.

It follows from these remarks that this principle is somewhat indefinite. But it does not follow that it is useless, for it is not altogether indefinite. It sets limits to the rules, and the actions, that are permissible. There are many (much too many) clear-cut cases of people being caused to suffer unnecessarily, either through thoughtlessness, selfishness, or deliberate design. It is true that, if an act likely to cause suffering can be justified on other grounds, if it is required by some other rule, then the suffering likely to ensue from it would not be regarded as unnecessary. It follows from this, though, that what this principle requires is that an act likely to cause suffering is one that requires justification, and that the justification must consist in showing that the suffering likely to ensue is unavoidable or not unnecessary.

Thus this principle has a moral rule *correlated* with it, to the effect that it is generally wrong to cause others to suffer. Similarly, the rule that stealing is generally wrong has a correlated moral principle, to the effect that stealing for the sake of stealing is always wrong. Correlated with the rule that lying is generally wrong is the principle that lying for the sake of lying (wanton lying) is always wrong, correlated with the rule that killing is generally wrong is the principle that killing for the sake of killing is always wrong, and so on. Consequently, there would appear to be at least two kinds of moral principles: those that have moral rules correlated with them, and those that do not. But there are of course other differences between moral principles: some refer more directly to actions, some to rules, some—as in the case of the three most recently mentioned—to the motives or intentions of actions; and some, as should be clear, can be derived from others.

3. What I have just referred to as correlated moral principles would seem to have something of an in-between status, without all the properties that I have attributed to principles. For example, though they *hold* in all circumstances, in the sense that violations of them are always wrong, they are not *relevant* in all circumstances. On the contrary, they are relevant only where the corresponding rule is relevant. The principle that it is always wrong to kill for the sake of killing is not relevant where killing is not involved. The principle of suffering has much the same status, since it also is not always relevant. It is evident from this that the distinction I have drawn between rules and principles is not hard and fast, since not all of the characteristic differences need always be present. Hence there are some precepts that cannot with certainty be placed in one class or the other.

Indeed, this is evident on other grounds. Consider cruelty. Cruelty is undoubtedly wrong, but is it always wrong, or is it sometimes justifiable? In other words, is this a moral rule, or a moral principle? In part this depends on what is meant by "cruelty." This term does not seem to describe a definite kind of action, at least in the way in which such terms as "stealing" and "lying" do. These latter terms can be much more precisely defined. But this is not the main source of the trouble. The term is really ambiguous. If "cruelty" is taken to imply malevolence, or sadism, an indifference to the suffering of others or even a positive delight in it, then cruelty is always wrong; for it consists in causing or allowing someone to suffer for the sake of doing so. On the other hand, if "cruelty" is taken to imply simply the causing of pain or grief or suffering, without this further implication of malevolence or indifference to it, then cruelty is not always wrong, because it is not always avoidable. In the latter sense of the term we can distinguish between cruelty and wanton cruelty, and hence between the rule that cruelty is generally wrong and the principle that cruelty for the sake of cruelty is always wrong. In the former sense of the term we cannot. But even so, no matter which sense of the term is adopted—whether we say that cruelty is always wrong, or whether we say only that wanton cruelty is always wrong—the principle of cruelty is more like the correlated moral principles than it is like the generalization principle, for it also is not always relevant. Cruelty is not always present, and not every wrong act involves malevolence, or the desire to see others suffer.

Given this difference between two kinds of moral principles, it may conduce to clarity to give them different labels. So let us call the correlated moral principles, the principle of suffering, and the principle of cruelty (however it is stated), as well as others of this nature, *moral laws*. Moral laws, as so identified, differ from moral rules in that they state that certain kinds of actions are always wrong (or obligatory) and do not admit of exceptions—they hold in all circumstances in which they are applicable—; and in that they cannot come into conflict with each other. They differ from moral principles in not being so abstract or comprehensive: they are not always relevant. But there is no need always to make this distinction explicit.

4. A question may arise about what is meant by a "violation" of a moral rule. It may be said that if someone is justified in doing some act then his act cannot violate any rule, even if it is a member of a class of acts that are generally wrong. But I am using the expression "violation of a rule" in a somewhat wider sense, so that any act of a type that is generally wrong can be said to violate a rule. (Synonymously with this, we can speak of an act conflicting with, or infringing, or breaking a moral rule, or of a discrepancy between an action and a rule.) Thus I shall say that to tell a lie is to violate the rule against lying, to steal something is to violate the rule against stealing, and so on. This is not to be interpreted as entailing, or as conclusively demonstrating, that the action is wrong. Also, if there is good reason to believe that someone

has stolen something, then there is good reason to believe
that his action violates the rule against stealing. In this sort
of case the action apparently violates the rule, and such an
action is in need of justification. One can justify himself in
this sort of case by showing that he did not *steal* the object,
that he had permission to take it, or that it was his in the
first place. But there is certainly a difference between showing
that one did not really steal, even though he appeared to, and
thus did not really violate a rule, and showing that in the circumstances one was justified in stealing.

The principle of justification states that any action that
violates a moral rule is in need of justification. I should say
that the converse of this is also true: an action that does not
violate a moral rule is not in need of justification. The question whether an act is justified would normally not arise unless there were such a conflict, either real or apparent. For the
demand that an act be justified implies or presupposes that
there is such a conflict, and would be unintelligible if there
were not. In other words, to claim that an act *requires* justification is to imply that it is in conflict with some rule, or that
there is some other reason for thinking it to be wrong. If
there is no such discrepancy, if there is no reason for thinking
the act to be wrong, then the act does not require justification. Hence there are cases where the demand that an act be
justified may itself require justification.

But, though an action may not require or be in need of
justification, it does not follow that it cannot be justified, or
that it makes no sense to speak of a justification of it. So it
seems to me necessary to distinguish two senses of "justification," a weak and a strong; or to distinguish those actions, or
kinds of actions, that demand justification, because there are
reasons for believing them to be wrong, from those that do
not demand it, and still can be justified or shown to be right.
An act can be justified (in the weak sense) though it is not
in need of justification (in the strong sense). In the former
sense of the term, to say that an act is justified is simply to say
that it is right, and not to imply that there is some reason
for believing it to be wrong. In some uses, to be sure, it seems

to imply more than this—it seems to imply that the act has been *shown* to be right. But the distinguishing feature of the two senses is that in the strong sense the term implies that there is some reason for believing the act to be wrong. This is the sense in which it can be said that an act demands or requires justification. Now the way in which an act that demands justification would be justified differs from the way in which an act that does not would be. One can justify an act of the latter sort merely by showing that there are reasons for it. In justifying an act that demands justification it would not suffice merely to give reasons for it; one would have to show, in addition, that these reasons outweigh the reasons against it.

But it still holds that a justification is not demanded for an action unless there is some question about it. And there is no need to insist on the distinction I have just elaborated. It may well be too artificial. Yet, without it, it would be necessary to recognize two different kinds of demands or requirements, which may be distinguished as those of practice and those of theory. For we can speak of the justification of rules, even where there is no reason against them, and hence no practical demand for it.

§ 3 §

There are at least three different kinds of moral rules that it is necessary to distinguish. Such rules as the ones against lying, killing, or stealing fall into a special class. These rules are fundamental moral rules. There are also what might be called "local" rules. This class includes various standards, customs, and traditions, peculiar to different groups or communities, as well as such rules as the rule that everyone ought to pay his taxes. Thirdly, there are what I propose to call "neutral norms," such as the rules of the road. All these rules are similar in that a violation of them requires justification. But they are related in somewhat different ways to the generalization argument.

What I have called local rules are less comprehensive, and

more closely tied down to their contexts and the purposes
that justify them, than fundamental moral rules. Apart from
being, as their name implies, more fundamental, the latter
do not depend on variations in social or geographical conditions in the way local rules do, owing, perhaps, to their greater
comprehensiveness and generality and relative freedom from
context. It makes no sense to say of the rule to keep promises,
for instance, that it may hold for one group of people and
not for another. It does make sense to say this of the rule to
pay taxes.[6]

But let us consider first what I have called neutral norms.
As an example of a neutral norm we may take the rule that
everyone is required to drive on the right-hand side of the
road. Such rules are *neutral* because it would make no moral
difference if their opposites were adopted. This is the important difference between this type of rule and other rules.
The rule just mentioned does not apply to people in England, where the rule is to drive on the left (and it might
very well have been made a rule to proceed on red and stop
on green). There is nothing antecedently wrong about any
of these activities. It is wrong, in some countries, to drive on
the left-hand side of the road, as a consequence of the fact
that the rule has been adopted and people are generally expected to obey it.

I have chosen the term "neutral norm" on the analogy of
Poincaré's term "neutral hypothesis." The characteristic of a
neutral hypothesis is that "the same conclusions would have

[6] This is by no means the only way of distinguishing between kinds of
moral rules. A very useful one has been set forth by J. D. Mabbott, in
"Moral Rules," *Proceedings of the British Academy*, vol. XXXIX (London: Oxford University Press, 1953), pp. 109-10: "Moral rules vary in
the degree to which they are constitutive or merely regulative. There are
some rules without which no civilized society would survive and few goods
could be achieved. The rules against killing and promise-breaking are of
this kind (and this may be the reason why they have been supposed to
be self-evident). Then there are rules essential to a particular institution
or a particular kind of society. . . . Then there are regulative rules, which
are alternative to others within a given society or institution and alterable
without completely changing its structure. . . ." It should be kept in
mind that, on either type of distinction, there will be borderline cases,
rules that do not clearly fall into one class or the other.

been reached by taking precisely the opposite," while it is necessary to make some assumption.[7] The characteristic of a neutral norm is that the same results would have been attained by adopting precisely the opposite, while it is necessary to adopt *some* rule. This is characteristic both of certain laws, which by themselves might seem arbitrary, and what we call conventions.

That it is necessary to have some rule is established by the application of the generalization argument. What would happen if there were no rules for directing and ordering traffic, if everyone drove on the same side of the road, or on the side of the road on which he happened to feel like driving? There is no need to specify the details. It is surely clear that this would be, to say the least, extremely inconvenient, and this is sufficient to show that not everyone ought to drive on the same side of the road, and that no one has the right to drive on the side of the road on which he happens, at the moment, to feel like driving. It follows that everyone ought to drive on the right, or on the left, whichever is in accordance with the rule of the community whose roads he is using; unless he has, as he might in special circumstances, good reason for the contrary. It also follows that there must be some rule to prevent catastrophe and serve the needs roads were built to serve. It is clearly indifferent which rule is adopted, so long as it serves this purpose, and is not, on other grounds, obviously unjust or inconvenient.

It should be evident that a neutral norm involves an essential reference to a social need or purpose, which is advanced by the general observance of the rule and would be defeated by the general disregard of it. It is in terms of this need or purpose that it would be disastrous, or undesirable, if there were no such rule, and it is in terms of this need or purpose that the rule must be justified. Of course, a reference to expectations is also involved in the explanation of why it is wrong to disregard such a rule. People generally expect others to obey these rules and normally rely upon their doing so. But

[7] Henri Poincaré, "Science and Hypothesis," in *The Foundations of Science* (Lancaster, Pa.: The Science Press, 1913), chap. IX, p. 135.

it is not wrong to violate such a rule *simply* because people expect and depend upon others to do so. This is no doubt part of the explanation. Yet if no one obeyed such rules, probably no one would expect anyone to do so. Hence the main reason it would be disastrous if no one obeyed such rules lies in the social needs such nonobservance would frustrate.

Now what I have called local rules also involve an essential reference to social needs and purposes, on which they depend and in terms of which they may be justified.

§ 4 §

One instance of a local rule is the rule requiring people to pay taxes. Not every government requires its citizens to pay taxes. The amounts to be paid, and the kinds of taxes to be collected, vary from time to time and from place to place, in accordance with different conditions and needs. At a time when there is no need for taxes to be collected, the argument "What would happen if no one paid taxes?" would be inapplicable. Thus such a rule depends on local conditions in a way in which fundamental moral rules do not. The fundamental moral rules are more like the preconditions for any society or government at all. One cannot avoid the obligation to keep promises or be honest without removing oneself from society altogether (and I do not mean in the merely physical sense).

I mentioned before that this class of rules also includes traditions and customs, as well as various standards, of which the standards of fair competition regulating certain business and other activities may be taken as representative. Also in this class are the rules that make up what are known as the "ethical codes" that prevail in different professions. Such rules do not have the comprehensiveness of fundamental moral rules. They apply only to certain groups of people: to those in a certain type of business, to the members of a certain profession, or to those in a certain location, and, in the case of a custom or tradition, to the members of the society of which it is the custom or tradition. (One who is not a doctor cannot sensibly be accused of "conduct unbecoming a doctor.") They also vary with different conditions. In one community it might be "unfair competition" to open a laundry within three blocks of another laundry; in another community the limit might be five blocks.

Many of these rules are no doubt cruel and unjust, not to say foolish. As with "vestigial relics" in the law, many of them continue to exist and govern conduct long after the need that brought them into existence has disappeared, or after the conditions have changed in which they were meant to apply. Nevertheless, these rules have a prima facie claim to acceptance. This is shown by what would happen if every one in a community disregarded its customs or traditions. "Imitation of the past," as Justice Holmes has said, "*until we have a clear reason for change*, no more needs justification than appetite." [8] To put it another way, these rules are binding simply because they are accepted by a dominant part of the group to which they apply. It may therefore be presumed that the members of the group expect and depend on other members to act in accordance with them. And the value of standards and codes for regulating conduct in need of regulation should not be underestimated. As with neutral norms, in many cases they actually determine what "ethical" or "unethical" conduct in a certain situation is.

It is no part of my purpose to compile a catalogue of various kinds of local rules. There are of course important differences between standards, traditions, and codes, but it would be an unnecessary digression to take account of them here.

---

[8] Oliver Wendell Holmes, *Collected Legal Papers* (New York: Harcourt, Brace and Company, 1921), p. 290. The phrase "until we have a clear reason for change" is important enough to warrant special emphasis. Compare, on this same general point, the following statement by Whately: "There is a presumption in favour of every *existing* institution. Many of these . . . may be susceptible of alteration for the better; but still the 'burden of proof' lies with him who proposes an alteration; simply, on the ground that since a change is not a good in itself, he who demands a change should show cause for it. No one is *called on* (though he may find it advisable) to defend an existing institution, till some argument is advanced against it; and that argument ought in fairness to prove, not merely an actual inconvenience, but the possibility of a change for the better" (Richard Whately, *Elements of Rhetoric* [7th ed.; London: John W. Parker & Son, 1857], Part I, chap. III, sec. 2, pp. 73-4).

What I wish to do here is merely to illustrate the way in which the generalization argument can generate (demonstrate the need for) and justify such rules. Thus what I propose to do is to present and comment on two actual examples of the application of this principle to establish a local rule.

In the first example, the principle is applied, under war conditions, to justify a certain military (or naval) policy.

> It was difficult to get yourself transferred from Alaskan vessels because of seasickness, for if such a policy had prevailed, there would have been no ships there, but it wasn't impossible. . . . Almost everyone on that duty was seasick some of the time, for the small escort vessels patrolled the whole winter long. . . .[9]

This example is almost self-explaining. I might just point out that this application of the argument presupposes that it was necessary, given the need to win the war, for there to be ships in Alaskan waters. If there were no war, or other emergency, there would be no need for such a drastic policy, which would then lose its justification. (To specify the point illustrated by the phrase "but it wasn't impossible" would be to underline the obvious.)

In the second example the argument is applied to justify a legal rule.

> "Two systems of water law are in force within the United States—the riparian and the appropriation systems." The system first named prevails in thirty-one of the forty-eight states. Its fundamental principle is "that each riparian proprietor has an equal right to make a reasonable use of the waters of the stream, subject to the equal right of the other riparian proprietors likewise to make a reasonable use." Some of the arid states of the west found this system unsuited to their needs. Division of the water "into small quantities among the various users and on the general principle of equality of right" would be a division "so minute as not to be of advantage to anybody." "It is better in such a region that some have enough and others go without, than that the division should be so

[9] Sloan Wilson, "Citation," The New Yorker, vol. XXVIII, no. 1 (February 23, 1952), p. 70.

minute as to be of no real economic value." The appropriation system is built upon the recognition of this truth. Its fundamental principle is "that the water user who first puts to beneficial use—irrigation, mining, manufacturing, power, household, or other economic use—the water of a stream, acquires thereby the first right to the water, to the extent reasonably necessary to his use, and that he who is the second to put the waters of the stream to beneficial use, acquires the second right, a right similar to the first right, but subordinate thereto, and he who is the third to put it to use acquires the third right, a right subordinate to the other two, and so on throughout the entire series of uses." [1]

It is worth making explicit the exact way in which the generalization argument is involved here. It is through the application of the generalization argument that the difference in the amounts of water available in, say, Arizona and Illinois is determined to be a relevant difference in the circumstances of riparians living in those states; a difference, that is, relevant to the question how rights to the use of the water should be distributed. The fact that one state may have more water than another is not by itself a relevant difference, so long as there is enough to satisfy the needs of all. But if every riparian in Arizona had the right to use as much water as he needs, there would not be enough to go around—none of them would obtain as much as he needs. Hence not every riparian in Arizona ought to have an equal right to the water of that state. On the other hand, since this sort of consequence would not result from allowing every riparian in Illinois to use as much water as he needs, and there is therefore no reason against it, every riparian in Illinois ought to have an equal right to the water of his state. It does not follow, however, that *no* riparian in Arizona should have the right to use as much water as he

[1] Benjamin N. Cardozo, *The Growth of the Law* (New Haven: Yale University Press, 1924), pp. 118-9, quoting from Bannister, "Interstate Rights in Interstate Streams in the Arid West," *Harvard Law Review*, vol. XXXVI (1922-23), pp. 960-2. Cardozo comments: "Here we have the conscious departure from a known rule, and the deliberate adoption of a new one, in obedience to the promptings of a social need so obvious and so insistent as to overrun the ancient channel and cut a new one for itself."

needs. For the consequences of this, presumably, would be equally undesirable. The fact that if everyone in Arizona had equal water rights, none would have enough water, sets a problem, which is to determine a fair way of distributing rights to the use of the water. The rule devised, which would be justifiable only under these conditions, is the one set down above.

This last example illustrates particularly well the way in which a local rule is more closely tied to its context, is less comprehensive, than a fundamental moral rule. The rule just mentioned applies only to people in Arizona (and other arid states). Different rules are required by the different conditions in the different states. If Illinois' water supply should sharply decrease, this would be a good reason for changing the rule. Note that these rules are not neutral norms. It is not indifferent which rule is adopted.

§ 5 §

Let us turn to the question of justifying fundamental moral rules. The procedure, as already indicated, is the same in every case. Moral rules are established by means of the generalization argument. A rule that cannot be derived from an application of the generalization argument cannot be justified.

Since the procedure in every case is the same, it does not matter which rule we select to exemplify it. Let us take the rule that lying is wrong. What is the proof of this? Since to justify a moral rule is equivalent to explaining why a certain kind of action is generally right or wrong, to justify the rule against lying is equivalent to explaining why lying is wrong. Thus it will be sufficient to answer the question "Why is it wrong to lie?"

I cannot refrain from pointing out how utterly fantastic it would be to answer the question "Why is it wrong to lie?" or any question of this kind, by saying, "Lying is wrong because I disapprove of it," or "Lying is wrong because most people disapprove of it." This would not be an answer at all. Lying is not wrong *because* it is disapproved of, that is, *regarded as wrong*. It would be more plausible to say that lying is regarded as wrong because it is wrong, for to explain why lying is wrong is to justify regarding it as wrong. But the fact that lying is disapproved of is as irrelevant to explaining why it is wrong as is the fact that one who lies is likely to be punished for it. It is no answer to say, "Lying is wrong because I'll hit you if you lie." This goes no way to show that, or why, lying is *wrong*. If someone should ask for a reason why he ought not to lie, the assertion that he will be hit or otherwise punished if he does might be a relevant consideration. The fact that someone will be punished if he does something may be a good prudential reason for not doing it. If what he can gain from the lying will not compensate for the punishment then he would be well advised not to lie. But this has no tendency to show that lying is morally wrong, that he has the duty not to lie. The child will be hurt if he touches the fire, and this is a good reason why he should not touch the fire. But this has no tendency to show that it would be morally wrong to do so. Similar considerations apply to the answer in terms of what is disapproved. This might serve as a device to keep someone from lying. We often have to use such devices. But it is irrelevant to the question why it is wrong to lie. For an act that is right might be punished or disapproved of. And it is wrong to lie even in those situations in which one can get away with it, without being punished or disapproved of. The perfect crime is one that goes undetected or unpunished. It is not one that is justified.

In some instances, to be sure, the fact that an act is generally disapproved of can create a presumption against it. But this fact, by itself, could not *make* it wrong, or constitute its wrongness. For this presumption, like others, can be rebutted, and to rebut it would be to show that the act is not wrong even though it is widely and strongly disapproved of. Morality is not the same as public opinion, nor is it always in accordance with it. The existence of a widespread disapproval of some practice is a major source of moral problems, and can be no automatic answer to them. The fact of social disapproval, furthermore, as the source (and sometimes the consequence) of customs and traditions, can establish only local rules, not fundamental ones.

The reason lying is wrong should be obvious from what has already been said. Lying is wrong because of what would happen if everyone lied. It would be nothing short of disastrous if everyone were to lie whenever he wished to, if lying became the rule and truth-telling the exception, which is, however it may seem, actually not the prevailing practice.[2] It follows that lying is generally wrong, or that no one has the right to lie without a reason, and that the mere wish or desire to lie is never a sufficient justification.

This last point, that the mere wish or desire to lie is never a sufficient justification, is shown by the further application of the generalization argument. For suppose that it were, and that I claimed the right to lie on the ground that I wanted to. Then every similar person, and that is, in this context, everyone who wants to lie, would thereby have the right to lie; that is to say, everyone would have the right to lie whenever he wanted to. The consequences of everyone's doing this, as I have already pointed out, would be nothing short of disastrous, and hence not everyone could have this right. But if not everyone can have this right, then no one can have it, without a special reason, and no special reason can here be given, for the desire to lie is not a distinguishing feature. To "reason" or try to justify oneself in this way really involves a contradiction, for it is to claim to be an exception to a rule on grounds that would make everyone an exception. Moreover, if everyone had the right to lie whenever he wanted to, then everyone would have the right to do whatever he pleases

2 The fundamental character of such rules is brought out quite vividly by Mill in the following passage: "The moral rules which forbid mankind to hurt one another (in which we must never forget to include wrongful interference with each other's freedom) are more vital to human well-being than any maxims, however important, which only point out the best mode of managing some department of human affairs. . . . It is their observance which alone preserves peace among human beings: if obedience to them were not the rule, and disobedience the exception, everyone would see in everyone else an enemy, against whom he must be perpetually guarding himself" (*Utilitarianism*, chap. V, par. 33, p. 55).

under any circumstances whatsoever, and this also is self-contradictory.

The argument just given is not restricted to lying, but actually establishes a further moral principle, one that is a useful supplement to the principle of justification: *One is never justified in violating a moral rule by the fact that one feels like it or just wants to.* This very same argument, furthermore, is sufficient to establish what I have called the correlated moral principles. To lie for the sake of lying, for instance, is to lie just because one feels like it, or wants to, or enjoys doing so; and if one is never justified in lying by the fact that one wants to, one is never justified in lying for the sake of lying. Now to say that one is never justified in this is to say that it is always wrong.

Lying, of course, differs from other wrong acts such as stealing and killing and promise-breaking in many important ways, and I would not be understood as asserting them to be in all essential respects alike. For one thing, no one can tell a lie without *intending* to do so, even though one can impart false information and even deceive someone without intending to, since to lie one must intend to deceive. But one can steal or kill or break a promise without intending to do so; and though the fact that one did not intend to do so may make one's act less reprehensible, and may even excuse it, it does not affect its nature. Furthermore, circumstances that might justify lying do not thereby justify theft or homicide.

Nevertheless, the rule against lying is a typical case, in that all moral rules are established by the undesirable, even disastrous, consequences that would follow if everyone were generally to act contrary to them. It follows from this that moral rules are not isolated or independent of each other; they are connected through the fact that they are established through the application of the generalization argument. But it does not follow that the consequences of the general violation of one rule may not differ in an important way from the consequences of the general violation of some other rule. It can be argued, for instance, that it would be impossible for lying to become the rule and truth-telling the exception, for on this supposition there could be no use of language, and thus no possibility of lying. Lying presupposes the practice of truth-telling, and therefore the institution of language, and is actually parasitic on it. If everyone were to lie, either regularly or promiscuously, so that it would be impossible to tell when anyone was speaking honestly, the institution would be undermined, and eventually no one could speak at all. We could not generally presume, as we do, that people's assertions are made honestly; yet the use of language is based on the assumption that, even though people are very often mistaken in what they say, and often use words to deceive, it is not so always or for the most part. No one could learn a language if those around him, on whom he must rely to learn it, were generally to lie to him; there would be no regularity in the use or reference of the words he is "taught," and hence no meaning to the words.[3] In the case of other rules, corresponding though somewhat different things can be said.

A word should be added about another class of fundamental rules. The rule to obey the law, or the rule to maintain law and order, is itself a fundamental rule, in virtue of which various rules and regulations become morally obligatory. This fundamental rule comprehends under it a large class of local rules. The same applies to the rule to conform to custom or tradition; only this is much weaker, and depends much more on the custom, and on the consequences of everyone's breaking it. For example, customs in dress may be broken with moral impunity. For if everyone dressed as he pleased, the community simply would have a custom of dressing as one pleases.

§ 6 §

It should be clear that the generalization argument does not establish moral rules as holding always or in all possible circumstances. This is a consequence of the generalization principle: If not everyone has the right to act in a certain way

[3] Cf. Max Black, *Problems of Analysis* (Ithaca: Cornell University Press, 1954), p. 45.

then no one has the right to act in that way without a reason. Hence, if it would be undesirable for everyone to lie, no one has the right to lie without a reason. This obviously implies that is is possible for the rule to have exceptions, for it implies that it is possible to have a justification for going against it. Whether a particular case is an exception to the rule is determined by specifying in a more detailed way the circumstances of the act in question. If the circumstances of the act are such that in those or similar circumstances it would not be undesirable for everyone to act in that way, then in those circumstances the act would not be wrong. (But this requires the qualifications elaborated in the last chapter. What is important is the principle on which the circumstances are specified, which must not imply that everyone's circumstances are exceptional.) Hence in justifying an exception one is actually justifying a *class* of exceptions, and is thus, in effect, modifying the understanding of the original rule by restricting its scope. As already mentioned, that moral rules can have exceptions, and thus do not always hold, is also required by the fact that they can come into conflict in particular instances. If moral rules are derivable from the generalization argument, as I have been maintaining, then to maintain of any moral rule that it holds without exception would be self-contradictory. It would, for instance, be self-contradictory to maintain that lying is always, and not just generally, wrong, because the reasons that establish the rule are the very same reasons that, in certain circumstances, would suffice to override it. And I should say, for reasons already given, that one who maintains that lying is always wrong, without giving any reasons in support of the assertion, is merely saying or indicating something about his attitudes or feelings towards lying.

I would not imply by this, however, that it is impossible for such reasons to be given. That such reasons can be given is clear from the fact that they have been, and it may be useful to examine, if only briefly, two different sets of such reasons, drawn from somewhat different areas of inquiry. For these reasons have seemed to some to be conclusive on the point at issue.

1. In the particular case of honesty or veracity, perhaps the most thorough discussion of the subject is a book by Dr. Richard C. Cabot, entitled *Honesty*, in which is contained an especially vigorous defense of the proposition that one ought never to tell a lie. What is perhaps the main argument advanced by Dr. Cabot is that "a lie is always wrong because it breaks a promise," since "truthfulness has been tacitly promised in the custom of language." [4] There is no need to take issue with this last statement. There is a sense in which it is true. But it does not really establish the point. It simply pushes the problem back to the question whether it is always wrong to break a promise, and this is even less plausible than the proposition about lying, since, while one truth cannot conflict with another (though two honest assertions can), one promise can conflict with another, in the sense that one cannot keep both, or keep one without breaking the other. There are also cases in which the keeping of a promise would violate some other rule, or inflict some avoidable harm, as well as cases in which one cannot keep a promise owing to circumstances beyond one's control. Suppose, for example, that in order for me to keep a promise I have made to you, say to meet you at a certain time and place, I must allow some child to drown. It is surely not obvious that in such a case one ought always to keep the promise. Indeed, it should be obvious that in such a case it is one's duty to help save the child.

One can, of course, agree to this and still maintain that the rule to keep promises is inviolable. One can do this by arguing that every promise is really conditional, no matter how it is actually expressed, and that in the case supposed not all the conditions on which the promise depends are met, so that in such a case the promise would not really be broken by stopping to save the child. There is something to this. But it does not save the position. In any ordinary sense of the term, if I do not meet you at the time I promised to, I have broken my promise—if I have not "broken" it, I certainly have not kept it. For I have not met you, as I promised to do, and thus I

---

[4] Richard C. Cabot, *Honesty* (New York: The Macmillan Company, 1938), pp. 21, 261-2.

have not done what I promised to do. The question is
whether in the circumstances the promise is morally binding,
and this point about the conditions of the promise merely
shifts the language in which we talk about the question. Furthermore, among the conditions on which a promise depends,
and which consequently define what one has actually promised, is the general condition that keeping the promise not
conflict with any other rule. But sometimes, when keeping the
promise would conflict with some other rule, one still ought
to keep the promise, and sometimes one ought not to.

Even apart from these points, however, the argument that
every promise is conditional still does not establish the invi-
olability of the rule against lying. For if every promise is conditional, then the general promise of truthfulness implicit "in
the custom of language" is conditional, and lying would then
be justified whenever the conditions of this general promise
are not met. By parity of reasoning one could argue that by
lying in certain circumstances the general promise of truthfulness has not really been "broken," since one did not promise
not to lie in these circumstances. Dr. Cabot asserts that "all
unconditional contracts and promises are dangerous," and
suggests that "their dangers should be avoided by thinking
out and by writing down as clearly as we can, the conditions
under which they ought to be broken, by mutual consent"
(p. 38). Now it may be that all such promises are dangerous,
but if so it is only because they are liable to conflict with the
requirements of other rules. It does not follow that they need
never be made, nor that it is always wrong to make one. And
the advice to write down the conditions under which they
ought to be (or may be) broken ignores the fact that it is not
always possible to specify in advance all the conditions on
which a promise depends and apart from which it cannot
justly be regarded as binding, and this is not due solely to
lack of time. Note that if every promise is qualified by conditions, then every tacit promise is, and if the promise is tacit,
the conditions will be tacit also. Suppose that one promises
to keep a certain secret, and that this can be done only by
lying. Dr. Cabot says that such a promise ought never to be

made (p. 39). But on what grounds can this be maintained? Even if such a promise would conflict with the general promise of truthfulness implicit "in the custom of language," it does not at all follow that such a promise ought never to be made, or that the general promise of truthfulness ought always to take precedence.

One who maintains that it is always wrong to lie will usually be found to be employing a special definition of "lying," in virtue of which the rule is, if not altogether tautological, yet nearly so. Thus one might admit cases in which it is not wrong to utter a false statement with intent to deceive, while refusing to call such legitimate deceptions "lies." I do not say that Dr. Cabot is actually following this procedure, but the definition he gives of "lying" certainly approximates to it. He defines a lie as simply "an attempt to deceive without consent," and by this definition is enabled to distinguish whole areas or classes of circumstances from the scope of the rule, as areas in which it is permissible to lie (or rather, to attempt to deceive), such as "in games, in jokes, in drama, and in conjuring," on the ground that people in these situations "consent to be deceived" (p. 21). That people in these situations really do consent to be deceived is not obvious, but it need not be disputed. The main trouble with this definition of "lying" is that it is not always clear when someone has consented to be deceived, and no indication is given of how disputes about this are to be settled. Are we to suppose that there are situations in which such consent can generally be taken for granted, so that we can speak of presumptive consent as opposed to explicit consent? If so, then suppose the other party to the transaction does not realize, or agree, that he is in such a situation? Moreover, it is by no means self-evident that it is always wrong to attempt to deceive another without his consent, or that consent is always necessary to justify an attempt to deceive. (Neither is it obvious that consent is sufficient.)

There is one other argument Dr. Cabot presents that must in all fairness be considered, even though I regard it as having the character of a last-ditch defense. "There is nothing peculiar," he says, "about the fact that honesty can admit no exceptions. No moral rule can admit exceptions and yet demand obedience" (p. 250); "exceptions undermine the rule" (p. 257). This is simply the result of a faulty analysis. Exceptions that are not admitted at one point are admitted at another, and this is precisely what is done by admitting cases in which it is not wrong to attempt to deceive someone who has consented to be deceived. Dr. Cabot continually insists that honesty ought to be automatic, and I presume that by this he means we ought to develop habits of honesty. But honesty can be automatic and still admit of exceptions, just as one habit, in certain circumstances, can be modified by another. If this were not so, then the admission of cases in which it is not wrong to attempt to deceive, since others have consented to be deceived, would mean that honesty could not be automatic. For one has at least to determine whether or not he is in such a situation. To be sure, one cannot effectively teach the rule if it is overloaded with exceptions. But this point does not apply to moral rules any more than it does to anything else, and we are dealing here not with the conditions of effective teaching, but with the conditions of adequate understanding. Now the main reason that Dr. Cabot gives for the claim that exceptions undermine the rule appears to be his statement that: "Even if I believed that there are exceptions to the rule just given I should be inclined to think that in times of temptation no human being can be trusted to make the exceptions fairly" (p. 243). But if this were true, then it would follow that in times of temptation no human being can be trusted *to obey the rule*, and this is clearly not true. And to talk about temptations, and times of temptation, is really beside the point. It ignores the fact that there are cases in which there is simply a conflict of rules, or in which one has to decide between conflicting interests or claims or obligations, without there being a conflict between a rule and a desire to act contrary to it. One can be in such a situation without being "tempted" one way or the other.

The conclusion seems inescapable that in the line of argument we have just considered all exceptions are regarded as necessarily arbitrary. By this time it need hardly be pointed out that this is mistaken.

2. The various arguments just considered relate mainly to the particular rule against dishonesty, though some of them could, by a natural extension, be applied to any other. But there is another line of argument, of a more abstract and general nature, which, if sound, would show that moral rules hold in all circumstances, and that there is never a sufficient justification for breaking one. Since this argument employs a rather impressive logical apparatus, it almost demands consideration.

The argument I have in mind is one advanced by G. E. Moore in the chapter of his *Principia Ethica* on "Ethics in Relation to Conduct," where he takes up the question of "the principles by which the individual should decide what he ought to do." This argument is based, in large part, on Moore's view of the nature of moral rules, which is itself derived from some more general features of his ethical theory. I do not propose to discuss this more general view here, because the argument especially relevant in the present context could be maintained independently and is intelligible without it. Still, it is not altogether out of place, and may even be useful, at least to mention what this more general view is. Moral rules, Moore holds, are "merely statements that certain kinds of actions will have good effects"; and this is itself a consequence of his theory that "our 'duty' . . . can only be defined as that action, which will cause more good to exist in the Universe than any possible alternative," that the results, *the total results*, of an action are the test, and the only test, of whether it is right or wrong.[5] This theory, no doubt, could be discussed at great length. Yet it does not really require expatiation. For it is shown to be false by two consequences that Moore quite properly draws from it: "We never have any reason to suppose that an action is our duty" (p. 149); and "No sufficient reason has ever yet been found for considering one action more right or more wrong than another" (p. 152). These two statements are *obviously* false. To be sure, they

[5] G. E. Moore, *Principia Ethica* (Cambridge: Cambridge University Press, 1903), pp. 146, 148.

are valid inferences from Moore's premises. But this only
shows these premises to be false.

Let us turn now to the argument I have mentioned. Moore
points out that: "Since . . . it is impossible to establish that
any kind of action will produce a better total result than its
alternative *in all cases*, it follows that in some cases the neglect of an established rule will probably be the best course of
action possible." But he then argues that no individual can
"ever be justified in assuming that his is one of these exceptional cases":

> For, if it is certain that in a large majority of cases the ob-
> servance of a certain rule is useful, it follows that there is a
> large probability that it would be wrong to break the rule in
> any particular case; and the uncertainty of our knowledge
> both of effects and of their value, in particular cases, is so
> great, that it seems doubtful whether the individual's judg-
> ment that the effects will probably be good in his case can
> ever be set against the general probability that that kind of
> action is wrong. . . . It seems, then, that with regard to any
> rule which is *generally* useful, we may assert that it ought
> *always* to be observed, not on the ground that in *every* par-
> ticular case it will be useful, but on the ground that in *any*
> particular case the probability of its being so is greater than
> that of our being likely to decide rightly that we have before
> us an instance of its disutility. In short, though we may be
> sure that there are cases where the rule should be broken, we
> can never know which those cases are, and ought, therefore,
> never to break it. . . .
>
> The individual can therefore be confidently recommended
> *always* to conform to rules which are both generally useful and
> generally practiced. . . .[6]

This is, it must be allowed, an impressive argument for the
maintenance of the *status quo*—for the preservation of any

---

[6] *Ibid.*, pp. 162-3, 164. The sentence left out of the first paragraph is
this: "Added to this general ignorance is the fact that, if the question
arises at all, our judgment will generally be biased by the fact that we
strongly desire one of the results which we hope to obtain by breaking
the rule." But, as we have just seen, this point is altogether irrelevant.
There are cases where the individual has no desire or inclination or
temptation to break the rule, and consequently need not be biased.

and every existing custom and social arrangement. For it applies, it should be noted, not simply to what I have called fundamental rules, but also to what I have called local rules.[7] Now I have admitted that any existing custom has an initial presumption in its favor. But this is no more than a presumption, and in some cases it may not be very strong. It means no more than that one ought to conform, unless there is good reason to the contrary, and the strength of the reason required will vary with the importance of the custom and the nature of the situation. There are surely many social customs and institutions that ought to be changed. This argument, however, would show that such rules ought never to be broken, that there is never good reason for going against them. It is therefore fortunate that it is fallacious.

If a certain kind of action is generally wrong, then any action of that kind may be presumed to be wrong; for, given that actions of that kind are usually wrong, or wrong in most cases, then it is probable that any action of that kind is wrong. But this gives no probability at all to the conclusion that every action of that kind is wrong. On the contrary, we know,

[7] Moore expressly restricts his conclusion, to be sure, to rules that "are both generally useful and generally practiced." He says (p. 164): "In the case of rules of which the general observance would be useful but does not exist, or of rules which are generally practiced but which are not useful, no such universal recommendations can be made." He goes on to say, however, that: "In many cases the sanctions attached may be decisive in favour of conformity to the existing custom," and adds that, "even apart from these, the general utility of an action most commonly depends upon the fact that it is generally practiced." The conclusion he draws from this is that: "In a society where certain kinds of theft are the common rule, the utility of abstinence from such theft on the part of a single individual becomes exceedingly doubtful, even though the common rule is a bad one. There is, therefore, a strong probability in favour of adherence to an existing custom, even if it be a bad one." It should be noticed that this conclusion is not restricted to theft, in which case it would sanction smuggling; but it would also sanction intolerance, persecution, and bigotry, as well as current advertising practices, in which the rule is "Sell the product, by any means." And the conclusion is plausible only so long as one uses the language of "utility." For there is some truth in the statement that "the utility of abstinence . . . on the part of a single individual becomes exceedingly doubtful." But it is not here a question of the utility of an act; the question is whether the act is right or wrong.

by hypothesis, that this is false. Now the probability or presumption established by the general rule holds only in those instances in which there is no reason to the contrary. Since probability always depends on the evidence available, in those instances in which there are reasons to the contrary this initial presumption can be outweighed, and may no longer apply. In other words, we are entitled to presume that the act is wrong, in the particular instance, only so long as all that we know about it that is morally relevant is that it is an instance of a kind that is generally wrong.

Now that there can be such countervailing reasons is shown by two facts. First, the claim was made that "though we may be sure that there are cases where the rule should be broken, we can never know which those cases are." But if we could never recognize any case as one in which the rule should be broken, then we could not be sure that there were any such cases, and in fact we are. Secondly, this argument completely ignores the possibility of conflicting rules. If one ought "*always* to conform to rules which are both generally useful and generally practiced," then what ought one to do in cases where two rules conflict, each of which is "both generally useful and generally practiced"? Since such cases can always arise, it is not possible "*always* to conform to rules which are both generally useful and generally practiced." Advice to which it is impossible to conform is worse than no advice at all.

It may be said that there are certain subsidiary rules, which are also both generally useful and generally practiced, which state what one ought to do in circumstances in which primary rules conflict, and that, in these circumstances, one ought always to conform to these rules. This still cannot save the position. For, in the first place, it admits that it is not the case that one ought "*always* to conform to rules which are both generally useful and generally practiced"; and, in the second place, though there may be some such subsidiary rules generally recognized as taking precedence in certain circumstances of a fairly common type, this is not so for all, or even for

very many, such circumstances. If it were, there would be no
moral disputes.

I conclude from this that we have been given no good
reason for supposing that we ought never to act contrary to
the established rules of our society, and I conclude further
that this opinion is false. Yet the emphasis I have given to
these points should not be misinterpreted as a recommendation for these rules to be generally violated.

§ 7 §

Given, then, that there are cases in which moral rules conflict,
as well as other sources of moral perplexity, it follows from
what has already been said that in cases in which rules conflict, in which there are conflicting claims or obligations, the
generalization argument provides the criterion for deciding or
mediating between them. For the action will be right in the
particular circumstances only if it would be right for anyone,
and everyone, in similar circumstances. Thus, to show that a
certain act in these circumstances is not wrong, one must
show that the consequences of everyone's acting in that way
in similar circumstances would not be undesirable. It can be
shown that it is a duty to act in that way, and hence wrong
not to, if the consequences of no one's acting in that way in
similar circumstances would be undesirable. The argument
must of course satisfy the conditions previously discussed.

The other sources of moral perplexity consist mainly in the
indefiniteness or vagueness of moral rules; it is not always
clear whether or not a certain rule applies in a certain situation. This itself is largely the result of the vagueness or the
ambiguity of such terms as "lying," "stealing," and "promising" (or "promise-breaking"). Where it is not, it is due to uncertainty about the facts of the situation. However, I should
say that the vagueness of moral rules can be eliminated or
cut down by the same process through which the rules are established. For in the question, "What would happen if everyone lied?" one can substitute any proposed definition or

analysis of "lying." And the same process can be applied to more or less complex concatenations of circumstances.

But what I am claiming about the generalization argument in relation to moral rules can perhaps be made clearer by some explicit indication of what I am not claiming.

In the first place, I am not claiming that in the situations just mentioned, in which there are conflicting claims or obligations, or in which it is not clear whether a certain rule applies or would be violated, or that even in the justification of an action generally, the generalization argument is in fact always invoked or explicitly appealed to. Nor am I claiming that it must be. It is not always or even regularly. Nor need it be. Nevertheless it is appealed to implicitly or tacitly. From the fact that a principle is not mentioned it does not follow that it is not used or presupposed. It was argued in a previous chapter that the generalization principle is involved in all moral reasoning. What I am urging now is that the generalization *argument* is also presupposed in every case in which an attempt is made to justify or give reasons for an action.

It should really be obvious that in giving a justification, or in moral reasoning generally, it is not necessary to make an explicit appeal to the generalization argument. There are times when at the very least it would be inappropriate, if not incongruous.[8] The generalization argument is in practice rarely appealed to except in cases in which rules conflict, in which there are conflicting considerations, or in which there seems to be no ordinary moral rule that is applicable. For it is very often sufficient merely to invoke a rule, or point out the existence of a right that some action would violate, or indicate how some action would lead to avoidable harm. Thus, if someone wants to know why it would be wrong for him to act in a certain way, it is often sufficient to point out that it would be a case of stealing, or lying, or hurting someone else, and that stealing, or lying, or hurting someone else, is wrong.

---

[8] This is nicely exemplified by a cartoon by Virgil Partch (*Collier's* September 15, 1951, p. 38), in which is seen a long line of marching soldiers, and a sergeant says to a half-dressed, sleepy soldier: "But, Kelly. What if *everyone* overslept?"

Again, it might be sufficient to point out how the action would lead to unnecessary suffering, or that its consequences would be undesirable. Yet, even though the generalization argument is not explicitly mentioned here, it is necessarily involved. For it is involved in the explanation of why stealing is wrong. And the argument just presented obviously presupposes that what is wrong in one case is wrong in all similar cases.

The generalization argument is often appealed to to establish a rule, and consequently may be used to bring home the reasons for some rule already in existence. Accordingly, it is often appealed to in connection with *breaches* of established practices, laws, or conventions.[9] In such cases the mere appeal to the rule is not thought sufficient. For the reasons that justify them are not always obvious, especially if particular breaches have no discernible effects. Consequently the argument can be used to show that certain conventions, laws, or practices should be abolished.

In the second place, I am not claiming that the generalization argument must be explicitly invoked in explaining why a certain *kind* of action is wrong. In many cases it suffices to point out the sort of consequences actions of the kind in ques-

---

[9] An instance of this is furnished by the following newspaper clipping:

GETS 3 MONTHS; HITS CYCLIST WITH PANTIES SHOWING
Derby, England———Percy Pothecary, 23, was driven berserk by the sight of a pretty cyclist's panties, his lawyer told a judge Wednesday.
Pothecary was charged with striking Margaret Jean Blair, 16. His lawyer said Miss Blair had cycled past Pothecary on a windy day. He added:
"The wind was blowing the girl's skirts above her knees, revealing her underclothes. Pothecary was shocked and upset by the spectacle. He can't bear to see young ladies indecently dressed."
Judge P. E. Sandlands sentenced Percy to three months in jail, remarking "if everyone who saw undies exhibited took the same course as you did, most young ladies in this country would be assaulted at one time or another."

This item was sent to me some time in the spring of 1953 by my friend Tom Green, and I am sorry to say that I do not now know either its exact date or the name of the paper from which it was taken. However, it does not matter. Anyone who thinks that it ought not to have been included, either for this or for some other reason, is entitled to treat it as nonexistent.

tion may reasonably be expected to have. Such acts as lying, stealing, breach of promise, and murder, generally have mischievous consequences in the particular case. Someone may reasonably be expected to suffer as a consequence of such an action. There would thus appear to be a significant difference between acts of this kind and acts like refusing to pay taxes or avoiding military service or, generally, failing to do one's part in a common enterprise the success of which depends upon the cooperation of everyone, or nearly everyone, concerned. For the mischievous effects of dishonesty are much more evident than the mischievous effects of a failure to vote or pay taxes. (And lying is wrong in itself, while failing to vote is not; to tell a lie one must *intend* to deceive.) It is in fact to actions of the latter kind that the generalization argument seems to be most often applied explicitly. The reason why lying is wrong seems more readily apparent than the reason why it is wrong not to pay one's taxes. The direct consequences of failing to pay one's taxes are obscure or seem so trifling.[1] Yet, if someone does not see why lying is wrong, or why it is wrong for *him* to lie, then there is room for appeal to the generalization argument, to make clear the reason for the rule. It is wrong to lie because of what would happen if everyone lied. And it is wrong for *him* to lie because it is wrong for others to lie to him. "How would you like it if everyone were to lie to you, or take away your property, or go out of his way to make your life miserable?" Though one can very well like to lie to others while not liking others to lie to him, one cannot sensibly claim that it would be wrong for others to lie to him yet not wrong for him to lie to them. In such a statement "wrong" could mean no more than "I wouldn't like it."

These considerations would appear to indicate that there is a difference between the types of actions involved in fundamental moral rules and those involved in other kinds of moral rules, or at least some of other kinds. In the case of lying, or stealing, or cruelty, there is a definitely assignable individual

[1] Cf. Thomas Fowler, *Progressive Morality: An Essay in Ethics* (London: Macmillan and Co., Ltd., 1884), pp. 146-50; also pp. 118-9.

or group of individuals whose rights or interests would be violated. In the case of attempting to avoid one's obligations to
one's government there is no assignable individual or group
whose rights would be violated. And few of us feel in ourselves the power to make the government suffer. Thus the
mischievous consequences of this sort of act are not so vividly
apparent, and may not even exist. One must appeal to a *principle*, and not merely to facts. "To do this is to take advantage
of others." Furthermore the act is not reciprocating: the government cannot do the same to us (though it can make us
suffer in other ways).

It would be a mistake, however, to suppose from this that
fundamental rules are to be distinguished from others on the
ground that the latter only are governed by the generalization argument, whereas the former are governed solely by the
principle of consequences. It is true that the generalization
argument has a more immediate or apparent application in
connection with the breach of local rules, or to rules that, described generally, require one to play his part in a common
enterprise that would fail if everyone concerned failed to do
his part. It is true also that fundamental rules are governed
by the (generalized) principle of consequences, so that the
generalization argument is not the only principle relevant to
them. Yet so are many local rules, and the principle of consequences, as we have seen, is itself involved in the generalization argument. Furthermore, where the consequences of the
violation of a moral rule in a particular case would not be
undesirable, the principle of consequences would not apply,
whereas the generalization argument very well might. If the
circumstances of the case are such that the consequences of
everyone's acting in that way in those circumstances would be
undesirable, then the act is wrong, and it is irrelevant that the
consequences of one person's acting in that way in those circumstances would not be undesirable. And, though this sort
of case is not governed by the principle of consequences, it
is governed by the rules themselves. For no one is justified in
violating a moral rule simply because the consequences of his
particular violation would not be undesirable. It is not even

sufficient for the consequences to be positively desirable. It must be shown for *whom* the consequences would not be undesirable, that it would not be unfair to others. But this requires appeal to a general rule or principle, and hence to the generalization argument.

It follows, then, from what has been said about the generalization argument that it is involved, and is decisive, in determining the relevance of the considerations that might be brought to bear in support of a moral judgment; that is to say, in determining whether some feature of a situation is relevant to what ought to be or may rightfully be done in that situation. This point has in fact already been discussed. For the question "How can you tell what is relevant?" is really the same as the question "How can you tell what is a reason?" And the formal principle is that a reason in one case must be a reason in all similar cases; that is to say, in all cases in which it applies. Otherwise it is not a reason at all. Hence what is relevant in one situation must be relevant in all similar situations. Otherwise it is not relevant at all. The question to be answered, therefore, is "How would it be if everyone, in a similar situation, or for similar reasons, were to act in the way said to be required or justified in this?"

Finally, I am not claiming, nor do I wish to imply, that the answer to this question can always be easily obtained, or that the application of the generalization argument to the situations I have mentioned is an easy or automatic process. The difficulty of applying it varies with the complexity of the situation. Hence, apart from the difficulty of determining what the consequences are likely to be, and of evaluating these consequences, there is the difficulty of determining just what the situation is, and of distinguishing relevant from irrelevant features. And there are various other difficulties about which I have so far said, if not absolutely nothing, certainly very little.

❊

THE APPLICATION
OF THE GENERALIZATION
ARGUMENT

In claiming that the generalization argument is valid, I have not of course claimed that its application is an automatic or self-certifying process. There are certainly many cases in which it is not. A particular application of the argument may be invalid, and even where it is valid it is not necessarily conclusive. Thus in this chapter I propose to consider some questions and difficulties that relate primarily to the application of the generalization argument, and not to its general validity. This will lead to a better understanding of the situations in which it does not apply, and of the conditions under which it does. These problems, however, merely illustrate difficulties that may arise in its application; they do not show it to be invalid. That this is so may not be obvious in all cases. Indeed, it is not in the very first instance that I shall consider. But this does not affect the situation.

§ 1 §

The first problem to be dealt with is one that often has been supposed to constitute an insuperable objection to the generalization argument, and I shall take it up first both for this reason and because it is so closely connected with the objections that I have already considered. This objection arises out of the fact that an act can be described in many different ways, that it can be, in other words, an instance of more than one kind of act. It follows from this, so it is argued, that depending on the way an act is described, the generalization argument will lead to incompatible results, and hence can be used to show both that the act is right and that it is wrong. If this were so, then it would clearly be invalid.

Objections along this line are frequently brought against Kant's categorical imperative, and are usually formulated with Kant's theory in mind. Consequently, this sort of objection is usually stated with reference to "maxims." As so framed, the objection is that it is possible to formulate the maxim of an action in many different ways; that, in particular, it is possible to formulate the maxim of one's action in so narrow or specific a way that it could apply only to that specific action, and that one can, by following this procedure, justify oneself in doing anything. As so stated, the point should begin to look somewhat familiar. Yet, in view of its usual affiliation with the categorical imperative, it will be necessary, in dealing with this objection here, to anticipate a bit the gist of some later discussions. This, however, is of no great moment. This objection, if relevant at all, is relevant here, and if it is decisive in the one case it is decisive in the other. Actually, it is decisive in neither.

This objection can best be dealt with by considering some actual examples of its formulation. One critic puts it this way, in explicit reference to Kant's theory:

> Any individual act is an instance of a class of acts which is a species of a wider class of acts which is a species of a still wider class; we can set no limit to the degrees of specification which may intervene between the *summum genus* "act" and the individual act. For example, if C tells a lie to the would-be murderer, this falls (i) under the species "lies told to murderous persons," (ii) under the species "lies," (iii) under the genus "statements. . . ."

We seem, then, to be in an impasse. The test of universalizability applied at one level of abstractness condemns the act; applied at another level of abstractness it justifies it. And since the principle itself does not indicate at what level of abstractness it is to be applied, it does not furnish us with a criterion of the correctness of maxims, and of the rightness of acts that conform to them.

This last point does not follow from the facts presented, and is actually not true. Before going on to deal with it, however, it will be useful to have before us another statement of this same objection, one that is stated even more forcibly:

> Any act falls under an indefinite number of classes and is described by an indefinite number of universals. . . . If any act is possible at all, one can formulate some class of which it is the only member, and thus lay down a universal rule applicable to it and free from inconsistency. . . . By a judicious selection of universal principles, one can demonstrate, on the basis of this theory, that anything is good or that anything is bad.[1]

There is undoubtedly a difficulty here. Yet it has by no means such damaging consequences as has been supposed. This objection is itself the result of an inadequate analysis, and the analysis of the preceding chapters will enable us to deal with it. For one thing, it rests on the assumption that the generalization argument is intended to provide a conclusive reason for its conclusion, whereas, as we have seen, it provides only a presumptive reason. It is not true, therefore, that "the test of universalizability applied at one level of abstractness *condemns* the act; applied at another level of abstractness it *justifies* it." But this is not the main defect of the objection we are now considering.

That one and the same act can be described in many different ways is an undoubted fact, to which I have already alluded at some length. This, notice, is just another way of saying that an act can be a member of many different classes of

---

[1] The first statement is by Sir David Ross, *Kant's Ethical Theory* (Oxford: The Clarendon Press, 1954), pp. 32-3; the second is by Felix S. Cohen, *Ethical Systems and Legal Ideals* (New York: Harcourt, Brace and Company, 1933), pp. 223-4.

acts. One's description of an action will be more or less detailed depending on whether one includes in its description more or less of its surrounding circumstances, or even of its consequences. And just as an act can be described in different ways, so can its circumstances, and the description of the circumstances can also be more or less detailed. Now, in the abstract, there is no one type of description that is more correct than any other, and consequently there is no unique description of an action. Similarly, there is nothing that can count as a "minimum description" of an action, which, presumably, would be a description of what the action "essentially" is, apart from its circumstances and consequences and the intention with which it is performed.[2] However, one description can be more adequate than another, for a certain purpose. This means that the action must be considered in its context, and so must the description.

But the fact that an act can be correctly described in a number of different ways does not show that the generalization argument is invalid or defective or that it leads to contradictions.

If an act is described in too specific or particularized a way in an application of the argument, the argument will be reiterable with respect to it, or with respect to the special characteristic in terms of which it is described, and hence invalid. This, as we have seen, rules out the possibility of justifying one's action by describing it in such a way that there could not possibly be more than one act of the kind described, or by de-

[2] One attempt to give a minimum description of an action, or to specify the essence of an act, was made by Oliver Wendell Holmes, Jr., in *The Common Law* (Boston: Little, Brown and Company, 1881), p. 91 (also p. 131): "An act is always a voluntary muscular contraction, and nothing else." But this will not do. For it can never count as an answer to the question, "What did he do?". To answer, "He voluntarily contracted his muscles," would be absurd. Nor can muscular contractions be regarded as a necessary condition for an act, though it is in most cases, since doing nothing at all can count as an act, and in this case there need be no muscular contractions. Cf. Hastings Rashdall, *The Theory of Good and Evil* (2nd ed.; London: Oxford University Press, 1924), vol. I, p. 87: "You cannot really distinguish an act from its present or foreseeable consequences. The consequences, in so far as they can be foreseen, are actually part of the act."

scribing one's circumstances in such a way that no one else could possibly be in those circumstances. If one person could argue in this way, so could everyone else.

On the other hand, if an action is described in too general a way in an application of the argument, the argument will be invertible, or else it will be altogether inapplicable. In neither case does any conclusion follow from it.

There are, to be sure, situations between these extremes, and here is where some difficulties can arise. This is actually all that follows from the present objection. As I just mentioned, what this objection overlooks is the elliptical nature of the conclusion justified by the argument. But it is only on this false supposition that this objection could be regarded as undermining the validity of the argument. For, as we have seen, the conclusion of the argument, in any one application, can be rebutted by a further argument of the same form, by what amounts to a reapplication of the generalization argument; and by this procedure one can justify acting in a way in which it would be undesirable for everyone to act. Now to show that one's circumstances are relevantly different from those in which the act is wrong, is in effect to redescribe one's action in a way that is more adequate to the purposes of moral judgment. For instance, though it is generally wrong to injure someone, it is not generally wrong to do so in self-defense. This is in fact a legitimate exception to the rule, and the generalization argument suffices to show this. What should be noticed here is that the expressions "to injure someone" and "to injure someone in self-defense" can both describe exactly the same action. For moral purposes, however, the latter is a more adequate description. And it does not matter in the least whether the latter is regarded as a more specific description of the action, taken apart from its circumstances, or whether it is regarded as a more specific description of the circumstances of the action.

Consider now an act that can be described as both a case of "doing x" and a case of "doing y," and suppose (1) if everyone did x the consequences would be undesirable; (2) if no one did y the consequences would be undesirable; and (3) if everyone did *y* the consequences would not be undesirable. Note that this last condition is necessary because if the consequences of everyone's doing *y* were also undesirable, with respect to doing *y* the argument would be invertible, and there would be no problem. Now this, presumably, is a situation of the sort regarded as objectionable. Is the act in question right or wrong? Should it be described as "doing *x*," or as "doing *y*"? When described as "doing *x*" it would appear to be wrong, and when described as "doing *y*" it would appear to be right.

The problem here, if not very simple, is still not very formidable. In the abstract, in reference to *x*'s and *y*'s, the question cannot be answered. But it is never necessary for it to be answered in the abstract. It is only necessary for it to be answered in particular cases, and in particular cases it can be answered. "Doing *x*" could be shorthand for "to kill," and "doing *y*" shorthand for "to kill in self-defense"; or "doing *x*" could be "to lie," and "doing *y*" could be "to lie to a murderer in order to save some innocent person from harm." In these cases, the act is justified, and "doing *y*" is the more adequate or appropriate description. But this does not hold in general—"doing *x*" could be "to vote more than once in the same election" and "doing *y*" could be "to vote," in which case the act would be wrong, and "doing *x*" would be the more adequate description. Thus it is possible for "doing *x*" to be a more specific description than "doing *y*," or for "doing *y*" to be more specific than "doing *x*." And it is also possible for the descriptions to be equivalent, in the context, in which case there is no problem at all. For example, "doing *x*" could represent "refusing to pay taxes," and "doing *y*" could be simply "paying taxes."

But it is really not necessary for the descriptions to be internally related, either as species to genus or in some other way. The two descriptions can be independent of each other. One and the same act can be of a kind that is generally right and also of a kind that is generally wrong, even where there is no other relation between the kinds. This is frequently the situation when there is a conflict of rules, leading to a moral problem. To describe the act in such a way as to obscure this fact about it is a mistake, and if it is not made honestly, is itself morally wrong. For it is to conceal an essential element in the situation. The problem of how the act is to be described is the problem of determining the relevant facts about it. All that can be said *in general* is that the way the act is to be described is determined by the conditions that generate the problem.

The possibility of competing descriptions, therefore, shows no more than that difficulties can arise in the application of the generalization argument.[3] But this we knew, or should have known, already. And it is worth remarking that this sort of objection, if taken as valid against the generalization argument as a moral criterion, would be valid against any moral criterion whatever.

§ 2 §

At the end of Chapter IV, I pointed out that the fact that not everyone will act in a certain way is irrelevant to the question whether it is right or wrong to act in that way. It is not a valid objection to the generalization argument, nor can it ever justify anyone in acting in the way in question. For the argument does not imply that everyone will act in that way, nor is this assumed in its application; and if this fact, that not everyone will act in that way, could serve as a justification, it would justify everyone in acting in any way whatsoever.

It is now necessary to recognize, however, that there are situations in which a fact or an assumption very much like the one just mentioned *is* relevant in the application of the generalization argument. In some applications of the argument it is presupposed that not everyone is in certain circumstances or has certain characteristics or is behaving in a certain way. For example, in dealing with the case of someone with a certain communicable disease who is engaged in producing food,

---

[3] Cf. A. C. Ewing, "What Would Happen if Everybody Acted Like Me?" *Philosophy*, vol. XXVIII (January 1953), pp. 26, 28; also J. Harrison, "Utilitarianism, Universalisation, and Our Duty to be Just," *Aristotelian Society Proceedings*, N. S. vol. LIII (London: Harrison & Sons, Ltd., 1953), pp. 114-16.

I remarked that the application of the argument to this case presupposes that not everyone has such a disease (see p. 80). For if everyone had such a disease the fact of having such a disease could not serve as a basis for distinguishing any one person from anyone else. It should be noticed that this is not the same as presupposing that not everyone will produce food, or that not everyone with such a disease will produce food. Again, in recognizing that having recently moved could be a justification for not voting in some election, or could justify a restriction on the right to vote (p. 85), I observed that this is so only if not everyone had recently moved. It is clear, then, that a presupposition of this sort is sometimes necessary, and many other such instances could be given. Suppose that everyone living on a pension, or that everyone in the armed forces, were exempt from paying income taxes. Reasons could be given to justify such exemptions, but not if everyone lived on a pension or were in the armed forces.

But the fact that some applications of the generalization argument involve presuppositions about other people—to the effect that not everyone is in certain circumstances, or will behave in a certain way—does not mean that the reply, "Not everyone will do it," is ever relevant either as an objection or as a justification. For what is being presupposed, in these cases, is not that everyone will act in the way in question, but that not everyone is in certain circumstances or has certain traits, which are claimed to be such as to distinguish the situation of one person from the situation of others. The cases where such a presupposition is necessary are those where one is attempting to justify his, or someone else's, acting in a way in which it would be generally wrong to act, or is attempting to justify the claim that someone has no right to act in a way in which it is not generally wrong to act, and is accordingly maintaining that his situation is different from that of others. Only if this is so, only if this presupposition holds, is there a genuine difference.[4] It it does not hold, if everyone, or practi-

4 Cf. the following remark by Dr. Johnson: "While learning to read and write is a distinction, the few who have that distinction may be the less inclined to work; but when every body learns to read and write, it is

cally everyone, is in the same situation, then the claim to be an exception has not been justified. For if everyone were in the same or a similar situation, then everyone would be an exception.

I have raised this point here because unless it is made perfectly clear we shall never be able to deal with the really important and difficult problems involved in the application of the generalization argument, and it is in fact a point on which there has been considerable confusion. Suppose that the consequences of everyone's acting in a certain way would be undesirable, but that the consequences of a single act, or of a limited number of acts, of that kind, would be beneficial, or at least not undesirable. Suppose, further, that someone has good grounds for believing, or even knows for certain, that his act will remain exceptional—that very few people, or perhaps no one else, will act in that way. Does this change the situation any? Would this justify anyone in acting in that way? My answer to this is that it would not. It was believed by Sidgwick, however, that it would, and since his argument on this is a subtle one, it will be instructive to examine it:

> It cannot be assumed as certain that it is never right to act upon a maxim of which the universal application would be an undoubted evil. This assumption may seem to be involved in what was previously admitted as an ethical axiom, that what is right for me must be right for "all persons under similar conditions." But reflection will show that there is a special case within the range of the axiom in which its application is necessarily self-limiting, and excludes the practical universality which the axiom appears to suggest: *i.e.* where the agent's conditions include (1) the knowledge that his maxim is not universally accepted, and (2) a reasoned conviction that his act will not tend to make it so, to any important extent. For in this case the axiom will practically only mean that it will be right for all persons to do as the agent does, if they are sincerely convinced that the act will not be widely imitated; and

---

no longer a distinction. A man who has a laced waistcoat is too fine a man to work; but if every body had laced waistcoats, we should have people working in laced waistcoats" (Boswell's *Life of Johnson* [London: Oxford University Press, 1953], 15 April 1772, p. 490).

this conviction must vanish if it *is* widely imitated. It can hardly be said that these conditions are impossible. . . .[5]

Though Sidgwick does not expressly mention it here, it is clear that he is taking it for granted that the consequences of the act will not be undesirable, in the particular case with which he is dealing, and later on he does actually say that he is dealing with a type of exception in which "the agent does not think it expedient that the rule on which he himself acts should be universally adopted, and yet maintains that his individual act is right, as producing a greater balance of pleasure over pain than any other conduct open to him would produce." [6]

Now what Sidgwick is assuming here is that the conditions he mentions are an essential part of the conditions under which one is acting; that if these conditions hold, one's circumstances would be relevantly different from those of others; and that therefore under these conditions one would be justified in acting in the way in question. But this clearly will not do. For these conditions will apply in nearly every case, and hence one could justify practically anything on this basis. Everyone could argue in the same way, for everyone can have good reason to believe that the act he is contemplating will remain exceptional, that his doing it will not tend to make it widespread. This sort of reasoning, therefore, is self-defeating. And I cannot see that it makes any difference whether one knows for certain, or merely has a reasonable belief, that his action will remain exceptional. No act can be justified simply on the ground that it will not tend to become widespread, even if it would have desirable consequences in the particular case, so long as it holds that *if it did become* widespread the consequences would be undesirable, and so long as the other conditions for the application of the argument are met. For if this reasoning would justify any one such action, it would justify every such action, and this is self-contradictory.

[5] Henry Sidgwick, *The Methods of Ethics* (7th ed.; London: Macmillan & Co., Ltd., 1907), pp. 318-19.
[6] *Ibid.*, p. 486. The same argument, in slightly different language, is repeated on pp. 486-7.

The argument we are considering, I have said, would justify anything. It would not merely justify the relatively harmless sorts of actions that Sidgwick may well have had in mind, but would justify such actions as murder, lying, and stealing. There is no reason to suppose that an isolated immoral act will have as its consequence the widespread performance of such acts, that it will "set a bad example" and hence cause everyone else to do the same. Indeed, we know very well that it will not. We know perfectly well that people will continue to behave in much the same way they have been behaving. Immoral behavior, though by no means the general practice, is still so rife and extensive that if the fact were otherwise, society would have perished long ago. Suppose, to take what I hope is a purely hypothetical example, you wish to get rid of your mother-in-law. You might reason that she will be better off dead, you will be better off with her out of the way, your wife will come into an inheritance—add any conditions you like. Now your murdering your mother-in-law has not the slightest tendency to make murder, even the murder of mothers-in-law, a widespread practice. (The reasons why are not important here. All that is important is the fact. But it seems worth pointing out that the reason why is not simply that not everyone feels this way about his mother-in-law.) Would these reasons justify your act? On the argument we are examining they would. It should be evident, however, that they would not. For precisely similar reasons would justify anything.

Suppose, again, that I am contemplating evading the payment of income taxes. I might reason that I need the money more than the government does, that the amount I have to pay is so small in comparison with the total amount to be collected that the government will never miss it. Now I surely know perfectly well that if I evade the payment of taxes this will not cause others to do so as well. For one thing, I am certainly not so foolish as to publicize my action. But even if I were, and the fact became known, this would still not cause others to do the same, unless it also became known that I was being allowed to get away with it. In the latter case the practice might tend to become widespread, but this would be a consequence, not of my action, but of the failure of the government to take action against me. Thus there is no question of my act being wrong because it would set a bad example. It would set no such example, and to suppose that it must, because it would be wrong, is simply a confusion. What would tend to cause people to evade the payment of taxes is a set of inequitable, or inequitably enforced, tax laws, but this is another matter. (One can legally evade the payment of taxes, provided one is rich enough. This is a result of the tax laws we now have.) Given all this, then if the reasons mentioned would justify me in evading the payment of taxes, they would justify everyone whatsoever in doing the same thing. For everyone can argue in the same way—everyone can argue that if he breaks the law this will not cause others to do the same. The supposition that this is a justification, therefore, leads to contradiction.

I conclude from this that, just as the reply "Not everyone will do it" is irrelevant to the generalization argument, so is the fact that one knows or believes that not everyone will do the same; and that, in particular, the characteristic of knowing or believing that one's act will remain exceptional cannot be used to define a class of exceptions to the rule. One's knowledge or belief that not everyone will act in the same way in similar circumstances cannot therefore be regarded as part of the circumstances of one's action. One's belief that not everyone will do the same does not make one's circumstances relevantly different from the circumstances of others, or relevantly different from those in which the act is wrong. Indeed, on the supposition that it does, one's circumstances could never be specified, for the specification would involve an infinite regress.[7]

---

[7] Cf. A. K. Stout, "But Suppose Everyone Did the Same," *The Australasian Journal of Philosophy*, vol. XXXII (May 1954), pp. 18-19: "If part of *my* special circumstances is my reasoned belief about how others will act in the same circumstances, then part of *their* special circumstances is their belief about how others, including myself, will act. In judging how they will act in their circumstances I must, then, judge how they believe I will act; and they in their turn must have a belief about what I believe they believe. And so on. Another way of putting this

What apparently led Sidgwick to this position was his belief
that there are "instances of conduct which Common Sense
holds to be legitimate solely on the ground that we have no
fear of its being too widely imitated." The example he takes
to illustrate this is "the case of Celibacy":

> A universal refusal to propagate the human species would
> be the greatest of conceivable crimes from a Utilitarian point
> of view . . . and hence the principle in question, applied
> without the qualification above given, would make it a crime
> in any one to choose celibacy as the state most conducive to
> his own happiness. But Common Sense (in the present age
> at least) regards such preference as within the limits of right
> conduct; because there is no fear that population will not be
> sufficiently kept up, as in fact the tendency to propagate is
> thought to exist rather in excess than otherwise.[8]

No doubt the reason why "a universal refusal to propagate
the human species would be the greatest of conceivable crimes
from a Utilitarian point of view" is that it would lower the
sum total of happiness, and indeed, would sooner or later
eliminate human happiness altogether. I should say that this
somewhat extravagant judgment indicates nothing so much as
that there is something radically wrong with a purely "utilitarian point of view." But let us discuss the question independently of utilitarianism. It provides us with an interesting test case. Is celibacy wrong, or would universal celibacy be
undesirable? The word "celibacy" may well be too formal and
solemn to be really appropriate here. We need not suppose
that people take vows, nor is there any necessary connection
between being unmarried and not having children. Let us simply raise the question in the form, "What would happen if
no one had children?" In all probability the race would die
out. Would this be undesirable? Anyone who finds it so has

---

logical difficulty is that as soon as you make the agent's belief about how
others will act a part of the special circumstances, you cannot properly
speak of others as in 'the same' or exactly similar circumstances. For
their belief includes a belief about me, and my belief does not include a
belief about myself."

[8] Sidgwick, *op. cit.*, p. 487. Cf. pp. 415-6.

it in his power to do something about it, provided he is physically able and can find someone of the opposite sex to share his labors. But suppose we agree that this would be undesirable. Does it follow from the generalization argument that everyone ought to have children? Is the case any different from that of producing food? Suppose everyone had children? This also would be undesirable. Even if we exclude those with certain transmissible defects and diseases, such as the feebleminded and the syphilitic, from our generalization, and apply the argument only to those without hereditary defects of a crippling nature, the consequences would still be undesirable. The dangers and evils of overpopulation are surely as great as those of underpopulation, and may be even worse. And if it is determined that everyone ought to have children, how is it determined how many one should have—should one have one, two, a dozen, twenty-four? I do not think the point needs further elaboration. We could go on to consider the situation of those too poor to care for their children properly, those constitutionally or psychologically incapable of doing so, those too stupid to do so, and so on. But it is not necessary. The conclusion seems to me inescapable that, just as it is with respect to "producing food," with respect to "producing children" the generalization argument is invertible. Thus all that follows from it is that some people, but not everyone, ought to have children. Hence it is not the case that failure or refusal to do so is "legitimate solely on the ground that we have no fear of its being too widely imitated." Neither is it the case that "the principle in question, applied without the qualification above given, would make it a crime in any one to choose celibacy as the state most conducive to his own happiness." The generalization argument is invalid in this application.

§ 3 §

I have been arguing that "not everyone will do it" is neither an objection to the generalization argument nor a justification of a course of conduct that may otherwise be presumed to be wrong, and that the fact that one may know or believe that others will not act in that way has no bearing on the situation. At the same time, I pointed out that there are cases where the circumstances or characteristics of others *are* relevant in the application of the generalization argument, that some applications of the argument presuppose that not everyone is in certain circumstances or has certain characteristics. It is now necessary to recognize that there are situations in which the *behavior* of others is also relevant. Suppose, not that not everyone will act in the way in question, or that most people will not, which is certainly the most common type of situation; but that everyone, or practically everyone, *is* acting in that way. Such situations are by no means nonexistent. Such situations are ones in which ordinary moral rules and practices are not generally observed, in which people generally, or else the members of a relatively well-defined group, can be counted on to lie, steal, cheat, or kill, or do anything else they think they can get away with. Let us call such situations "state of nature situations." Any reader of Hobbes will understand the reason why. In such situations there seems no point in asking, "What would happen if everyone acted in that way?" For practically everyone already is acting in that way, and the situation already is undesirable. Now what ought one to do in such a situation? Is one under any obligation to conform to ordinary moral rules in dealing with people who do not themselves observe them? "Suppose that I live in a society in which the spoken word is seldom to be relied on or men go about in constant fear of their lives. . . . What is my obligation?" [9] Does the generalization argument apply here? If so, how?

In order to answer such questions we must determine more precisely what the situation is. The situation I am envisaging is not one of utter chaos, of unrestricted and ever increasing enmity and violence, or of a war to the death of "every man against every man." Such a state could certainly not exist for long, supposing it could exist at all, and, indeed, can

[9] R. F. Harrod, "Utilitarianism Revised," *Mind*, vol. XLV (April 1936), p. 151. See also J. Harrison, *op. cit.* (note 3), pp. 125-30.

hardly be imagined. At best—or at worst—the chaos could be only partial. As Hume has pointed out, in examining much the same hypothesis, "Whether such a condition of human nature could ever exist, or if it did, could continue so long as to merit the appellation of a *state*, may justly be doubted. Men are necessarily born in a family-society, at least; and are trained up by their parents to some rule of conduct and behavior." [1] The situation, then, cannot be one in which absolutely everybody generally or almost always violates the fundamental rules of morality, or, in other words, in which absolutely everybody habitually lies to everybody else, or attempts to cheat, steal from, or kill everybody else, or does whatever he wants to whenever he wants to and thinks he can get away with it. *This* would be absolute chaos—a situation in which everyone was insane. It is true that in such a situation there could be no question of right and wrong, and thus no question of applying the generalization argument. But neither could there be any question about anything else. Our supposition, therefore, in order to serve as the basis for a problem, must be considerably restricted.

Let us suppose, then, with Hume,

> that it should be a virtuous man's fate to fall into the society of ruffians, remote from the protection of laws and government; what conduct must he embrace in that melancholy situation? He sees such a desperate rapaciousness prevail; such a disregard to equity, such contempt of order, such stupid blindness to future consequences, as must immediately have the most tragical conclusion, and must terminate in destruction to the greater number, and in a total dissolution of society to the rest. He, meanwhile, can have no other expedient than to arm himself, to whomever the sword he seizes, or the buckler, may belong: To make provision of all means of defence and

[1] David Hume, *An Enquiry Concerning the Principles of Morals*, L. A. Selby-Bigge, ed. (2nd ed.; Oxford: The Clarendon Press, 1902), sec iii, part i, p. 190. Hume adds: "But this must be admitted, that, if such a state of mutual war and violence was ever real, the suspension of all laws of justice, from their absolute inutility, is a necessary and infallible consequence." For reasons to be given, I do not think that this is true, in any sense in which it means something different from saying that the "laws of justice" are not in fact observed.

security: And his particular regard to justice being no longer of use to his own safety or that of others, he must consult the dictates of self-preservation alone, without concern for those who no longer merit his care and attention.[2]

Hume's particular brand of utilitarianism, it is evident, leads him to the conclusion that since, in a situation of this type, the rules of justice or morality are of no use, they are therefore suspended or inapplicable, and the implication of this is that, in such a situation, one is justified in doing anything. This, I shall argue, is not the case. In such a situation one is justified in doing whatever is necessary to the preservation of one's own life, person, or property, or those of one's friends and allies, and therefore is justified in taking whatever steps are clearly necessary for this purpose. But this clearly is not a justification for doing anything whatsoever; the rules of morality, therefore, are not altogether inapplicable. And if we consider the matter more closely we shall see that the generalization argument is not either.

What I am imagining is that one is in a situation in which he has to confront or have dealings with a group of people who habitually lie to him whenever they deem it to their advantage, or would cheat, steal, assault, torture, or even kill under these same conditions. Would it be right or wrong for him to act in the same ways toward them, for him to treat them as they would treat him? Now it is true that there *seems* no point in asking, in connection with such situations, "What would happen if everyone acted in that way?" For it seems as if everyone, or practically everyone, already is acting in that way, and the situation already is undesirable. But this is only what seems! It is not true that the generalization argument is inapplicable here. What is true is that it is not applicable in an unrestricted manner, and from this it does not follow that it is not applicable at all. That certain other people are acting or may reasonably be expected to act in certain ways is part of the context in which the generalization argument is applied. To put it another way, that certain other people are acting in ways in which it would be undesirable for everyone to act, in ways that are generally wrong, is part, and an essential part, of the circumstances in which one is acting. Thus the question whether one has, say, the right to lie to them, is not about lying simply, but about lying as a means of self-defense or self-preservation. One has the right to lie as a means to the preservation of one's own life or person or property, or in defense of those of others, provided that it really is necessary to do so or may reasonably be considered so. For if everyone *in such circumstances* were to do *this*, the consequences would not be undesirable. Indeed, it may be that this is the only way of ending this abysmal state of things, and if it is, it is one's duty to do so, and to attempt to bring about a situation in which law and order prevails. It may be necessary to fight fire with fire, force with force, and deception with deception. But in the nature of the case the advantage one would gain by replying in kind must be only temporary, so long as the situation continues; one's primary duty, therefore, must be to attempt to change the situation. Yet from the fact that one has no right to take unfair advantage of others, it does not follow that anyone is under the obligation of allowing others to take unfair advantage of him.

(This, incidentally, is the basis of society's right against criminals. What is called "punishment" is primarily a means to the preservation of society, and though it may justly be made to serve other purposes, this is its primary justification. But this is by no means a wholesale justification of any punishment that may in fact be meted out, of all the devices that have been used as punishments, or of the laws of every society. For it does nothing to answer the question whether a society or government is worth preserving, and it is clear that not all of them are.)

This, however, does not justify unrestricted lying, theft, or violence. The argument presented merely establishes the right of self-defense, and does not give anyone a general right to do these things, a right to do them whenever he pleases. In general, one would have the right to do these things only to those who would do them to oneself or to others, and then only as a means of self-defense. Of course, there are exceptions to this rule also, but I cannot see that even these reasons would ever justify such things as rape or pillage. Furthermore, though one may have the right to kill as a means to the preservation of one's own or someone else's life, and consequently may also cheat, lie, or steal in order to achieve the same purpose, it does not follow that one would have the right to kill or assault or injure another who would merely attempt to gain some advantage over one by lying or cheating. For in this case the means is disproportionate to the end and goes beyond what the end would justify. It would seem, then, that some gradations of priority can be set up among the actions here enumerated.

It may be wondered why the actions of others should be relevant here and not in other situations, why the fact that other people are acting, or may be expected to act, in certain ways can be a relevant difference in one's circumstances, while the fact that not everyone will act in certain ways is not. The answer is that if it were not for this fact, that others are behaving in certain immoral ways or are disregarding moral rules, the question whether one has the right to act towards them in the same way would not arise. This fact both defines the situation as a state of nature situation and generates the question. There would be no such problem if it were not for this. In other situations, on the other hand, this is not the case. The fact that "not everyone will do it" can only lead me to suppose that I can get away with it, or that the consequences will not be so terrible, and not that I have a right to do it.

A state of nature situation, in short, is just a generalization of a situation in which one has to defend oneself or help another, and everything said about it would apply to a situation involving just two people. A has no right to lie to B, but A has the right to lie to B in self-defense.

The state of nature situations considered so far may be characterized, generally, as those in which certain people, or the members of a certain group, habitually violate certain fundamental moral rules, in such a way and in such numbers as to bring instability, disorder, and uncertainty into society.

As we have seen, one who for any reason finds himself in the midst of a "society" of thieves or murderers or maniacs is in such a situation. This general description is also exemplified in the relations existing between the criminal elements of a society on the one hand, and its police or law-abiding elements on the other—between any society and its underworld—as well as in the relations between two warring groups or nations. But there will be many variations depending on the exact nature of the situations and the nature of the opposition between the groups. Now, however, what we have to notice is that this term can usefully be extended to cover situations in which there is merely no established practice or convention or tradition, or in other words, no local rule, governing people's actions on a certain matter, and yet there ought to be one. It can be said that there ought to be such a rule when, in order for action to be effective in achieving some desirable end, or in the elimination of some intolerable evil, it must be organized, at least sufficiently so for one to have reasonable assurance that others in one's situation will join in the effort. And it must be a sufficient number of others, for, by hypothesis, the situation is one in which one person alone, or too small a group, cannot expect to achieve the aim of the activity. Only so can there be reasonable assurance that the aim will be achieved, and without this the risks, either of failure or reprisal, may be too great to make such action sensible. Of course, some people can afford to take such risks, but not everyone can.

Suppose you are a worker who is contemplating going out on strike, either in protest against miserable working conditions or to attain a living wage, and suppose that there is no union to organize the activities of workers. Unless you are fortunate enough to possess some skill that makes you indispensable to your employer or that will enable you to find other employment easily, you are clearly in such a situation. Or suppose you are a teacher who, on moral grounds, objects to being required to sign a "loyalty oath." Whether loyalty oaths are good or bad is not the question here. Suppose, for the sake of argument, that they are bad, and that no one ought to sign one or be required to sign one. Yet, unless a sufficient number of other teachers in your institution or school system or state also refuse to sign, your refusal is likely to lead to nothing but the loss of your job, and may also prevent you from obtaining another. If you are sufficiently well known and respected, your refusal may possibly have some good effects and you may possibly be able to afford to refuse. But it is unlikely that you are. It is clear that what is needed here is some degree of organization and mutual understanding, but this does not always exist and is not always attainable.

Now what should one do in such situations as these? That there ought to be, in such cases, some rule or agreement in terms of which activity can be organized and people enabled to count on the support of others, is easily established by the application of the generalization argument, by a procedure we have already examined. But suppose there is no such rule. What should one do then? One thing that seems clear is that even without some assurance that others in the same circumstances will join in one's action, it is not, generally, wrong for one to do so oneself. One would, as a rule, have a right to do so, if one wants to take the risk or thinks it worth taking. Yet one also has a right not to, since one has no duty to sacrifice oneself for others if the sacrifice has no reasonable expectation of achieving its end. Hence it is largely a matter of prudence here. But it is not wholly so, for one may and very often will have obligations to others, say to support one's family, that would be inconsistent with imprudent action. For these reasons, among others, I do not think that the question here is one to which any general answer can be given. Each case must be considered in its own right, and will reveal complications that any general solution must gloss over. Hence, I do not think that even any general presumption can be established. It does not follow, however, that the generalization argument is inapplicable in such situations. With suitable restrictions and qualifications, it is, and where it is not, the question is not one of morality, but of what course is the most prudent or likely to prove the most effective.

Suppose the question is whether the government should be resisted, or even be overthrown. It must be emphasized that this question has no tint of appropriateness unless the government is intolerably bad or has enacted despotic or repressive laws of an intolerable nature. Even so, as we have seen, the presumption is against it, and this presumption is especially strong if there are legal or constitutional means, as there are in our system, for repealing or changing the law, or eliminating those in power. Even without such provisions the presumption is still against rebellion, for the consequences of general rebellion will generally be worse than the consequences of general obedience. Nevertheless, there are circumstances in which this presumption can be outweighed and rebellion justified. Some governments not only have no right to exist, but may be so bad as not to be worth preserving even if the consequences of rebellion would be a long period of anarchy and terror. It might be argued in certain circumstances that if everyone refused to obey the law it would either be repealed or the government would collapse, and that this, on the whole, would be a good thing, or at least not undesirable; whereas if everyone were to obey the law or help keep the government in power the consequences would be on the whole distinctly undesirable. There are circumstances in which this might hold, and if it does, then it is one's duty to break the law, unless one has, as one might, some special reason for not doing so. But suppose it is known that others will continue to obey the law, even though it is oppressive, that they have been so cowed into submissiveness as to make disobedience or rebellion futile; and suppose further that anyone who refuses to obey the law will be shot and that the members of his family will be sold into slavery. What should one do then? If the facts mentioned are truly the facts of the case, then the situation is really intolerable, and it would seem that one's only hope is to conform to the law while attempting to organize resistance. If this hope should be taken away, then one's situation is absolutely hopeless, and any general advice would be both presumptuous and dangerous. At this point the matter would no longer be one of right and wrong.

Before leaving this topic there is one point that needs special emphasis. It is not every occasion on which others are violating the rules of society, or acting immorally, that gives one the right to do so as well. The fact that other people are engaging in smuggling, or the breaking of rationing restrictions, does not mean that anyone has the *right* to do so, and consequently does not mean that I have. Similarly, if I live in a society in which the majority regularly persecute or intimidate some minority group, in which intolerance and bigotry are generally practiced and generally approved of (that is to say, practiced and approved of by the majority of people or by a highly articulate and powerful minority), this does not give me the right to do so as well, and it certainly does not mean that I have any duty to do so. It is only if my conforming to the rules would be obviously and dangerously imprudent, only if it would place me in a perilous or precarious position, or would lead to great and avoidable harm, that it would be right for me to break them. For here it can be said that if everyone in circumstances similar to mine were to break the rules, the consequences would not be disastrous. Indeed, they might be disastrous otherwise.

§ 4 §

This brings us to a further class of situations that must be considered, which I shall call "competitive situations." These are situations in which variety, diversity, freedom of action, and competition are permissible, or even desirable. To put it another way, these are cases where not everyone ought to do something, while yet someone must or ought or has the right to. The reason why not everyone ought to may be either that it is impossible or undesirable. In either case, there can be no doubt that situations of this kind exist, and that there are areas or kinds of action with respect to which diversity is desirable, or even necessary, and uniformity either undesirable or impossible. In part, as we shall see, this may result from the way such an action is described. But the facts just mentioned are not, as they may appear to be, in conflict with the generalization argument. We can best see this by reviewing a series of examples.

One example of this kind, which has already been considered, was that of Mr. and Mrs. Jones (see p. 32). This was a case, it will be remembered, in which everyone has a right to do something, namely have sexual relations with some one definite person, that no one else has a right to do. While this situation might not involve competition, nevertheless it does involve individualization. Everyone, who meets certain conditions, is assigned a specific right that no one else has, on the basis of a general rule in accordance with which everyone is assigned a similar right. As we saw, this is not incompatible with the generalization principle, and it is therefore not incompatible with the generalization argument, though this fact may be obscured if the situation is wrongly described. A comparable case is provided by the duty to raise and provide for one's own children.

Another example is that of winning a race. Not everyone can win, and it would certainly be undesirable if everyone could. Yet someone ought to win. Otherwise there would be no point to the running of races. Does everyone have the right to win? Well, everyone, at least everyone with the qualifications for entering, has the right to try. But the one who wins does not thereby, merely by winning, violate the rights of the others entered. He would do so only if he violated the rules of the race, which determine when a race is fairly won. The winner of the race is determined by the running of it, and by the rules in accordance with which it is run (and sometimes, of course, when the outcome is close, or doubtful points arise, by the judges who administer the rules). Corresponding points apply in the case of any contest or competitive sport, as well as to such activities as running the government or commanding the army. Not everyone can rule or be in a position of authority, and yet someone must. This does not mean, however, that everyone who is in fact in a position of authority has a right to be, has fairly obtained the position, or is fairly administering it. These are other questions entirely.

Now in none of the cases mentioned is there any conflict with the generalization principle or the generalization argument. The reason is, that with respect to all the activities mentioned the generalization argument is invertible. In some cases, of course, it is also reiterable. With respect to a race, for example, both the consequences of everyone's winning and the consequences of no one's winning would be undesirable. The argument, therefore, is not applicable to the act of running a race, or the achievement of winning one, at least not directly. It is, however, the basis of the rules that govern the running of races, and of the standards that determine what is and what is not fair competition. It is clear, therefore, that the generalization argument is not incompatible with treating certain circumstances or certain persons as unique or as having a unique status. In some cases it even demands it. For it is actually through the application of the generalization argument that a situation is rightfully determined to be of the type that I am calling competitive. It is so only if the argument is invertible with respect to it, or else is altogether inapplicable, in which case, of course, one has the perfect freedom to do the act or not as one pleases.

Another clear case of what I am calling a competitive situation is one that was dealt with previously, at length, in connection with the condition of invertibility. I refer to the activity of producing food. As has already been mentioned, though not everyone ought to produce food (or make clothes or build houses or have children), yet someone must. In such a case as this, the principle of the division of labor, according to capacity, interest, and opportunity, may be permitted to operate, as, in our society, it usually does. This is not to say that it always operates fairly, beneficially, or efficiently. It clearly does not. And there is always the danger that either too many people or not enough will enter some occupation or engage in some activity.[3] In such cases society

[3] The following passage provides a somewhat amusing commentary on this: "It's a good thing for us chartists there aren't more of us. If you got too many people investing by this method, their operations would begin to affect stock prices, and thus throw the charts off. The method

must offer specific inducements either to leave it or to enter it. If the situation becomes drastic, as it might in wartime, specific laws may be passed to require people to perform certain services or to remain in their jobs. For if the job is distasteful enough, the normal inducements may not be sufficient.

The cases just mentioned differ from those mentioned before in that in those just mentioned it is clearly not sufficient for just one person to be engaged in the activity. What is required is a certain number of people, a number sufficient to meet the needs of society. This number of course will vary with the conditions and needs of society and with changes in technology, and could hardly ever be specified with exactitude. But this is not a difference of principle.

In all competitive situations it is necessary that there be certain standards of fairness to determine the limits between fair and unfair competition. Variety of interest, diversity of function, freedom of action, and competition between individuals are permissible or desirable only within certain limits. Competition, with its consequent freedom of action, does not *per se* involve violation of the rights of others. It does so only if it violates the rules or standards of fairness governing the activity. A lawyer who wins a case, or a salesman who makes a sale, has not thereby violated the rights of the opposing lawyer or salesman; though he would have done so if he had, say, bribed the jury, or misrepresented his competitor's product. But these rules of fairness, as I have called them, are, generally, local rules. Thus, though they have an initial presumption in their favor, they may themselves be unjust. Many that actually prevail are merely the results of custom, or of the influence of some dominant class, and could hardly withstand reflection. Thus there are two questions that can arise in the case of any competitive activity. There is the question whether the activity conforms or comes up to certain rules or standards, and there is the question whether these rules or standards can themselves be justified. Questions of this sort are de-

would become self-defeating" (from an article by John Brooks, in *The New Yorker*, vol. XXXII, no. 18 [June 23, 1956], p. 46).

cided every day by courts and administrative agencies; and sometimes, of course, these two questions cannot in fact be distinguished. For sometimes the problem is to formulate and establish a rule not previously acknowledged or recognized. And very often the determination of these questions involves decisions of great difficulty. For it involves drawing a line between competing activities, or conflicting sets of rights, and where it should be drawn is not always clear.

If what has been said about competitive situations is sound, then it follows that the generalization argument has in connection with them two distinct and equally important applications. In the first place, it provides the criterion for determining whether a situation or an activity that is actually competitive is rightfully or truly so; and it is not obvious that its judicious application would justify every existing social or economic arrangement. In the second place, it can be used to determine the limits of fair competition, or whether the standards governing some activity are themselves justifiable. I take it that the first point has already been sufficiently established; for the notion of a "competitive situation" has actually been defined by reference to the generalization argument and the condition of invertibility. The second point can only be established by showing how the argument can be so used, and I shall show this by presenting an actual example of its use for this purpose. (But this is actually not the first such example; see pp. 117-119.)

The example to be presented is taken from a judicial opinion, that of Mr. Justice Jackson, in the case of *Douglas* v. *Jeannette* (319 U.S. 157). Through a mere technicality, Justice Jackson's opinion is concurring in the *Douglas* case; it is, however, dissenting in a whole series of similar cases decided at the same time (including *Murdock* v. *Pennsylvania*, *Martin* v. *Struthers*, and, by implication, *Jones* v. *Opelika*),[4] and on the substantial legal issues involved, it must be regarded as a dissenting opinion.

[4] 319 U.S. (*Supreme Court Reports*) 105, 319 U.S. 141, and 319 U.S. 103. This last case was first decided in 1942; the decision was reversed when these other cases were decided, May 3, 1943.

The facts and issues involved in these cases, which are all closely related, are, as might be expected, fairly involved, and it would be too much of a digression to detail them here. They are well and fully recited in Justice Jackson's opinion, much more fully and clearly, in fact, than in any of the many other opinions presented in this series of cases. Yet some brief indication of the facts is a necessity. These cases all deal with the proselytizing activities of members of the sect of Jehovah's Witnesses, which came into conflict with certain municipal ordinances that were applied to limit or restrict them. In the *Murdock* case, the ordinance, of the city of Jeannette, was one requiring a license tax of all persons canvassing for or soliciting orders for goods or merchandise of any kind; in the *Struthers* case the ordinance was one declaring it "unlawful for any person distributing handbills, circulars or other advertisements to ring the doorbell, sound the door knocker, or otherwise summon the inmate or inmates of any residence to the door for the purpose of receiving such handbills. . . ." In all these cases there was organized activity by members of this sect—one instance involved over one hundred of them—that was clearly in violation of these ordinances, and the outcome was that these ordinances were declared unconstitutional by the Supreme Court of the United States (though it is not clear whether they were invalidated as such or merely in their application to what was referred to as "religious practices"). It may be worth mentioning that on these cases the Court divided five to four.

These are merely the bare bones of the facts. Yet the record is available for anyone who wishes to inquire further, and my main interest here is not in these cases or their outcome, but in certain points made in the dissenting opinion of Justice Jackson. Justice Jackson is quite clear that the issue in these cases is one of conflicting rights. He speaks of "the problem of those in local authority when the right to proselyte comes in contact with what many people have an idea is their right to be let alone" (p. 166), and of the problems of weighing "the conflicting claims of rights in the related cases today decided" (p. 167); and says that, "Doubtless there exist fellow spirits who welcome these callers, but the issue here is what are the rights of those who do not and what is the right of the community to protect them in the exercise of their own faith in peace" (p. 177). He says further:

Our difference of opinion cannot fairly be given the color of a disagreement as to whether the constitutional rights of Jehovah's Witnesses should be protected in so far as they are rights. These Witnesses, in common with all others, have extensive rights to proselyte and propagandize. These of course include the right to oppose and criticize the Roman Catholic Church or any other denomination. These rights are, and should be held to be, as extensive as any orderly society can tolerate in religious disputation. The real question is where their rights end and the rights of others begin. The real task of determining the extent of their rights on balance with the rights of others is not met by pronouncement of general propositions with which there is no disagreement (pp. 178-9).

With these preliminaries, then, the following application of the generalization argument should be almost self-explanatory:

A common-sense test as to whether the Court has struck a proper balance of these rights is to ask *what the effect would be if the right given to these Witnesses should be exercised by all sects and denominations.* If each competing sect in the United States went after the householder by the same methods, I should think it intolerable. If a minority can put on this kind of drive in a community, what can a majority resorting to the same tactics do to individuals and minorities? Can we give to one sect a privilege that we could not give to all, merely in the hope that most of them will not resort to it? Religious freedom in the long run does not come from this kind of license to each sect to fix its own limits, but comes of hardheaded fixing of those limits by neutral authority with an eye to the widest freedom to proselyte compatible with the freedom of those subject to proselyting pressures.

For a stranger to corner a man in his home, summon him to the door and put him in the position either of arguing his religion or of ordering one of unknown disposition to leave is a questionable use of religious freedom.[5]

Now I regard this application of the argument as not only decisive, but as unanswerable. It is neither invertible nor re-iterable; and given the facts presented, the somewhat ellipti-cal language in which it is stated is perfectly clear. It is worth noting that it was not in fact answered, or even alluded to, in the various opposing opinions, although some other points made by Justice Jackson were. And the fact that it was used to support a dissenting judgment, and did not in fact deter-mine the law of the land, seems to me of no moment what-ever.

But I would not imply by this that such an argument can be used *by itself* to effect a sound determination of such issues. These issues are too complicated to be resolved in so simple a manner. Note that before it could be applied in the present instance it was necessary to establish that the problem was one of effecting a balance between conflicting rights, or of specifying a limit to activities otherwise permissible. This re-quired a rather lengthy recital of a complicated set of facts, for it was necessary to establish the nature of the activity in question, and of the activities and interests with which it con-flicted. In order to put one's opinion beyond doubt, it is also necessary, though it is not always sufficient, to meet other ar-guments that bear the other way, and this in fact took up a good portion of the opinion with which I have been dealing.

These limitations and provisos, however, are not really de-bilitating. From the fact that the application of the generaliza-tion argument is not *all*-sufficient, it does not follow that it is not sufficient. It only follows that, as we knew before, its ap-plication is not self-justifying or necessarily conclusive. Yet what should be clear beyond doubt is that the case just pre-sented is truly an instance of what I have been calling a com-petitive situation. For with respect to an activity described simply as "proselyting," or as "attempting to convert others

[5] 319 U.S. 157 at 180 and 181 (italics added).

to the practices and tenets of one's own religion," the generalization argument is either invertible or altogether inapplicable. What was needed then, in the instant case, was a more adequate description of the activity in question, a more relevant specification of it. This, then, is but further confirmation of some points made before.

§ 5 §

We have considered state of nature situations and competitive situations. Let us consider now the case of punishment, which bears some affinities to both. It provides an interesting test case.

Punishment, of course, can take many forms, and can be inflicted in various degrees. None of these details need detain us. To punish is to inflict pain or evil or suffering or inconvenience on someone for some crime or fault or offense. Speaking generally and formally, it is to deprive someone of life, liberty, or property. How, on our principles, is it possible for this to be justified?

According to the generalization principle, or so it appears, if not everyone ought to act or be treated in a certain way, then no one ought to act or be treated in that way. But then how is it possible to justify punishment? For surely not everyone ought to be punished.

This dilemma, if dilemma it is, rests on a simple misinterpretation of the generalization principle. It is true that not everyone ought to be punished. But what follows is, not that no one ought to be punished, but that no one ought to be punished *without a reason*. (Of course, here there is no question of one having *a right* to be punished. We say, "So and so *ought to be* punished," and if anyone has a right here it is the community, or those in authority.) It is right for A to be punished if, and only if, it is right for every similar person in similar circumstances to be punished. In other words, if A ought to be punished, then, not everyone, but every similar person in similar circumstances ought to be punished, in the same way. Reference to a reason is essential in order to determine the conditions of similarity. So the question is, why ought A to be punished? If it is because he has committed some wrong or infringed some rule, then everyone who has done the same ought to be punished, and if they are not then it is wrong for A to be punished for this reason. In general, "A ought to be punished because he did *x*" implies "Anyone who does *x* ought to receive the same punishment," unless there is some further relevant difference in the backgrounds or natures of the parties or in the contexts of their actions. (One, for example, might have an extensive background of past offenses, which would justify more severe treatment in his case.) This is the prime condition for fairness.

Whether the reason given in any particular case actually justifies the punishment given is determined by the generalization argument. If it holds that the consequences of everyone who has committed such and such an offense being punished for it would not be undesirable, whereas the consequences of no such person's being punished would be undesirable, then everyone who has committed such and such an offense ought to be punished. Note how this leaves open the possibility of extenuating circumstances. Note also how the condition of restricted universality operates here: not everyone is within the scope of the argument.

Why is punishment necessary at all? There are many who have begun to doubt whether punishment has any of the effects, such as deterrence or reform, that have been claimed for it. Perhaps punishment should be replaced by some other arrangement, alleged to be more humane, such as treatment or the attempt to cure, on the ground that criminals are really more sick than evil? This, no doubt, has something to be said for it, in specific cases. Perhaps certain types of punishments do not have the deterrent or reforming effects, in certain cases, that they are supposed to have. But as a general policy this idea is absurd. What would happen if no one were ever punished for wrongful or unlawful acts, if everyone were permitted to do whatever he pleased with impunity? It seems obvious that this would be disastrous, and that no one could re-

gard this as desirable. For we should then be in a state of
nature situation, and this would be intolerable. This says nothing whatever about the justice or necessity or efficacy of this
or that type of punishment, of the rules that actually prevail,
or about the purposes or aims of punishment. These are all
questions of detail, mixed questions of fact and morals, requiring separate treatment. In particular, it says nothing about
the morality of capital punishment.

Furthermore, not every instance or type of punishment
can be justified, as is shown by the same line of reasoning. If
the consequences of everyone who has committed such an act
being treated in that way would be undesirable, then no one
ought to be treated in that way, without a special justification.
This shows why it is wrong for anyone to be punished for
something he has not done. One can justly be punished only
for something he has done that he ought not to have done. For
without this condition anyone would be subject to punishment
for any reason at all, and we should be again in a state of nature situation. This situation would be equivalent to one in
which everyone would have the right to do whatever he pleases
with anyone or to anyone he pleases, and this is self-contradictory. Thus it is wrong for anyone to be punished for reasons of
whim, or because he is disliked or unpopular or has unpopular opinions.

Can one be willing to be punished? Could anyone regard it
as desirable that he be punished? This is no doubt possible,
but it is not likely to happen with any frequency. It is, in
any case, irrelevant. The preceding arguments have shown
that punishment must be administered under a system of
rules, and must not depend on the desires of a specific individual. One can regard it as desirable that everyone who
commits an offense of such and such a nature be punished
(be deprived of certain rights); and we are supposing that it
would be undesirable if no one who commits such an offense
were to be punished for it. One who has committed such an
offense and is punished for it cannot thereby deny this. He
may dispute the justice of *his* punishment, he may deny that
be committed the offense, just as he may wish and attempt

to evade detection. But he does not thereby deny the necessity or justice of *punishment*.

<h1 style="text-align:center">§ 6 §</h1>

This chapter may fittingly be concluded with some specimen applications of the generalization argument, in order to illustrate further some of the points already discussed, and to settle some further questions, not already discussed. For this purpose I shall select two examples for further comment.

1. The question, "What would happen if no one voted?" has been used several times as an instance of the generalization argument. I shall therefore take it for granted that the argument establishes, as a general rule, that everyone ought to vote, or rather, that everyone who has the right to vote should exercise that right. But now suppose the question is raised, "What would happen if everyone voted for your party (or candidate)?" One consequence would probably be that the "two party system" would break down, and one party would be left in control with no effective opposition and no effective criticism. Assuming that this would be a bad thing, as it probably in fact would be, does it follow that it is morally wrong to vote for the party (or candidate) in question?

It should be clear that it does not, that the generalization argument does not at all have this consequence, and that this is not, therefore, as it would otherwise be, a genuine counterexample to it. In the first place, the argument is reiterable: if it is wrong to vote for this party, because of what would happen if everyone did, it would be wrong to vote for that party, because of what would happen if everyone did, and it would be wrong to vote for some other party, for exactly the same reason. It follows from this that it would be wrong to vote for any party, and this implies that it would be wrong to vote. But this contradicts the conclusion that everyone ought to vote, and consequently the argument is invertible. And it can be shown to be invertible independently of the fact that it is reiterable, and that the case is quite different from the case of just not voting. For the consequences of no one's voting for X would be just as undesirable as the consequences of everyone's voting for X.

The question, then, whether one ought to vote for such and such a candidate, as contrasted with the question whether one ought to vote, is not one to be answered by the application of the generalization argument. The situation here is one that is properly competitive, and everyone ought to vote as he sees fit, and for the candidate or the party that best represents his political convictions. This does not mean that moral questions do not enter into the question how one ought to vote. What it means is that the question is not *per se* a moral one. But neither does it mean that it does not matter how one votes, nor that it is wrong to attempt to change or to sway the vote of another.

The rule just laid down, of course, like other rules, is subject to exceptions. There are cases where it could be argued that it would not be undesirable if no one voted for a certain candidate, as where he is, say, a member of the lunatic fringe. Similarly, there are cases where it could be argued that it would not be undesirable if everyone voted for a certain candidate, on the ground that the opposing parties should be repudiated. But such cases must remain rare; otherwise we should constantly be in a state of nature situation.

As the rule just mentioned is subject to exceptions, so is the rule that everyone ought to vote, and there are many factors that would justify a failure or a refusal to vote. Moreover, the force of the rule, and consequently the force of the countervailing factors, will vary with the importance of the election. But it is perhaps worth mentioning that one may be justified in refusing to vote by the fact that one wishes to register a protest against the choices that he has been offered. This is a positive refusal to vote, for which one has reasons, and is quite different from just "not feeling like voting." The latter is never a justification. But I see no need to enter into the further complications of this very complex matter. My purpose was not to add ammunition to the arsenal of political campaigners, but to obviate a difficulty with respect to the generalization argument.

2. Consider now the question about military service. This is another example that has been used before, and what I wish to do now is to complicate it. The first thing to notice about this application of the argument is that it must be sharply restricted. If everyone refused to serve, we would lose the war, or supposing that there is no war, invite an attack that would be devastating. But if everyone did serve in the armed forces, there would be no one left to run the country and to do the other jobs essential to the maintenance of armed forces. It follows that not everyone ought to be in the armed forces, and whether one ought to or not depends on one's age and physical fitness, and the other functions that one is, or is capable of, performing. The determination of these limits, in turn, will vary with the needs and conditions of the time, and with the complexity and flexibility of the society. But of course I am taking it for granted that the society is worth defending, and that if it were not defended it would be destroyed. It is evident, then, that the question, "What would happen if everyone refused to serve?" must be restricted to those of proper age, not obviously unfit, not performing some essential and irreplaceable function, and so on. If there is a compulsory service law, these limits will be determined by the law, and there will be an added and much more exact criterion for determining who is attempting to take unfair advantage of others.[6] But there is not always such a law, and the question I am dealing with here can be taken

---

[6] The framing and administering of such a law presents difficulties of its own, to which the generalization argument is not entirely irrelevant. Consider the following discussion by Hanson W. Baldwin in *The New York Times* (February 23, 1951): "Another feature of the emerging draft law has given many scientists and educators considerable concern. These observers fear that the universal-service feature of the act may be applied in a shortsighted manner to the detriment of the nation's ultimate strength. The development of scientists . . . would be interrupted or the numbers would be materially reduced under the legislation now contemplated. Higher education in general would suffer. The problem is not easy to solve, for it is clear that each special group and category believes that its efforts are of paramount importance to the country and hence should not be interrupted by the exigencies of national emergency. Yet if all were deferred there would be no soldiers, and yet if any are to be called it is obviously fairer to call all."

as applying to any situation in which volunteers are needed
for some essential task.

So much for these preliminaries. Suppose now that someone argues, as a means of justifying his failure or refusal to
serve, that if no one joined *any* armies, if everyone on both
sides refused to go to war, there would be no wars, and thus
no need to serve. This sort of defense is by no means un-
heard of, and is in fact widely used; it occurs frequently in
practice, and is consequently reflected in theory.[7] But it is
none the better for this. It is unsound, and the reason why is
that it overlooks the fact that the situation in which armed
forces (as well as police forces) are needed is one that bor-
ders on a state of nature situation, if it does not in all respects
fully answer to the description. If it were not for the fact that
other people in other countries have joined their countries'
armies, and that the country is under attack or is threatened
by attack, the question whether one ought to serve or has the
right not to would not arise. The question arises, in other
words, because the need exists, and would not arise apart
from it. Granted that if everyone in the world refused to go
to war, there would be no wars, the fact remains that not
everyone in the world will refuse to go to war, and that is
why men are needed to defend the country. (Similarly, if
everyone were moral and always did what he ought there
would be no need for deception and other protective devices,
perhaps no need for police or government, and perhaps moral
questions would not arise at all, or at least to the extent to
which they do. But this is to suppose that men are angels.) It
is this fact, that others, in opposing countries, can be counted
on to act in certain ways, that calls for this application of the
generalization argument, and it would surely be curious if it
were to defeat it. It is true, of course, that if a number
sufficient to meet the need could be counted on to volunteer,
either because they were attracted by adventure and the
military life, or were induced by the pay and other bene-

---

[7] A good instance of this error occurs in C. D. Broad, "On the Function
of False Hypotheses in Ethics," *The International Journal of Ethics*, vol.
XXVI, (April 1916), pp. 390-1.

fits—and not because they felt an obligation to—the question would also not arise. But we are supposing that this is not the case, as, in fact, it is not. For we are supposing that the question arises.

The question, "What would happen if everyone refused to serve?" must therefore be understood with a further restriction. It must be restricted not only to those of proper age who are not physically unfit and so on, but also to those who are citizens of or residents in one's own country. Hence a further defect of the sort of defense we are considering is that it goes beyond the scope of the original argument. It is consequently irrelevant to it. It violates, in other words, the condition of restricted universality.

The fact that others in other countries can be counted on to join their countries' armies is a relevant fact about the situation. But the fact that others in one's own country can be counted on to join one's own army is not, and is not a justification for refusing to serve. For if this fact could justify me in refusing to serve, it would justify everyone in my situation, and this is self-contradictory. Similarly, the fact that *my* refusal to serve would not have very bad consequences, the fact that it would not cause us to lose the war, is not a justification for refusing. For this fact also would justify everyone in refusing.

Of course I am supposing that not everyone would be justified in refusing, and this, it must be pointed out, is not always so. Not all wars are justified, just as not all countries are worth defending. But to claim that the war is unjustified and should be ended, or that the country is not worth defending and that no one should defend it, is not to claim that one is an exception to a rule that applies to others. It is to claim that the rule does not apply, and this is quite a different matter.

One final point. The argument we are examining may be understood in a somewhat different sense. Instead of being understood as merely a justification of refusing to serve, it may be understood as implying that if everyone in the world refused to join his country's army, the consequences would be desirable, and that therefore everyone *ought* to refuse to serve. Understood in this sense it is not, as it may appear to be, an application of the generalization argument. It is, rather, an instance of what I shall call the *obverse* of the generalization argument: If the consequences of everyone's acting in a certain way would be *desirable*, then everyone ought to act in that way. I shall argue in the next chapter that this is not in general a valid mode of argument, that an application of it is valid only where it happens to coincide with an application of the generalization argument. Given this conclusion, then, the present argument, as so understood, is still altogether irrelevant.

❀

CHAPTER VII

MORAL PRINCIPLES
AND THE PRINCIPLE OF
UTILITY

Suppose someone were to argue that if no one paid ransom to kidnapers, there would be no kidnaping, or at least no kidnaping for the sake of ransom, and that therefore no one should pay ransom. Would this be sound? Let it be admitted, for the sake of argument, that the premise is true, that if no one paid ransom there would be no kidnaping for ransom. It may also be admitted, and about this there can be no doubt, that this would be a good thing. Does this then provide a good reason for concluding that it is wrong to pay ransom?

The argument just presented is of the same type as the one presented at the end of the last chapter, to the effect that "If everyone refused to go to war, there would be no wars; therefore, everyone ought to refuse to go to war." It is an instance, not of the generalization argument, but of what I have called its *obverse*. This is not, in any sense, the other side of the generalization argument; it is not the generalization argument from another point of view or stated in a different way. It is its opposite. Both these lines of argument, of course, involve the generalization principle. They both involve generalization, the consideration of what would happen if everyone acted in a certain way. In the generalization argument, however, the reference is to the undesirability of the consequences of everyone's acting in a certain way; here the reference is to their desirability. Now these two lines of argument are distinct, and not equivalent. They have quite different, and even contrary, implications. This is so even though they are often confused together. It will be my contention that this is not, in general, a valid form of argument; a conclusion drawn from it will be reasonable only if it could also be derived from an application of the generalization argument. To put it another way, the principle that "If the consequences of everyone's acting in a certain way would be desirable, then it is one's duty to act in that way," is not a sound moral principle.

In order to show this it will be useful to consider first what may by analogy be called the obverse of the principle of consequences: "If the consequences of A's doing x would be desirable, then A has the duty to do x." This is related to the obverse of the generalization argument as the principle of consequences is related to the generalization argument. Consequently if it were sound the obverse generalization argument could readily be derived from it. What I shall argue is that it is not sound, and that it is neither equivalent to nor deducible from the principle of consequences. From the proposition that it would be wrong to do that which would have bad or harmful consequences, it by no means follows that it is a duty to do that which would have good or beneficial consequences. Yet this is an assumption that has frequently been made.

This point, it will be apparent, has some connection with utilitarianism, and with its central principle, the principle of utility. This is one good reason for considering this principle, and the connections between the view I am maintaining and utilitarianism. It is not utilitarianism, nor even a variety of it, and the generalization argument is not a Utilitarian argument. Utilitarianism, in fact, cannot officially recognize it. The generalization argument and the principle of utility, however, are not altogether unrelated.

The discussion of these various principles, or alleged principles, has an importance that is not just intrinsic. On the one hand, it will enable us to distinguish the generalization argument, and the other principles that I regard as sound, from those that I regard as unsound but with which they might easily be confused. On the other hand, it will be relevant to the problem of the justification of moral principles, which will be dealt with in the last chapter of this book. On what basis can one principle be said to be sound and another unsound? On the basis, obviously, of the considerations that show one to be sound and the other unsound. It will be well to keep this in mind.

§ 1 §

The obverse of the principle of consequences, or what may also be called "the principle of consequences in its positive form," states that: "If the consequences of A's doing *x* would be desirable, then it is A's duty to do *x*." It may also be stated in its generalized form: "If the consequences of doing *x* are generally (or usually) desirable, then it is one's duty to do *x*," where "*x*" refers, not to a specific act in specific circumstances, but to a kind of action. But to simplify the argument, which will be complicated enough, let us consider this principle simply in the form in which it asserts: "If the consequences of A's doing *x* would be desirable *on the whole*, then A ought to do *x*." Now this principle, in one form or another, has had an extraordinarily wide acceptance, and is widely regarded as either intuitively or demonstratively certain. It is, for example, central to traditional utilitarianism, which maintains that we have the duty, not simply to minimize unhappiness or pain, but to maximize happiness or pleasure; and that it is everyone's duty to do that act, of all those open to him in a given situation, which would produce the greatest amount of happiness on the whole. The acceptance of this idea, however, by no means depends on an acceptance of hedonism; what is essentially the same doctrine is maintained by "nonhedonistic utilitarians": those utilitarians who do not accept the identification of "the good" with "pleasure." Thus it has been held, by one such writer, that it is "quite self-evident that it must always be our duty to do what will produce the best effects *upon the whole*, no matter how bad the effects upon ourselves may be and no matter how much good we ourselves may lose by doing it. . . . . It must always be the duty of every agent to do that one, among all the actions which he *can* do on any given occasion, whose total consequences will have the greatest intrinsic value. . . ." But neither does the acceptance of this idea depend on an acceptance of utilitarianism, the doctrine that the morality of an action depends solely on the consequences of that specific action. Thus it has been held, by a writer who is not a utilitarian, of either variety, that: "Even if Utilitarianism is not true, it is still the case that it is *one* of our main responsibilities to produce as much good as we can. . . . If something is good there is a *prima facie* obligation to produce it, and an actual obligation unless some more stringent *prima facie* obligation intervenes." [1]

This principle, however, has been asserted much more frequently than it has been supported; it is usually not argued for at all, but left at the level of "self-evidence" or intuitive obviousness. This is unfortunate, for once it is so accepted the tendency is to leave its implications unexamined. Thus the author just quoted says: "It seems self-evident that if there are things that are intrinsically good, it is *prima facie* a duty to bring them into existence rather than not to do so, and to bring as much of them into existence as possible," and adds that the proposition "that there is no *prima facie* duty to produce as much that is good as we can . . . hardly admits of argument but seems to me plainly false." [2] Yet it is not at all

---

[1] G. E. Moore, *Ethics* (Home University Library; London: Oxford University Press, 1947), p. 143; Sir W. David Ross, *Foundations of Ethics* (Oxford: The Clarendon Press, 1939), pp. 67, 271.

[2] W. D. Ross, *The Right and The Good* (Oxford: The Clarendon Press, 1930), pp. 24, 25. On p. 27 it is asserted that, in virtue of "the general principle that we should produce as much good as possible," we have such duties as the duties of beneficence and self-improvement. See also p. 39: "If we are ever under no special obligation such as that of fidelity to a promisee or of gratitude to a benefactor, we ought to do what will produce most good . . . even when we are under a special

self-evident, and there are actually fairly strong reasons against it. Before going on to give these reasons, however, there is one argument in support of this principle that should be considered, both because it is fairly typical, and because it is such a splendid example of logic-chopping, on a par with the arguments of Parmenides.

The argument I have in mind is one that has been presented to prove that "the assertion 'I am morally bound to perform this action' is identical with the assertion 'This action will produce the greatest amount of good in the Universe,' " a "fundamental point" which, it is insisted, is "demonstrably certain":

> It is, in fact, evident that, however valuable an action may be in itself, yet, owing to its existence, the sum of good in the Universe may conceivably be made less than if some other action, less valuable in itself, had been performed. But to say that this is the case is to say that it would have been better that the action should not have been done; and this again is obviously equivalent to the statement that it ought not to have been done—that it was not what duty required.[3]

The first thing to notice about this argument is that it simply takes it for granted that it makes sense to speak of "the sum of good in the Universe," or of "the greatest possible amount of good in the Universe." In the absence, however, of any specification of what sense it makes, this is not a supposition that can reasonably be granted. It is on a par with that of traditional utilitarianism, which speaks of "the sum of pleasure" or "the greatest amount of happiness." Such a conception results from reifying pleasure, or "good," and thinking of it as though it were like money, which can be thought of and spoken of in abstraction from the people whose money it is, and thus can in a sense be said to have an independent existence. It would make sense to speak of the

obligation the tendency of acts to promote general good is one of the main factors in determining whether they are right."

[3] G. E. Moore, *Principia Ethica* (Cambridge: Cambridge University Press, 1903), pp. 147-8.

amount of money in the universe, for it makes sense to speak of the amount of money in the country, and it makes sense because there is a method of calculating it. But it makes no sense to speak of the amount or the sum of good (or pleasure), no matter where we suppose it to be located. And the fact that we can speak of the amount or the number of *goods* that someone possesses does not enable us to make sense of the notion of an amount or a sum of good. (Goods are fungible: "good" is not.) I would add that the fact that we can ask, and sometimes answer, such questions as "How much good did it do?" and "Would this be better than that?", gives no title to the phrase "the sum of good in the Universe" or to the notion of a sum or an amount of good.

But let us grant, for the sake of argument, that it does make sense to speak of "the sum of good in the Universe." Then, presumably, to say of some action that it would "increase the sum of good in the Universe" would be merely another way of saying that its consequences would be desirable, on the whole. On this interpretation, then, to say that by some action "the sum of good in the Universe would be made less than if some other action had been performed" is to say that the consequences of performing the latter would be more desirable, on the whole, than the consequences of performing the former. It is not to say that the consequences of performing the former would be bad; it is merely to say that the consequences of performing the latter would be better. Even so, it is not at all obvious that "to say that this is the case is to say that it would have been better that the action should not have been done," nor is it obvious that this is "equivalent to the statement that it ought not to have been done—that it was not what duty required." It depends on what is meant by such an expression as "it is better to do *b* than *d*," which, as we have seen (p. 36), is of a rather complicated nature. If it is taken to mean simply that the consequences of doing *b* would be better than the consequences of doing *d*, then it does not necessarily imply that one ought to do *b* rather than *d*, or that it would be wrong to do *d* and not *b*—so long as the consequences of doing *d* would not be undesirable. This, at any rate, is the very point at issue. On the other hand, if "it is better to do *b* than *d*" is taken to be identical with "one ought to do *b* rather than *d*," then it does not necessarily imply that the consequences of doing *b* would be better than the consequences of doing *d*. All that follows from it is that the consequences of doing *b* rather than *d* would not be undesirable. For it is possible for the consequences of *not* doing *b* to be worse than the consequences of *not* doing *d*. Thus it is possible for the consequences of doing *d* to be better than the consequences of doing *b*, and for it to be wrong to do *d*. Most often, of course, as I indicated once before, a statement like "it is better to do *b* than *d*" is a mixed judgment and evaluation, in which a moral judgment of the action is combined with an evaluation of the consequences. So understood, such statements do not imply that it would be wrong to do *d*, but simply that it would be better to do *b*, and these two are not the same.

So the argument just considered does not establish the coincidence of what is right (in the sense of being mandatory) with what would have the best consequences, and therefore it does not prove that if the consequences of A's doing *x* would be desirable then A ought to do *x*.

But so far I have only attempted to show that this proposition has not been established, and have not yet given any reasons against it.

One major objection to this principle is that, if consistently adhered to, it would lead to moral fanaticism, to the idea that no action is indifferent or trivial, that every occasion is momentous. That this is so is borne out by the fact that one supporter gladly accepts such a consequence: "It is obvious that any of the acts that we do has countless effects, directly or indirectly, on countless people, and the probability is that any act, however right it be, will have adverse effects (though these may be very trivial) on some innocent people. Similarly, any wrong act will probably have beneficial effects on some deserving people. Every act, therefore, viewed in some aspects, will be *prima facie* right, and

viewed in others, *prima facie* wrong." [4] Now this, I submit
with all due respect, is nothing less than absurd. Not every
occasion of life is momentous, nor is every choice we make or
thing we do. To suppose otherwise is to suppose that every
occasion of life gives rise to a moral problem, and that everything we do requires justification, and this is simply false. One
who consistently thought so would die from moral perplexity.
Unless the question whether some act is right or wrong
actually arises, through some conflict, either real or apparent,
with some moral rule, it is senseless to raise it. For there
would then be no possibility of answering it.

The problems to which this principle would give rise are
exemplified by the problem of "the concert ticket": "Suppose I had one ticket for a concert, and suppose I knew that
Q would appreciate the concert just as much as I should and
no more. Ought I to give him my ticket or go myself?" This
is a problem that logically arises on the principle presented.
Yet there is absolutely no reason why I ought to give Q the
ticket, and even if Q would appreciate the concert much
more than I should, there would still be no reason. Of course,
there *might* be a reason. If, for example, I had promised Q
to give him the ticket, then there would be a reason; and if,
for some reason, I was unable to go, and was unable or unwilling to sell the ticket, then there would be a reason. But to
say that there might be a reason is not to say that there is, and
given the circumstances described, there is no reason whatever. Indeed, to suppose that there is, and that I *ought* to
give Q the ticket, say on the ground that this would be an
instance of benevolence or generosity, would lead to an inescapable paradox. For, if I ought to give Q the ticket, then,
for the very same reason, Q ought to give it right back to me,
and the very same reason would be a reason why we ought to
spend the rest of the evening trading it back and forth, each
insisting that the other have it, with the consequence that

[4] Ross, *The Right and the Good*, p. 41. Cf. pp. 31, and 33-4: "There
is probably no act . . . which does good to any one without doing harm
to some one else, and *vice versa.*" This is absurd. It would be true if
restricted to "acts of a legislature," but this is clearly not what its author
had in mind.

neither of us would get to the concert. If this is not lunacy, it is a good imitation of it. Of course, if I *want* to give Q the ticket, I have a perfect right to, supposing it is mine to give and that I have not promised it to anyone else. Given such conditions as these, there would be nothing wrong in my giving him the ticket, and if I have an especially generous disposition, I very well might. But likewise there would be nothing wrong in my not giving him the ticket, and if I do not want to, I have a perfect right not to. For Q has no claim on me, and in keeping the ticket myself I have not violated anyone's rights. To suppose otherwise would actually lead to contradiction. For I am not different from anyone else in this respect, and if I ought to give Q the ticket, then everyone else, in a similar situation, ought to act in the same way. But then it would follow that everyone ought to give whatever he has, and not just a concert ticket, to anyone else who would enjoy it as much or more. But this implies that whatever anyone does is wrong, for he *might* have done something better; and this is not just false—it is self-contradictory.

Some of the points I have just made clearly require elaboration, and this can best be given them by specifying as clearly as possible just what is involved in my denial that the obverse of the principle of consequences is a sound moral principle. In the first place, in denying that one has the duty to do that which would have good consequences, I am not saying that such action would be wrong. What I am saying is that one has the right not to, so long as the consequences of not doing so would not be undesirable. So what I am denying is that generosity or benevolence is a duty. No doubt benevolence is a good thing, and it would be a good thing if there were more of it; and no doubt an act of generosity or benevolence is praiseworthy and admirable. But this does not mean that it is obligatory.

In the second place, in denying that one has the duty to do that which would have good consequences, I am not denying that one often has the duty to do that which would *in fact* have good consequences. What I am denying is that one has the duty to do that which would have good consequences *for that reason alone*. If an act would have consequences that would be on the whole desirable, it does not follow that the act ought to be done. If the act ought to be done, it is for some other reason, and obviously there are many actions that are obligatory and which would also have good consequences.

In the third place, my denial of this principle must not be taken to mean that our duties are "merely negative," that there are no actions that one ought to *do* but only actions that one ought *not* to do, nor can it be taken to mean that one need not help others who are in need of help. On the contrary, that one has the duty to help others in need of help is a consequence of the principles already elaborated. And it follows from the principle of consequences in its *negative* form that a person may have the duty to sacrifice his time, his convenience, his interests, or even his life, in order to save the life or protect the interests of another. This will be so if the consequences of not doing so would be undesirable. It will not be so, however, if the consequences of not doing so would not be undesirable.

The fact is that these two principles, the principle of consequences and its obverse, coincide in most cases, and consequently in most cases would require the same conduct. It is most often the case that if an act is such that if it is *not* done the consequences would be on the whole *un*desirable, then it is also such that if it *is* done the consequences would be on the whole desirable; and the converse proposition also holds. This fact, that these two principles usually coincide, may account for whatever plausibility the obverse principle may appear to have. For in a case where the consequences of doing some act would be desirable, on the whole, it is easy to suppose that this is the reason why it ought to be done; whereas the true explanation is that the consequences of not doing it would be (on the whole) undesirable.

But even though these two principles usually coincide, they do not do so always, and it is in the cases where they do not that the obverse principle breaks down and leads to the paradoxes mentioned. For it may hold true, in some instance, that the consequences of A's not doing x would be undesirable, in which case A ought to do x, even though the consequences of his doing x would not be positively desirable. It might be alleged that in such a case the consequences of A's doing x must necessarily be desirable, on the ground that in doing x the undesirable consequences of not doing it would have been avoided. This is a possible way of looking at the matter. Its only defect is that it would tend to make the two principles equivalent. And what I wish to insist on is that there is a genuine difference between what might be called positive loss and the absence of positive gain, between an act's being merely not harmful and its being positively beneficial. "To throw out of cultivation land already productive, is a *positive* loss. *Leaving* waste-land as it is, is merely the absence of a possible gain. The one procedure, if carried on to any considerable extent, would cause ruin to the occupiers, and distress to the whole community; the other is merely *negative*, and hurts nobody." [5] Given this difference, then, it is possible for some act not to be harmful to anyone even though it is not beneficial to anyone, and it is possible for the consequences of not doing some act to be undesirable even though the consequences of doing it would not be positively desirable.

But then, in exactly the same way, it is possible for the consequences of doing some act to be positively desirable even though the consequences of not doing it would not be undesirable. Here again it might be alleged that the consequences of not doing it must be undesirable because the positive benefits of doing it would not have been achieved. In some cases this will be a solid consideration. But in many it is not. For though an act may not be beneficial to anyone (aside from the agent, who presumably wishes to perform it), it does not follow that it is hurtful to anyone. You would no doubt be benefited (though I am afraid not to any very great extent) if I assigned to you half my income; it does not follow that you would be harmed if I do not. Now it is in just

[5] Richard Whately, *Paley's Moral Philosophy: With Annotations* (London: John W. Parker & Son, 1859), pp. 100-1.

these cases that there is not only not a coincidence between these two principles, but something of a conflict between them. For let us suppose that the consequences of A's doing x would be desirable; and let us also suppose that the consequences of his not doing x would (on the whole) not be undesirable. Then it follows from this last statement that A has the right not to do x, if he so chooses, and this conclusion conflicts with, and, I should say, outweighs, the conclusion that A ought to do x, derived from the obverse of the principle of consequences.

Let us now consider the obverse principle of consequences in relation to the generalization argument. Suppose that the consequences of A's doing x would be desirable. Does it follow that A ought to do x? There are at least two possibilities here. Suppose (1) that the consequences of no one's doing x would be undesirable. Then it follows that A ought to do x, but this follows from this application of the generalization argument, which implies that everyone (within the scope of the argument) ought to do x, and not from the obverse of the principle of consequences. On the other hand, suppose (2) that the consequences of everyone's doing x would be undesirable. Then it follows that no one ought to do x, without a reason; and this conclusion conflicts with that obtained from the obverse principle. One might have such a reason. But, as I have already argued, such a reason is not provided by the mere fact that the consequences of one's doing x would be desirable. It would have to be shown, in addition, that one's circumstances differ from those of others in some other respect than this.

So much, then, at least for the present, for the obverse of the principle of consequences. I do not think that any one of the arguments I have used against it is conclusive by itself. But taken together they have a cumulative force that I regard as considerable. And at least I may have succeeded in throwing some doubt upon it. If I have, then, though this will not have shown the obverse of the generalization argument to be unsound, it will have removed one of its means of support. For one of the arguments I used to establish the generalization argument was to show how it can be derived from the principle of consequences. Consequently, if the obverse of the principle of consequences has been shown to be unsound, a corresponding argument cannot be used to establish the obverse of the generalization argument.

§ 2 §

The obverse of the generalization argument states that, "If the consequences of everyone's doing x would be desirable, then everyone ought to do x." In considering whether this is sound, there are three possibilities to be taken account of. Suppose that the antecedent holds, and that the consequences of everyone's doing x would be desirable. Then suppose (1) that the consequences of *no one's* doing x would be *un*desirable. Then it does follow that everyone ought to do x, but this conclusion follows from this application of the generalization argument, not from its obverse, and what we have here is simply an instance in which the generalization argument and its obverse coincide. There are undoubtedly many such instances, but this does not establish the obverse of the generalization argument as a valid line of argument. Again, suppose (2) that the consequences of no one's doing x would be desirable. This corresponds to the situation in which the generalization argument is invertible. As any instance of the generalization argument that is invertible is invalid, the same may be presumed to be so with respect to its obverse. Finally, suppose (3) that the consequences of no one's doing x would not be undesirable. Then, according to the procedure we have been following, everyone has the right not to do x, and hence in this case also it does not follow that everyone ought to do x.

Furthermore, the obverse argument does not account for established moral rules and acknowledged obligations, nor is it needed for this purpose, and this same point applies as well to the obverse of the principle of consequences. Whereas the generalization argument by itself can be used to establish and justify moral rules, the obverse of the generalization argument, by itself, cannot, and its only color of plausibility arises from those cases in which the two lines of argument coincide. It might be supposed that the generalization argument establishes only negative rules, and that its obverse is needed to establish positive rules, or rules in their positive form. But this is not so. The same line of argument that establishes that we ought not to lie establishes that we ought to tell the truth. "We ought to tell the truth because of what would happen if no one did." It is often indifferent whether a rule is stated negatively or positively. Of course, often it is not, for often a rule is more definite in its negative form, and may actually have somewhat different implications. From the fact that I ought not to lie, it does not follow that I ought to tell the truth, for the rule leaves it open to me to be silent. The main difference appears to be that a positive rule is open to more defenses and exceptions. Nevertheless, if a rule in its positive form is justifiable, it is justifiable by the application of the generalization argument, and the obverse argument is not needed for the purpose. This is the case, for example, with the rule to help others in need of help, which is extremely indefinite and requires numerous qualifications. Qualifications or no, what has to be considered is what would happen if no one helped anyone who was in need of help, and not what would happen if everyone did.

Let us consider, finally, some of the difficulties in the way of applying the obverse argument. In particular, let us consider its application to a state of nature situation. It might be argued that if everyone acted in accordance with moral rules, and refrained from lying and stealing and so on, the consequences would be desirable, and that therefore *in such a situation* one ought to obey the rules. Would this be sound? It is not even so much as relevant. To argue in this way is completely to ignore the facts of the case. No doubt it would be a good thing if everyone obeyed the rules. But a situation in which everyone obeyed the rules would not be a state of nature situation, as we are supposing this one to be. Thus the argument is irrelevant to the question it supposedly is intended to answer. No doubt everyone ought to obey the rules of morality, and thus do what is right, but what ought one to do in a situation in which others are not acting as they ought? Since this sort of question arises precisely because others are not obeying the rules, the argument just presented is irrelevant to it, and has no force whatever. It is, however, typical of an unreal type of moralizing, which can appropriately be labeled sentimentalism.

A similar conclusion follows even if we suppose the argument to be restricted in its application, and to be intended to apply, not to those who are already acting immorally, but only to those who find themselves confronted by the immoral behavior of others, who find themselves *in* a state of nature situation and are either not responsible for it or would prefer to be out of it. If every such person in such a situation continued to obey the rules the consequences would quite definitely not be desirable. By so doing they would, as Hobbes so aptly put it, merely "make themselves prey to others and procure their own certain ruin." If this is the consequence of the obverse of the generalization argument, it is another good argument against it.

This analysis may now be applied to the examples with which we started. Supposing that a universal refusal to pay ransom would lead to the elimination of kidnaping for ransom, is this a good reason for concluding that it is wrong to pay ransom? Granted that a universal refusal to bear arms would lead to the extinction of war, does it follow that it is wrong to bear arms in order to defend one's country? Since the form of the argument is invalid, both these conclusions are invalid. The example of military service has already been dealt with. It ignores the facts of the case, out of which the need and the problem arises. But so does the other example. The important question here is whether, if everyone in such a situation did pay ransom, the consequences would be undesirable, and I cannot see that they would. (To anticipate a bit, this would certainly not defeat the purposes of doing so, though it might not attain them either.) The argument here would thus appear to be what I have called altogether inapplicable. If it is, then the question whether one ought to pay ransom is not, as it stands, a question of morality, but a

question of prudence. It is a question of the most effective
means to the end, which is, I am assuming, both to obtain the
safe return of the person who has been kidnaped, and to lead
to the apprehension of the kidnapers. The answer, of course,
will vary from case to case, though it is an unfortunate fact
that those who are kidnaped for ransom rarely escape un-
harmed, or even alive, whether ransom is paid or not. But to
agree to pay ransom in order to rescue one's child is not in
any legitimate sense to encourage kidnaping, any more than
it is an encouragement of robbery to agree to hand over one's
money in order to escape with one's life. Whether a law
should be passed outlawing the payment of ransom, as a possible means of eliminating kidnaping, is another question,
which I see no need to consider.[6]

§ 3 §

Utilitarianism, defined most generally, is the view that whether
an act is right or wrong depends, solely, on its (actual or
probable) consequences. On this view, an act is right if and
only if it produces, or is likely to produce, at least as much
"good" as any other act open to the agent; whereas an act
is obligatory if, and only if, it produces, or is likely to produce, more "good" than any other act open to the agent;
hence on this view an act is wrong if and only if it produces,
or is likely to produce, less "good" than any other act open
to the agent (which includes the case where the consequences
of the act are on the whole bad). This, then, is the principle
of utility, which, in one form or another, is common to all the
varieties of utilitarianism. The different varieties of utilitarianism are merely different views of the proper way of determining the value or worth of the consequences, for determining

[6] A number of points I have made about the generalization argument
and its obverse are nicely summed up in a cartoon by Dana Fradon (*The
New Yorker*, vol. XXXIII, no. 35 [Oct. 19, 1957], p. 126), in which one
hobo says to another: "You know something? If everybody in the country
gave us just one stinking penny, we'd have over a million and a half
bucks."

what is "good" and how this is to be estimated.[7] Thus he-
donistic utilitarianism, which is utilitarianism in its traditional
form, maintains that pleasure, or happiness, is the one and
only thing that is good in and for itself, nothing else being
good except as a means to it. Nonhedonistic (or "ideal")
utilitarianism, on the other hand, maintains that pleasure is
not the one and only thing that is good in itself; and hence,
depending on the view that one adopts, that it is just one of
a number of things that are good in this sense, or that "the
good" is something else entirely, or that it is just one element
in the total complex that is "the good."

But the principle of utility, as the principle for determining
the morality of actions, is the same in all these varieties, which
differ only in their standards for "evaluation." They all determine the morality of actions by their utility, and only differ in
their ways of estimating and defining this "utility," the "ultimate end to which our actions contribute." This being so,
there is no need in dealing with this principle to keep distinguishing between these different varieties of utilitarianism,
nor is there any need, for present purposes, to treat them
separately. For our purposes it is indifferent whether the criterion provided by the principle of utility is specified as
conduciveness to "the greatest amount of *good*" or to "the
greatest amount of *happiness*." It is equally defective in either
interpretation. Since this is the case, I shall for reasons of convenience deal mainly with the principle in its traditional form,
with its emphasis on human well-being or welfare.

Now actually I have already shown that the principle of
utility is unsound, both in remarks made along the way, and
in my discussion, earlier in this chapter, of the obverse of the

[7] There are, of course, other lines of variation, as I tried to indicate in
my reference, above, to "actual or probable consequences." Some utilitarians maintain that whether an act is right or wrong depends only on
its *actual* results. This is paradoxical. If one is to talk in this way one
might as well omit all reference to human behavior and speak only of
"Acts of God." Traditional utilitarianism refers solely to the tendency of
an action. Bentham, for example, says that: "The tendency of an act is
mischievous when the consequences of it are mischievous; that is to say,
either the certain consequences or the probable" (*An Introduction to the
Principles of Morals and Legislation* [2nd ed., 1823], chap. XII, par. 2).

principle of consequences. It should be evident without argument that the principle of utility is equivalent, in effect, to the combination of the principle of consequences with its obverse, though its emphasis is definitely on the obverse principle. Its other defects are all comprehended in its claim to be the sole or the fundamental principle of morality. It should be evident that it is not, and could not be. From the point of view of producing a greater amount of happiness or "good" than any alternative action could produce, it would often be useful, or expedient, to violate someone's rights. Is it obvious, for example, that slavery, a system in which one group of people is held in subjection to the wishes and the orders of another, does not and cannot produce a greater amount of happiness on the whole than any alternative system? It can be argued, on any utilitarian method you please, that, provided that the number of slaves is kept relatively small, the benefits produced by the system, even where it involves willful cruelty, may be greater in amount and extent than the unhappiness produced by it. Thus it is at least conceivable that the sum total of happiness might be increased by such a system. Yet it cannot conceivably be justified. In order for such an arrangement to be justified there would have to be a difference between these two groups of people, those who are enslaved and those who are not, that is both relevant to this difference in treatment and sufficient to justify it. There is no such difference.

Examples of this nature, which show that an act can be wrong even though it is useful, and that an act can be right even though it is not useful, have been presented so often in the literature of the subject that there should be no real need to develop them further. But apparently there is, so let us consider again an example that has been already developed in the course of this work. If someone refuses to pay his taxes, the consequences of his particular act may be beneficial; it may produce more good than harm, and it may produce more good than would be produced by his paying them. Still it would be wrong, because of what would happen if everyone refused to pay his taxes, which is something that the agent himself would not be willing to have happen. As was mentioned before, from the fact that the consequences of everyone's acting in a certain way would be undesirable, it does not follow that the consequences of anyone's acting in that way would be undesirable. But it does follow that it would be wrong for anyone to act in that way, unless he can justify his conduct; and an appeal to the consequences of his particular act would not be a justification. Here again, one must appeal to a principle, and not merely to consequences. It follows, however, from the principle of utility that the act is right, since its consequences are good.

Actually no utilitarian would in practice say this. But that is hardly an argument for the theory. Mill, for instance, says:

> In the case . . . of things which people forbear to do from moral considerations, though the consequences in the particular case might be beneficial . . . the action is of a class which, if practiced generally, would be generally injurious, and . . . this is the ground of the obligation to abstain from it.[8]

This is an obvious appeal to the generalization argument. Yet on the utilitarian principle this simply cannot be "the ground of the obligation to abstain from it." On that principle it would not be a ground of obligation at all. For if "the consequences in the particular case are beneficial," that is the same as saying that they are useful, and it would follow from the principle of utility that the act is right, and ought not to be abstained from. To be consistent, a utilitarian would have to argue that the consequences in the particular case would not really be beneficial, because, as is so often said, one who acts in that way would be setting a bad example for others. Since he would be leading others to do the same, since others would do the same as a consequence of his act, the consequences of his act would really be undesirable. This may be so in some instances, but as a general proposition it is simply false. It suffices to point to cases of wrong acts that no one ever hears

---

[8] John Stuart Mill, *Utilitarianism* (Everyman's Library ed.; New York: E. P. Dutton and Company, 1910), chap. II, par. 19, pp. 17-18.

about. Indeed, this way of arguing puts the cart before the horse (and it is surely more useful to put the horse before the cart). For it consists in arguing that the consequences in the particular case must be undesirable, because the act would be wrong. But then the principle of utility is no longer functioning as a criterion. It is ludicrous to suppose that anything that anyone does has a tendency to cause everyone else to do the same. It does not, any more than it tends to cause the agent to do it again in the future. Yet this is what is presupposed by this way of arguing.

Although it is not directly relevant to the topic, I cannot refrain from pointing out a definite ambiguity in the utilitarian standard, which, in view of the seriousness of its consequences, deserves wider recognition than it has in fact received. The utilitarian standard has been stated to be that of conduciveness to the "general happiness" or "the greatest amount of happiness on the whole." But it has also very often, and perhaps even more frequently, been stated to be "the greatest happiness of the greatest number." Now these expressions actually represent different criteria for the interpretation of the utilitarian standard, which may be called, respectively, "the greatest happiness criterion" and "the greatest number criterion," and they are by no means equivalent. In most cases, no doubt, they would coincide, and no distinction would be apparent. But there is no necessity for this. We can easily describe circumstances in which they would conflict. Imagine two acts, *a* and *b*, which are alternative to each other, and suppose (taking small numbers for convenience, and waiving the point whether such neat and exact calculations can be made) *a* would produce four units of happiness for each of twelve persons, while *b* would produce eight units of happiness for each of eight persons. On the basis of the principle of utility, which ought to be done? It is impossible to say, for the criterion of "utility" is here ambiguous, and it cannot be determined which of the two is the more "useful." On the greatest number criterion, *a* ought to be done, for it produces happiness for a greater number of people. But on the greatest happiness criterion, *b* ought to be done, because it produces, presumably, 64 units of happiness, whereas *a* would produce only 48, and hence it produces a greater amount of happiness on the whole. Now this issue cannot be decided by appeal to the principle of utility. Indeed, to plump for one or the other of these two criteria would be essentially arbitrary.

But this is not all. The greatest happiness criterion itself is not free from ambiguity. It can mean either "the greatest *total* amount of happiness" or "the greatest *average* amount of happiness," and one action can produce a greater total amount of happiness, though a smaller average amount, than another. Imagine an action *c*, which will produce a total of fifty units of happiness for five people, an average of ten units apiece; whereas an alternative action *d* would produce a total of 56 units of happiness for a group of seven people, an average of eight units apiece. Which would be right? Indeed, which would be better? Here again the decision would be arbitrary. Certainly no utilitarian reason can be given for saying that one situation would be better than the other. And the ramifications of this sort of thing are practically endless. For a conflict can arise between the greatest average criterion and the greatest number criterion. For example, compare action *c* with action *a*. It follows, then, from the existence of these conflicting criteria, that the principle of utility is not the "first principle of morals," or the "fundamental principle of morality," since some other principle is needed to resolve these conflicts, when they arise. As it stands, it is not even acceptable as a principle, much less as the fundamental one, by ultimate reference to which all questions of morality are to be decided.

It may be thought that the difficulties just noted are purely academic, of the sort that could never arise in practice. This is not true. It is true that the examples selected are artificial, artificially abstract as well as artificially exact. But this does not mean that difficulties of this type could never arise. Such a difficulty could arise in any situation in which one would have to choose between doing something that would benefit a very large number of people each to a very small extent,

and doing something that would benefit a relatively small
number of people each to a very large extent; and such difficulties are almost always present, though they may not always
be recognized, in considering any proposed piece of legislation. I do not say that such issues are undecidable. I say that
they are undecidable on the principle of utility.

Consider the question of population. It was maintained by
Sidgwick, it will be remembered, that "from a utilitarian point
of view . . . a universal refusal to propagate the human species would be the greatest of conceivable crimes," [9] and his
reason for maintaining this was that it would decrease the
amount of happiness in the world, and eventually eliminate
it altogether. Now what view ought a utilitarian to take with
respect to the *increase* of population? It would seem that, if
quantity of happiness is the end, or even the greatest happiness of the greatest number, population ought to be increased
to the greatest possible extent consistent with bare subsistence. For the more people who have happiness, even if they
have only a little happiness, the more happiness there is, and
given that it is a duty to increase happiness, then it is a duty
to increase the population. This, at any rate, is the view maintained by Paley, an earlier (that is, a pre-Malthusian) utilitarian:

> The final view of all rational politics is to produce the great-
> est quantity of happiness in a given tract of country. . . .
> The happiness of a people is made up of the happiness of
> single persons; and the quantity of happiness can only be aug-
> mented by increasing the number of the percipients, or the
> pleasure of their perceptions. . . .
> Notwithstanding that diversity of conditions, especially dif-
> ferent degrees of plenty, freedom, and security, greatly vary
> the quantity of happiness enjoyed by the same number of in-
> dividuals; and notwithstanding that extreme cases may be
> found, of human beings so galled by the rigours of slavery,
> that the increase of numbers is only the amplification of
> misery; yet, within certain limits, and within those limits to

[9] Henry Sidgwick, *The Methods of Ethics* (7th ed.; London: Macmillan & Co., Ltd., 1907), p. 487.

which civilized life is diversified under the temperate governments that obtain in Europe, it may be affirmed, I think, with
certainty, that the quantity of happiness produced in any
given district, *so far* depends upon the number of inhabitants,
that, in comparing adjoining periods in the same country, the
collective happiness will be nearly in the exact proportion of
their numbers, that is, twice the number of inhabitants will
produce double the quantity of happiness; in distant periods,
and different countries, under great changes or great dissimili-
tudes of civil condition, although the proportion of enjoyment may fall much short of that of the numbers, yet still any
considerable excess of numbers will usually carry with it a
preponderation of happiness; that, at least, it may, and ought
to be assumed in all political deliberations, that a larger portion of happiness is enjoyed amongst *ten* persons, possessing
the means of healthy subsistence, than can be produced by
five persons, under every advantage of power, affluence, and
luxury.

From these principles it follows, that the quantity of happiness in a given district, although it is possible it may be increased the number of inhabitants remaining the same, is
chiefly and most naturally affected by alteration of the numbers: that, consequently, the decay of population is the greatest evil that a state can suffer; and the improvement of it the
object which ought, in all countries, to be aimed at, in preference to every other political purpose whatsoever.[1]

It is to be noted that the statement, "a larger portion of
happiness is enjoyed amongst *ten* persons, possessing the
means of healthy subsistence, than can be produced by *five*
persons," does not mean that *each* of the ten will be happier than each of the five, nor does it mean that the larger
group will contain a greater number of happy people. What
it means is simply that the total amount of happiness (the
collective amount) will be larger in the larger group, as this
total might be obtained by the imaginative abstraction of
multiplying the number in the group by the average amount
of happiness. Why not, if happiness is like money? If each of

[1] William Paley, *The Principles of Moral and Political Philosophy*
(7th ed.; London: R. Faulder, 1790), vol. II, bk. VI, chap. XI, pp.
345-7.

the five has two dollars, and each of the ten has one dollar, the groups will each have the same amount of money; add one more such person to the ten, and that will be the "richer group."

What is, perhaps, a more careful (though certainly a no sounder) statement of this doctrine respecting population has been provided by Sidgwick:

> Assuming . . . that the average happiness of human beings is a positive quantity, it seems clear that, supposing the average happiness enjoyed remains undiminished, Utilitarianism directs us to make the number enjoying it as great as possible. But if we foresee as possible that an increase in numbers will be accompanied by a decrease in average happiness or *vice versa*, a point arises which has not only never been formally noticed, but which seems to have been substantially overlooked by many Utilitarians. For if we take Utilitarianism to prescribe, as the ultimate end of action, happiness on the whole, and not any individual's happiness, unless considered as an element of the whole, it would follow that, if the additional population enjoy on the whole positive happiness, we ought to weigh the amount of happiness gained by the extra number against the amount lost by the remainder. So that, strictly conceived, the point up to which, on Utilitarian principles, population ought to be encouraged to increase, is not that at which average happiness is the greatest possible,—as appears to be often assumed by political economists of the school of Malthus—but that at which the product formed by multiplying the number of persons living into the amount of average happiness reaches its maximum.[2]

But this implies that the number of people ought to be increased even at the expense of decreasing the average happiness, as long as this increase in numbers leads to a greater amount of happiness on the whole, and the question is, Why? Why ought this criterion to be adopted, and not, say, the criterion of the greatest average? This question, clearly, cannot be answered by an appeal to "utility" (or "happiness," or "good"), for it is precisely what "utility" is that is in question, as well as its credentials for serving as a standard. It is worth

[2] Sidgwick, *op. cit.*, pp. 415-16.

noting, in addition, that if this is the utilitarian standard, then what it bids us aim at is not the promotion of the happiness of human beings, but the ramification of an abstraction, the mere increase of a statistic. Consider again the analogy of money. "On utilitarian principles," we may paraphrase this doctrine, "the point up to which population ought to be allowed to increase, is not that at which the average wealth is the greatest possible, but that at which the product formed by multiplying the number of living persons by the amount of average wealth reaches its maximum—the point at which, in other words, the total amount of money is the greatest possible." On this view, it is just as good for there to be a million people in a community each with a dollar to his name, as it is for there to be a thousand people each with a thousand dollars to his name.

Would it be reasonable to conclude, then, that the greatest average criterion is the one to be adopted? I do not think so. An average, after all, is just an average, and indicates nothing about distribution. The average amount of wealth in a community may be very high, though half its members are penniless, and in debt to the rest; so too, indeed, can the total amount of wealth. Some can be very rich, and some can be very poor; a very few can be very rich, and very many very poor; and the utilitarian principle will sanction it, provided only that the total amount is very high, or else that the average amount is very high—taking into account, of course, the amount of money possessed by all the people, even those who have none. "The bigger the better," and "the more the merrier." What it would be reasonable to conclude is that none of these criteria ought to be adopted, since none has any real relevance to human welfare, and since none can really be sanctioned on moral grounds. The criterion to be adopted, it would appear, is not that of *maximizing* welfare (or happiness, or "good"), whether in respect to the total amount or in respect to the average amount. Nor is it that of *equalizing* welfare. Of course, neither is it that of *minimizing* welfare. It is, rather, to secure the conditions under which everyone would be assured a certain *minimum* welfare, so far as this is attainable by the efforts of human beings. This, to be sure, requires extensive elaboration, which I am not about to give it. But nothing else can be sanctioned by the principle of justice. The general welfare is the welfare of people; it is not a "brooding onmipresence in the sky." This means that justice is an essential component of it.[3]

§ 4 §

Utilitarianism, it is evident, bristles with difficulties, and the principle of utility, when interpreted in the way that has been described, is certainly unsound. But there is really no good reason why it must be interpreted in this way, or why it must be applied in the manner that has been indicated. Though this is the usual and traditional way of interpreting it, it is not the only way. There is another, which may have something more to be said for it.

To bring this out, I propose to distinguish between two forms or types of "utilitarianism," two ways of interpreting and applying the principle of utility, which I shall call "Direct Utilitarianism" and "Indirect Utilitarianism." On Direct Utilitarianism, as I am calling it, the principle of utility refers to individual or specific actions; one applies it *directly* to an individual action, evaluates the consequences of the specific action in the specific circumstances, and by such means determines its morality. It is this interpretation that I have been discussing so far, and I think there is nothing to be said for it. On Indirect Utilitarianism, on the other hand, the principle does not apply directly to individual actions, but only to kinds of actions; one applies it directly to the kind or type of action, and hence only *indirectly* to the specific instance. One thus considers the consequences that actions of that kind may generally be expected to have, and by such means di-

[3] The motto, "Let justice be done, though the heavens fall," has had some pretty hard things said about it, in its time. But is it any worse than the motto, "Let the consequences be good, though the heavens fall," or "Let the consequences be good, no matter whose rights are violated"? I submit the latter to the attention of those who pride themselves on not being "formalists."

rectly determines the morality of that *kind* of action. Through this process, then, and hence only indirectly, one determines the morality of the specific action. On this interpretation, the morality of a specific action does not depend on its specific consequences, but on the kind of action it is and the consequences that actions of that kind generally have. It is clear then that on Indirect Utilitarianism the principle of utility is applied to establish rules, to the effect that a certain kind of action is generally right or generally wrong, in virtue of the consequences that it generally has; and it is these rules, and not the principle itself, that apply directly to individual actions. For unless some such rule is involved, no question would arise that would call for the application of the principle.

What I am calling Indirect Utilitarianism is still utilitarianism, though it may not seem so. This can be seen from the fact that it is quite definitely presented by Mill, though not clearly and not unambiguously, and can even be said to correspond with what he really intended to say. Thus Mill's definition of "morality" is not, as might be expected, "behavior in accordance with the principle of utility," but rather: " 'the rules and precepts for human conduct,' by the observance of which an existence such as has been described might be, to the greatest extent possible, secured to all mankind." [4] Thus, the principle of utility, being "the standard of morality," is the standard of these "rules and precepts," and not of individual actions. And Mill makes frequent reference to moral rules, which he indifferently calls "intermediate generalizations," "secondary principles," "subordinate principles," and "corollaries from the principle of utility":

> The corollaries from the principle of utility, like the precepts of every practical art, admit of indefinite improvement, and, in a progressive state of the human mind, their improvement is perpetually going on. But to consider the rules of morality as improvable, is one thing; to pass over the intermediate generalizations entirely, and endeavor to test each

[4] Mill, *Utilitarianism*, chap. II, par. 10, p. 11. The quotations that follow are from pars. 24-5, pp. 21-4.

individual action directly by the first principle, is another. It is a strange notion that the acknowledgement of a first principle is inconsistent with the admission of secondary ones. . . .

Thus individual actions are to be tested by these intermediate generalizations, and it is these intermediate generalizations, or moral rules, that are established by the principle of utility, and that determine our rights and obligations. These rules, however, do not hold without exception. In view "of the complicated nature of human affairs . . . rules of conduct cannot be so framed as to require no exceptions, and . . . hardly any kind of action can safely be laid down as either always obligatory or always condemnable." It is only when these rules conflict that the principle of utility must be resorted to, and it is these "cases of conflicting obligation" that "are the real difficulties, the knotty points both in the theory of ethics, and in the conscientious guidance of personal conduct. . . ."

It can hardly be pretended that anyone will be the less qualified for dealing with them, from possessing an ultimate standard to which conflicting rights and duties can be referred. If utility is the ultimate source of moral obligations, utility may be invoked to decide between them when their demands are incompatible. Though the application of the standard may be difficult, it is better than none at all. . . . We must remember that only in these cases of conflict between secondary principles is it requisite that first principles should be appealed to. There is no case of moral obligation in which some secondary principle is not involved; and if only one, there can seldom be any real doubt which one it is, in the mind of any person by whom the principle itself is recognized.

In one of Mill's lesser known essays, this distinction is made even more explicit: "Prudence, indeed, depends on a calculation of the consequences of individual actions; while, for the establishment of moral rules, it is only necessary to calculate the consequences of classes of actions—a much easier matter."[5]

[5] John Stuart Mill, "Dr. Whewell on Moral Philosophy," in *Dissertations and Discussions* (Boston: William V. Spencer, 1868), vol. III, p. 156.

It has not been my intention to give a full or even an adequate account of Mill's moral philosophy. My intention has been merely to show that the distinction I have drawn between these two ways of interpreting the principle of utility, the direct and the indirect, is actually part of utilitarianism as it has historically been presented; and my reason for this is that, by means of this distinction, utilitarianism is able to surmount a good many of the more obvious objections to it. One such obvious objection is based on the obligation to keep a promise. It has often been pointed out that the obligation to keep a promise cannot rest simply—if it rests at all —on the consequences of keeping it or breaking it in a particular case. To proceed in this way, and consider only the consequences, would be to ignore the fact that one has made a promise, and has thus voluntarily incurred the obligation to do something. The fact that one has made a promise is a new element in the situation, in virtue of which the situation is different from what it otherwise would be. One has the obligation to keep a promise because one has promised, and has thus antecedently agreed, not only to do the act in question, but not to consider the relative advantages and disadvantages when the time comes to keep it. One who would do this is already untrustworthy. Now it is clear that we must have reference here to a rule, the rule that promises ought to be kept, and one advantage of indirect utilitarianism is that it is able, at least to some extent, to account for this.

Yet this distinction between direct and indirect utilitarianism cannot meet all of the difficulties to which the principle of utility is subject. Why would it be wrong to break a rule, in a case where the consequences of doing so would not be undesirable? To break a moral rule is merely to do that which is generally wrong, and on the principle of utility the reason why an act is generally wrong is that it generally or usually does lead to undesirable consequences. To use a locution of a kind referred to once before, actions of that kind frequently lead to bad results, and hence actions of that kind frequently are wrong. But suppose that in a particular instance an act of that kind would not lead to undesirable consequences, so that its consequences would not be what they are generally. Why should not the rule be broken? After all, on the principle of utility the rule is merely a guide, a guide to what the consequences are likely to be, and since it holds only in most cases, why should one be bound by it in a case in which it obviously does not apply? This question cannot be answered by reference to the principle of utility. Indeed, on the basis of the principle of utility it would seem that if the consequences would be, on the whole, useful, the rule ought to be broken, and that if they are merely not undesirable, one need not keep it. But this will not do. As we have seen, one is not justified in breaking a moral rule merely by the fact that the consequences of doing so, in the particular case, would not be undesirable. This may be necessary, but it is not sufficient. What needs to be shown, in addition, is that the act would be right in all similar instances, and these similar instances cannot be defined as simply those in which the consequences would not be undesirable.

Furthermore, even in this indirect application the principle of utility cannot by itself show why it is wrong, let us say, to refuse to pay taxes. Such an act is usually wrong, but are the consequences of acts of this kind usually harmful? This is far from clear. What is required for the moral argument is the generalization argument, and hence the generalization principle. The relevant question is not, "What would happen if I refuse to pay taxes?" but "What would happen if everyone refused to pay taxes?" and to ask this question is not to appeal to utility. By itself, one person's taxes have very little utility, and may have none at all. The substance of this point is actually admitted by Mill, in a passage previously quoted, in which he admits that certain acts are wrong, even though "the consequences in the particular case might be beneficial": "In the case of . . . things which people forbear to do from moral considerations, though the consequences in the particular case might be beneficial . . . the action is of a class which, if practiced generally, would be generally injurious, and . . . this is the ground of the obligation to abstain from it." But such actions are not, or need not be, "generally injurious"; they are so only "if practiced generally." The appeal here is not to the principle of utility, but to a principle that is independent of it, and more fundamental.

Of the principles elaborated earlier in this work, the one that corresponds most closely with the principle of utility, in this present interpretation, is the generalized principle of consequences. Now, as I pointed out before, though many moral rules, and especially what I called fundamental rules, are governed by the principle of consequences, not all of them are. Furthermore, every moral rule that is governed by the principle of consequences is also governed by the generalization argument. Therefore, though indirect utilitarianism is a great improvement on direct utilitarianism, and, given the necessary qualifications, is a necessary part of an adequate theory of morality (provided we waive the difficulties about "happiness"), it is not sufficient. One necessary qualification is that the principle be interpreted in what might be called a "negative" manner, rather than a "positive" one. The other is this. Mill maintains that "only in these cases of conflict between secondary principles is it requisite that first principles be appealed to," that since "utility is the ultimate source of moral obligations, utility may be invoked to decide between them when their demands are incompatible." He therefore implies that in cases in which rules conflict, in which moral problems arise, the principle of utility must be resorted to, and that it must be applied directly to the case. I argued before that this is not so. The question to be asked here is not simply, "What would happen if I break this rule in this situation?" but "What would happen if everyone were to break this rule in a situation of this kind?" For the question is not which course of action would be the most useful, but rather which course of action would be right.[6]

[6] This is actually maintained by Mill, though he was not aware of how far he was thereby straying from his official doctrine. See *ibid.*, pp. 159, 160: "If one person may break through the rule on his own judgment, the same liberty cannot be refused to others; and, since no one could rely on the rule's being observed, the rule would cease to exist. . . . The essential is, that the exception should be itself a general rule; so that, being of definite extent, and not leaving the expediencies to the partial

§ 5 §

Even if this distinction between direct and indirect utilitarianism be accepted, and even if the latter be accepted as a great improvement over the former, it is evident that utilitarianism cannot be made either adequate or consistent without the most drastic modifications and revisions. Inconsistency, it might almost be said, is a built-in feature of utilitarianism, if it is to be taken seriously as a comprehensive and all-sufficient moral doctrine, as it claims to be. Mill, for one, is not consistent with this distinction, and often attempts to stretch the principle to cover cases to which it manifestly does not apply. This is often done by claiming that an act, apparently useful, really is not useful, that it *must* have detrimental consequences that are undetected. What is the reason for this?

Consider the psychological doctrine from which utilitarianism takes its rise. It starts from the idea that since every action aims at some end, there must be some "ultimate end" at which every action aims, and to which every subsidiary end is subservient. This ultimate end is happiness. This ultimate end, then, must be the criterion for the judgment of actions. Thus an action is right if it conduces to happiness, and wrong if it does not conduce to this ultimate end; and actions that have this property, of conducing to happiness, are said to be useful, while those that do not are said not to be useful. This therefore must be *the* moral principle, the criterion on which actions are to be judged; and since this involves identifying what is "useful" (for this purpose) with what is right, utility becomes the measure of right and wrong.

Now what happens in practice, when this line of reasoning comes to be applied, is this. When one who adopts this line of reasoning encounters an action that he does not doubt is wrong, even though it appears, on all the evidence available, to be useful or to be conducive to the "ultimate end," he will

---

judgment of the agent in the individual case, it may not shake the stability of the wider rule in the cases to which the reason of the exception does not extend."

almost invariably argue that it cannot really be useful, that it must have consequences that, though they are not at first glance apparent, make it, in the end, not useful. This is what leads to the notion that the principle is to be used to establish rules, and that the action is useful because it is an instance of a rule that is useful. This is also what leads to the notion that the action has certain "secondary effects," not immediately apparent, which are on the whole detrimental, such as setting a bad example for others, or such as its effects on the agent's character; and another secondary effect that must be considered is that the act does involve the breaking of a rule, the violation of which, "for a present advantage . . . is not expedient."

But this clearly will not do. For if these "secondary effects" apply in any case, they apply in all, and if they show of any act that it is not really "useful," no matter how useful it may appear apart from them, then they would show this of every act. It would follow that every moral rule holds without exception, or that no rule ought ever to be broken, and this contradicts the view that rules "cannot be so framed as to require no exceptions, and that hardly any kind of action can safely be laid down as either always obligatory or always condemnable." Legitimate exceptions remain, yet on this view they cannot be distinguished from others. This line of reasoning, furthermore, really begs the question. It is not, as it ought to be, "This act is not useful; therefore it is wrong." It is, "This act is wrong; therefore it cannot be useful." The principle of utility, therefore, is not really being used as a criterion. The conviction that an act is wrong and therefore is only *apparently* useful is not derived from the principle of utility, but from some other principle.

This difficulty has not gone unnoticed. In an attempt to meet it, Paley, in a once celebrated but now little read work, drew a distinction, well worth considering, between the *general* and the *particular* consequences of an action. When properly defined, the distinction is a useful one. The system resulting, however, is no longer utilitarianism.

The basis of Paley's system, so far as we need consider it, is the doctrine that "actions are to be estimated by their tendency," their tendency to promote or diminish the general happiness, and that, as he puts it, "Whatever is expedient, is right."

"But," says Paley, "to all this there seems a plain objection, *viz.* that many actions are useful, which no man in his senses will allow to be right." Some instances are the following:

> There are occasions, in which the hand of the assassin would be very useful. The present possessor of some great estate employs his influence and fortune, to annoy, corrupt, or oppress all about him. His estate would devolve, by his death, to a successor of an opposite character. It is useful, therefore, to dispatch such a one as soon as possible out of the way; as the neighborhood will exchange thereby a pernicious tyrant for a wide and generous benefactor. It may be useful to rob a miser, and give the money to the poor; as the money, no doubt, would produce more happiness, by being laid out in food and clothing for half a dozen distressed families, than by continuing locked up in a miser's chest. . . . Must we admit these actions to be right, which would be to justify assassination, plunder, and perjury; or must we give up our principle, that the criterion of right is utility? [7]

The question is fairly put. It is evident that these objections are of the same type raised above. But Paley's answer, as might be expected, is that "it is not necessary to do either," since "these actions, after all, are not useful, and for that reason, and that alone, are not right." This point is made out by means of the distinction mentioned:

> The bad consequences of actions are twofold, *particular* and *general*. The particular bad consequence of an action, is the mischief which that single action directly and immediately occasions. The general bad consequence is, the violation of some necessary or useful *general* rule. ·
> Thus the particular bad consequence of the assassination above described, is the fright and pain which the deceased

[7] Paley, *op. cit.* (note 1, p. 200); the quotations presented in the text are from bk. II, chaps. VI, VII, and VIII, which are entitled, respectively, "Utility," "The Necessity of General Rules," and "The Consideration of General Consequences Pursued."

underwent; the loss he suffered of life, . . . the prejudice
and affliction, of which his death was the occasion, to his family, friends, and dependents. The general bad consequence is
the violation of this necessary general rule, that no man be
put to death for his crimes, but by public authority.

Although, therefore, such an action have no particular bad
consequence, or greater particular good consequences, yet it is
not useful, by reason of the general consequence, which is of
more importance, and which is evil. And the same of the other
two instances, and of a million more, which might be mentioned.

Now this distinction as it has just been stated is perfectly
straightforward, and Paley goes on from this to argue for
"the necessity of general rules," on the ground that:

You cannot permit one action and forbid another, without
showing a difference between them. Consequently, the same
sort of actions must be generally permitted or generally for-
bidden. Where, therefore, the general permission of them
would be pernicious, it becomes necessary to lay down and
support the rule which generally forbids them.

Yet the distinction does not do the job it was intended to do.
Why is the general consequence "of more importance" than
the particular consequence? Granted that the act would violate a general rule, not every act that violates a general rule is
necessarily wrong, since rules can have exceptions. From what
does it follow that the act is "not useful," given that it has
"no particular bad consequence, or greater particular good
consequences"? Paley says that it follows "by reason of the
general consequence, which is of more importance." But this
is what has to be shown. Let it be granted that the violation
of a rule is one bad feature of an action; this is still only one
bad feature. Why may it not be outweighed by the "particular" good features? If we are to go by the system from which
we started, then it would have to be shown that the violation
of a general rule always, or almost always, causes more harm,
creates more misery, is more detrimental, has a greater tendency to diminish the general happiness, than conformity to
it. This can hardly be maintained, and is certainly not obvious

from the instances presented. If we are to estimate the *utility* of the action *for the purpose mentioned* (and apart from a purpose there is no sense in speaking of "utility"), and if this is all we are called upon to estimate, then we should have to say that, even though the act has certain bad features, it is still useful. Otherwise "utility" becomes a weasel word.

The fact is that the term "general consequences," as Paley presents it, is ambiguous, and he unwittingly uses it in more than one sense. He gives, in fact, three definitions of the term, all of which are distinct. The first is the one that has already been presented, that "the general bad consequence" of an action is "the violation of some necessary or useful general rule" (Chapter VI). The second, which is given a few paragraphs later (Chapter VII), is this: "the general consequence of an action, upon which so much of the guilt of a bad action depends, consists in the *example*." Though this definition may be closely connected with the first, it is still distinct from it. Paley was apparently reasoning here in the following way: the reason why the violation of some necessary or useful general rule is so important a feature of the action, and is thus to count for so much in estimating its utility, is that it will set a bad example for others; it will as a consequence lead others to do the same; hence one of the consequences of violating a rule is that so many others will be led to do the same that the rule will tend to break down. Now if this were true, it certainly would be an important consequence of the action; and, depending on the importance or the utility of the rule, it usually would outweigh "the particular good consequences of the action." But, as I argued before, though this proposition may hold true to some extent, and in some instances, it is not true in general, and certainly not to the extent supposed.

This second definition of "general consequence," moreover, that it "consists in the example," immediately leads to a difficulty. For, as Paley recognizes, "it should seem, that, if the action be done with perfect secrecy, so as to furnish no bad example, that part of the guilt drops off." This is only partly true. In the cases being considered it would seem that "all of the guilt drops off." For if the action is kept secret, or if for any other reason does not set a bad example for others, then by the definition given the action has no general bad consequences, and ought therefore to be regarded as useful. However, Paley does not accept this conclusion, and at this point departs from his utilitarianism. For this leads him to give a third definition of "general consequence," quite different from the other two, a point of which he was apparently unaware. Thus he says, in answer to the objection "that if the action be done with perfect secrecy, so as to furnish no bad example," then it has no general bad consequences, that:

> those who reason in this manner do not observe, that they are setting up a general rule, of all others the least to be endured; namely, that secrecy, whenever secrecy is practicable, will justify any action.

This is quite true, but the argument here is not a utilitarian argument. The fact remains that if the action is kept secret, or if for any other reason it sets no bad example to others, it will not lead others to do the same, and thus will have no general bad consequence. If the particular consequences are useful, then why is the act not useful? If grounds of utility are all that can be given, secrecy would justify the action, for it would make it useful.

Yet the rule against secrecy, that secrecy will never justify any action otherwise not justifiable, is perfectly sound. Indeed, it is more than a moral rule. It is a moral principle, of the sort that I called before a "moral law." Just as one is never justified in violating a moral rule by the fact that one wants to, one is never justified in violating a moral rule by the fact that one does so secretly or by the fact that no one else will know about it. But this cannot be established by the principle of utility. It can be established only by appeal to the generalization argument.

This is in fact the argument that Paley uses, and it is by reference to the generalization argument that he frames his third definition of "general consequences": "The general consequence of any action may be estimated, by asking what would be the consequence, if the same sort of actions were generally permitted" (Chapter VIII). It should require no argument to show that this definition, the one Paley actually uses in the course of his work, is fundamentally different from the others. To suppose otherwise would be to confuse what I called before the generalized principle of consequences with the generalization argument; it would be to confuse the statement "the action *a* frequently leads to bad results" with the statement "the frequency of the action *a* would lead to bad results."

To bring this point home, we may consider one or two of the "string of instances" that Paley subjoins, "in which the particular consequence is comparatively insignificant; and where the malignity of the crime, and the severity with which human laws pursue it, is almost entirely founded upon the general consequence":

> The particular consequence of coining is, the loss of a guinea, or of half a guinea, to the person who receives the counterfeit money; the general consequence (by which I mean the consequence that would ensue, if the same practice were generally permitted) is, to abolish the use of money.
>
> The particular consequence of forgery is, a damage of twenty or thirty pounds to the man who accepts the forged bill; the general consequence is, the stoppage of paper currency.
>
> The particular consequence of sheep-stealing, or horse-stealing, is, a loss to the owner, to the amount of the value of the sheep or horse stolen; the general consequence is, that the land could not be occupied, nor the market supplied with this kind of stock. . . .

Yet Paley still maintains the slogan from which he started, which his own examples have proved fallacious:

> "Whatever is expedient is right." But then it must be expedient upon the whole, at the long run, in all its effects collateral and remote, as well as in those which are immediate and direct; as it is obvious, that in computing consequences, it makes no difference in what way or at what distance they ensue (Chapter VIII).

What Paley has now defined as the "general consequences" of an action, however, are not in any ordinary sense consequences, either actual or probable, either of the action or of the kind of action. They are not collateral or remote effects, as contrasted with immediate and direct. They are not even "secondary effects," such as its influence on others, or on the character of the agent. To determine the general consequences of an action, as the term has now been defined, is not a matter of considering its consequences on the whole or in the long run. Neither is it a matter of determining what sort of consequences usually do ensue from (individual) actions of that kind. To think otherwise is to be misled by a word.

❀

CHAPTER VIII

THE CATEGORICAL
IMPERATIVE

We have now dealt sufficiently with the principle of utility. It is, in a sense, only fair to take up the categorical imperative next. For this principle also has frequently been identified with the generalization argument. In this case the identification is happier.

The categorical imperative states: "Act only on that maxim whereby thou canst at the same time will that it should become a universal law." This principle (and any formulation of the categorical imperative involving the notion of universality) may also be called Kant's first moral principle, or *the principle of universality*. One disclaimer is necessary: I propose to deal with this principle *as a moral principle*, apart from the further complexities of Kant's ethical theory, and the complexities of his metaphysics. This means that I shall not be mainly concerned with Kant's ethical theory as such or on the whole, with all the details of what Kant actually said or may really have meant; though I shall, of course, have some occasion to refer to these other matters. This mode of treatment is rarer than one might think. The idea has taken on almost the status of a tradition that Kant's ethics is "excessively formalistic," and consequently empty or sterile, so that the categorical imperative is incapable of being used to establish any moral rule or to settle any concrete question of conduct. This, I shall argue, is not so.

The relation of the categorical imperative to the generalization argument will be taken up in the next chapter, along with a number of other questions and difficulties, many of which relate mainly to its application. In this chapter I shall attempt to remove what is perhaps the most persistent and the most important of the misunderstandings connected with it. Kant's ethics has traditionally been thought of as issuing in "categorical imperatives," which take no account of individual situations, personal differences, or extenuating circumstances. Thus Kant has effectively been stereotyped as an "ethical absolutist," or "ethical formalist": one who holds, for example, that it is always wrong to lie, no matter what the circumstances or consequences. There certainly is this element of rigorism in Kant's view. But there are other elements as well, which are more important. Kant's rigorism, I shall argue, has no essential connection with the categorical imperative, since it is actually inconsistent with it. But to show this it will first be necessary to consider carefully the exact nature of the difference between a hypothetical and a categorical imperative.[1]

[1] To facilitate reference, in this chapter and the two following Kant's works will be cited as follows. Kant's *Grundlegung zur Metaphysik der Sitten*, the *Groundwork* (or *Fundamental Principles*) *of the Metaphysics of Morals*, is cited simply as "*Grundlegung.*" The translation used is that of H. J. Paton, which is contained in his book entitled *The Moral Law* (London: Hutchinson's University Library, 1948). The pages referred to are those given in the *margin* of Paton's book, which are those of the second edition of the *Grundlegung* (1786). After the reference to Paton's translation, I have given the corresponding reference to the translation by T. K. Abbott, in *Kant's Critique of Practical Reason and Other Works on the Theory of Ethics* (6th ed.; London: Longmans, Green & Co., 1909). The pages cited are those Abbott inserts in the body of the text (and in brackets at the top of each page), which refer to Rozenkranz and Schubert's edition of Kant's works. Kant's *Critique of Practical Reason* is cited simply as "*Practical Reason.*" The translation used is Abbott's. Here also the pages referred to are those Abbott places in the body of the text. The translation used of Kant's *Philosophy of Law* (*Metaphysische Anfangsgründe der Rechtslehre*) is the one by W. Hastie (Edinburgh: T. & T. Clark, 1887). In the cases where the same passage

§ 1 §

Kant's distinction between hypothetical and categorical imperatives is one of the fundamental features of his ethics. Unfortunately, it has been almost universally misunderstood. This is not surprising, for, owing to the unfortunate terminology in which he expressed it, Kant himself was seriously misled by it. Yet the distinction, when properly understood, is perfectly sound. It is, basically, nothing more than the distinction between prudential and moral rules or judgments.

As Sidgwick has pointed out, "It is important to take separately the two species of judgments . . . distinguished as 'moral' and 'prudential.' . . . In ordinary thought we clearly distinguish cognitions or judgments of duty from cognitions or judgments as to what 'is right' or 'ought to be done' in view of the agent's private interest or happiness. . . ." [2] Now what is the nature of this distinction? Roughly this: what would be prudent or imprudent, wise or foolish, for someone to do depends on his wants or desires in a way in which what would be morally right or wrong for him to do does not. It is essential to the nature of an obligation that no one can get rid of his obligations by not wishing to perform them. The fact that someone does not want to do something is irrelevant to the question whether he has the duty to do it. But the fact that someone does not want to do something is not similarly irrelevant to the question whether it would be prudent for him to do it.

This is so far not a very precise criterion. But it can be made more precise by only a slight modification. Note that such terms as "ought," "right," and "wrong" are ambiguous

---

appears in Abbott's edition, the corresponding reference is given to the *regular pages* of Abbott's book, *not* to the inserted page numbers. The regular page numbers of Abbott's work are also used in referring to the other writings of Kant included in it. The abbreviation used in such cases is simply "Abbott, p.—." The edition used of Kant's *Lectures on Ethics* is the translation by Louis Infield (London: Methuen & Co. Ltd., 1930).

[2] Henry Sidgwick, *The Methods of Ethics* (7th ed.; London: Macmillan & Co., Ltd., 1907), pp. 25-6.

between their prudential and moral senses (though this is
more usual, perhaps, with "ought" than with the other two).
A statement of the grammatical form "A ought to do *x*" can
express either a moral judgment or a prudential judgment. It
can mean either that it would be immoral, or that it would
be imprudent, for A not to do *x*. Of course, it can mean both,
at one and the same time. Yet there is a difference. How can
this difference be made out in particular cases? One way,
clearly, is by reference to the way such a statement would be
justified or substantiated. What sort of reasons are offered in
support of the statement? If the statement is supported by
reference to the agent's own desires or inclinations, to his
own interest, then the judgment is a prudential one. If it can
be shown, for instance, that if one does not do the act in question he will not obtain something he wishes to have, that he
will be made unhappy or be seriously inconvenienced, then
by not doing the act he will be acting foolishly, unwisely, irrationally, or imprudently, but not necessarily immorally. The
fact that an imprudent act can also be immoral is strictly irrelevant. The reasons specified show that the statement in
question expresses a prudential, and not a moral, judgment.
They show that the act is imprudent, and not that it is immoral. On the other hand, if the statement is supported, not
by reference to the agent's own interest, but by reference to
the needs or wants of *others*, or to the rights of or one's
obligations to others, or by pointing out what would happen
if everyone failed to act in that way, then the judgment is a
moral judgment. For instance, if the assertion that one ought
not to act in a certain way is supported by the claim that as a
consequence of one's doing so someone else will be injured
or seriously inconvenienced, then it is an assertion of a moral
judgment. None of this, it should be noted, settles the question of its validity.

Thus, if in the statement of the reasons supporting the
assertion that something is right or ought to be done it is
necessary, and sufficient, to specify the needs, wants, desires,
or the interest of the agent—or the effects on the agent of
failing to act in the way specified—then the judgment is a

prudential one. In this case what is being claimed is that it would be imprudent not to act in this way.

Now it is in a way closely corresponding to this that Kant distinguishes between hypothetical and categorical imperatives: a hypothetical imperative is a rule (or "counsel") of prudence; a categorical imperative is a moral rule (or "law").

> Skill in the choice of means to one's own greatest well-being can be called *prudence* in the narrowest sense. Thus an imperative concerned with the choice of means to one's own happiness—that is, a precept of prudence—still remains *hypothetical*: an action is commanded, not absolutely, but only as a means to a further purpose.[3]

Kant says that a hypothetical imperative (precept of prudence) is based on a condition or presupposition, and distinguishes hypothetical from categorical imperatives on the ground that the latter are not based on or limited by any condition. This is by no means as obscure as it may seem, nor does it mean what it has usually been supposed to mean. What it means is that a statement of the form "A ought to do *x*" (which Kant calls an imperative) may be supported or based on A's desire for some end, which may or may not be expressly mentioned. In such a case the statement "A ought to do *x*" is elliptical for "If A desires *y* (and he does), then he ought to do *x*" (which in turn is based on the proposition that doing *x* is an indispensable condition for the attainment of *y*). In this case the "imperative," that "A ought to do *x*," is hypothetical. It is asserted hypothetically or contingently upon A's desire for *y*, which is the condition upon which it is based. As Kant says, "we can always escape from the precept if we abandon the purpose." [4] On the other hand there are

---

[3] Kant, *Grundlegung*, Paton 42-3, Abbott 40. There is no need to take account here of the distinction Kant draws between two kinds of hypothetical imperatives, counsels of prudence and rules of skill. As Kant himself says, the imperative of prudence "differs from the imperative of skill only in this—that in the latter the end is merely possible, while in the former the end is given . . . both command solely the means to something assumed to be willed as an end. . . ." (Paton 48, Abbott 44). Thus either, indiscriminately, can be called a rule (or judgment) of prudence.

[4] *Grundlegung*, Paton 50, Abbott 45.

statements of this same form ("A ought to do *x*") which are
not based on or conditioned by any desire or purpose of A.
In such a case the imperative is not asserted hypothetically or
conditionally upon any of A's desires, and this is what Kant
would call a categorical imperative. A categorical imperative is
a moral imperative. It is not one from which we can escape by
abandoning some purpose. For it is not conditional upon any
purpose of the agent. As Kant says, "an unconditioned command does not leave it open to the will to do the opposite at
its discretion. . . ."

> Wherever an object of the will has to be put down as the
> basis for prescribing a rule to determine the will . . . the im-
> perative is conditioned, as follows: "*If*, or *because*, you will
> this object, you ought to act thus or thus"; consequently it
> can never give a moral—that is, a categorical—command. . . .
> This relation, whether based on inclination or on rational
> ideas, can give rise only to hypothetical imperatives: "I ought
> to do something *because I will something else*." As against
> this, the moral, and therefore categorical, imperative, says: "I
> ought to will thus or thus, although I have not willed some-
> thing else." [5]

It should be evident from this that Kant's distinction between hypothetical and categorical imperatives is the same as
that between prudential and moral judgments, as well as the
one that can be drawn on the same grounds between prudential and moral rules. But this, incidentally, does not mean
that Kant would draw this distinction in exactly the same way,
or at exactly the same place. A statement or imperative of the
form "A ought to do *x*" can express either a prudential or a
moral judgment (either a hypothetical or a categorical imperative), depending on the sort of reasons that are offered

---

[5] *Ibid.*, Paton 93, 88-9; Abbott 76, 72. Cf. *Practical Reason*, 146: "All
the matter of practical rules rests on subjective conditions, which give
them only a conditional universality (in case I *desire* this or that, what I
must do in order to obtain it) . . ." See also *Lectures on Ethics*, p. 37:
"A moral law states categorically what ought to be done, whether it pleases
us or not. It is, therefore, not a case of satisfying an inclination. If it
were, there would be no moral law, but everyone might act according to
his own feeling."

for it. If it is supported by reference to the desires, or to what
is in the interest, of the agent, then it is a judgment of prudence, or hypothetical imperative.[6]

§ 2 §

But Kant's notion of "a categorical imperative" has not always been interpreted in this way. And with some justification. For Kant himself shifted his use of the term, without
making this shift explicit. He did not always use the term in
the way in which he defined it. From a sense of "categorical"
in which a categorical imperative is simply a moral imperative,
as contrasted with a prudential one, he shifted to a sense in
which a categorical imperative is one that is inviolable, one
that holds under all circumstances or conditions and admits
of no exceptions. This is Kant's ethical rigorism or absolutism,
for which he has so often been censured. One of the sources
of it appears to be the unfortunate terminology he chose to
express the distinction between moral and prudential rules,
that of "categorical" and "hypothetical." From "categorical"
as opposed to "hypothetical" it is a short step to "unconditional" as opposed to "conditional." And from an unconditional *rule* it is but a short step to an unconditional *duty*, one
that holds irrespective of conditions or circumstances, which
is what Kant asserts the duty of veracity to be. But when Kant
first speaks of a categorical imperative, he says that it is not
conditioned by, or conditional upon, any purpose of the
agent, and he distinguishes it from a hypothetical imperative
precisely on the ground that the latter is conditional upon

---

[6] That this, incidentally, was what Kant had in mind by the distinction
between hypothetical and categorical imperatives was clearly recognized by
Sidgwick (*op. cit.*, pp. 6-7): "We frequently prescribe that this or that
'ought' to be done or aimed at without any express reference to an ulterior
end, while yet such an end is tacitly presupposed. It is obvious that such
prescriptions are merely, what Kant calls them, Hypothetical Imperatives:
they are not addressed to any one who has not first accepted the end.
. . . A physician assumes that his patient wants health: he tells him that
he *ought* to rise early, to live plainly, to take hard exercise. If the patient
deliberately prefers ease and good living to health, the physician's precepts fall to the ground: they are no longer addressed to him. . . ."

some purpose of the agent. Thus what he seems to have done is to have shifted from thinking of a categorical imperative as one not conditional upon any purposes of the *agent* to thinking of it as not being conditional upon *anything at all*. Yet, from the fact that a statement of the form "A ought to do *x*" is not based on or "conditioned by" any of A's purposes, it does not follow that it may not be based on or conditioned by someone else's purpose, for whose sake A ought to do *x*. Nor does it follow that it is not based on or conditional upon other circumstances or factors. The "imperative," "If A promised B to loan him the money he asked for, then A ought to loan B the money he asked for," for instance, is not a hypothetical imperative in the sense in which Kant defined this term. It is not conditional upon any of A's desires. But it is still conditional. The imperative "A ought to loan B the money he asked for" is, in this instance, based on or conditional upon a prior promise. One cannot be required to loan money to anyone who asks him for it. Thus Kant seems to have been misled by his own unhappy choice of language.

This may sound odd. Yet others have been misled by the same faulty terminology. The following passage is just one instance:

> Customary moral rules consist largely of such practical imperatives. But modern philosophers have tried to draw a sharp distinction between the two on the ground that moral rules are absolutely binding, while the others are conditional. The rules of economy, of prudence, or of hygiene are conditional in the sense that we must follow them *if* we wish to achieve certain ends. But we may not care for these ends, and in that case we do not need to follow the rules. Moral rules, such as that against lying, are thus absolute in the sense that we must follow them under all circumstances without regard to likes or preferences. Now there is no doubt that many moral rules are felt by a good many people to be absolute in this sense. . . . But reflective people who are in the habit of asking for the reasons for customary moral rules do not always accept their absolute character. Few, for instance, agree with . . . Kant in regarding the rule against lying as absolute in the

sense that it must not be violated under any circumstances whatsoever, not even to save human life.[7]

The fact that the authors of this passage do not regard themselves as agreeing with Kant does not save them from committing Kant's error. From the fact that moral rules "hold under all circumstances without regard to" *the agent's* "likes or preferences," it does not follow that "they must not be violated under any circumstances whatsoever," nor does it follow that they must be observed without regard to the likes or preferences of others. From the fact that moral rules are not "conditional in the sense that we must follow them if we wish to achieve certain ends," it does not follow that they are "absolutely binding."

Kant did not always fall into this confusion, and this actually supports the interpretation that I am here presenting. His distinction between "perfect" and "imperfect" duties, for example, is based on the fact that some duties are conditioned by or depend on the desires or purposes of others. Thus he says: "We distinguish the law that merely furnishes a *principle* of obligation from that which is really obligatory; as, for instance, the law of what man's *wants* require from me, as contrasted with that which their *rights* demand, the latter of which prescribes essential, the former only non-essential duties. . . ." [8] Kant also claims that we have a duty to promote the happiness of others, and this could hardly be the case unless at least some of our duties were "conditioned by" the purposes of others.[9]

It follows, then, if my argument is sound, that it is no part of the meaning of the term "a categorical imperative" that a

[7] Morris R. Cohen and Ernest Nagel, *An Introduction to Logic and Scientific Method* (New York: Harcourt, Brace and Company, 1934), p. 365.

[8] *Practical Reason*, 309-10.

[9] Cf. the Preface to the *Metaphysical Elements of Ethics*, Abbott, pp. 303-4. In this connection the following statement is worth noting: "That one should sacrifice his own happiness, his true wants, in order to promote that of others, would be a self-contradictory maxim if made a universal law. This duty, therefore, is only *indeterminate*; it has a certain latitude within which one may be able to do more or less without our being able to assign its limits definitely."

categorical imperative must be inviolable. A categorical imperative is simply a moral rule, and it involves a shift in the use of the term to suppose that a categorical imperative may under no circumstances be violated, that it is absolutely binding under any and all conditions. To suppose this is to confuse *a* categorical imperative, in the sense of a moral rule, with *the* categorical imperative, which is a moral principle.

Perhaps the most famous instance of Kant's rigorism is his almost fanatical insistence that it is always wrong to lie, that one may not lie even to save someone from being killed. But it can be illustrated by many passages from his *Philosophy of Law*, in which this phase of his view found its most forceful expression. In this work, Kant maintains that the precept, "Obey the authority which has power over you," "is a Categorical Imperative . . ." which "forbids investigating into how this power has been attained, at least with any view to undermining it," and says that "resistance on the part of the people to the supreme legislative power of the state, is in no case legitimate. . . . It is the duty of the people to bear any abuse of the Supreme Power, even though it should be considered to be unbearable." [1] Again, he speaks of "The Categorical Imperative of Penal Justice, that the killing of any person contrary to the Law must be punished with death . . . ," and makes such pronouncements as: "Even if a civil society resolved to dissolve itself with the consent of all its members— as might be supposed in the case of a people inhabiting an island resolving to separate and scatter themselves throughout the world—the last murderer lying in prison ought to be executed before the resolution was carried out." [2]

It is not to the present purpose to inquire whether Kant really meant what he seems here to be saying, or what the particular grounds were that led him to make these pronouncements. I think it will generally be found that, in his philosophy of law at any rate, Kant does, in one way or another, qualify them to some extent when he comes to apply

[1] *Philosophy of Law*, pp. 256-7, 176-7.
[2] *Ibid.*, pp. 204, 198.

them or consider their bearings on one another.[3] But what is of importance here is the relation between Kant's rigorism and his first moral principle, *the* categorical imperative, "Act only on that maxim whereby thou canst at the same time will that it should become a universal law," and what has generally been inferred about this principle from these characteristically "Kantian" pronouncements. For what has generally been inferred is that the principle of universality must be wrong, if not simply absurd. Thus one critic writes:

> The notion of the test of universalization as a practical criterion has been unanimously rejected by the critics, and doubtless with good reason. The arguments against it are probably familiar to every student in the elementary stages of moral philosophy. We have all been introduced very early to the figure of the innocent man pursued by murderers whose life can be saved by a timely lie. There is no need to work over this well-trodden ground again.[4]

Now this view is thoroughly mistaken. The most grotesque fallacies often arise out of the assumption that some ground has been "well-trodden." What has happened is that Kant himself misapplied his own principle, and it has been in-

[3] It is noteworthy that Kant would admit cases in which it is not wrong to utter a false statement with intent to deceive, only he would not call such statements "lies." See *Lectures on Ethics*, pp. 227-8. For the dictum, "Thou shalt not lie, be the circumstances what they may," *ibid.*, p. 13.

[4] G. C. Field, "Kant's First Moral Principle," *Mind*, vol. XLI (January 1932), p. 19; reprinted in Field's *Studies in Philosophy* (Bristol: J. W. Arrowsmith, 1935), p. 179. For the assumption that the principle of universality necessarily leads to rigorism, cf. Edward Caird, *The Critical Philosophy of Immanuel Kant* (Glasgow: published by James Maclehose, 1889; copyright by Jackson, Son & Co., Ltd.), vol. II, pp. 188-90: "Kant's way of connecting the principle with the particular rules of morality seems to involve that each such rule should be treated as in itself universal, as an absolute law which may not on any occasion be set aside. . . . Kant . . . just because he takes as the universal principle of morality the merely formal principle of self-consistency, is obliged to conceive each of the moral rules as an absolute law; for the formal principle cannot be used to determine the relations of different rules which express the different interests in the moral life; but if it admits a particular rule as having any kind of obligation, it must consecrate it as an absolute law." There can be no better sample of these almost canonical mistakes.

ferred, *without any independent examination,* that the *principle* cannot be valid. But ethical rigorism, the view that certain moral rules hold absolutely or in all circumstances, simply does not follow from Kant's first moral principle, any more than it does from the generalization argument. I do not propose to repeat here the arguments that have already been given on this matter. I propose instead to put the point beyond all reasonable doubt by examining directly Kant's arguments in the famous essay "On a Supposed Right to Tell Lies from Benevolent Motives," in which his view that it can never be right to tell a lie was most vehemently maintained.[5]

§ 3 §

Kant wrote this essay in reply to a criticism by Benjamin Constant, whom he quotes as saying:

> The moral principle that it is one's duty to speak the truth, if it were taken singly and unconditionally, would make all society impossible. We have the proof of this in the very direct consequences which have been drawn from this principle by a German philosopher, who goes so far as to affirm that to tell a falsehood to a murderer who asked us whether our friend, of whom he was in pursuit, had not taken refuge in our house, would be a crime (p. 361).

To consider Constant's arguments against this, and Kant's direct replies to these arguments, while it might possibly be of interest, would simply tend to obscure what is most important in the present context. Let us consider only Kant's positive remarks on what he calls "the unconditional principle of veracity" (pp. 363-64). Along these lines he claims:

> Truth in utterances that cannot be avoided is the formal duty of a man to everyone, however great the disadvantage that may arise from it to him or any other; and although by making a false statement I do no wrong to him who unjustly compels me to speak, yet I do wrong to men in general in the

[5] This essay, which first appeared in 1797, is translated in Abbott, pp. 361-5. The references of the following section, unless otherwise specified, will be to these pages.

most essential point of duty . . . that is, so far as in me lies
I cause that declarations in general find no credit, and hence
that all rights founded on contract should lose their force;
and this is a wrong which is done to mankind. . . .

A lie . . . always injures another; if not another individual,
yet mankind generally, since it vitiates the source of justice
. . . (p. 362).

It is to be noted that Kant is really begging the question here.
It seems as if he is maintaining that lying in this case would
be wrong because, even if it does not injure another individual, it would injure mankind generally. But he is really doing nothing of the sort. What he is really maintaining is that
to tell a lie, even in a situation of the sort described, *must* injure mankind generally, because it would be wrong. But
whether it would be wrong is precisely the point in question.
The claim that a lie must be wrong because it vitiates the
source of justice, or would help destroy the foundations of
the law of contract, is similarly question-begging. It can be
met by the reply that failing to lie in such a situation would
be wrong because it would help destroy the bonds of human
trust, in terms of which one person may be relied on to shield
another against an oppressor.

But all this is really beside the point. What is most important here is that this argument is certainly not an application
of the categorical imperative. In fact, Kant does not apply
the categorical imperative at all in this essay. A fallacious inference as to what the results of applying it would be can
hardly be construed as an application. If Kant were applying
his first moral principle to this case he would be arguing that
it would be wrong to lie in such a situation because it could
not be willed to be a universal law that everyone do so. Instead of doing this, he contents himself with such assertions as
the following: "To be *truthful* (honest) in all declarations
is therefore a sacred unconditional command of reason, and
not to be limited by any expediency . . ." (p. 363).[6] "The

---

[6] The use of the word "therefore" in this sentence may be taken as a
sign that Kant is arguing rather than baldly asserting. And so, in a way,
he is: "Whoever . . . tells a lie, however good his intentions may be,

duty of veracity . . . is an *unconditional duty* which holds
in all circumstances"(p. 364). The rule of veracity, he continues, "in its nature does not admit of exceptions, since to
do so would be self-contradictory"(p. 365).

Now none of these assertions is in any degree warranted
by the principle of universality. What Kant is apparently assuming here is that since the rule of veracity is a categorical or
unconditional imperative, in the sense of not being a hypothetical imperative, it would be self-contradictory to speak of
a justifiable exception to it. And he is assuming that this rule
has been established to be a categorical imperative, in the
sense of a rule admitting of no exceptions, by some previous
application of *the* categorical imperative. But these assumptions are simply false. Nothing of the sort has been established.

Consider the famous illustration in the *Grundlegung* in
which Kant applied the categorical imperative to the case of
lying (or making a lying promise). What was established by
this application of the principle? What was established was
that the maxim in this case ("whenever I believe myself
short of money, I will borrow money and promise to pay it
back, though I know that this will never be done")

> can never rank as a universal law and be self-consistent, but
> must necessarily contradict itself. For the universality of a law
> that every one believing himself to be in need may make any
> promise he pleases with the intention not to keep it would
> make promising, and the very purpose of promising, itself im-
> possible, since no one would believe that he was being prom-
> ised anything, but would laugh at utterances of this kind as
> empty shams.[7]

---

must answer for the consequences of it, even before the civil tribunal, and
must pay the penalty for them, however unforeseen they may have been;
because truthfulness is a duty that must be regarded as the basis of all
duties founded on contract, the laws of which would be rendered uncertain and useless if even the least exception to them were admitted."
Though this may be an argument, it is certainly not an application of the
categorical imperative.

[7] *Grundlegung*, Paton 54-5, Abbott 48-9. Cf. 19 (Abbott 24): "I can
indeed will to lie, but I can by no means will a universal law of lying; for

Kant's point here is that if such a rule were universally followed there could be no promises at all. It would be self-contradictory to say that everyone has the right to make a lying promise whenever he feels like it. It is essential to the nature of a promise that when one promises to do something he can generally be presumed to intend to do it. If no one intended to carry out his "promises" no one could be said to have promised; the phrase "I promise" would lose its meaning—it could not be used to make a promise. And since the act therefore could not be right for everyone, it would not be right for anyone, at least without a special reason. But it does not at all follow that it is *always* wrong to lie or make a false promise. All that Kant has shown is that it is generally wrong (and surely this is enough). He has not shown that *no matter what the circumstances*, the supposition that everyone could make a lying promise in those circumstances would have this consequence. But this is what would have to be shown in order to show that lying, or false promising, is always wrong, no matter what the circumstances. And the fact is that this cannot be shown. For it is possible to imagine circumstances such that everyone may make a false promise in those circumstances without thereby making "promising, and the very purpose of promising, itself impossible," either in those circumstances or in general. Indeed, it would be self-contradictory to maintain that lying is always, and not just generally, wrong, *because*, as I have already argued, *the reasons in terms of which the rule is established are the very same reasons which, in certain circumstances, would suffice to override it.*

Now the case in which it is proposed to tell a lie in order to save an innocent person from harm is precisely of this type. The circumstances of the case have already been sufficiently described in the quotation given above. But to make it more

by such a law there could properly be no promises at all, since it would be futile to profess a will for future action to others who would not believe my profession or who, if they did so over-hastily, would pay me back in like coin; and consequently my maxim, as soon as it was made a universal law, would be bound to annul itself."

precise, so that it cannot be said that one has the alternative
of refusing to speak at all, let us imagine that the situation is
the following. A is hiding in B's house. The murderer arrives
and asks B, who happens at the moment to have C for company, whether A is in the house, and says that if B does not
answer he and C will be killed. B can do one of three things.
He can tell the truth, in which event A will be murdered; he
can refuse to answer, in which event he and C, who is just as
innocent as A, will be murdered; or he can tell a lie calculated
to save the life of A, as well as his own and C's. Now the
question Kant should have raised in his treatment of this
question is, "Could it be willed to be a universal law that
everyone should lie in this sort of situation?" But he did not
in fact do this. Instead of raising such a question, he simply
assumed that his previous applications of the categorical imperative established the duty of veracity as "an *unconditional duty* which holds in all circumstances." Instead of applying the categorical imperative to these particular circumstances, he applied this hard and fast rule. There is no process
of reasoning by which it can be deduced from this that the
categorical imperative is somehow defective. What is defective
is the way Kant used it. What is more, the result of applying
the categorical imperative to this sort of situation would be
quite different from what both Kant and his critics so uncriti-
cally assumed. For it would not be self-contradictory or self-
defeating for everyone to lie in the specified circumstances.
And the question is about lying *in the specified circumstances*,
not about lying in general. Since this is the case, supposing everyone to lie in a similar situation, the lie would be
self-defeating—the murderer would fail to believe it—only if
the murderer knew what the circumstances were, that is to
say, only if he knew that his victim was in the house. But if
he knew this the whole question would not arise in the first
place. In addition, it should be noted that what it is proposed
be done in this situation is to save an innocent man from
harm by telling a lie to a murderer. The question "Could it
be willed to be a universal law that everyone should lie in
order to save an innocent man from harm?" practically an-

swers itself. There is more ground for saying that it is impossible to will the opposite.

§ 4 §

There is another line of reasoning Kant might have used (though he does not appear to have done so) to support his claim that it would always be wrong to lie, even in a situation of the type described. He might have invoked his principle of humanity or personality: "Act in such a way that you always treat humanity, whether in your own person or in the person of any other, never simply as a means, but always at the same time as an end." For in applying this principle to the case of the lying promise Kant had said:

> The man who has a mind to make a false promise to others
> . . . is intending to make use of another man *merely as a*
> *means* to an end he does not share. For the man whom I seek
> to use for my own purposes by such a promise cannot possibly
> agree with my way of behaving to him, and so cannot himself
> share the end of the action.[8]

Hence Kant might have argued that since the murderer could not possibly agree to having a lie told to him, could not possibly share the end of the action, it would therefore be wrong to lie to him. For, on Kant's view, to lie to someone is always, no matter what the purpose of the lying, to treat him (or "humanity in his person") merely as a means. Thus he speaks of "this respect-inspiring idea of personality which sets before our eyes the sublimity of our nature (in its highest aspect) . . . ," and asks, rhetorically:

> Has not every even moderately honourable man sometimes
> found that, where by an otherwise inoffensive lie he might
> either have withdrawn himself from an unpleasant business,
> or even have procured some advantage for a loved and well-
> deserving friend, he has avoided it solely lest he should de-
> pise himself secretly in his own eyes? When an upright man
> is in the greatest distress, which he might have avoided if he

[8] *Ibid.*, Paton 67-8, Abbott 58.

could only have disregarded duty, is he not sustained by the consciousness that he has *maintained humanity in its proper dignity in his own person* and honoured it . . . ? [9]

Kant is actually maintaining that one who tells a lie is not only treating the person lied to as a mere means, but is mistreating "humanity in his *own* person"—he is treating himself as a mere means.

But this simply does not show that it is always wrong to lie. What it shows, if anything, is that there is something defective about the principle of personality. Indeed, the vagueness of this principle has often been pointed out. "What does it mean to treat every individual as an end in himself? Does it mean that a government has no right to conscript a man against his will and make him kill some fellow man in battle or be killed himself? Does it mean that in building a road or bridge we may not expropriate individuals who are attached to their ancestral homes?" [1] This principle, however, is not just vague. In the context of Kant's ethics, it is fundamentally equivocal. For Kant's notion of an "end" is habitually equivocal between "rational" or "objective" ends, and subjective ends, which depend on inclinations or desires.

Suppose it were said that to tell the truth, in a situation of the sort described, would be to treat the victim merely as a means to the ends of the murderer, ends he, as a victim, cannot be expected to share, and that therefore it would be wrong not to tell a lie. This is probably what would be said on any ordinary interpretation of the principle. But Kant would have a ready reply. To tell a lie, even to save the man from death, would be to subject his humanity, his rational or *noumenal* self, to his merely sensuous or *phenomenal* desires. Only as a person in the phenomenal world, one with sensuous inclinations or desires, would one wish a lie to be told. As a member of the noumenal world one would will that the

[9] *Practical Reason*, 216; italics added.
[1] Morris R. Cohen, "A Critique of Kant's Philosophy of Law," in *The Heritage of Kant*, ed. by Whitney and Bowers (Princeton: Princeton University Press, 1939), pp. 298-9; reprinted in Cohen's *Reason and Law* (Glencoe, Ill.: The Free Press, 1950), p. 124.

truth be told, in this and every other situation, for that is what would be willed by a perfectly rational being, whose will is unaffected by any sensuous inclinations or external causes. And what a perfectly rational being, one without any sensuous inclinations, *would* do in this situation, is what *ought* to be done.

The equivocation in this principle, then, is between purely "rational" or "noumenal" ends, and merely subjective or "phenomenal" ones. But this makes the principle, as so interpreted, absolutely useless. It is not a moral criterion at all. It is an *ad hoc* device, serving only to give rational respectability to a judgment about what ought to be done made antecedently to its application. It is impossible to tell before the issue has already been decided on some other standard which way of acting would be treating someone merely as a means to "ends" he cannot himself share. The line of reasoning involved is not, as it seems to be, "This would be treating someone merely as a means; therefore it is wrong." It is "This would be wrong; therefore it would be treating someone merely as a means." But in the case in question, as in many others, this simply begs the question.

There can be no doubt that Kant regarded the principle of universality as equivalent to the principle of personality. He says, for instance, that "the aforesaid . . . ways of representing the principle of morality are at bottom so many formulations of precisely the same law. . . . The principle 'So act in relation to every rational being (both to yourself and to others) that he may at the same time count in your maxim as an end in himself' is . . . at bottom the same as the principle 'Act on a maxim which at the same time contains in itself its own universal validity for every rational being.' "[2] And the principle of personality very often has been regarded as in some sense better or more adequate than Kant's first moral principle, which has been thought too "formal" and empty. But if the preceding arguments are sound, both these ideas are false. Kant's first moral principle is not equivalent to his second, for, given Kant's peculiar dialectic be-

[2] *Grundlegung*, Paton 79, 82; Abbott 66, 68.

tween the phenomenal and noumenal worlds, they can conflict with each other. And it is the latter principle that is
too "formal" and empty. It is not a criterion at all, for just
what it would require in a particular situation is indeterminate until it has been determined whose ends are to count as
"rational." It has more of an emotional uplift than a definite
meaning.

Suppose, however, that the principle of personality is ex-
tracted from its context in Kant's ethics, and considered independently. It would then not be subject to this equivocation between objective and merely subjective ends, and it is
clear that the particular criticism just made of it would then
no longer apply. For while it might still be vague and indefinite, it would not be equivocal and empty. Suppose, then,
that we restate it in some such way as the following: "No one
ought ever to treat anyone else merely as a means to ends of
one's own, without at the same time treating him as a person
with his own ends and plans" (that is, "as an end"); or, "Everyone ought always to treat others, not merely as means to the
achievement of his own purposes, but as persons with ends
or purposes of their own." (Note that I have eliminated any
reference to "mistreating humanity in one's *own* person"; for
I do not see how anyone can treat *himself* as a mere means.)
In other words, the principle states that, while it is allowable
to treat or use others as means or instruments to the achievement of one's own ends, it is not allowable to treat them
merely as means, for this is to treat them merely as things and
not as persons with ends of their own. So understood, there
are certain practices that this principle clearly rules out as immoral, such as human exploitation and slavery. And so understood it may be that it can be added to our list of moral principles, for it seems unlikely that it can come into conflict
with any of the principles that I have already elaborated. It
may even be that, so understood, it is equivalent to the principle of universality, at least in the sense that it cannot
conflict with it.

This principle, however, is still vague, and in need of
further examination. For example, does it or does it not re-

quire some such qualification as "without a reason or justification," and can there be a justification for treating another person merely as a means? In other words, is it *always* wrong to treat someone merely as a means, or is it presumptively wrong, and sometimes justifiable? And how is it determined whether or not someone "can share in the end of the action"? How, for instance, does it apply to punishment, and to capital punishment? Can one who is to be executed possibly "share in the end of the action"? What this principle requires, clearly, is examination and clarification *as a moral principle*, and not just as a feature of Kant's ethics, and I do not know that it has ever received it. But I see no need to embark on this here.

§ 5 §

I have been arguing that Kant's ethical rigorism or absolutism is not only not warranted by his first moral principle, but is actually incompatible with it. It will be well to make this argument more explicit.

Rigorism is the view that there are certain moral rules that hold in all circumstances or under all conditions. On this view, then, certain actions are always wrong, no matter what the circumstances, and no matter what their purposes. Thus Kant, in this mood, holds that lying is an action of this type.

Now the categorical imperative is advanced as a principle for determining whether any act is right or wrong. But it cannot be applied to an action taken apart from any determinate context. It must always be applied to an action considered as taking place in certain circumstances, or for a certain purpose. The proof of this is that a reference to the circumstances and purpose of an action is necessarily involved in the "maxim" of the action. And it is the maxim of an action that Kant continually insists is what must be willed to be a universal law, not the action taken apart from some determinate maxim, that is, apart from some determinate purpose or circumstances. "Actions must," he says, "be considered, in the first place, according to their subjective principle, but whether this principle is also valid objectively, can only be known by the criterion of the categorical imperative." [3]

But if this is the case, then the rule derived from the application of the categorical imperative holds only for the circumstances to which it is applied, and, of course, for anyone in the same or similar circumstances, and does not thereby hold for all possible circumstances. Because it could not be willed to be a universal law that everyone should act in a certain way under certain circumstances, it does not follow that it could not be willed to be a universal law that everyone should act in that way under certain other circumstances. Indeed, on the basis of the categorical imperative, an act which would be wrong in certain circumstances may well be right in other circumstances. Kant overlooked the fact that lying merely for one's own personal convenience, and lying in order to save the life of some innocent person, are two different sorts of actions, actions whose maxims are quite different. Thus Kant's ethical rigorism is neither a consequence of nor compatible with the principle of universality.

Rigorism is, therefore, purely arbitrary. The particular rules selected as holding absolutely are selected arbitrarily. There is no good reason for selecting this one instead of that, nor saying that it is always wrong to lie, but not always wrong to kill or to fail to help another human being in distress. Kant's ethical rigorism is thus no argument against the validity of the categorical imperative as a moral principle.

[3] *Philosophy of Law,* p. 34; in Abbott, p. 281.

❄

CHAPTER IX

THE APPLICATION
OF THE CATEGORICAL
IMPERATIVE

What I have shown so far about the categorical imperative is that it does not have certain consequences that it has generally been supposed to have. This, however, merely shows that one important argument against it is unsound, and is not to establish its validity. Even apart from this argument the consensus would appear to be that it is "seriously defective" and "woefully inadequate." This, I maintain, is very far from the truth. The categorical imperative, when properly understood, is perfectly valid. Yet before this can be regarded as established there are a number of other important and persuasive objections that must be disposed of. It is only through this process, in fact, that the proper interpretation of it can be effectively brought out.

The general method of these criticisms consists in citing examples of maxims or actions that (a) can be universalized, and yet are wrong, or (b) cannot be universalized, and yet are not wrong. If either of these charges could be sustained it would show either that the categorical imperative leads to wrong actions or that it does not adequately distinguish between right and wrong. Thus the principle would be definitely refuted. But in each case, it should be noticed, there are two distinct questions to be dealt with. First, is it true that the maxim can, or cannot, be universalized? Secondly, supposing that this is true, what is the basis of the claim that the act in question is, or is not, right. Is this claim a sound one? Surely it is not enough to point to an action that is regarded as wrong, or right, by many people, or in many places, but which cannot be determined to be so by the categorical imperative. There are many people who regard it as wrong to dance or wear lipstick. That there is no basis for this in the categorical imperative does not show the principle to be defective. *Is* it wrong—morally wrong—to dance, or wear lipstick? This is, in fact, just a taboo, with no rational basis.

As an example, with only a slight variation, of this general critical procedure, which as a general method, of course, is unexceptionable, consider the following argument, which claims that Kant's principle is "not an adequate statement of the nature of obligation," because, among other things:

> it is possible to generalize into universal rules all sorts of maxims which nobody (and certainly not Kant) would hold to be obligatory. For instance, I could perfectly well hold that every purchaser of a new book should write his name on the flyleaf when he acquires it. There is nothing self-contradictory about this maxim; but it remains morally neutral—we neither feel an obligation to inscribe our names or to abstain from inscribing them. . . .[1]

This is not only a good instance of a typical mode of criticism, it is also an instance of a typical misunderstanding, which it will be useful to eliminate at the outset. If the maxim of an action *cannot* be willed to be a universal law, then it is wrong to act on it, we have the duty or obligation not to, and it can be said that we ought not to. However, if a maxim *can* be willed to be a universal law, it does not follow that it is obligatory to act on it or that it would be wrong not to. What follows is that it is permissible to do so, or not wrong (and thus right in the permissive sense), and hence that it cannot

[1] W. T. Jones, *A History of Western Philosophy* (New York: Harcourt, Brace and Company, 1952), vol. II, p. 855. The phrases "seriously defective" and "woefully inadequate" come from here.

be said that we ought not to—which is not the same as saying that we ought to. Does it follow that the categorical imperative is only a "negative principle," from which we can determine, perhaps, what we ought not to do, but not what we ought to do? This has often been said, but it is none the better for that. If it is wrong to do a certain act, then we ought not to do it; but if it is wrong not to do it, then we ought to do it, and there are many actions that can be determined to be obligatory on the basis of the categorical imperative. If, however, it is neither wrong to do a certain act nor wrong not to, then there is no question of a moral obligation with respect to it. To ask for something more than this, to complain "I agree about what I ought *not* to do, but I still don't know what I *ought* to do," is to confuse the moral "ought" with the prudential, and to suppose, speciously, that there are no morally indifferent actions.

It would be easy to cite a number of passages in support of this interpretation of Kant.[2] Yet I see no real need to do so. Suppose, what I do not believe for a moment, that Kant really had made this mistake, and had regarded it as morally obligatory to act on every maxim that can be universalized? What would this prove? Only that in this Kant was mistaken, and not that the categorical imperative is defective. Even if it could be shown that this idea is necessarily involved in *Kant's* interpretation of the categorical imperative, it would not follow for a moment that it must be involved in our interpretation of it. Yet this type of criticism is all too common, the categorical imperative being identified with everything Kant said (or is thought to have said) about it, it then being all too easy to deduce its absurdity.

Consider another instance of the method of criticism that I have mentioned. After concluding that the instance given "shows that universalization cannot be a positive criterion of duty," the author just quoted goes on to claim that neither "is it a negative criterion. There are many actions, con-

---

[2] See for instance, *Grundlegung*, Paton 86, Abbott 70; *Philosophy of Law*, pp. 29-31 (Abbott, pp. 277-9); and cf. H. J. Paton, *The Categorical Imperative* (Chicago: The University of Chicago Press, 1948), pp. 141-2.

demned by Kant (and many other people), whose maxims can be universalized. It is our duty, Kant thought, not to commit suicide; but there is nothing self-contradictory about a prospective suicide's willing that everyone else commit suicide." Now I agree that the categorical imperative does not show suicide per se to be immoral, and I think that Kant's argument against it is singularly unsuccessful, and even sophistical. Indeed, his argument against it does not even involve a genuine application of the categorical imperative. There is no reason why it cannot be willed to be a universal law that everyone may take his own life "if its continuance threatens more evil than it promises pleasure," provided that in doing so one does not violate the rights of another, for there is no reason why the universal adoption of this maxim would be self-defeating. (One's maxim in the case, it should be noted, is not simply to commit suicide, but to commit suicide if future life appears to be unbearable.) But this shows nothing, except that Kant was mistaken. The question to be asked is, is suicide immoral? What is the evidence for this? It is true that a good many people say so. But this does not settle the matter. There is hardly anything that has not been regarded as immoral at one time or another by a good many people. Suicide, of course, may be immoral. It definitely is so where it involves shirking an obligation to another, and it so happens that a great many cases do. But where no one else's rights are violated, what ground is there for maintaining it to be wrong? I do not mean by this to imply a recommendation of suicide. Where it is not immoral, it is almost always senseless or imprudent, or may be presumed to be so. It is usually the act of an unbalanced mind. Yet some acts of suicide are also acts of the greatest heroism, and some are as coolly and deliberately undertaken, for perfectly honorable reasons, as the acts of the most calculating egoist. There is thus good reason to believe that the question has not been adequately thought out. At any rate, a requirement that a criterion must agree with what everyone or nearly everyone thinks is an impossible one.

Such is the general type of the criticisms to be considered.

But to consider various criticisms is not the only object of this chapter. In addition to this, we have still to determine how the categorical imperative is related to the generalization argument. Are they equivalent principles, or are they essentially different? What I shall be primarily concerned with is the criteria for determining whether or not the maxim of an action can be universalized, and with the moral relevance of this both in general and in particular cases. But first it is necessary to discuss further the notion of a "maxim." Not only is this a notion of central importance, but the fact that the categorical imperative involves a reference to a maxim is one of the two respects in which it differs, or appears to differ, from the generalization argument.

§ 1 §

Kant defines a maxim as "a subjective principle of action." It is "a principle on which the subject *acts*," and is contrasted with "an objective principle valid for every rational being," which is one "on which he *ought* to act." [3] A maxim is thus a certain kind of rule, and to speak of the maxim of someone's action is to speak of the rule in accordance with which he acted. As Kant says, "the rule of the agent or actor, which he forms as a° principle for himself on subjective grounds, is called his maxim"; and the subjective grounds on which one's

---

[3] *Grundlegung*, Paton 51, Abbott 46, note. Cf. Paton 15 (Abbott 21), note: "A *maxim* is the subjective principle of a volition: an objective principle (that is, one which would also serve subjectively as a practical principle for all rational beings if reason had full control over the faculty of desire) is a practical *law*." Kant also says (Paton 60, Abbott 52) that a subjective principle, or personal maxim, is "one on which we have a propensity and inclination to act." It should be noted that Kant often uses the term "principle," or "practical principle," in the sense of a motive or disposition, as, for instance, when he speaks of "the determining principle of the will." Thus he speaks (*Practical Reason*, 200) of: "a subjective determining principle, that is, a motive to this action." Cf. *ibid.*, 125: "Practical principles are propositions which contain a general determination of the will, having under it several practical rules. They are subjective, or *maxims*, when the condition is regarded by the subject as valid only for his own will, but are objective, or practical *laws*, when the condition is recognized as objective, that is, valid for the will of every rational being."

maxims are founded are one's inclinations or habitual desires.[4] As an example of a maxim we may take the one stated by Kant in his example of "the lying promise": "Whenever I believe myself short of money, I will borrow money and promise to pay it back, though I know that this will never be done."

Kant's statements of a maxim are not usually as explicit as this, and it is not clear that even this one is a wholly accurate statement of the maxim actually involved in the case. Nevertheless this indicates, to some extent, why Kant places so much emphasis on the maxim of an action. To say that someone is acting on a certain maxim is to imply (if not to say) that he is acting for a certain purpose, or with a certain end in view, or with a certain intent; and to specify the maxim is to specify the purpose or intent of the action, as well as something of its circumstances. Thus one of the things that Kant wishes to emphasize, in his emphasis on maxims, is the intent or purpose of the action. This is borne out by the fact that the statements of the categorical imperative given in the *Lectures on Ethics* refer, not to the *maxim* of the action, but to the *intent* of the action: "If the intent of the action can without self-contradiction be universalized, it is morally possible; if it cannot be so universalized without contradicting itself, it is morally impossible. . . . That action is immoral whose intent cancels and destroys

[4] *Philosophy of Law*, p. 33, Abbott, p. 281. In *Practical Reason*, 189, Kant speaks of "the maxims which everyone founds on his own inclinations." Cf. also *Grundlegung*, Paton 62 (Abbott 54), where Kant says that maxims arise from desires and inclinations, "with the co-operation of reason." But Kant really distinguishes between two kinds of maxims, those which are founded on inclinations or subjective ends, which he calls "material," and those which are not, which he calls "formal": "Practical principles are *formal* if they abstract from all subjective ends; they are *material*, on the other hand, if they are based on such ends and consequently on certain impulsions" (*Grundlegung*, Paton 64, Abbott 55). Cf. also Paton 14, Abbott 20. If it is part of the meaning of the term "maxim" that maxims are founded on inclinations, as Kant sometimes seems to imply, then what we have here is not so much two different kinds of maxims as two different senses of the term. But this is not clear. At any rate, I am dealing here solely with "material" maxims, for it is these that are to be tested by the application of the categorical imperative.

itself when it is made a universal rule. . . ." [5] It clearly makes
no difference if in these statements the term "maxim" (or
even "purpose") is substituted for "intent."

It seems clear, then, that one of the reasons Kant empha-
sizes maxims—or at least one of the consequences of this
emphasis—is to ensure that the acts to which the categorical
imperative is applied are morally determinate, acts to which
moral terms are applicable. Since to specify the maxim of an
action is to specify something of its circumstances and its purpose, to specify the maxim of an action is part of the process
I described in a previous chapter as "filling in the context of
the act." Thus to specify the maxim of an action is really to
specify more clearly the nature of the action. Just as the same
kind of action can be performed in different contexts or circumstances, it can be performed on different maxims or for
different purposes; and, similarly, its morality—whether it is
right or wrong—can depend on its maxim.

But this is not all that Kant means by a maxim. Kant holds
the view that every act is purposive; that "every action has its
end." [6] Thus Kant holds that every time someone acts he is
acting on some maxim, in the sense of acting for a purpose
or in order to attain some end. On this view, then, no one
can be said to act, in the sense in which he can be held responsible for his actions—in the sense in which his acts are
"free"—unless he is acting in accordance with some plan or
policy. What is more, it would seem that the plan must be
one that the agent has consciously formulated. Kant sometimes implies by his use of the term "maxim," in other words,
that everyone always acts on a rule that he consciously and
deliberately adopts. He says, for instance, that maxims are
"self-imposed rules"; [7] and this is clearly the way the term

[5] *Lectures on Ethics*, p. 44.
[6] Preface to the *Metaphysical Elements of Ethics*, Abbott, p. 295. Cf.
Paton, *The Categorical Imperative*, p. 75: "According to Kant every action aims at a result or end or object."
[7] *Grundlegung*, Paton 84, Abbott 69. Cf. *Philosophy of Law*, p. 35
(Abbott, p. 282): "A maxim is . . . a subjective principle of action,
which the individual *makes a rule for himself* as to how in fact he will
act" (italics added).

must be interpreted in such statements as "Suppose . . . I have made it my maxim to increase my fortune by every safe means," and "One may make it his maxim to let no injury pass unrevenged. . . ."[8] In this sense a maxim is a plan or resolution or policy that one consciously adopts beforehand as to how one will act in a certain kind of situation.

I do not know whether Kant ever expressly says that a maxim must be conscious. Clearly some maxims are, but it is not certain that all of them are. It does not seem to me that Kant is very clear on this matter. He not only does not say very clearly just exactly what he means by a maxim, but he is often very careless in his statements of them. Thus he never seems aware that it is often a very difficult matter to formulate with accuracy the maxim of an action. Yet it is not necessary for us to dwell on these questions. For it seems plainly untrue that everyone always acts in accordance with some predetermined plan, whether conscious or not, or that everyone always acts purposively. Moreover, and this is much more important, these assumptions are not necessary for the purposes of moral judgment. What is necessary is that an act be voluntary; an involuntary act is not one for which one can be held responsible, and in a sense can be said not to be an act at all. But it is not necessary that an act be purposive, or that it be undertaken in accordance with (or in violation of) some self-imposed rule. (Note that there is a difference between saying that someone acted *purposely*, and saying that he acted *purposively*; between saying that someone did something *on purpose*, and saying that he did it *for a purpose*.) One may act aimlessly, or thoughtlessly, in accordance with habit, or with no clear idea of why he is doing something or even of what he is doing, and can still be held responsible for his action (or failure to act). For it may be one's duty in certain situations to know what he is doing, or to have a definite aim or purpose. This is shown by the fact that the generalization argument, and hence the categorical imperative, is applicable to such actions—"What would hap-

[8] *Practical Reason*, 137, 126. In this sense of the term we can speak of maxims in abstraction from actions.

pen if everyone drove along aimlessly, without looking where he was going?" or "How would it be if everyone in your situation failed to realize what he is doing?"

Along with actions, which may be based on maxims, there are such things as omissions, which need not be; just as one can be blamed for certain performances, one can be blamed for nonperformance (such as nonperformance of contract); and a nonperformance or omission need not be deliberate or undertaken in accordance with an actual decision. There is a difference between a refusal to act, which must be deliberate, and simple failure to act, which need not be deliberate. One can be guilty of negligence, and negligence need not be deliberate, or conscious, or even intentional.

It follows that the reference to maxims in the categorical imperative is not really necessary, and in so far as it implies that every action must be based on a maxim, it can be seriously misleading.

I said before that just as the same kind of act can be performed in different contexts, the same kind of act can be performed on different maxims, or for different purposes. Now in so far as to specify the maxim of an act is to specify its context, the notion of a maxim is already incorporated in the generalization principle. For the function it performs is already performed by the qualification "similar persons in similar circumstances." What is more, the distinction between an act and its purpose or intention is not as sharp as insistence on the use of this notion would seem to imply. While we sometimes say of two persons that they did the same thing, only with different motives or intentions, we can also say of them, owing to the difference in their intentions, that they did entirely different things. And very often the description of someone's action will involve a reference to what, in terms of a less informative description of the action, would be called his intention or purpose. Lying merely for one's own personal convenience and lying in order to save the life of some innocent person are two different sorts of actions, actions whose maxims are quite different. Similarly, the actions of hitting someone in order to take his money and of hitting someone in order to save one's own life are, in a sense of the term that is quite proper and not at all unusual, different actions, even though the physical movements involved may be identical. Of course, they can just as properly be said to be actions of the same kind performed for different purposes, or on different maxims. But outside of special contexts, such as in a court of law, there simply is no precise criterion governing this usage. The notion of an action is elastic, and the description of an action may include more or less of what, in terms of some other description of the action, would be regarded as its circumstances or purpose.

Thus it is not necessary always to specify the "maxim" of an action as something apart from the action itself. And it is worth noting that Kant does at times use the term "action" in this way, so that he finds it unnecessary to specify the maxim of the action. The following passage is a case in point:

> The rule of the judgment according to laws of pure practical reason is this: ask yourself whether, if the *action* you propose were to take place by a law of the system of nature of which you were yourself a part, you could regard it as possible by your own will. Everyone does, in fact, decide by this rule whether *actions* are morally good or evil. Thus, people say: If everyone permitted himself to deceive, when he thought it to his advantage; or thought himself justified in shortening his life as soon as he was thoroughly weary of it; or looked with perfect indifference on the necessity of others. . . .[9]

The fact that the categorical imperative is here applied directly to actions, and not to the maxims of the actions, makes absolutely no difference. As I mentioned in the first chapter, in an application of the generalization argument it makes no difference whether one says "If everyone did that . . . ," "If everyone acted in that way . . . ," "If everyone acted on that rule . . . ," or "If everyone acted on that maxim. . . ." For the very same reasons it makes no difference in an application of the principle of universality.

[9] *Ibid.*, 192 (italics added). It should be noted that the principle of personality makes no reference to maxims.

The introduction of maxims, however, does have certain definite advantages. It enables us to see that the principle of universality can be used, not simply as a test of individual actions, but also as a test of maxims or rules of action. Even though we do not always formulate a policy in advance, and thus do not always act on rules that we make for ourselves, nevertheless we sometimes do; and we often adopt rules or policies of action whether we act on them or not. I might resolve, for example, to rise early every morning in order to exercise; a statesman might make it a rule never to give out interviews on the telephone; someone might adopt the maxim always to be polite to people; someone else might resolve never to take another drink. There can be no doubt that people often do adopt such rules or maxims for governing their future behavior (and not always on New Year's Eve, or the morning after), with at least the intention of acting on them. Now the categorical imperative, and the generalization argument as well, can be used to determine not simply whether a particular action, which may or may not accord with someone's self-imposed rule, is right or wrong, but also whether such rules or maxims are right or wrong. This can be done by determining what would happen if everyone, or everyone in certain circumstances, adopted such a maxim, or decided to act on such a rule. Here we are considering the *rule or maxim*, apart from some particular action that might be undertaken in accordance with it (Whether this is simply to consider a certain *kind* of action, as opposed to a particular action, is a question that I do not decide.) It should be noticed, however, that the ambiguity of "action" is paralleled by an ambiguity of "maxim." Sometimes the statement of a maxim already incorporates a purpose, in which case it makes no sense to ask for its purpose, or the purpose of adopting it; sometimes it does not, in which case it does make sense to ask for its purpose. This, apparently, is a function of how fully or explicitly a maxim is stated. But more on this later.

§ 2 §

The fact that the generalization argument does not refer to what one can "will" is the other respect in which it differs from the categorical imperative. What does this difference amount to? What is the criterion involved here, and what is the moral relevance of it?

Kant actually has two criteria for saying that the maxim of an action cannot be universalized, one of which, the narrower, entails the other:

> We must *be able to will* that a maxim of our action should become a universal law—this is the general canon for all moral judgement of action. Some actions are so constituted that their maxim cannot even be *conceived* as a universal law of nature without contradiction, let alone be *willed* as what *ought* to become one. In the case of others we do not find this inner impossibility, but it is still impossible to *will* that their maxim should be raised to the universality of a law of nature, because such a will would contradict itself.[1]

Let us consider first the narrower criterion. Kant is saying that there are certain ways of acting, or certain maxims of action, that could not possibly become universal. I have already given reasons for believing that this is the case with respect to certain kinds of actions, such as lying as a regular rule, or whenever it seems convenient. (As Alice pointed out, if no one spoke until he was spoken to, no one would speak.) Yet of all the features of Kant's ethics this is one that has been most often and most vehemently—and it may be added, most thoughtlessly—condemned. For example, Mill claims that Kant "fails, almost grotesquely, to show that there would be any contradiction, any logical (not to say physical) impossibility, in the adoption by all rational beings of the most outrageously immoral rules of conduct.

---

[1] *Grundlegung*, Paton 57, Abbott 50. Kant adds that "the first kind of action is opposed to strict or narrow (rigorous) duty, the second only to wider (meritorious) duty." This distinction corresponds, apparently, to that between perfect or determinate duties, and imperfect or indeterminate duties.

All he shows is that the *consequences* of their universal adoption would be such as no one would choose to incur." [2] Yet Mill himself fails, almost grotesquely, to understand what Kant was driving at. He had in this, however, plenty of company, and rather strange company indeed. Hegel's criticism of Kant is a famous one:

> The proposition: "Act as if the maxim of thine action could be laid down as a universal principle," would be admirable if we already had determinate principles of conduct. That is to say, to demand of a principle that it shall be able to serve in addition as a determinant of universal legislation is to presuppose that it already possesses a content. Given the content, then of course the application of the principle would be a simple matter. In Kant's case, however, the principle itself is still not available and his criterion of noncontradiction is productive of nothing, since where there is nothing, there can be no contradiction either. . . .
> The absence of property contains in itself just as little contradiction as the nonexistence of this or that nation, family, etc., or the death of the whole human race. But if it is already established on other grounds and presupposed that property and human life are to exist and be respected, then indeed it is a contradiction to commit theft or murder; a contradiction must be a contradiction of something, i.e., of some content presupposed from the start as a fixed principle. . . .[3]

Now this objection of Hegel's is almost incredibly simpleminded. For it entirely ignores the fact that the maxim of an action, which is what the categorical imperative is designed to

---

[2] Mill, *Utilitarianism* (Everyman's Library ed.; New York: E. P. Dutton and Company, 1910), chap. I, par. 4, p. 4. Cf. chap. V, par. 22, p. 49: "that a rule even of utter selfishness could not *possibly* be adopted by all rational beings—that there is any insuperable obstacle in the nature of things to its adoption—cannot be even plausibly maintained. To give any meaning to Kant's principle, the sense put upon it must be, that we ought to shape our conduct by a rule which all rational beings might adopt *with benefit to* their collective interest" (italics in text).

[3] Hegel, *The Philosophy of Right*, translated by T. M. Knox (Oxford: The Clarendon Press, 1942), addition to par. 135, p. 254; par. 135, p. 90. Bradley follows the master almost slavishly on this. See his *Ethical Studies* (2nd ed.; Oxford: The Clarendon Press, 1927), essay 4, especially pp. 154 ff.

test, is itself a "determinate principle of conduct" and "already possesses a content." Hegel assumes that the categorical imperative is supposed to be applied in a vacuum—or in other words, is not to be applied to anything, with the possible exception of itself—and it is this same assumption that vitiates the common charge that Kant's ethics is an "empty formalism." Given that someone proposes to adopt a certain maxim, or to act in a certain way in certain circumstances in order to achieve a certain purpose, then we "already have a determinate principle of conduct," something that "already possesses a content," to which the categorical imperative can be applied. Hence we are "given the content," but unfortunately "the application of the principle" is not always a simple matter.

Hegel, moreover, seems to realize that if everyone stole, whenever and whatever he pleased, there would be no such thing as property and hence the purposes of stealing would be made impossible. This, at any rate, is what is implied by his reference to "the absence of property." Yet he seems utterly confused as to why it would therefore be wrong to steal. Kant never says that "the absence of property contains in itself" a contradiction. He never says, in other words, that the existence of property is a logical necessity. Nor does he say that "it is a contradiction to commit theft or murder," or anything remotely resembling this. Kant's point (and this holds even though he does not actually use this example) is a relatively simple one, which is perhaps why the profundities of Hegel are so far from the mark. It could not be willed to be a universal law that everyone could steal whenever he wished to, for if everyone stole whenever he wished to, or took for his own anything he happened to want, there would be no property and hence nothing to steal—there would be nothing he could call his own. Stealing presupposes that there is such a thing as property—something to be stolen—and this presupposes some measure of stability in society. Someone who wishes to steal something presumably wishes to keep it as his property; but if everyone were to act in this way no one would be able to keep anything as his property, and hence there would in effect be no such thing as property. Not only would the purposes of one's act be defeated if everyone were to do the same, but not everyone *could* act in the way in question. To put it another way, if everyone were to act in this way, no one would be able to. (Just as, if everyone had a right to everything, no one would have a right to anything.) Hence not everyone has the right to act in this way. But since not everyone has the right to steal, *no one* has the right to steal, and stealing is therefore wrong. Now this last step of the argument is governed by the generalization principle: what is right for one person must be right for every similar person in similar circumstances. The conclusion "no one has the right to steal" must accordingly be understood as elliptical for "no one has the right to steal without a reason or justification." If Kant went wrong anywhere it was in overlooking this qualification. For if the circumstances or purposes of the act are such that everyone could steal in those circumstances or for those purposes, then this criterion is inapplicable (though another one may still be applicable).

To take another example, one who refuses to pay his taxes "could not will it to be a universal law that everyone do so." For if everyone refused to pay taxes the very ends one would hope to achieve by not paying his would be made incapable of achievement. One's purpose in refusing to pay taxes, presumably, is to have more money for one's own use or one's own purposes. This therefore must be thought of as part of one's maxim and hence of one's action. Now, if no one paid taxes, the government would collapse, along with all the services it provides, the monetary system would break down, and the money one would have saved would be of no use. Indeed, it would no longer be money, but only so many worthless coins or pieces of paper. The ends one hopes to achieve by not paying his taxes depend on a system of law and order (including a complex credit system) that would be destroyed if everyone did the same. Thus by refusing to pay his taxes he is taking advantage of others. He is claiming a privilege for himself he would not be willing to grant to them, since his very livelihood depends on others not doing the same. This is, indeed, the reason why his act is wrong.

There are two qualifications to be attached to this argument, and they might as well be made now as left for later. First of all, the example of refusing to pay taxes might seem unrealistic, since, as everyone knows, there is a law against it, and, in this country at least, the law is fairly effectively enforced. So, quite apart from the question of its morality, which no realistic person bothers with anyway, it is quite likely to prove imprudent. One runs a good chance of getting into trouble, and this is the reason why he ought to pay taxes. "He'd better, or else." This is substantially true (ignoring the reference to *"the* reason"). But only substantially, since it tends to exaggerate the imprudence of cheating the government. Many people, and very many corporations, evade taxes with impunity. The risks vary from time to time, from country to country, and with one's individual situation. All this, however, is really irrelevant, since I have chosen to abstract from the fact that one is legally required to pay taxes, and consequently also from the fact that the mere existence of such a law is morally relevant, in view of the rule that it is generally wrong—and not just imprudent— to break the law. The question here is whether it is morally wrong to refuse to pay or evade the payment of taxes—quite apart from the question whether it is advisable—and on what grounds. So the example is not really as unrealistic as might be supposed. We need not imagine someone announcing his refusal to pay taxes, and thus challenging the government to come and get him. And one might have a question about the morality of the law itself, under which *he* is required to pay taxes. Secondly, one who refuses to pay taxes is not *necessarily* guilty of cheating. One's purpose need not be to have more money for his own use. One may refuse on principle—because he regards some particular tax as wrong, or because he regards it as wrong to support the government that exacts it. Such a person could, and usually would, be quite willing to have everyone else do the same.

This would not defeat his purposes in refusing, but would bring about the very result he wishes to achieve, though it might also bring about some others that he had not wished for. Thoreau is an example of one who refused to pay a certain tax because he disapproved of the actions of the government (the war with Mexico), and hoped that enough other people would do the same to force the government to revise its actions. But this point does not conflict with anything that has been said. What the argument in question establishes is that one has to justify a refusal to pay taxes, and not that it is always and everywhere wrong. To claim that one refuses as a matter of principle is to claim that one is justified (morally, of course, and not legally). This has at least the form of a justification. Whether the claim can be made out is something else again. The same point applies to all the rules than can be established by the application of the principle of universality.

Consider, as another example, one that was actually used by Kant (and which I discussed in the previous chapter), that of the lying promise. To make a false or lying promise is to make a promise without the intention of keeping it. Hence to make a true or honest promise is to make a promise *with* the intention of keeping it. This distinction, notice, is quite distinct from the question whether a promise is actually *kept* or not. It is, therefore, part of the meaning of "a promise" that one who promises to do something intends to do what he has promised to do. This is what one conveys, or attempts to convey, by saying "I promise" or engaging in any of the other behavior by which promises are made. Thus it is essential to the nature of a promise (as I said before) that one who promises to do something can generally be presumed to intend to do it. This is a built-in and essential feature of the practice or institution of promising. Now this does not mean that it is impossible to make a promise without the intention of keeping it, or that in such a case one would not actually have promised. (What one asserts that is false, when one makes a lying promise, is not that one has made a promise—for one has, whether one intends to keep it or not—but that one intends to do what one has promised to do.) Nor does it mean that every promise must be presumed to be made honestly; I am not supposing that we are all such fools as that. What it means is that this is a presumption that ordinarily or usually operates, in the absence of special knowledge to the contrary, without which promising would be something other than it is and would not be a human practice. If the opposite presumption prevailed, how could one then convey his intentions, and how could one then make a promise? Just as it would be impossible for every circumstance to be exceptional, even though this or that circumstance can be exceptional (and just as it would be impossible for every statement to be meaningless, even though this or that statement can be meaningless), it would be impossible for every promise to be made without the intention of keeping it. Without this general presumption that promises are made honestly, if we could not ordinarily assume that a promise that was made to us was made with the intention of keeping it, "there could properly be no promises at all." Hence it could not be willed to be a universal law that everyone "may make any promise he pleases with the intention not to keep it," in Kant's words, for such a law "would make promising, and the very purpose of promising, itself impossible."

These very same reasons apply, not just to promises, but to other forms of agreements between human beings, such as contracts, covenants, and treaties. And a closely parallel argument applies to the *keeping* of promises and agreements. As it is essential to the nature of a promise that it can generally be presumed that a promise is made honestly, it is just as essential that it can generally be presumed that a promise will be kept. If everyone were to break "any promise he pleases"—if everyone broke his promises whenever he felt like it or whenever it seemed inconvenient to keep them—then promises would usually be broken, and this "would make promising, and the very purpose of promising, itself impossible." Thus it could not be willed to be a universal law that everyone may break a promise any time he pleases, and one who wishes to do so could not be willing to have everyone else do the same. If everyone else did the same it would be impossible to make any promises at all (including the one that one now wishes to break), for a promise is a transaction involving at least two parties; and one could not be willing to have other people break their promises to him, which is what would happen if no one had any scruples about breaking promises.

Another way of looking at the matter is this. One who breaks, or wishes to break, any promise he pleases does not regard promises as binding, at least on him. But if promises are not binding on him, then they are binding on no one, and this is self-contradictory. Similarly, if everyone were to break any promise he pleases, then no one would regard promises as binding. Is this possible? Then what could be meant by a promise?

We come now, as our last example, to the use of language in general. A lying promise, indeed, is just a special case of lying, which is asserting as true what one knows or believes to be false with the intention of deceiving, and Kant, in fact, did not distinguish the two. They are not identical, however, since one can lie without promising (unless one regards using language as committing one to the implicit promise not to lie), and promising has features not found in all uses of language. In one respect they are identical: it is essential to the use of language as an instrument of communication that most assertions be made honestly, without the intention of deceiving. For otherwise we could not presume that people normally speak the truth, and would not believe anything that anyone said, or anything that we read, without undertaking a special investigation to determine the truth of it. But there is no point in repeating here the argument against lying that was given previously (in Chapter V). What I shall do instead is consider an objection to it, which may help to bring out more clearly what this argument involves.

If for the rule, "Speak the truth," we could substitute the rule, "Tell Lies," it is quite true that neither language itself nor the simplest of existing social institutions could have been developed. To invert the rule of truth would imply such a change as would necessitate a modification of some of the apparently most essential attributes of humanity. Yet even in this case the rule, "Deceive," is not in a formal sense more contradictory than the rule, "Do not deceive," and perhaps it would be possible to imagine conditions under which mutual deception might be profitable to a race. Undoubtedly such a race would have to do without language, and without many other things which are essential to society as we know it. The state of truthfulness is as essential to society as you please, but it is illegitimate to confound this doubtless important statement with the statement that the opposite rule is logically impossible. Universal lying is not self-contradictory; it is only impossible within the whole range of our knowledge.[4]

There is a point here, but there is also some serious confusion. The arguments already given are sufficient to show, I think, that it would be impossible for lying to become the rule and truth telling the exception, since this would break down the use of language (or any system of communication), without which it would be impossible to lie. Lying, therefore, must remain exceptional (note that this does not mean infrequent), if it is to exist at all. It is true that the rule "Tell lies" is not a *formal* self-contradiction. But what does it matter? It is impossible for everyone to act on it, for everyone to lie as a regular rule, and this is enough. What is odd is that the passage under review seems to admit this, with its admission that "such a race would have to do without language." But, given this, then how is it "possible to imagine conditions under which mutual deception might be profitable" to it? For without the use of language how would it be possible for these people to deceive each other? Of course conditions might be imagined under which deception—even mutual deception— might be profitable or necessary for survival (though it would be good to have these conditions stated), but it would still not be possible if it were the regular practice, from which no one was immune. Language is thus not just a useful social in-

[4] Leslie Stephen, *The Science of Ethics* (London: Smith, Elder, & Co., 1882), chap. V, sec. 32, pp. 206-7.

stitution, it is a necessary one. Without it there could be no other social institutions at all. To be sure, the reason why lying is wrong is *not simply* that it could not become universally adopted and regularly practiced; it is wrong because, given this fact, the purposes of lying would be frustrated by everyone doing the same, so that one who wants to lie could not will the maxim of his action to become a universal law. (But note that this may depend on just what the maxim is.) This, again, does not mean that lying is always wrong. It means that it is usually wrong. (For it is possible for one's maxim to be such that it *could* be willed to be a universal law.) But this is sufficient to establish the rule against lying, which requires that any lie must be justified, and not that every lie must be wrong. What more is needed?

With this I conclude, for the present, my discussion of what I have called Kant's "narrower criterion" for determining whether the maxim of an action can be universalized. It is not necessary to assume that all of Kant's applications of this criterion are sound. Certainly some of them are not— perhaps the outstanding example is his argument against suicide, but there are others. Nor does it make any difference whether the impossibility of everyone acting in a certain way is or is not a *logical* impossibility, determined solely *a priori*, with no reference to empirical facts. It is sufficient for it to be impossible in some weaker sense.[5] For if, as a consequence of everyone's trying to act in a certain way, no one would be able to, then no one has the right to act in that

[5] Could Kant admit this? Why not? It is perfectly consistent with his practice, with what he actually says in the examples in which his principle is applied (whether or not it is consistent with his professed intentions). He says, in his example of the lying promise: "it would be futile to profess a will for future action to others who would not believe my profession or who, if they did so over-hastily, would pay me back in like coin"; and again, "no one would believe he was being promised anything, but would laugh at utterances of this kind as empty shams." It is clear that when Kant says that this maxim could not become a universal law, this is the evidence to which he appeals. It therefore must be taken as evidence of what he meant. But for purposes of understanding the categorical imperative as a moral principle it does not really matter whether or not Kant could or would admit this, and it would be good if this came to be understood.

way, without a special reason. As long as this criterion applies,
the nature of the disability involved is immaterial.

§ 3 §

But, as Kant points out, this criterion is not applicable to all
cases. It is to these further cases that the more inclusive criterion, that of the impossibility of *willing* that everyone act in
a certain way, without it being impossible for everyone to *act*
in that way, is intended to apply. Now this criterion *as Kant
applies it* is complicated by his view that there are certain
essential ends of humanity, or certain essential (or necessary) ends or purposes of nature. On Kant's view, there are
certain ends that every rational person, in virtue of his rationality, would necessarily "will," certain purposes that every
rational being necessarily has. It is this view that governs his
applications of this criterion, at least in some cases. For example, Kant says of the person who does not wish to cultivate
his talents that "he cannot possibly *will* that this should become a universal law of nature or should be implanted in us
as such a law by a natural instinct. For as a rational being he
necessarily wills that all his powers should be developed, since
they serve him, and are given him, for all sorts of possible
ends." [6]

This idea is no doubt extremely puzzling, and even somewhat mysterious. It is perhaps fortunate, therefore, that
for present purposes it is not necessary to examine it. For
Kant's criterion of "the impossibility of willing" can be eluci-
dated apart from this notion of essential or rational ends. Indeed, I do not think it can be properly understood, and certainly not usefully applied, unless it is taken apart from this
idea of "what a rational being would necessarily will."

Thus in order to understand what is involved in this criterion it is not necessary to agree that there are certain essential purposes of humanity, or that "a rational being would
necessarily will that all his powers should be developed." It is

[6] *Grundlegung*, Paton 55-6, Abbott 49.

not necessary to agree, for example, that "there are in humanity capacities for greater perfection which form part of *nature's purpose* for humanity in our own person." [7] This simply obscures what is important in this criterion, and what should be clear is that this criterion does involve a reference, albeit an oblique one, to the undesirability of the consequences of everyone's acting in a certain way. Kant's notion of essential purposes is then simply a particular and not very plausible view of the proper standard for determining these consequences to be undesirable. When Kant says that it is impossible to will that a certain maxim should become a universal law, he *at least* means that the consequences of everyone's acting on that maxim would be undesirable. He may— and certainly does—mean more than just this, but he cannot mean less.

What more than this Kant means is, perhaps, not really so mysterious as it may seem. H. J. Paton has suggested that what Kant has in mind here is a standard of "a systematic harmony of purposes." As Paton has stated it:

> If we wish to test the maxim of a proposed action we must ask whether, if universally adopted, it would further a systematic harmony of purposes in the individual and the human race. Only if it would do this can we say that it is fit to be willed as a universal moral law. . . .
>
> When we ask whether we can *will* a proposed maxim as if it were to become thereby a law of nature, we are asking whether a will which aimed at a systematic harmony of pur-

[7] *Ibid.*, Paton 69, Abbott 59 (italics added). This is said, incidentally, in reference to the same example, that of the duty of developing one's talents, only in connection with the application to it of the principle of personality. Kant holds, by the way, that "the natural end which all men seek is their own happiness." (Cf. *Lectures on Ethics*, pp. 4, 17.) But his view that there are certain "essential" or "rational" ends is at the root of the equivocation noted previously in his principle of personality. Cf. Paton, *The Moral Law*, p. 141, 69 n. 1: "The *purpose* (or *end*) of *nature* for humanity is to be sharply distinguished from the natural *purpose* (or *end*) which all men seek," which is their own happiness. "The first conception supposes nature to have a final end or aim which is not to be found in nature itself. The second rests on observation of nature and can be confirmed by such observation."

poses in human nature could consistently will this particular maxim as a law of human nature. . . .[8]

This is a possible, and even plausible, interpretation; and even though Kant never actually says that this is what he has in mind, it is supported by some things that he does say. For example: "Whereas in other cases a universal law of nature makes everything harmonious; here, on the contrary, if we attribute to the maxim the universality of a law, the extreme opposite of harmony will follow, the greatest opposition, and the complete destruction of the maxim itself, and its purpose." [9] There is, furthermore, an interesting passage in the *Lectures on Ethics* that brings out this idea even more clearly:

> If the will is subordinated to the dictates of ends universally valid, it will be in harmony with all human purposes, and herein is to be found its inherent goodness . . . Moral goodness consists . . . in the submission of our will to rules whereby all our voluntary actions are brought into a harmony which is universally valid. Such a rule, which forms the first principle of the possibility of the harmony of all free wills, is the moral rule. . . . Our actions must be regulated if they are to harmonize, and their regulation is effected by the moral law. A pragmatic rule cannot do this. Pragmatic rules may make our actions consistent with our own will, but they will not bring them into harmony with the wills of others. . . .[1]

[8] Paton, *The Moral Law*, p. 31; *The Categorical Imperative*, p. 151.

[9] *Practical Reason*, 137-8. This idea of a systematic harmony would seem to be involved in Kant's concept (which is, he says, "admittedly only an Ideal") of "a kingdom of ends": "I understand by a 'kingdom' a systematic union of different rational beings under common laws. Now since laws determine ends as regards their universal validity, we shall be able—if we abstract from the personal differences between rational beings, and also from all the content of their private ends—to conceive a whole of all ends in systematic conjunction (a whole both of rational beings as ends in themselves and also of the personal ends which each may set before himself); that is, we shall be able to conceive a kingdom of ends which is possible in accordance with the above principles" (*Grundlegung*, Paton 74, Abbott 62). Kant says, incidentally (Paton 84, Abbott 69), that "a kingdom of ends would actually come into existence through maxims which the categorical imperative prescribes as a rule for all rational beings, *if these maxims were universally followed*."

[1] *Lectures on Ethics*, p. 17. Kant adds: 'We must have rules to give our

This in itself is sufficient to show the absurdity of the view that Kant regards, and must regard, the consequences of an action as completely irrelevant to the question whether it is right or wrong. For it is clear that he holds that whether an act is right depends on "what would happen" if everyone acted in that way, and this is an appeal to consequences. If any more instances are wanted, the following examples of the application of the categorical imperative, in which no reference is made to "the impossibility of willing" (or even to maxims), should suffice.

> It is inhuman to hate and persecute one from whom we have reaped a benefit, and if such conduct were the rule, it would cause untold harm. Men would then be afraid to do good to anyone lest they should receive evil in return for their good. . . .
> If one country breaks the peace this does not justify the other in doing likewise in revenge, for if it did no peace would ever be secure. . . . If a man spreads false news, though he does no harm to anyone in particular, he offends against mankind, because if such a practice were universal, man's desire for knowledge would be frustrated.[2]

These arguments clearly presuppose, where they do not assert, that the consequences of such conduct becoming the rule would be disastrous or undesirable.

It would be a mistake, however, to infer from this that there is really no essential difference between the categorical

---

actions universal validity and to mould them into a general harmony. These rules are derived from the universal ends of mankind, and they are the moral rules."

[2] *Ibid.*, pp. 219, 227. Cf. pp. 203, 215. The idea that Kant does not, or has no right to, consider the consequences of an action as in any way relevant to moral judgment, undoubtedly stems from his well-known insistence that ethics must be *a priori*, not empirical. But though this insistence is well known, it is by no means as well understood. For in saying this Kant was distinguishing what he regarded as the supreme principle of morality, which is what he held must be established *a priori*, and not by reference to its consequences, from the *applications* of the principle. In the application of the principle Kant regarded empirical considerations, and therefore the consideration of consequences, as not only relevant but necessary. (Cf. *Grundlegung*, Paton vii, 32 note, and 35; Abbott 6, 33 note, and 35.)

imperative and the generalization argument. The major trouble with this interpretation is that it does not bring out what is really important and distinctive about the principle of universality and this criterion of "being able to will." For this criterion does not merely involve an appeal to the undesirability of the consequences of everyone's acting in a certain way. It also provides a method for determining when one *must regard* the consequences of everyone's acting in a certain way as undesirable, when it would be unreasonable or illogical not to, and this is what is really important and distinctive about it. I propose therefore to consider the matter anew, apart from Kant's idea of "nature's purposes for humanity" or of what "a rational being would necessarily will," and even apart from this idea, or ideal, of "a systematic harmony of purposes."

§ 4 §

What could be meant by saying that "we must *be able to will* that a maxim of our action should become a universal law"? The phrase is difficult, because it is unfamiliar, and Kant never really says just what he means by it. But it is not beyond elucidation. One thing that Kant means, for example, in saying that "we must be able to will," is that we must be able to will *without self-contradiction*. This is quite clear from his statement that "it is impossible to will . . . because such a will would contradict itself."

This, however, though it tells us something, does not really tell us very much. We have still to determine what it is *to will* something, and, in particular, what it is *to will that* a maxim become a universal law.[3] One plausible suggestion is that we think of this in connection with *being willing*. Thus the question "Can you will that your maxim should become a

---

[3] Kant says that "The will is conceived as a power of determining oneself to action *in accordance with the idea of certain laws*" (*Grundlegung*, Paton 6, Abbott 55). "To will a certain action," then, is to determine oneself to act in a certain way (on some maxim or other). But what is it to will *that*, or to will *that* a maxim become (or should become) a universal law?

universal law?" can be interpreted to mean "Would you be willing to have everyone adopt your maxim?" or "Could you be willing, without inconsistency, to have everyone act in the way you propose to act?" Again, "Do you really think that everyone, in your circumstances, should be permitted to act in that way?" That such interpretations are not really foreign to Kant's meaning is indicated by such passages as the following: "*Should I really be content* that my maxim (the maxim of getting out of a difficulty by a false promise) should hold as a universal law . . . ? And *could I really say to myself that everyone may* make a false promise if he finds himself in a difficulty from which he can extricate himself in no other way?" [4]

But this, perhaps, gives us only equivalent phrases, and not an explanation. So let us consider, instead, some examples in which there is clearly "a contradiction in the will," no matter how one would choose to describe it.

My first example may be thought somewhat odd, and I do not intend it as a serious possibility. I use it simply because it brings out the point so nicely. Is it possible for there to be someone of such a lascivious mind as to be able to will that everyone, including himself (or herself), be raped? It should be clear that it is not. For notice that being raped involves being subjected to violence involuntarily—that is, *against one's own will*—and if the individual we are imagining were willing to have this happen to everyone, including himself, then, by hypothesis, it would not be against his own will, and would not be *rape*. One may be willing to have someone else subject one to his lewd purposes. But it does not follow that one can will that everyone be raped. All that follows is that one can will that *everyone, who is similarly not un-*

---

[4] *Ibid.*, Paton 19, Abbott 23 (italics added). What Paton calls "the formula of the law of nature": "Act as if the maxim of your action were to become through your will a universal law of nature," which is Kant's alternative way of stating the principle of universality, may be relevant here. Thus what Kant is saying can perhaps be put this way: "Suppose that, as a consequence of your acting in this way in these circumstances, (it would become a regular law that) everyone would always act in the same way in the same circumstances; would you then want or be willing to act in this way?" But I mention this merely as a possibility.

willing, be treated in this way, and this is surely not to will rape as a universal law.

The difficulty with this example, of course, is that the contradiction appears in the particular case, apart from universalization. For since it is impossible for anyone to will that he himself (or she herself) be raped, universalization here is just redundant. In order to avoid this difficulty, therefore, let us modify the example just a little. Let us imagine, instead of someone who wishes "to be raped," someone who wishes to rape. For this, unfortunately, we do not need such vivid imaginations. Could such a person be willing to have everyone act in this way? Since no one can rape himself, everyone, or everyone who rapes, would have to rape someone else. But if everyone were to rape someone else (that is, someone not himself) the consequence would be that everyone would be raped. I do not mean that this is an absolutely necessary consequence; it is sufficient that it is not impossible. Now this is no doubt a possible state of affairs, though it is hardly a desirable one. For the reasons just given, however, it is impossible for anyone to will that it take place. No one, therefore, could be willing for everyone to rape whomever he pleases, for no one could be willing to be raped himself. This, incidentally, is the reason why such a state of affairs would not be desirable. It would not be *desirable* because it *could not be desired*.

The principle involved in the foregoing examples can quite readily be generalized: it is impossible for anyone to be willing to be treated in a way in which he is unwilling to be treated, or to be willing to do anything that he is unwilling to do. Thus no one could be willing to be *forced* to do something, that is, to do something against his will. This is sufficient to show the immorality of such things as sadism and human exploitation, and such institutions as slavery. One who wishes to force another to do something against his own will could not be willing to have everyone do the same, for he could not be willing to be forced to do something against *his* own will, and this is what this would almost certainly involve. Rape, indeed, is just a special case of this general rule.

And it will not do to say that one can will that "everyone except me" be treated in this way, for not only is this not to will this mode of treatment as a universal law, but it contradicts the generalization principle. Everyone else can say the same. Thus what has to be shown is how one is an exception, and one is not shown to be an exception by the fact that he does not wish to be so treated. Forcing another to do something against his will is wrong, therefore (except in special circumstances), because one who wishes to act in this way would not be willing to have others do so as well (and, in particular, could not be willing to have anyone do so to him), and is thus claiming for himself a privilege that he would not be willing to grant to others. But if it is right for him then it must be right for every similar person in similar circumstances —hence if it is not right for everyone it is not right for anyone, without a special reason.

What has been said in connection with these examples is sufficient, I think, not only to bring out what is involved in speaking of a "contradiction in the will," or in saying that it is impossible to will that a certain maxim become a universal law, but also to make clear the relevance of this notion to moral judgment. It will therefore be useful in connection with an example actually used by Kant, which has been the subject of much controversy and considerable misunderstanding. The example I refer to is the one about the man who "is himself flourishing," yet refuses to do anything to help others in need of help. "Now admittedly," says Kant,

> if such an attitude were a universal law of nature, mankind could get on perfectly well—better no doubt than if everybody prates about sympathy and good will, and even takes pains, on occasion, to practice them, but on the other hand cheats where he can, traffics in human rights, or violates them in other ways. But although it is possible that a universal law of nature could subsist in harmony with this maxim, yet it is impossible to *will* that such a principle should hold everywhere as a law of nature. For a will which decided in this way would be at variance with itself, since many a situation might arise in which the man needed love and sympathy from

others, and in which, by such a law of nature sprung from his own will, he would rob himself of all hope of the help he wants for himself.[5]

Now it has been objected to this argument that no "contradiction in the will" has actually been made out, that it involves an illicit appeal to self-interest, and thus only shows that it would be imprudent to refuse to help others, and that it involves an appeal to empirical knowledge about human beings which, on Kant's view, should be inadmissible. These objections, however, where they are not altogether wrong, are simply irrelevant.

It must be admitted that Kant's statement of the argument is not very careful, and this is particularly so in the case of the maxim involved, which is not definitely stated at all. Yet it is not difficult to determine that what we are presented with is the case of a person who, because he is not in need of help himself ("is himself flourishing"), refuses to help others who are. ("What does it matter to me?" he says.) His reason for so deciding, it is clear, is to avoid the inconvenience and possible sacrifices that helping others would involve; and given that he is not in need of help himself, he sees nothing to be gained from helping them that would compensate for this inevitable inconvenience. Note that this implies that he would put himself out for the sake of a reward or payment, or in return for something that he wishes to have; but we are supposing that this is not in question here. Now the maxim involved here may be stated in at least two alternative ways: it may be (a) "Never to help anyone who is in need of help"; or it may be (b) "Whenever I am not in need of help myself I will refuse to help anyone who is." But it does not matter which of these maxims we suppose to be operative, for in the context they come to the same thing, the second merely containing explicitly a condition presupposed by the first. (We could, if we wished, go on to state the maxim in an even more complicated fashion: "Whenever I am not in need of help myself I will refuse to help anyone who is, unless I am

[5] *Ibid.*, Paton 56, Abbott 50.

promised something that I wish to have in return for my services." But this is not necessary.) In neither case can the maxim be willed to be a universal law. The first maxim when universalized would read: "No one need ever help anyone who is in need of help"; the second: "Everyone who is not himself in need of help may refuse to help anyone who is." Now it has been pointed out that "If a man shows kindness only on condition that others are kind to him, his maxim of kindness is such that, if it were made into a law, it would remove the possibility of kindness altogether. For if every one makes his kindness depend on another's being kind to him, it is obvious that there is no possibility of anyone being kind at all." [6] A precisely analogous, though not identical, point is applicable here.

Supposing that I wish to adopt this maxim, as I very well might, I could still not will it to become a universal law, for even though I am not now (let us suppose) in need of help of any sort, it is possible that a situation will arise in which I am. I certainly have no control over this. But if I should ever be in a situation in which I do need help (and the fact that I am not now is irrelevant), I would have willed, in the second case, that *everyone who is not in such a situation* need not help me—and in the first case, that no one at all need help me. Now I could not be willing not to be

---

[6] Julius Ebbinghaus, "Interpretation and Misinterpretation of the Categorical Imperative," *The Philosophical Quarterly*, vol. IV (April 1954), p. 105. The following passage from this essay will be of some use here: "Equally astray is the contention that if we feel ourselves immune from need, we can perfectly well will *the maxim of indifference* as a law. This maxim *as a law* would run as follows—Every one who feels himself immune from need may be deaf to the need of others. It is manifest that however immune from need we may imagine ourselves to be, we *cannot* will this law. The reason is that the universalized maxim of the hardhearted, let him turn and twist as he will . . . does not hold subject to the condition on which he agreed to . . . it, namely, that *he* should be immune from need. *Everybody* is authorized by the maxim to refuse help so far as he himself is immune from need—without regard to the position of the man to whom help is refused. Consequently a will which wills the maxim of hard-heartedness as a law necessarily contains in itself a will to be abandoned in the not absolutely impossible case of the agent's own need, and therefore it is a will in conflict with itself."

helped if I should ever be in a situation in which I do need help, and, to repeat, that I am not now in such a situation makes no difference.

The reasoning here, notice, is perfectly general. The reasons why I cannot will this maxim to become a universal law— could not be willing to have everyone act on it—do not apply especially to me, and therefore show that no one, certainly no one who wishes to adopt this maxim, could be willing to have this maxim universally adopted. It is true that some people do not need help as often as others, that there are some people who would prefer not to be helped in situations where others immediately or eventually call for it, and that some people are more self-sufficient than others. But all this is irrelevant, just as it is irrelevant that different people in different situations need help of different kinds. No one, no matter how wealthy, strong, or self-sufficient, can so order and determine things as never to be in need of help of any kind or degree. Hence no one, no matter how wealthy, strong, or self-sufficient, could be willing for others to ignore his need *when he is* in need of help. It follows, then, that it is wrong, generally, to refuse help to others who are in need of it, when one is in a position to give it; and that it is always wrong to refuse or fail to help another merely because one is not in need of help oneself. The fact that one does not need help oneself, in other words, is not a justification.

The rule just stated, of course, does nothing to determine just what sort of help, or how much, must be given, or just when it should be given or what form it should take. All this will depend upon the situation, and the variations are too numerous to be conclusively codified. Hence the rule is relatively indefinite (as Kant would put it, this duty is only inde-terminate). But there is no warrant for restricting the rule to any one kind of help, for supposing, say, that it applies only to financial help. It most emphatically does not. Indeed, I should say that the occasions on which it requires financial help are relatively rare. I would not be justified in refusing financial help to one who needs it on the ground that I do not, any more than he would be justified in refusing to save me from drowning on the ground that he is not about to drown. No one can legitimately maintain that the rule applies only to those kinds of help that he needs (or might possibly need) himself, and that since he does not need help of a certain kind he is under no obligation to give it to anyone who does. For everyone can argue in the same way, and hence the argument can be reiterated for any kind of help. The reason, therefore, for restricting the rule to any one kind of help —if there is any—must be something other than this. But the rule is simply that it is wrong to refuse or fail to help someone in need of help, when one is able to give it (provided that giving it would not be *too* dangerous or inconvenient), and such an act or omission always requires justification. For many purposes, no doubt, as in the decision of a concrete case, this rule as just stated is extremely indefinite. For present purposes, however, it need be no more definite than it is.

Let us turn, now, to consider some of the objections that have been made to this argument, at least to this argument as presented by Kant. Some of the most intelligent and characteristic of these have been made by Sidgwick, who says, in the first place, "that every man in need wishes for the aid of others is an empirical proposition which Kant cannot know *a priori*." [7] I regard this point as irrelevant, since there is no reason why Kant must know it *a priori*. But I also regard it as mistaken, and even confused. The catch lies in the phrase "every man in need"; and the question to be asked is: "in need of what?" The argument just given does not imply that every man in need, say, of food, or a new suit of clothes, must "wish for the aid of others." The need referred to by the argument is simply the need for help, and not a need for anything else. Thus, with respect to needs, all it involves is the proposition that everyone *in need of help* is in need of help, and this is surely harmless enough. By itself, of course, this does nothing to determine when someone is in need of help, and as we have seen all sorts of variations and individual dif-

[7] This and the two following quotations from Sidgwick are from *The Methods of Ethics* (7th ed.; London: Macmillan & Co., Ltd., 1907), p. 389.

ferences are possible here, but this is irrelevant. Must everyone in need of help "wish for the aid of others"? The answer is that he must, in so far as he is in need of help. If in order for me to achieve some end that I wish to achieve, it is necessary for me to have the aid of others, then in so far as I desire to achieve the end I desire the aid of others. To say that some-one in need of help does not wish to receive any help is to say that he wishes he were not in such a situation, and this is something else again. So is the fact that someone in need of help may be too proud to ask for it.

Sidgwick's second point is this: "We can certainly conceive a man in whom the spirit of independence and the distaste for incurring obligations would be so strong that he would choose to endure any privations rather than receive aid from others." For my part I cannot, and I doubt that anyone can. No doubt some men are more independent than others and more reluctant to receive aid than others, but this does not prove the point. Sidgwick may have been led astray here by thinking exclusively of *financial* aid and *financial* privations, but there is no reason for this restriction. I can conceive of someone who would rather starve than receive any financial assistance from anyone (or who at least would say that he would), but I cannot conceive of anyone who, when set upon by a band of gangsters, would prefer to be beaten, robbed, tortured, and killed, rather than be assisted to escape. To sup-pose this is to suppose someone who would renounce all his ends rather than be assisted in the attainment of any of them, and this is impossible. It is possible for someone to renounce some particular end in order to avoid being assisted in its attainment. But it is not possible for anyone to renounce all his ends, for to suppose that it is leads to contradiction. One of the ends of such a person, surely, and it would appear to be a paramount end, is not to be assisted by others. But suppose that in order to achieve *this end*, that is, in order to ward off the well-meant but unwanted assistance of some, it is neces-sary for him to have the help of others (even if it is only a "Cease and desist" order from a court). What would he want then? What we are being asked to imagine is someone who could say, honestly and truly, *"The only thing* I want is not to be helped by anyone else." Helped to do what? Taken strictly this is not a desire or a possible end at all, and this is shown by the fact that such a person may want and desire and need the assistance of someone else in order to achieve it.

Sidgwick's last point is: "But even granting that every one, in the actual amount of distress, must necessarily wish for the assistance of others; still a strong man, after balancing the chances of life, may easily think that he and such as he have more to gain, on the whole, by the general adoption of the egoistic maxim; benevolence being likely to bring them more trouble than profit." The difficulty here is in the reference to benevolence. The obligation to help others in need of help (to try to save someone from drowning, to bring aid to protect someone from robbers and murderers) is not a matter of benevolence. It may be that Kant thought of it in this way. That is immaterial. Benevolence—the doing of good to others —goes beyond what one can morally be required to do. This is not to say that it must be wrong, but only to say that it is not mandatory. Helping another in need of help, however, when one is in a position to do so, is mandatory. No doubt an egoist "may easily think that he and such as he have more to gain, on the whole, by the adoption of the egoistic maxim," and in this he may well be right. This is not to say that it is moral. The egoistic maxim is the maxim not to help others when one is not in need of help oneself without receiving some tangible return. One can act on this maxim; it may be, on the whole, prudent for someone to do so; yet one who does so is immoral. For no one could be willing to have it adopted by others at his expense. Thus no one could will it to be a universal law that everyone act on it. The arguments already given are sufficient to show this, and this last point of Sidgwick's raises no new doubts about it. But it is worth mentioning that these arguments are also sufficient to show how very mistaken it is to suppose that an egoist "can will that everyone be an egoist," and that Kant's principle therefore fails to rule out egoism. Leaving aside the difficulty of specifying exactly what is meant by "an egoist"; if an egoist is someone interested solely in his own advantage, and in that of others only in so far as it is conducive to his own, then an egoist is certainly the last person in the world who could will egoism to be a universal law.

This reference to egoism brings us to our final objection to this argument, the charge that it involves an illicit appeal to self-interest, so that Kant has shown only that refusing to help others is imprudent and not that it is immoral. This charge is based on a confusion. For Kant never says that the reason why I ought to help those in need of help is that if I do not they will refuse to help me when I am in need of help. He never says, in other words, that the consequence of *my* refusal to help others will be that they will refuse to help me, and that this is the reason why I ought to help them. But this is what he would have had to say in order for his argument to be even plausibly interpreted as an appeal to self-interest. Kant's appeal is to what would happen if *everyone* adopted this maxim, and not to what would happen if *I* do. There is all the difference in the world between this and merely prudential reasoning, and this is not denied, and should not be obscured, by the fact that Kant's principle involves an appeal to what one could be willing to have happen. The appeal in the moral argument is not to the imprudence of so acting, but to its unfairness.

A particularly good instance of this confusion, though it is not in reference to this example, is presented by the following passage:

> It is true that if everyone told lies habitually, no one would believe anything another had to say. It is also true that while one can will a lie, one cannot will that lying be universal. But if we should refrain from telling lies only because if universalized lying would defeat itself, that would be the same as saying, "Don't be a fool, it doesn't pay." It is this kind of reasoning which justifies Mill's criticism: "all he shows is that the consequences of their universal adoption would be such as no one would choose to incur. . . ." Does not Kant say that I ought not to lie because if everyone lied no one could deceive because no one would be believed; and

if that is why one should never tell a lie, what is the difference between saying that lying is immoral and saying that it is imprudent? [8]

But it is not at all true that "if we should refrain from telling lies only because *if universalized* lying would defeat itself, that would be the same as saying, 'Don't be a fool, it doesn't pay.'" It is true that the purposes (and even the possibility) of lying would be defeated *if everyone* were to lie; but from this it does not at all follow that a particular lie must be self-defeating or that lying "doesn't pay." It would be manifestly absurd to suppose that if one person adopts a policy of lying this will cause everyone to do so, yet it is only on such an assumption that such an inference could be made. The rhetorical question with which this passage ends requires no answer, nor even, at this stage, any analysis. The "difference between saying that lying is immoral and saying that it is imprudent" is actually determined by the principle of universality.

§ 5 §

The generalization argument states that if the consequences of everyone's acting in a certain way would be undesirable, then no one has the right to act in that way—without a reason or justification. The principle of universality, as I have been interpreting it, states that if, as a consequence of everyone's acting or trying to act in a certain way, no one would be able to, then no one has the right to act in that way—without a reason. This is in fact the essential difference between them. On the latter criterion an act is wrong, not because the consequences of everyone's acting in that way would be undesirable, but because not everyone *could* act in

[8] A. E. Teale, *Kantian Ethics* (London: Oxford University Press, 1951), pp. 106-7. Another delightfully confused account appears on pp. 154-5, where it is said that Kant "tries to show that there is a contradiction involved in borrowing money with no intention of repaying. Here he has an easy task: for no one would lend money if he knew that the borrower had no intention of repaying. But the contradiction is not, as Kant alleges, between self-love and vain promises; it is between appealing to good faith from bad faith."

that way; or, supposing that everyone could, no one would be willing to have everyone do so, because this would defeat the very purposes of doing so, and anyone who wishes to achieve these ends cannot at the same time be willing to have these ends defeated.

But this at the same time explains why any rational person must regard the consequences of everyone's acting in such a way as undesirable. It is not necessary for him to feel horror at the contemplation of them; neither is it necessary for him to have a positive desire that they not occur. All that is necessary is to realize that if everyone were to act in that way, no one would be able to, and that this would defeat *his* purpose in wanting to. Given that these are his purposes, he must regard their frustration as undesirable.

It is this notion of *the purpose* of acting in a certain way (or of adopting a certain maxim), which would be defeated if everyone were to do the same, that is really of paramount importance. Not only will it be useful in allaying any remaining doubts about the argument for the rule to help others, but it will be useful in coordinating what I have heretofore distinguished as the two criteria for determining whether or not a maxim can be universalized. It will, in addition, be of some importance in disposing of the objections still remaining to the categorical imperative as a moral principle.

> There are a number of maxims which are such that what might be termed the "natural" or "normal" purpose—though not just any purpose—of anyone's adopting them would be defeated if they were adopted by everybody. . . . If my purpose in making it a rule to make promises I cannot keep is to obtain services from others without doing anything in return, my purpose will be defeated if everyone adopts my maxim. . . . If my purpose in making it a rule not to help others in distress is to benefit from the help of others without doing anything in return, then my purpose will be defeated if everyone adopts my maxim.[9]

[9] Jonathan Harrison, "Kant's Examples of the First Formulation of the Categorical Imperative," *The Philosophical Quarterly*, vol. VII (January 1957), p. 59.

This passage seems to me incontrovertible. The facts presented in it are instances of the following criterion: If the purpose of adopting a certain maxim would be defeated as a consequence of everyone's adopting it, then it is wrong for anyone to adopt that maxim. For it is clear in the cases presented that one who proposes to adopt the maxim for the purpose stated could not will it to become a universal law (could not be willing, in other words, to have it adopted by everyone), since this would defeat his purposes in adopting it. Now given that this is the normal or natural or usual purpose of adopting such a maxim, then it is the purpose one may be presumed to have. Hence it may be presumed that no one could will it to be a universal law; and from this it follows that adopting the maxim may be presumed to be wrong.

The criterion that has just been stated, that of the impossibility of willing that a maxim should become a universal law, is what I earlier referred to as Kant's more inclusive criterion. This criterion may be applicable even though the narrower one, that of the impossibility of everyone's acting on the maxim, is not. It is clearly possible, for example, for everyone to adopt the maxim "never to help others in distress," and even to act on it, even though the consequence of everyone's adopting it will be that the purpose—the very point—of adopting it would be made impossible. Thus, to use Kant's language, this maxim, *as so stated*, can be conceived as a universal law without contradiction, but it cannot without contradiction be willed to become one.

This distinction, however, is merely a function of how fully or explicitly the maxim is stated. I pointed out earlier, in my discussion of maxims, that the notion of a maxim, like that of an action, is a fluid one, that sometimes the statement of a maxim already incorporates a purpose, and that sometimes it does not. Thus, instead of speaking of someone adopting the maxim "never to help others in distress," and then mentioning his purpose in adopting it, we can say that he adopted the maxim "never to help others in distress in order to benefit from the help of others without doing anything in return." No doubt to state a maxim in this way will often result in an excessively complicated and unrealistic statement. But it can be done. One's purpose in adopting a certain maxim is his reason for adopting it, the end he hopes to achieve by adopting it, and to specify the purpose is to specify the circumstances under which the maxim is applicable; thus all this is part of the wider policy of which the narrowly stated maxim is only a part. Now, if the maxim is stated in this more explicit way, so that it not only states how one proposes to act but also states when and why one proposes to act in that way, then Kant's narrower criterion will be applicable in every case in which the more inclusive one is. Not only will it be impossible to *will* that everyone should adopt the maxim, but it will be impossible for everyone to adopt it or successfully to act on it—if everyone were to adopt it then no one would be able to do so.

It appears, then, that these two criteria for determining whether a maxim can be universalized are not so distinct as we might at first have supposed. And it should be clear that the situation is the same if we refer, not to the maxims of actions, but to the actions themselves. This has actually already been illustrated in the examples given before of refusing to pay taxes in order to have more money for one's own use and of appropriating for one's own use and enjoyment whatever one happens to want (pp. 252-55). We could, if we want, specify maxims for these actions; but it is not necessary —the descriptions of the actions already involve a reference to a purpose. If I steal something merely because I happen to want it for my own use, then, whether I know it or not, I am acting in accordance with the rule or maxim of appropriating for my own use whatever I happen to want. This is so whether or not I consistently or regularly act on this maxim —that is, act in this way—and even if I have never done it before and will never do it again. It is so even if I never *intend* to do it again.

This is sufficient to show, I think, the importance of the purpose or intent, as well as the circumstances, of an action. It is also sufficient to show that not all actions that cannot be universalized, in the sense of being performed by everyone, are thereby wrong. For the purpose of acting in a certain way may be *achieved*, and not defeated, as a consequence of everyone's acting in that way, in which case the act would not be wrong, since there would be no reason against it. Failure to see this is the source of a number of mistaken objections to the categorical imperative, which I shall now pass in review.

§ 6 §

1. Suppose that everyone were to refuse to take a bribe. It would follow that no bribes would ever be taken, and eventually, no doubt, that none would ever be offered. Bribery as a human practice would disappear. But this would make it impossible to *refuse* to take a bribe, since none would ever be offered. Does it follow from the categorical imperative that it is wrong to refuse a bribe? It seems to me obvious that it does not. Yet it has not seemed so to everybody. According to one writer, Kant's view is that:

> Borrowing money without the intent to repay is immoral . . . because if the maxim were willed universally and thus if all borrowing were without the intent to repay, all lending and thus all borrowing would cease, and the principle that it was willed universally would be contradicted by itself. When Kant's theory is applied to the case where a man refuses to accept a bribe, the result is rather sensational. Would universal refusal prevent all offers and thus all refusals of bribery? If so, according to Kant, refusal would be wrong, for the universalization of the maxim of this act would contradict the universalization of it.

And according to another critic, Kant was forced by his principle

> to entangle himself in elaborate and sometimes intricate and even fallacious discussions in order to determine what, precisely, *is* just in a particular case. Deposits, for instance, must be restored to the owner; for if they were universally not restored, no further deposits would be made and thus the commandment "Do not restore deposits!" would destroy itself. . . . Franz Brentano used to refute this argument by a

reductio ad absurdum. In the same way, he said, we might prove that bribes, when offered, must be accepted; for should they be universally rejected, no further bribes would be offered, and thus the commandment "Do not accept bribes!" would destroy itself.[1]

The author says that he regards this "reductio ad absurdum" as "amusing." So do I, but for entirely different reasons.

If everyone refused to take a bribe then no one would be able to, since, we are assuming, bribes would, eventually, no longer be offered. Suppose this is true? What then? This would not defeat the purposes of refusing to take a bribe, as in the case of lying, or stealing, or refusing to pay taxes. One who wants to steal wants to keep the stolen goods as his property or use and enjoy them as his own; but if stealing were the rule this would be impossible, since there would be no security and no stability of ownership. This does not apply in the case of refusing to accept a bribe; on the contrary, one's purposes in refusing to accept a bribe would be completely achieved if everyone did the same. Thus one could not regard the extinction of bribery as undesirable, and thus there is no reason why one could not will the maxim of this action to become a universal law. Again, one who refuses to pay taxes does so in order to have more money for his own use. But if everyone were to refuse to pay taxes, no one would have any money at all, since the monetary system would break down. This then would defeat the purpose of refusing to pay taxes, and this also does not apply in the case of bribery.

Of course, I am supposing here something about the "maxim" of the person who refuses to accept a bribe: I am supposing that he does so on moral grounds, because he disapproves of bribery or regards it as wrong. This is absolutely essential. It is only on some such assumption as this that the consequence taken for granted in this objection can even plausibly be supposed to follow. It is only this (or some sim-

[1] Gardner Williams, *Humanistic Ethics* (New York: Philosophical Library, 1951), p. 29 note; Heinrich Gomperz, *Philosophical Studies* (Boston: Christopher Publishing House, 1953), p. 194, note 3.

ilar) maxim, in other words, the universalization of which
would lead to the extinction of bribery. It is significant that
the passages I have quoted do not mention the maxim of the
person who refuses to accept a bribe. (The first passage mentions that there is a maxim, but does not say what it is.) If
one's reason for refusing to accept a bribe is simply that it is
not high enough, then his maxim is "Never to accept a bribe
that is not high enough"—which, of course, implies that he
would accept a bribe that is—and the universalization of this
maxim would not lead to the extinction of bribery. At most it
would lead to the elimination of bribes that are not high
enough, but even this is not certain. Again, if one's reason for
refusing to accept a bribe is that it is, in the circumstances,
too risky, then his maxim is "Never to accept a bribe that is
too risky," which implies of course that he would accept a
bribe when he thinks the chances of his not being caught are
good. But the universalization of this maxim would also not
lead to the extinction of bribery. And it will not do to suppose that one's reason for refusing to accept a bribe is that he
regards *this particular* bribe as wrong, though not bribery in
general. For even supposing that this supposition makes sense,
which is only barely possible, this maxim can be universalized
without eliminating bribery. Then the situation would simply
be that everyone will refuse to accept a bribe that he happens
to regard as immoral. Thus it is easy to see that one's reason
for refusing to accept a bribe must be that he regards it as
wrong to accept a bribe, and not simply that he regards it as
wrong to accept *this* bribe; his maxim must be "I will never
accept a bribe because I regard it as immoral to do so," and
not "I will never accept a bribe that I regard as immoral."
Otherwise the consequence in question—the elimination of
bribery—would not ensue. When this maxim is universalized,
it will take the form "Everyone will refuse to accept a bribe
because he regards it as wrong to do so," and not "Everyone
who regards it as wrong to accept a bribe will refuse to do so."
Now it is perfectly obvious that this maxim can be universalized without defeating the purpose of adopting it, that it

would not be self-defeating or impossible for everyone to act on it, and that it therefore can be willed to become a universal law.

Another example somewhat analogous to the one about bribery is the following: If everyone refused to buy pork, no one would sell it, and eventually no one would be able to refuse to buy it, because there would then be no opportunity of refusing. This, however, would not be self-defeating, or disruptive of the purposes one might have in refusing to buy pork, even though it would, for a time, create hardship for those engaged in producing and selling pork. But it would not even be self-defeating in the sense of eliminating the possibility of its own occurrence. The catch is in the way the action has been described, as *refusing* to buy pork. Just as I cannot *refuse* to vote in an election in which I have no opportunity of voting, I cannot refuse to buy something I have no opportunity to buy. So naturally if no pork is sold no one would have the opportunity of *refusing* to buy it. If, instead of describing the action as one of *refusing* to buy pork, we describe it simply as one of "not buying pork," the difficulty is totally eliminated.

This shows that the argument we have been examining rests on a verbal anomaly. Suppose that instead of speaking of "refusing to accept a bribe," or of "rejecting the offer of a bribe," we describe the action simply as one of not accepting a bribe. Then instead of asking "What would happen if everyone refused to accept a bribe?" we would ask "What would happen if no one accepted a bribe?" This may eliminate all offers of bribes, and thus make it impossible to accept one (as it would make it impossible to refuse to accept one). But it would not make it impossible not to accept one; in other words, it would not make it necessary to accept a bribe. Thus it is false that "the commandment 'Do not accept bribes!' would destroy itself."

2. One of the passages quoted just before contains a reference to "deposits," and an interpretation of why, on Kant's view, it is wrong not to restore a deposit to its rightful owner. Now Kant actually does deal with such an example,

and his argument is worth reproducing, not only because
what Kant says about it is not exactly what it has been alleged
to be, but also because it is an especially noteworthy application of the categorical imperative. What Kant says is the following:

> Suppose . . . that I have made it my maxim to increase
> my fortune by every safe means. Now, I have a deposit in my
> hands, the owner of which is dead and has left no writing
> about it. This is just the case for my maxim. I desire, then, to
> know whether that maxim can also hold good as a universal
> practical law. I apply it, therefore, to the present case, and ask
> whether it could take the form of a law, and consequently
> whether I can by my maxim at the same time give such a law
> as this, that everyone may deny a deposit of which no one can
> produce a proof. I at once become aware that such a principle,
> viewed as a law, would annihilate itself, because the result
> would be that there would be no deposits.[2]

There is, it is evident, a definite error here. The result would
not be that there would be no more deposits. At most every
deposit would have a proof. Thus such a law would not make
it impossible to entrust a deposit with anyone; it would only
make it impossible to entrust a deposit without at the same

[2] *Practical Reason*, 137. Bergson gives a simply marvelous account of
what Kant says here (*The Two Sources of Morality and Religion* [New
York: Henry Holt & Co., 1935], p. 77): "When Kant tells us that a
deposit of money must be handed back because, if the recipient appro-
priated it, it would no longer be a deposit, he is obviously juggling with
words." Someone is obviously juggling with words, but it is not Kant. The
only other version of what Kant said that is, to my knowledge, at all
comparable with Bergson's is the one handed down by Hegel in *The
Phenomenology of Mind* (trans. Baillie, 2nd ed.; London: George Allen
& Unwin Ltd., 1931), pp. 452-3: "Suppose a deposit has been made over
to me on trust, it is the property of another, and I recognize it because
it is so, and remain immovable in this relation towards it. But if I keep
the deposit for myself, then, according to the principle I use in testing
laws—tautology—I undoubtedly do not commit a contradiction; for in
that case I do not regard it any longer as the property of another. To keep
anything which I do not look on as the property of some one else is perfectly consistent. . . . Just as I can—as I do, when I give something away
as a present—alter the view that something is mine into the view that it
is the property of another, without being thereby guilty of a contradiction,
so too I can proceed the other way about." Well, in Bradley's famous
phrase, "in a sense, but not as such."

time retaining a record of it that could be used as proof. But in either case it is hard to see how the universalization of this maxim would annihilate itself, or be at all self-defeating. It may be that what Kant had in mind was that one could not will this maxim to be a universal law (though he does not actually use this criterion here)—could not be willing that "everyone may deny a deposit of which no one can produce a proof," because it is possible that he might want himself some day to entrust a deposit with someone, and "by such a law of nature sprung from his own will, he would rob himself of all hope" of the opportunity he wants for himself. But this seems very farfetched: one with so few scruples about other people's money is not at all likely to entrust his own to another.

Are we to conclude here that we have with this a genuine counterexample to the categorical imperative, from which we can definitely deduce its inadequacy? For it seems unquestionably wrong to appropriate for oneself a sum of money entrusted to one simply because its rightful owner is dead and no one can prove that it is not one's own; and the categorical imperative does not appear capable of showing this. I think not. A deposit, after all, is something entrusted to the care or safe-keeping of another. The action in question, therefore, is clearly within the scope of a number of rules, all of which are clearly established by the categorical imperative. It is, in the first place, a breach of trust, and in being so is also a breach of promise, for the act of accepting a deposit (agreeing to hold on to something for somebody) necessarily involves an implicit promise to return it. But the act is also a case of stealing, for it involves appropriating for oneself something that belongs to another, and that one knows to belong to another. It is, finally, a form of lying, for it involves maintaining the deliberate untruth that the deposit in question is rightfully one's own (and may also involve the explicit denial that the object has been entrusted with one for safe-keeping). Does it make any difference that no proof is available? The only difference it makes is that in fact, or under law, one may be able to get away with it. But this is morally irrelevant.

One would not be justified in breaking a promise, for example, simply because there is no independent proof that he has made one. If one person would be justified in doing this simply for this reason, then so would everyone else. But what would happen if everyone did the same? There is no need to spell it out.

3. There is another alleged counterexample to the categorical imperative, closely analogous to the one about bribery, which is interesting enough, and complicated enough, to be worth considering. One writer on the subject maintains that "maxims can be cited which are incapable of being made into universal laws but which do produce what most people regard as right actions," and gives as an example

the maxim to vaccinate against communicable disease. Supposing that in the case of a given disease, the only source of the vaccine fluid was persons who already had the disease and supposing that the disease could be contracted only by communication from diseased persons, it is clear that if such vaccination were practiced universally, the disease would be stamped out and the vaccine would be no longer available. Vaccinating people against the disease would, then, no longer be possible. Nor would it any longer be necessary—a consequence which would be regarded generally as justifying the use of the vaccine. But the fact that a general application of the maxim to vaccinate would make universal vaccination an impossibility would, by a strict application of Kant's imperative, seem to show that to will this maxim is to will a contradiction. . . .[3]

[3] Lucius Garvin, A Modern Introduction to Ethics (Cambridge, Mass.: Houghton Mifflin Company, 1953), p. 420. This same example is also used by Frank Chapman Sharp, in his Ethics (New York: The Century Co., 1928), p. 317, from which Garvin appears to have derived it: "Suppose it could be shown . . . that a given kind of action would become impossible by becoming universal. What of it? This fact would not make anyone feel an obligation to refrain from it unless he wished, on one ground or another, its continued existence. Suppose, for example, that vaccine fluid could be obtained only from human beings who were suffering from smallpox. Suppose, furthermore, that vaccination were an unfailing protection against the onset of this disease. Suppose, finally, that smallpox propagated itself only through contagion, having its source in other cases of the same disease.

Though I much admire the ingenuity that went into the construction of this complex example, I cannot say the same for its accuracy, and it is perhaps needless to say that I regard the conclusion here as an error. The main difficulty here, as in the example about bribery, is that the universalization of "the maxim to vaccinate" would not defeat the purpose of adopting it, and hence there is no difficulty at all in willing this "maxim" to become a universal law—such a will would by no means "be at variance with itself." But a subsidiary difficulty, which helps to explain how the main one arises, is that we are not given any determinate maxim, and thus are not really told with any clarity what the action in question is. In some cases this may not be very important, but in this case it is. "The maxim to vaccinate against communicable disease" is not really a *maxim* at all, but a precept. Whose maxim are we to suppose that it is? Who are we to imagine as acting in accordance with it? This information is essential if we are to determine what is to be universalized, and what form it will take when it is. If we are to make any sense at all out of this example it is clear that we must suppose that what we are dealing with is not a way of *acting*, but a way of *being treated*. The action then must be, not *vaccinating*, but *being vaccinated*, and what we are to imagine, in imagining this universalized, is not "everyone vaccinating"—which can be immediately ruled out—but everyone *being vaccinated*. Now it is clear, from the (hypothetical) facts presented, that not everyone could be vaccinated against this disease, for when the disease is "stamped out . . . the vaccine would be no longer available." But an action (and certainly this is Kant's view) as well as a mode of treatment is not morally determinate apart from some determinate maxim. One's purpose in wishing to be vaccinated against a disease, presumably, is to become immune to it. Hence one's maxim here must be something like: "I will be vaccinated against this disease in

---

Under such circumstances universal vaccination would, in time, destroy the possibility of all vaccination. So far from condemning the practice on this ground, we should regard it as the most impressive consideration that could be urged in its favor." Exactly.

order to become immune to it." It ought to be obvious, even on the hypothesis presented, that this maxim can be willed to become a universal law without self-contradiction. Furthermore, even this maxim is too specifically stated. Does one want to be protected merely against *this* disease, and not against any other? This is not only irrational, it is implausible. Yet if we state the maxim of one's action in the more general way that this point requires, the example presented will lose all shred of plausibility. In the language appropriate to the generalization argument, which is perfectly appropriate here, we can say that in application to this maxim, or way of acting, *as so described*, the argument is reiterable.

4. Precisely the same difficulties affect the other examples of this nature that have from time to time been presented. Thus the author just quoted goes on to say that:

> The same situation . . . would appear to arise in connection with measures that might be proposed for ridding the world of various other evils—such as slavery, ignorance, poverty, or war. Consider, for example, the maxim, "Give half your wealth for distribution among the poor." Or the maxim, "Love your enemies." If everyone followed these maxims, there would presumably be no more poor to provide for and no more enemies to love. Success of the attempt to make these maxims universal would mark also the failure of that attempt. Hence they cannot be conceived without contradiction as universal laws of nature.[4]

It should be noted that the particular "maxims" cited here present peculiar difficulties of their own. They are presented, of course, as worthy "maxims" to follow, it being presupposed that it would be a good thing for everyone to act on them—otherwise they could not function as counterexamples. I am so far from thinking this that I do not even regard them as

[4] Garvin, *op. cit.*, pp. 420-1. Cf. Bradley, *Ethical Studies*, p. 155: " 'Succour the poor' both negates *and* presupposes (hence posits) poverty. . . . If you are to love your enemies, you must never be without them; and yet you try to get rid of them. Is that consistent? In short, every duty which presupposes something to be negated is no duty; it is an immoral rule, because self-contradictory." Again, "in a sense, but not as such." Indeed, not even in a sense.

making sense, at least without considerable elaboration. As they stand, they are not really *maxims* at all, in Kant's sense of the term, but precepts or recommendations to others; and unless we can deal with a maxim the categorical imperative is inapplicable and so is any criticism of it. In order to approximate to this, we must imagine a person who proposes to give half his wealth for distribution among the poor. But what is his reason for this—his purpose, his motive, the end he wishes to achieve? And what are the conditions under which he proposes to do this? What, in other words, is his situation? To ask questions of this sort is to ask what the maxim of the action is, and this is only to determine more particularly and precisely the nature of the action. The possible answers to this question are indefinite in number. One man may propose to give away half his wealth because he hates to pay taxes, and hopes in this way to cut down the amount he has to pay; another because he wants to spite his relatives; another for a number of reasons; and another for no sensible reason at all (or, what comes to the same thing, for purely sentimental reasons). There is no need to elaborate on this. The difficulty is to determine just what is to be universalized. For as it stands the "maxim" makes no sense, and makes even less sense if we suppose it universalized. Are we to imagine everyone giving away half his wealth for distribution to the poor? Suppose I am poor myself, and have only a dollar to my name? Am I to give half of this away for distribution to the poor? What is the sense in that? Furthermore, when is the process to stop? After I give away half my wealth, am I then to give away half of what is left, and then half of that, and so on, indefinitely? Of course, this is absurd. But if we take the "maxim" as it stands this is what its universalization would require. As Kant has said, "that one should sacrifice his own happiness, his true wants, in order to promote that of others, would be a self-contradictory maxim if made a universal law." [5] This is precisely the situation here. If *everyone* is to give away half his wealth for distribution to the poor, to whom is it to be distributed? Suppose, then, that the rule

[5] Preface to the *Metaphysical Elements of Ethics*, Abbott, p. 304.

is restricted so as to apply only to those who come up to a certain standard of wealth, while it is understood that only one such donation is required by each. As so restricted, the rule is unjust. For it requires only those who have more than a certain amount of money to give away half of it. But then it will make these people poorer than those who just fail to come up to the standard. Would this eliminate poverty? No. It would only eliminate great wealth.

Consider now the "maxim," "Love your enemies." Apart from the question whether there can be a duty to love, that is, to have a certain affection, are we to suppose that one who adopts such a rule is to restrict it to his enemies, and is thus not to love his friends and relations? This is absurd. The rule should be, not "Love your enemies," but "Love everyone, including your enemies," and (waiving the point about what "love" could possibly mean here, and thus what the rule requires) the universalization of this rule could not possibly eliminate its object—people to be "loved"—and hence would not be self-defeating.

There is no need to consider separately such other precepts as "Free the slaves," "Help the destitute," "Cure the sick," "Educate the ignorant," "Clothe the naked," "House the homeless," "Feed the hungry," and "Pull the teeth," any of which might be advanced as the basis of an objection of this type. All such objections are specious, and some are intrinsically absurd.

5. I want now to consider an objection of a somewhat different type, which will take us back to the rule against lying, and thus enable us to deal with some further questions that still require to be answered. It was maintained previously that it would be impossible for lying to become the accepted practice of society, and for truth telling to become the exception, and I all along took it for granted that this is what would happen if everyone lied whenever he pleased. But now suppose that everyone were to lie whenever he wanted to—but only whenever he wanted to. Does this mean that everyone (or nearly everyone) would lie as a regular rule? And does it follow that the possibility and thus the purposes of lying would

then be destroyed? This is disputed in the following subtle and ingenious argument:

> Does our formula mean quite literally "everyone," or rather "Everyone that wishes to"? Apparently the former. . . . Take, for example, the case of lying. If, every time everyone used his vocal organs, he lied, no one would pay any attention to what anyone else said. Speech, and with it untruthful speech, would disappear. But, as a matter of fact, in most of our ordinary conversation we have no motives whatever for lying. Accordingly, if men lied only when they wanted to deceive, this would not happen often enough to render all communication impossible; it would merely result in very serious harm. If the Kantian formula, therefore, is to supply us with the ground for condemning unveracity, it must take the term *everyone* seriously and interpret its imperative to mean: That action is wrong which would be self-destructive if performed by everyone every time he had an opportunity and whether he had any desire to perform it or not.[6]

Consider, in the first place, the assertion that "in most of our ordinary conversation we have no motives whatever for lying." This is, of course, a question of fact, but since it has been raised it is necessary to deal with it. Is this true? I do not think that it is. What is true is that in most of our ordinary conversation we usually do not lie; and this holds for all of us except for those habitual or incorrigible liars who are almost always found out. But this does not mean that we ordinarily have no motives for lying. I should say that we ordinarily have a great many different motives or reasons for lying, that these temptations or incentives arise all the time, and that no one is wholly free of them. What it means is that these motives usually do not prevail—they are in fact usually outweighed by one or more of a number of countervailing motives, such as the desire not to be caught in a lie (egoistic motive), the desire to preserve one's reputation (prudential motive), the desire not to harm or deceive someone else (benevolent motive), the belief that lying is wrong

6 Sharp, *op. cit.*, p. 316.

(moral motive). Since all of these motives and more are usually present, our motive for lying is usually outweighed, and the average person lies relatively infrequently.

Now in raising the question "What would happen if everyone lied whenever he wanted to?" I am not thinking of "wanting to lie" solely in terms of lying for its own sake, or of a direct desire to lie, though I am including this case. I am also including those cases where someone might feel that he did not really *want* to lie, in the sense that he would have preferred not to, but lied simply to attain something else that he wanted to achieve. "It was the only way I could get him to agree," "It was the only way I could get him to stop asking those foolish questions," and so on. Thus what the question really amounts to is: "What would happen if everyone lied whenever he had any reason or motive or incentive whatever for lying?" Now my claim is that what would happen is that lying would become the regular rule, and that, since the ordinary scruples against lying would no longer operate, no one would believe what anyone else was saying. This would not merely result in very serious harm—although it is true that it would result in this. It would also render communication impossible and thus make lying, as well as truth telling, almost totally ineffective. This, of course, adds to the harm. But it does more than that. It also ensures that the harm would not just be restricted to others, but would affect the one who proposes to act in this way as well. This is why one could not consistently will the maxim of his action to become a universal law. One might think that it is all right for him to act in that way, but no one could think that it is all right for others. If everyone lied whenever he pleased, no one would regard the rule against lying as binding, at least on himself. But then no one could consistently regard it as binding on others, hence no one could regard it as binding. This is self-contradictory.

Consider now the assertion with which this passage ends, that the criterion involved in the categorical imperative must be that "That action is wrong which would be self-destructive if performed by everyone every time he had an opportunity and whether he had any desire to perform it or not." This is put in a very paradoxical way. Even so, as it stands it *is* sufficient to establish a general rule, to the effect that such an action is wrong, *provided that* there is some desire on the part of someone to perform it. Without this proviso there would be no purpose or desire that would be frustrated by everyone acting in that way, and thus no reason why that way of acting could not be willed to become a universal law. Indeed, the question would never arise. Yet this way of putting the matter overlooks the fact that for Kant it is always the maxim of the action that must be universalizable, and the maxim always does involve a reference of some sort to a desire to perform the action—either for its own sake or as a means to some further end or as a part of some comprehensive policy. It is sufficient for moral judgment if the purposes of adopting the maxim (or of so acting) would be defeated if everyone did the same, that is, if everyone acted in such a way for such a purpose.

6. We come now to a still different type of objection.

Any conduct can be universalized provided one does not care what happens. Kant says that lying cannot be made a law because otherwise promises would not continue to be made. But why *should* promises be made? Obviously because we presuppose that the cooperative human life, which requires for its maintenance a measure of good faith, is itself good and desirable; and this we could not do without appealing back to the natural basis of desire which Kant has thrown overboard. If we did not already think cooperation good for something, all we should need to do would be to decide to get along without it, and no bar to making lying a universal law would remain. . . . Kant's method of procedure will not work at all, then, except as the universal form of morality presupposes ends already taken as worth while.[7]

This type of criticism, which stems from Hegel, can probably never be totally eradicated, since there will probably always be someone new to rediscover it. It is none the better for this. It

[7] Arthur Kenyon Rogers, *The Theory of Ethics* (New York: The Macmillan Company, 1922), p. 67.

is true that for the categorical imperative to be applicable there must be a desire on the part of someone to act in a certain way. The reason is that otherwise there would be no occasion for a moral judgment about that way of acting, and moral judgment always requires an occasion. If no one ever had any desire to act (or not to act) in a certain way, or if there were never any need for such an act to be performed, no moral question about so acting would ever arise. Thus if no one ever desired to tell lies, break promises, or take something that belongs to another without his permission, there would be no occasion for a moral judgment of such behavior, since the question whether such conduct is right or wrong, whether anyone is ever justified in acting in such a way, would never arise. But all that this means is that the categorical imperative must always be applied to some determinate maxim of action, and unless there were some desire to act in a certain way, some purpose that such action is intended to achieve, there would be no maxim for it to be applied to, and thus no question of applying it. It does not mean that it must be antecedently presupposed that such modes of conduct are undesirable, or that the institutions of property, promising, and language are good and desirable. They may be as desirable or as necessary as you please, but that they are so is not presupposed by the application of the categorical imperative, though something like this is presupposed by the application of the generalization argument. The reason why one cannot without contradiction will it to be a universal law that everyone may break his promises whenever he pleases, is not that this would eliminate a useful and desirable practice (though it would), but that this would defeat the very purposes of promising, including those of the person who wishes to break one. One would not be able to break a promise unless one has made one. By the very fact that one has made a promise, therefore, one indicates that he regards the practice as a useful one, whether he now wishes to break a promise or not, and thus that he would regard the elimination of the practice as undesirable. For this would destroy the opportunity of making one, and make it impossible to achieve the purposes that promises are intended to achieve, some of which he himself must be presumed to have. Now one cannot rightfully claim for himself the privilege of breaking promises unless he is willing at the same time to extend it to others. But this is what one cannot do, without self-contradiction.

It is, of course, possible for there to be someone who does not care whether promises are made or not, who would never himself make one or have any desire to (or at least any desire that would not be outweighed by a contrary aversion). But I cannot see the significance of this. If there is anyone who never makes a promise, then there would be no question of his ever breaking one. The categorical imperative does not require that everyone ought to make promises.

7. Is it true, then, that "*any* conduct can be universalized provided one does not care what happens," or that one can will almost anything provided he does not care what happens? The point of such a claim, no doubt, is that:

> Much depends on what one could so will, and this in turn depends not only upon rational consistency but also upon the character of one's desires and valuations. When one's purposes become abnormal, what he could will as a universal law is no reliable criterion of right; and when they become extremely distorted, Kant's principle is of virtually no use at all.[8]

Yet such a claim is itself intrinsically absurd: one who does not care what happens could not will anything at all. Could there really be such a person—a human being who does not care about anything that happens, either to himself or to anyone else? I know that people occasionally *say* this. "I don't care what happens. I don't care about anything." But do they mean it, literally? People say this in the depths of despair, or in the heat of the moment. It is an expression of anguish, and the very fact that people say it indicates that they do care. A human being who did not care about anything at all would be one who had no wants, desires, needs, concerns, wishes,

---

[8] Thomas E. Hill, *Ethics in Theory and Practice* (New York: Thomas Y. Crowell Company, 1956), p. 69.

purposes, plans, aims, or ends, and this, I should say, is self-contradictory. Such an entity would not be a human being, and morality applies to human beings, not to flaccid seaweed. Neither does it apply to angels, or to raving or even silent lunatics.

§ 7 §

In my discussion of the categorical imperative I have concentrated mainly on those respects in which it differs from the generalization argument, and thus primarily on the notion of being able to will that a maxim of an action should become a universal law. Accordingly I have considered in this chapter only those objections and criticisms that apply peculiarly to it, and have not dealt further with those that would apply to both. Since the only important difference between them is that the application of the generalization argument presupposes that the consequences of everyone's acting in a certain way would be undesirable, whereas the application of the categorical imperative does not, it should be evident that, with this one exception, all the objections to the generalization argument are also objections to the categorical imperative, and these have already been dealt with. But it should also be evident that, with this one exception, all the conditions for the application of the generalization argument are also conditions for the application of the categorical imperative, and I have, in fact, been taking this for granted throughout this chapter. For, as should be readily observable, the relation between them is such that *if the categorical imperative is a valid moral principle then so is the generalization argument.* This relation, however, does not hold the other way around.

Some review of these conditions, as they apply to the categorical imperative, may be useful. Since both these principles involve the generalization principle, all the qualifications that attach to it are required by these other two principles. This means, in particular, that the categorical imperative is also subject to what I have called the condition of restricted universality, and that the conclusion of any application of it is, generally, rebuttable by another argument of the same form; and I have tried, on occasion, to illustrate this. Again, any application of the categorical imperative that is invertible is invalid, and so is any application that is reiterable. In connection with the categorical imperative the definitions of these conditions no doubt require some modification, but this is easy to supply. Thus, the categorical imperative is *invertible* with respect to a certain maxim (or action) if neither that maxim nor its opposite (its contrary) can be willed to be a universal law—if it cannot be willed to be a universal law that everyone do *x*, and if it also cannot be willed to be a universal law that no one do *x*. And the categorical imperative is *altogether inapplicable* with respect to *x* if it can be willed to be a universal law that everyone do *x* and also that no one do *x*. This should be sufficient to bring out what I mean, and these various conditions require no separate discussion here.

This applies equally to what I previously called the problem of competing descriptions, which is almost always brought up as an objection to the categorical imperative. In reference to the categorical imperative, of course, this objection will be framed in terms of the different ways in which one's maxim can be formulated, rather than in terms of the different ways in which one's action can be described. But the principle is the same, and so is the answer to it. All such objections ignore the fact that an application of the categorical imperative, in order to be valid, must be neither reiterable nor invertible.

There is some notion afoot that the determination of the maxim on which someone is acting is an arbitrary matter. But while it may be a difficult matter to formulate the maxim of an action, just as it may be a difficult matter to determine just what sort of action it is, it is not an arbitrary one. One cannot change the maxim on which one has acted, any more than one can change the circumstances and purpose of the action. In particular, it is not open to one to formulate the maxim of his action in such a way that it could (logically) apply only to him in just these circumstances. For everyone else can do the same, and thus the argument can be reiterated for every maxim of this same type. And in practice the type is not really very difficult to determine. It is true that there are cases in which the maxim of an action can be formulated in alternative ways, and that certain problems can arise if it is formulated in one particular way rather than another. But these are all problems of application, analogous to determining the facts of the case. I do not mean that these problems are trivial, but only that they do not affect the validity of the principle as such.

A good example of this notion comes to hand in the following passage:

> Suppose a student has borrowed $9.81 from his roommate, and is considering whether he should repay it. He finds it impossible to universalize the maxim, "When you have borrowed money, don't repay." But there are somewhat more specific maxims, which he can equally well regard as maxims of his act. He happens upon this one: "Whenever one student in a small coeducational college borrows exactly $9.81 from another student who is his roommate, and on the day of the loan the borrower is exactly —— years old (corresponding to his own age), and the creditor is exactly —— years old, and the borrower's weight is exactly —— and his height exactly ——, and if the borrower finds it very inconvenient to repay, then let him not repay the money." The student finds himself heartily in favor of universalizing this maxim. Hence, he concludes it is morally permissible to ignore the debt.[9]

The fallacy involved here has already been exposed in several places, in relation to both the generalization principle and the generalization argument, and with respect to the categorical imperative the point is the same. This conclusion is wrong, for the same argument can be reiterated for every maxim of this same type, and this would imply that it is morally permissible for anyone to ignore his debts, which is

[9] Richard B. Brandt, *Ethical Theory* (Englewood Cliffs, N.J.: Prentice-Hall, Inc., 1959), p. 34.

clearly not so. Since this application of the principle is re-iterable it is therefore invalid, and so is any application of this kind. It should be self-evident that what the kind is, is not really difficult to determine.

A related myth that needs dispelling is the idea that the categorical imperative is supposed to be applied in a moral vacuum, in complete ignorance of any moral rules or of any other ideas of what is right and what is wrong. It is true that Kant's language may tend to suggest this, and that he often talks as though there were no other relevant moral principles whatsoever. But this is simply an irrelevant extravagance. It is also true that many examples of its application are discussed as though there were no moral rules and no other moral principles on the basis of which the case could be decided. But this is done solely for illustrative purposes. I have actu-ally already shown how the categorical imperative can be used to establish and clarify moral rules, and it follows from this that there are many cases where it need not be applied directly to an action. Indeed, it need never be applied in abstraction from moral rules, unless the question be about some rule (or alleged rule) itself. Now many of the objections brought forward against it, especially those arising out of the possibility of alternative descriptions, are based on this no-tion, and can be eliminated by attention to this fact. When-ever a particular maxim is mentioned that seems clearly wrong, and which the categorical imperative does not seem capable of showing to be so, in view of the way in which the maxim is formulated, the question to be asked is: Is there any moral rule, itself derivable from the categorical impera-tive, on the basis of which the act in question may be presumed to be wrong? If not, then what reason is there for regarding it as wrong? If so, then the act in question requires justification: Are the conditions specified in the maxim mentioned sufficient to justify it? When these difficulties are looked at in this way, they will, I am certain, assume a dif-ferent aspect.

These points may be applied to the following objection:

When we have a rule that we can universalize without inconsistency in our conduct it does not follow that what it allows is right. A person subjected to blackmail might, without inconsistency in his conduct, will that it should be a universal practice that every such victim should murder his blackmailer if he can; but it would not follow that the murder of blackmailers is right. We may agree that a rule is *wrong* if it can *not* be universalized, but it does not follow that it is *right* if it *can*.[1]

This is an ingenious example, more complex than it appears, but I do not think it establishes its point. There is no reason why the "rule" here should be restricted to those subjected to blackmail. There is nothing that special about blackmail. By the same token, it could be alleged that one whose property is being trespassed upon could will it to be a universal law that every victim of trespassing murder the trespasser, if he can. Essentially the same argument can be reiterated for anyone who is subjected to danger or fear or inconvenience by another. But then the maxim in the case will be: "Whenever anyone subjects me to fear or danger or inconvenience, which I can eliminate by killing him, I will kill him." And this maxim cannot be willed to become a universal law. For it would entail the complete breakdown of law and order, and hence the perpetual presence of fear and danger and inconvenience. The fact that one is being blackmailed is not a sufficient justification for killing anyone—not even the blackmailer—provided one is not in a state of nature situation to start with. I will admit, however, that the universalization of such a maxim would be an effective way of eliminating blackmail from society. This may be a point in its favor.

I conclude, then, in the light of the various arguments presented, that the principle of universality, when properly understood, is perfectly valid. Its proper understanding, however, requires that it be taken together with the other principles elaborated in this work.

[1] A. Campbell Garnett, *Ethics: A Critical Introduction* (New York: The Ronald Press Company, 1960), p. 201.

❀

CHAPTER X

THE
BASIS OF MORALITY

What, then, have we accomplished? Have we established the basis of morality? What is the basis of morality? Does morality have a basis? Or is it merely, as it has been so often alleged, a matter of convention, tradition, taste, or opinion?

The principles set forth in this work are sufficient to provide an answer to this question, and all that remains is to elaborate it. To establish the rationality of these principles is to establish the rational basis of morality. For these rational moral principles are themselves the basis of morality—not of *any* morality, or of anything that might go by the name of morality, but of rational morality. Any morality contains elements of custom, convention, and tradition, some more and some less. Many rules are inexplicable apart from these factors. Accounting for a particular moral code is thus in many ways like accounting for a particular legal system. But a rational morality is one the basic rules and principles of which are supported by reasons. And this is what we are dealing with, not with taboos, or parochial moral prejudices.

This does something to isolate our question, but it does nothing to establish these principles themselves. Do they have any rational basis? Given that moral rules can be established by appeal to moral principles, and that both are involved in determining the morality of actions, how can moral principles themselves be established? Perhaps they themselves are matters of convention, arbitrary "decisions of principle," or ultimate presuppositions, unsupported by reasons. This is frequently asserted. "It is now pretty generally accepted by professional philosophers," says a professional philosopher,

> that ultimate ethical principles must be arbitrary. One cannot derive conclusions about what should be merely from accounts of what is the case; one cannot decide how people ought to behave merely from one's knowledge of how they do behave. To arrive at a conclusion in ethics one must have at least one ethical premiss. This premiss, if it be in turn a conclusion, must be the conclusion of an argument containing at least one ethical premiss. And so we can go back, indefinitely but not for ever. Sooner or later, we must come to at least one ethical premiss which is not deduced but baldly asserted. Here we must be a-rational; neither rational nor irrational, for here there is no room for reason even to go wrong.[1]

I do not know whether this opinion is "pretty generally accepted by professional philosophers," and do not much care. I suspect that our author may be thinking primarily of the circles he frequents. But it does not matter. This opinion, in any case, is mistaken. It is not true that "ultimate ethical principles" must be arbitrary, for none of the principles I have tried to defend are. The mistake is to suppose that a principle, to be rational, must be deduced from self-evident premises, and that if it is "not deduced" it must be "baldly asserted." The rationality of the principles defended in this work is actually shown by the arguments used to support them, and these arguments do not show them to be any the less principles or any the less "ultimate."

We shall come back to this in due course. First we must lay the groundwork. There are some other topics remaining, relating both to the generalization argument and the cat-

---

[1] Brian Medlin, "Ultimate Principles and Ethical Egoism," *The Australasian Journal of Philosophy*, vol. XXXV (August 1957), p. 111.

egorical imperative, which must be dealt with before our inquiry can be concluded. This will have the effect of bringing out more clearly what rational morality is and what it consists in.

§ 1 §

Let us consider again the distinction between prudence and morality. Up to now I have emphasized the distinction. Now I wish to bring out the relations between them.

The meaning of prudence has been well brought out by Whately: "Whatever is done wholly and solely from motives of personal expediency—from calculations of individual loss or gain—is always accounted a matter of prudence, and not of virtue."

> When any persons submit to the will of another merely because it is their interest, or because they dare not resist, we never speak of this submission as a matter of *duty*, but merely of prudence. If robbers were to seize you and carry you off as a slave, threatening you with death if you offered to resist or to escape, you might think it *advisable* to submit, if you saw that resistance would be hopeless: but you would not think yourself bound in *duty* to do so. Or again, if you were offered good wages for doing some laborious work, you might think it *expedient* to accept the offer, but you would not account it a moral duty. . . . And we judge the same in every case where a man is acting solely with a view to his own advantage.[2]

But prudence is not the same as selfishness. A prudent person is not necessarily an egoist, one who acts *solely* with a view to his own advantage, without due regard to the interest of others. Neither is an egoist or a selfish person necessarily prudent. In some instances, indeed, selfishness may be decidedly imprudent.

Prudence, of course, always involves reference to *one's own*

[2] Richard Whately, *Paley's Moral Philosophy: With Annotations* (London: John W. Parker & Son, 1859), pp. 68, 89-90.

interest, one's own needs, wishes, or desires—or else to the interest of a person or group or organization that one is representing, and with which, so far as one is acting in that capacity, one's interest is identified. The other element in prudence is the exercise of intelligence or rationality or fore-thought with respect to that interest. To act imprudently is to act foolishly or irrationally (or even stupidly), from the point of view of one's own interest or aims, or from the point of view of the interest that one is representing. Yet to act with reference to one's own interest, and thus to attempt to achieve or to safeguard one's own ends, is not necessarily to act at the expense or to the disadvantage of anyone else, since one's own interest need not be in conflict with that of others. Egoism is immoral; prudence is not. Prudence is more like *rational* or *enlightened* self-interest than it is like mere self-interest, which may be shortsighted and unenlightened.

But, even though prudence is not immoral, neither is it, at least in general, morally mandatory. For neither is impru-dence immoral. The two concepts are distinct, and we can distinguish prudential from moral reasons, prudential from moral judgments, and prudential from moral actions—as well as imprudent from immoral actions. In evaluating the pru-dence of an action, we must consider its effects on the agent. But its morality depends on its effects on others. The fact that an act would tend to harm oneself is a reason for regarding it as imprudent, but not a reason for regarding it as immoral; the fact that an act would tend to harm others is a reason for regarding it as immoral, but not a reason for regarding it as imprudent.

The reason I emphasize this so much is that confusion be-tween the two is so prevalent. If any instances are wanted (and some have already been given), a particularly good one is provided by the following passage, in which we have first a bit of stilted dialogue, and then a comment on it. First the dialogue:

A: It is your duty to vote.
B: No, my vote will make no difference to the final outcome.

A: You could scarcely wish that all others should adopt your ways!

Now the comment:

> A's rejoinder, reminiscent of Kant's categorical imperative,
> unquestionably has its place in common-sense arguments.
> How may its relevance be explained? Although it does not
> name any direct consequence of B's stand, it is fertile in
> suggesting many indirect ones. B may set a precedent to others
> which he will not welcome. Or he may nullify his influence
> in *inducing* others to vote, for people are temperamentally
> suspicious of those who "do not practice what they preach."
> Or he may develop habits of noncoöperation, which . . .
> may have effects that extend far beyond the present case.
> These observations are clearly a part of the explanation of the
> force of A's reason; and to continue the explanation in this
> way, rather than in Kant's way, seems only in keeping with
> the principle of parsimony.[3]

It seems a shame to blame this exercise in irrelevance on the
principle of parsimony; its judicious application should hardly
lead to absurdity. Yet, in the context, this appeal to the principle of parsimony is but an appeal to prejudice (in technical parlance, an *argumentum ad populum*). The claim is
made that someone has a duty to vote. By not voting, it is
true, B *might* "set a precedent to others which he will not
welcome." But, if so, this would show only that it would be
advisable for him to vote, and not that it is his duty; it is a
prudential, and not a moral reason. The same goes for the
other "indirect" consequences "of B's stand." In the light of
what has already been said on this matter further comment

3 Charles L. Stevenson, *Ethics and Language* (New Haven: Yale University Press, 1944), pp. 121-2. The question "How may its relevance be
explained?" really means, it should be clearly understood, "How may its
psychological effect be explained?"; for, on Mr. Stevenson's view, "*Any*
statement about *any* matter of fact which *any* speaker considers likely to
alter attitudes may be adduced as a reason for or against an ethical judgment" (p. 114), and this same statement can be used to explain what, on
this view, would be meant by "relevance." This point, however, is simply
further evidence of the irrelevance of this type of view.

would be superfluous. These irrelevant observations can do
nothing to explain the "relevance" of this argument. They
are, rather, in need of explanation themselves. Why these
consequences, which are really most improbable, should be
regarded as "indirect" and not as "direct" is more than I can
fathom. Is "indirect" here a synonym for "unlikely," or for
"irrelevant"?

The fact of a distinction between prudence and morality
does not deny the existence of border-line cases. In fact there
are many. One and the same act can be both imprudent and
immoral (or both prudent and morally right). A statement of
the form "A ought to do x" can express both a prudential and
a moral judgment, and a reason why A ought to do x can
at one and the same time be a reason why it is imprudent, and
a reason why it is immoral, for A not to do x. Thus cases
can arise in which it may be impossible to tell just what one
has in mind, and it is, I think, one of the strengths of the
criterion given earlier (Chapter VIII, sec. 1) that it is fully
capable of allowing for this. I said before that if a statement
of the form "A ought to do x" is supported by reference to
the needs or wants of others, then it is the expression of a
moral judgment. It may be thought that reference to the
needs or wants of others is not sufficient to make a judgment
a moral judgment, but it is, so far as it goes. For this does not
mean that such reference is sufficient by itself to establish the
judgment or to prove that the act is wrong; it is a moral reason, though it may not be a conclusive one. Neither does it
mean that this same judgment may not be at the same time a
prudential judgment. It may. Is the relation rather that reference to the needs or wants of others is *necessary* for the
judgment to be a moral judgment? Only if it is understood
that such reference may be implicit. One may simply point
out what would happen if everyone acted in that way, without
actually specifying how others would be harmed or their
interests adversely affected.

Suppose it is said that you ought to do something or other
because your mother wants you to do it, so much so that she

will be made unhappy if you do not, and that you want your mother to be happy. Would this be a moral or a prudential judgment? It could be both; there is no reason to suppose that it must be only one. One can have a desire for the benefit of another. The reference here to your desire for your mother's happiness makes the judgment a prudential one; but it is not sufficient to show that not acting in the way in question must be imprudent. On the other hand, the reference to your mother's desire is sufficient to show that the judgment is a moral one; but it is not by itself sufficient to show that the omission of the act must be immoral. We must distinguish between a reason for concluding that a certain judgment is a moral judgment, which says something about the sort of claim the judgment makes, and a reason for concluding that an act is immoral.

Thus there are border-line cases, and this is not surprising, in view of the general coincidence between prudence and morality. In our society, as presently constituted, and in any society that is not sick to the roots, there is a general coincidence between what is prudent and what is moral, between what is imprudent and what is immoral. The degree and extent of this coincidence will vary from time to time and from place to place; yet some degree of coincidence is actually necessary for a society to exist at all. The following passage says just about all there is to be said on this:

> I think it altogether superfluous to dilate upon the old test that honesty is the best policy. The point has been so much laboured, that, although there is abundant room for rhetoric, there is little need of argument. Considering how closely we are dependent upon our neighbors and upon their good opinion, and the enormous difficulty of retaining that good opinion without deserving it, there can be no serious doubt that, on the average, every man will find his account in observing the accepted moral code and acquiring the corresponding instincts. To be on good terms with your family, to avoid picking and stealing, to be decently sober, industrious, and good-natured, are rules of conduct so obviously expedient upon all grounds, that I will not burn daylight by insisting upon them.

I assume a general coincident between the dictates of morality and of prudence. . . .[4]

Yet even though there is this coincidence between prudence and morality, it is only general, and not universal; there is also an area of conflict.

When we turn to contemplate the actual tyrannical usurpers, wicked statesmen, successful leaders of unwarranted rebellion, and, speaking generally, the great criminals whose position raises them out of the reach of legal penalties, it does not appear that the moral odium under which they lie must necessarily count for much in an egoistic calculation of the gain and loss resulting from their conduct. For this disesteem is only expressed by a portion of the community: and its utterance is often drowned in the loud-voiced applause of the multitude whose admiration is largely independent of moral considerations. Nor are there wanting philosophers and historians whose judgment manifests a similar independence.[5]

Thus it is not always imprudent to be immoral. And one need not be selfish, evil, or malevolent to be in a situation in which the prudent course conflicts with what would be morally right, in which one's interest, in other words, conflicts with one's duty. Suppose, for example, that you have witnessed a murder, and that you are threatened with death or some other disaster if you testify in court. Many people who are themselves honest and law-abiding have been in just such a situation. What should be done then? The prudent course would appear to be to refuse to testify in order to preserve one's life and family—though of course this might lead to the loss of one's reputation and self-respect, one might become known as a coward or as a protector of criminals, and the consequences of this might, in the end, be even worse. On the other hand, it is to the interest of every law-abiding citizen (and even of others) that lawbreakers, especially murderers and gangsters, be caught and punished. But if no one testified

4 Leslie Stephen, *The Science of Ethics* (London: Smith, Elder, & Co., 1882), pp. 403-4.
5 Henry Sidgwick, *The Methods of Ethics* (7th ed.; London: Macmillan & Co., Ltd., 1907), pp. 166-7.

against them, they never would be; and if everyone so threatened refused to testify, no one would ever testify. Hence one morally ought to testify, whether one is threatened or not. Thus the question here is not really unanswerable. But the decision is often hard, and where the threat is really serious, the circumstances may be extenuating. This is especially the case if the police are corrupt, or in league with the gang, or if one has no real confidence in their ability to protect him (though this verges on a state of nature situation). Should one then take the prudent course? (But note this use of "should." In such circumstances what course would be prudent? Would there be a prudent course?)

It is impossible to maintain that in society as it is presently constituted such conflicts could never occur. It is a fact, unfortunate perhaps, but nevertheless a fact, that it is not always to one's interest to do what is morally right (unless one's interest is so defined), and that people can and often do profit by doing what is morally wrong—and it is about time this fact was recognized. As it is, almost the only people who recognize it are those who profit by it. I do not mean simply that immoral acts occur, or that people perform them under the delusion that they will be profitable or that they can get away with it, and that this belief often turns out to be false, to the ultimate discomfiture of the agent. What I mean is that some immoral actions, in some circumstances, really do turn out to be profitable to the agent, in the long run as well as in the short run. "The attempt to establish an absolute coincidence between virtue and happiness," it has been said, "is in ethics what the attempting to square the circle or to discover perpetual motion are in geometry and mechanics. I think it better frankly to abandon the hopeless endeavour." [6] This seems to me undeniable. Yet this fact is not one in which we must acquiesce. The situation as it is is undesirable, and a better one is certainly conceivable, and even to some extent attainable. If it makes sense at all to speak of an ideal society, the ideal society would be one in which prudence and morality would never conflict, in which it

[6] Stephen, *op. cit.*, p. 430.

would never be to the interest of anyone to do what is morally wrong, and in which it would never be detrimental to the interest of anyone to do what is morally right. Such at least would be the structure of the ideal society, whatever would be its content, and though such a state of affairs is only an ideal, it is not unrealistic. It is something that we can and do approximate to in the process of harmonizing conflicting desires, reconciling conflicting aims, and compromising conflicting programs, when this is done in a way that is at all reasonable or enlightened. This ideal, furthermore, provides a standard for the evaluation of social institutions, which is, namely, that of considering to what extent they contribute to the attainment of this ideal.

But the difference between prudence and morality is not defined simply by the fact that there is an area in which they conflict. Prudence has a wider range, so that there is an area of activity where they do not connect at all. What I mean is that there are many actions that are morally indifferent or permissible, that we have a right to do or not to do as we please; so that whichever we do, it would not be morally wrong. Hence many actions are perfectly all right to do in the sense that there is no moral reason against them, and moral considerations will be inoperative. Yet prudential considerations will still apply, for many such actions will still be either prudent or imprudent. This is another proof that it is not always immoral to be imprudent.

It cannot be said, however, that it is never immoral to be imprudent. There are some circumstances in which prudence itself is morally obligatory. A clear case of this is where one has undertaken to represent or to act in the interest of another, or is acting as a representative or as an official of some group or organization. With respect to the interest one is representing one is morally bound to be prudent. A lawyer, for example, representing a client, a government official representing the government, is morally bound to exercise prudence in his official or public acts, in those of his acts that affect the interest he has undertaken to protect.

But these are not the only circumstances in which prudence

is morally obligatory. One need not be acting for others, or in some official or representative capacity, in order to come under the rule. Certain acts that involve harm to oneself, and that are consequently imprudent, may not only involve harm to another but may be such as are likely to do so. If the act is of such a nature that under the circumstances it may reasonably be expected to cause harm to another, then it is a moral fault. Note that it is not sufficient for the particular act to be such that it *in fact* causes harm to another. This may be no more than coincidence or misadventure, for which one cannot properly be held responsible. The harm to another must be reasonably foreseeable as arising out of the imprudence. And it is not necessary that there be actual intent to harm. In such cases one's actual intent is irrelevant to the morality of the act. The nitwit who drives through a crowded residential district at sixty miles an hour may not actually intend to harm anyone, any more than he may intend to harm himself. He may simply like the thrill of driving fast, or the feeling of causing consternation, or he may not be aware of his actual speed or of the nature of his surroundings. This makes no difference. Provided that he is a moral agent, and not really insane, the act is still immoral. Here the question of intent relates only to the judgment of character, and not to the morality of the action. Such a person may not actually be wicked; his act is none the less immoral. One is morally bound to exercise prudence in driving a car. Thus it is sufficient if there is simply negligence, thoughtlessness, lack of due care or forethought—in a word, imprudence. When such an act can be reasonably foreseen as likely to result in harm to another, it is morally wrong. The fact that one may not actually have foreseen the harm, or the likelihood of harm, is not a legitimate defense. For, given that the harm was reasonably foreseeable, so that it would be unreasonable not to expect it, one ought (morally) to have foreseen it. One's defense must be that his circumstances were actually such that he *could not* have foreseen it, or could not reasonably have been expected to; or else that, though he was aware of the risk, it was justified in the circumstances. This does not relate to intent.

Differences of opinion on such questions as these, which are almost inevitable, cannot undermine the general rule, or defeat the presumption based upon it.

Now the criterion that is applicable here is actually provided by the generalization argument: What would happen if everybody in such circumstances as these were to fail to exercise due care, were negligent, thoughtless, or imprudent? Where the consequences would be undesirable, prudence is morally obligatory. This, indeed, merely reflects the commonly received opinion that in certain circumstances, or when acting in certain capacities, one ought to exercise due care and forethought; and there are many rules or standards, more or less vague but nonetheless applicable, for determining not only when one is required to exercise due care, or prudence, but also what due care *is* in various circumstances. These standards, of what a reasonable man, or a man of ordinary prudence, would do or know or expect in certain circumstances, are not merely features of our law. They are also features of morality. They are not merely legal standards; they are also moral standards. That this is so is established by the generalization argument.

§ 2 §

This discussion of prudence leads naturally to the question whether there are any duties to oneself. Many have thought so. One of the commonest divisions of duties is that based on the distinction between those that one has "to oneself" and those that one has "to others." Thus it is often said that it is a duty that one owes to oneself to preserve one's own life or develop one's talents or preserve one's self-respect. Consequently it is often held that suicide and sloth are morally wrong, on the ground that they violate one's duty to oneself. Few, perhaps, would go so far as Kant in claiming that "Our duties towards ourselves are of primary importance and should have pride of place . . . the prior condition of our duty to others is our duty to ourselves. . . ." [7] Yet many

[7] Kant, *Lectures on Ethics*, pp. 117-8.

would agree that the distinction is both genuine and important, and it seems well embedded both in traditional moral philosophy and in ordinary moral thinking.

Nevertheless, it is actually impossible, as I shall argue, for there to be any duties to oneself, in any literal sense, for, if taken literally, the idea involves a contradiction. What are called "duties to oneself" are either not genuine moral duties at all, or, if they are, they are not duties *to oneself*. This leaves, of course, the question of what can be meant by the various expressions in which such "duties" are imputed, for I am certainly not arguing that such expressions are essentially meaningless or ought never to be used. My answer to this question will follow directly.

There are certain duties that we can quite clearly regard as being relative to persons, in the sense that we can speak of a duty *to someone* to do or forbear from doing certain acts. This is especially true of duties (or obligations) arising out of contracts or agreements, although it is not restricted to such cases.[8] If I have promised you to do something, then I have a duty to you to do what I have promised, and you are the person to whom I have the obligation. If I have borrowed money from you, then I owe it to you and not to anyone else (unless you have assigned the debt to another), and I can be said to have a duty to you—namely, to pay back what I have borrowed—and I do not thereby have a duty to another. (This, of course, is what is said more simply and idiomatically in the statement that I owe you a certain sum of money.) Now, if I have a duty to you, then you have a right against or with respect to me. Thus, if I owe you a certain sum of money, then you have a right to receive and demand that money from me. In general, if A has a duty to B, then B has a right against or with respect to A.[9] But it follows from this that to

[8] Although for certain purposes such a distinction might usefully be made, I am not here distinguishing between duties and obligations. Cf. H. L. A. Hart, "Are There any Natural Rights?," *The Philosophical Review*, vol. LXIV (April 1955), p. 179 note; also pp. 180-1.

[9] This statement by no means exhausts the subject of the relations between rights and duties. It is not intended to. The subject is complex, yet I cannot forbear mentioning that the question whether and how rights and

have a *duty to oneself* would be to have a *right against one-self*, and this is surely nonsense. What could it mean to have a right or a claim against oneself? (Could one sue oneself in a court of law for return of the money one owes oneself?)

Yet my argument does not rest simply on the claim that it is nonsense to speak of a right against oneself, and that this is a necessary consequence of speaking of a duty to oneself. It is really more fundamental than this. It is essential to the nature of an obligation that no one can release himself from an obligation by not wishing to perform it or by deciding not to perform it, or, indeed, in any other way whatsoever. In other words, no one can release himself from an obligation, just as no one can release himself from a promise. To be sure, one can *break* the promise or the obligation. One can refuse to perform it. But this is not to release oneself. One can, however, *be released* from an obligation by the person to whom he has the obligation, just as one can be released from a promise by the person to whom he has made it. For one can give up his right against someone, or decide not to exercise it, and by this means release someone else from an obligation. But a duty to oneself, then, would be a duty from which one could release oneself at will, and this is self-contradictory. A "duty" from which one could release oneself at will is not, in any literal sense, a duty at all.

The situation is the same in the analogous case of a promise to oneself. Can one *promise* oneself to do something? Such language is frequently used. People say "I have prom-

duties are correlative has been clouded, not only by a failure to distinguish between different senses of "correlative," but also by a failure to distinguish different kinds of rights. There are, I think, at least three: (a) *action rights*, which are rights to *do* certain things, or to act in certain ways; (b) what may be called *receivatory* or *treatment rights*, which are rights to *receive* certain things, or *to be treated* in certain ways; and (c) *property rights*, which are rights *in* or *to* something. (These first two types of rights correspond, it may be observed, to what I before distinguished as the two sides of the generalization principle.) These different kinds of rights are related to each other in different ways, and they are also related in different ways to obligations, so that what holds of one may not hold for another. Cf., for an analogous distinction, Roscoe Pound, *An Introduction to the Philosophy of Law* (New Haven: Yale University Press, 1922), pp. 191-2.

ised myself to. . . ." (Note that the operative expression is in the past tense.) But a promise to oneself would be a promise from which one could release oneself at will, and thus not a genuine promise at all. The language here must be metaphorical. To say "I have promised myself to . . ." is to say "I have strongly resolved to. . . ." It is to express a settled determination to do the act in question, and in some cases the wish not to be dissuaded from it. Thus, though a "promise to oneself" is in some respects like a promise, it is not a genuine or in any literal sense a promise. For one can make a genuine promise without resolving or intending to do what one has promised, just as one can intend to do something without promising to do so. In the former case one would have made a false or lying promise, but one would still have made a promise. There is no analogue here with a "promise to oneself." To promise oneself to do something just *is* to be strongly resolved to do it, and if one were to change one's mind and not do what one intended one would not have broken any promise.

Consider also such expressions as "I owe it to myself to . . ." or "You owe it to yourself to. . . ." Can one literally *owe* something to oneself, be in debt to oneself? Here again the language must be metaphorical. To say "I owe it to myself to . . ." is both a way of emphasizing one's *right* to do something and of expressing one's *determination* to do it. To tell someone that he owes it to himself, say, to take a vacation, is an emphatic way of asserting that he has a right to do it and of expressing one's belief that it would be decidedly imprudent for him not to. Thus it says no more than that he ought to, in the sense that it would be imprudent for him not to ("You need a vacation, you'd be foolish not to take one"), only it says it more forcefully. Similarly, no one can literally threaten or command or forcibly restrain himself, though such language can on occasion be psychologically or even socially useful.

These very same points apply to the notion of a duty to oneself. To say that someone has a duty (or owes it) to himself to do something is an emphatic way of asserting that he has a right to do it—that there are no moral considerations against it—and that it would be foolish or imprudent for him not to. It is, to be sure, to say that he ought to do the act in question, but only in the prudential sense of "ought." Thus, to suppose that one can actually have a moral duty to oneself, in any literal sense, is to confuse both a right to do something with a duty to do it, and an imprudent act with an immoral one.

If my argument is sound, then such expressions as I have considered cannot be given a literal interpretation. Yet they serve an interesting function in discourse. To say "I have promised myself to . . ." can often be a way of warding off objections to one's announced course of action and of enabling one to withstand them, as well as a way of *reinforcing* one's determination to do it. If we come to think that we have a duty to do something this can often save us from the onerous task of having to make up our minds what to do. To tell someone else that he owes it to himself, or has a duty to himself, to do something, can often be effective in persuading him to do it. For it can convey the idea that here is a case where both self-interest and duty combine in demanding a certain course of action. Apparently, then, what we have here is an appeal to self-interest disguised in the language of duty.

The argument that I have presented, against the idea that there are self-regarding duties, rests essentially on the following three propositions: (1) If A has a duty to B, then B has a right against A; (2) If B has a right against A, B can give it up and release A from the obligation; and (3) No one can release himself from an obligation. I must confess that I do not see how these propositions can rationally be denied. Yet one possible objection against the thesis I have presented might take the following form: In not every case can one be released from an obligation or duty. This may hold only where the duty arises out of a contractual relationship or some other voluntary undertaking. But not all duties arise out of contracts or promises or voluntary undertakings. Hence it may be that self-regarding duties are not duties of the sort from which one can be released.

My answer to this objection is that the relation I am presupposing as holding between rights and duties—proposition
(1) above—is only asserted as holding for those duties or
obligations that one can be said to have *to* someone.
Consequently, if one could sensibly be said to have a duty *to*
oneself, one would have a right against oneself that one could
give up, thereby releasing oneself from the duty, which would
contradict proposition (3), and be, in effect, self-contradictory.
Now I can see no good reason for supposing that every duty
must be a duty *to* someone. Many duties, to be sure, are thus
relative to persons, are duties *to* some assignable individual
or group, and this feature, as I have said, is characteristic of
duties arising out of contracts or promises. But not all duties
arise out of contracts or promises. Why then must all duties
be supposed to have this characteristic? It is important here
not to confuse the person *to whom* one is under an obligation
with the person *regarding whom* one is under the obligation
—that is, the person who stands to benefit by its performance
—for they are not always one and the same.[1] A may have a
duty *regarding* C without having a duty *to* C. Thus A may
have a duty to B to pay C a certain sum of money, in which
case it is B, and not C, who has the correlative right against A.
It may be that it is this latter confusion that is responsible for
the confusion about self-*regarding* duties. It may be that so-
called "duties to oneself" are duties, or alleged duties, *regarding* oneself—in the sense that it is oneself who would be
primarily or in the first instance affected by their performance
or nonperformance—rather than duties *to* oneself. But this
would not make this language any the less misleading, and I
doubt whether the distinction can really be sustained along
these lines.

[1] Cf. Hart, *op. cit.*, p. 181: "It is important for the whole logic of rights
that, while the person who stands to benefit by the performance of a duty
is discovered by considering what will happen if the duty is not performed,
the person who has a right (to whom performance is *owed* or *due*) is discovered by examining the transaction or antecedent situation or relations
of the parties out of which the 'duty' arises." See also, on this distinction,
W. D. Lamont, *The Principles of Moral Judgment* (Oxford: The Clarendon Press, 1946), pp. 80 ff.

What has just been said is sufficient to dispose of another possible objection to the argument I have been presenting, which may be derived from the arguments by which certain alleged duties are alleged to be duties. I have my doubts whether, to take the examples that are most usually given, it is a duty, in general, and apart from special circumstances, to preserve one's life or develop one's talents. But suppose that it is, and that it is morally wrong to commit suicide or waste one's talents. It would not at all follow that these are duties to oneself, merely because they would be duties with respect to oneself. Someone under military discipline may have the duty of keeping his shoes shined and his hair cut, and, in general, of maintaining a trim and neat appearance. But these are not duties to himself, nor are they alleged to be. Kant's arguments to show the immorality of suicide and sloth (his first and third illustrations of the categorical imperative) have not the slightest tendency, even if sound, to show that these are breaches of one's duty to oneself. That there are duties to oneself is a supposition from which Kant starts, not a consequence of his argument. In effect, then, the question whether all duties are relative in the sense specified is not a matter of inordinate importance. A duty that cannot be said to be relative in this way to some specifically assignable individual or group still need not be supposed to be a duty to oneself. It can be regarded, if one so chooses, as a duty to one's society, or to mankind generally. (In that case, it would be what might be called a general duty, correlative to a general or "real" right, rather than a special duty [or obligation], correlative to a special or "personal" right.) Such, for example, is the case with the duty to pay taxes or to vote. Hence, if it really is a duty to preserve one's life, this can be regarded as a duty to mankind generally (if not to one's family). But this presupposes another classification of duties than the one mentioned at the outset.

In denying that there are duties to oneself, in any literal sense, I am not of course denying that there are what might be called self-regarding faults or vices. Similarly, in denying that one can literally promise oneself, owe anything to one-

self, or threaten, command, or forcibly restrain oneself, I am
not denying that one can harm oneself, or hurt oneself, defeat
one's own purposes, or do what is detrimental to one's own
best interest. Of course one can. A vice, after all, is a defect
or an undesirable trait of character, a habit that it would be
desirable not to have. Smoking, for example, is often said to
be a vice. Suppose that it is. If it is, it is because, on the
evidence available, it is likely to prove harmful to the agent
and is thus a habit which, from the point of view of his own
best interests, it would be desirable for him not to have. But it
does not follow that it is a *moral* vice. In saying that a vice
is an undesirable trait or habit, we must distinguish the interests with respect to which it is undesirable, the person or
group of persons *for whom* it is undesirable. If it is harmful to
the person who has it, then it is undesirable with respect to
his interests, and thus it is undesirable from the point of view
of prudence. It is, consequently, a self-regarding or prudential vice. On the other hand, if it is harmful to another or to
society, then it is undesirable with respect to their interests,
and is thus morally undesirable. It is, consequently, a moral
vice. But not all vices, and so not all virtues, are moral ones,
and it may be suspected that those who have crusaded, on
moral grounds, against just such things as smoking, have been
guilty of just this sort of obfuscation. On this matter, I think,
Mill has said very nearly, though not quite, the last word:

> Self-regarding faults . . . are not properly immoralities,
> and to whatever pitch they may be carried, do not constitute
> wickedness. They may be proofs of any amount of folly, or
> want of personal dignity and self-respect; but they are only a
> subject of moral reprobation when they involve a breach of
> duty to others, for whose sake the individual is bound to have
> care for himself. What are called duties to ourselves are not
> socially obligatory, unless circumstances render them at the
> same time duties to others. . . .[2]

[2] John Stuart Mill, *On Liberty* (Everyman's Library ed.; New York:
E. P. Dutton and Company, 1910), chap. IV, par. 6, p. 135.

§ 3 §

This brings us to the question of motivation, the question "Why should I be moral?" This question may appear to be simple and straightforward. It is very far from that. It is, in fact, decidedly ambiguous and confused, and it is for this reason that it has always appeared so difficult to answer.

Suppose we put it first in the form "Why ought I to do what I ought to do?" To be moral, after all, is to do what one ought to do, and "should" is equivalent to "ought." In this form the question is simply self-contradictory, and omniscience would not suffice to answer it. To ask such a question is not to ask, for example, "Why ought I to do what *you say* I ought to do?" If this were all that were meant, it would be a simple request for the reasons for a moral judgment, and would raise no special problems whatsoever. It is, rather, to ask "Why ought I to do what I *admittedly* ought to do?" and to ask this is, on the one hand, to agree about what one ought to do, and to accept the reasons from which this follows, while, on the other hand, it is to demand a further reason for accepting this and for so agreeing. The question thus contradicts its own implications. It is as though one were to say: "I agree that this is what I ought to do, and I am convinced that these are the reasons why I ought to do it. Now tell me further, why ought I to do it?" The question is irrational (if it is not a manifestation of deafness). Perhaps all that can be said in reply is, "Because you ought to, and that is all there is to it." But that really amounts to saying that there is no reason, or no further reason, why one ought to do what one ought to do. All the reasons have already been given.

To put it in another way, to ask such a question is to demand a moral reason for accepting any moral reasons at all. This, of course, is an impossible demand. By the very terms of the question, anything that could count as a moral reason is itself an instance of what is being asked about, and thus is itself an instance of what one is demanding a reason for accepting. Thus the question could not possibly be answered. One who is not already prepared to accept and act on moral

considerations cannot be given a *moral* reason for doing so;
a moral reason is just the sort of consideration he is not prepared to accept.

When someone asks simply why he ought to do this, that,
or the next thing, the question is perfectly intelligible and is
of a type that can be answered. Sometimes, no doubt, the
answer will take the form that he ought not to; and sometimes
that he need not, as there is no good reason why he ought.
But often the question can be answered as it stands—
reasons can be given why he ought to and the questioner can
be satisfied. Yet this can occur only if he is prepared to accept
something as a moral reason. If he is not, if there is nothing
that he would so accept, he cannot possibly be satisfied. His
question is then a senseless one, and is, at best, the product of
confusion. (But this presupposes that the question actually
expresses a genuine puzzlement, and this may well be too
optimistic.) There is thus an enormous difference between
asking why I ought to do this or that particular act, or why
I ought to conform to this or that particular rule, and asking
why I ought to do what I ought to do, or why I ought to do
anything at all.

Consider an analogous question. Suppose someone were to
ask, "Why should I be reasonable?" or "Why should I be rational?" There is no way at all in which such a question
could be answered. Such a question, to be sure, would probably never be intended to be taken literally, but this is irrelevant. To be rational is to govern one's conduct and beliefs by reasons or rational considerations; it is thus to be
prepared to accept reasons for or against a belief or an action,
and this implies a readiness to "listen to reason." But you
cannot possibly give anyone who is not prepared to do so a
reason for being reasonable. One who is totally unreasonable could not be reasoned with; it is the merest tautology
that one who is not prepared to listen to reason is not prepared to listen to reason. One can be given a reason for believing this or that. One can even be given a reason for being
more reasonable than he is. But one cannot be given a reason
for believing anything at all, or for accepting anything as a

reason. Such a person would be irrational, and that is all there is to it.

It may well be that there is no one (outside of an institution) who is totally and completely unsusceptible to rational considerations. Certainly it would be rare to hear such a question raised in the very general and all-embracing form in which I have stated it. Whether this is so or not does not matter. If there is anyone who is not prepared to accept any reasons at all on any subject whatever, then there is no possibility of giving him one, no possibility of reasoning with him, and no possibility of convincing him of anything. Of course, he *ought* to be rational, just as he ought to be moral, but he does not think so, and there is no way of making him think so. A reason is not a restraining force. A reason is an appeal to reason. The use of force is something else. So one can continue to be irrational, or immoral, no matter how many reasons there are against it.

This point would hardly be worth making if it were not so often overlooked. Confusion about it, I am convinced, is at the very basis of moral skepticism. It is often supposed that the very fact that people disagree on moral questions, or that some people are unaffected by moral considerations, is sufficient to cast doubt on the objectivity or rational character of morals, and shows that moral judgments must be subjective. Thus one often hears it said that two people could agree on all the facts of a case, and still disagree in their moral judgments about it (or in their "attitudes" towards it), and it is supposed to follow from this that moral judgments must be subjective (or emotive, or incitive-emotive, and so on). This is simply absurd. The fact that two people can *in fact* do this, that such disagreements can occur, proves nothing. For what has to be shown is that neither party to the dispute is being irrational or unreasonable in so disagreeing, and this does not follow from the mere fact of disagreement. Just as some people are immoral, some people are irrational. One could not hope to convince a Caligula that he ought to be moral, or that he ought to have done this rather than that, not because there are no good reasons here, but because a Caligula is immoral. There is certainly nothing in the facts of any case to *force* people to agree in their moral judgments about it, any more than there is anything in the facts about the present international situation to force people to agree about its outcome, about what will happen next. (Are all predictions therefore subjective, or emotive, or expressive of attitudes?) The absence of universal or even widespread agreement, therefore, is no refutation of a moral judgment or a moral doctrine, and is certainly no criterion of the subjectivity or nonrational character of moral judgments in general.

Given, then, that some people are immoral, and that some people are irrational, and that none of us always acts morally or believes reasonably, we should not be surprised to find disagreement on moral questions. We can find disagreement on all sorts of questions. There seems to be some blithe notion afoot that on questions of logic, and on questions of empirical fact—"the sorts of things that can be dealt with by science"—it is possible to arrive at universal agreement; that these matters are therefore objective; while on questions of ethics and morals and "values" it is not possible to arrive at universal agreement, so that these matters are therefore not objective or capable of being rationally decided. This view can only be the product of worldly innocence. For it is not itself an empirical fact, or even supported by empirical means, but a philosophical dogma. ("How do you know that it is possible to attain universal agreement on these matters? Surely it has not been attained? Because this statement is true and that one is false, and you can prove that this statement is true and that that one is false? But surely not everyone agrees that this statement is true and that one is false? Oh, everyone *ought* to agree, because it can be proved? But should not the fact that not everyone agrees, that not everyone accepts your proof, throw some doubt on your statement? Does it not affect the validity of your proof? If it does so in morals, why not in Science? Indeed, why not in Logic?") Actually there is no good reason to suppose that universal agreement is attainable on all questions, or even on all types of questions, even supposing, what is not at all certain, that it is worth attaining. What we must do is distinguish between reasonable and unreasonable disagreement, and to do this we must go beyond the mere fact of disagreement. Now one's disagreement or refusal to come to a certain conclusion will be reasonable to the extent to which one can support one's opinion by reasons. Otherwise it is not even relevant. Moral questions, it should be kept in mind, are not the only ones about which disagreement arises, and moral disputes are not the only ones that lead to heated and abusive words, or even to blows. Neither is it characteristic of moral disputes that they lead to abusive words. The question "Why should I be moral?" like the question "What's it to me?" is therefore no defense for moral skepticism. It is not even an excuse for it.

But let us return, now, to the question of motivation. I have so far been interpreting the question "Why should I be moral?" as meaning "Why ought I to do what I (admittedly) ought to do?" and have pointed out that in this interpretation it is senseless, since it is self-contradictory. This is, however, by no means the only thing it can mean, nor is it, perhaps, the fairest or most likely interpretation of it.

Another interpretation of it is this. One might be identifying "being moral" with conforming to the standards or the code of some particular group, or with conformity to some particular rule. This would certainly be a limited use of "being moral," but it is not an impossible one, and in fact it occurs with some frequency. In this sense the question "Why should I be moral?" is identical with "Why should I do what is *called* 'moral' in this group or that?" and in this sense it can certainly be answered. Since it does not have the all-embracing character of the previous interpretation, it is by no means a senseless question. It is simply a demand for the justification of the standards or code or rule in question, and moral reasons can be given one way or the other. It is thus equivalent to asking "Why ought I to do what *it is said* that I ought to do?" and, as such, it raises no special problems that have not already been dealt with. As before, sometimes it will turn out that one ought not to do what it is said that one ought to do, and sometimes that one need not, and in these cases this common opinion, or the standards or code in question, will turn out not to be justifiable.

Again, the question "Why should I be moral?" might mean simply "What's in it for me?" Since the term "ought" is ambiguous between its moral and prudential senses, the question "Why ought I to do what I ought to do?" is not necessarily self-contradictory. It might mean "Why (prudentially) ought I to do what I (morally) ought to do?" and this at least is intelligible, and might even be what would most frequently be meant by it. Yet even here the question is not altogether unambiguous, and cannot always be given a satisfactory answer. If one means simply why *in general* he ought, from the point of view of prudence, to do what he morally ought to do, he can be answered by pointing to the general coincidence between prudence and morality. "On the whole, honesty is the best policy to follow." If, however, one means to ask why *in this particular case* he ought from the point of view of his own self-interest to do what he morally ought to do, there may be no way of answering him, since there is no *necessary* coincidence between prudence and morality. Honesty is not always the best policy; sometimes people have profited, even in the long run, from being dishonest. Perhaps all that can be said is that his own interest is not all-important, that there is no reason why there should be something in it for him, and no reason why he should expect there to be, and that if he does not do what he ought he is simply being immoral. Certainly he would not be willing to have everyone adopt that attitude. "Why should there be something in it for you, and what difference does it make whether there is or not? How would you like it if everyone had that attitude, and only did what he ought when he thought it would be to his advantage?" This may or may not be effective. If it is, it will be because he will have been led to ask a different question from the one he had been asking. If it is not, there is no dialectical recourse, though there may be psychological or rhetorical ones.

This ambiguity of "ought," incidentally, leads to another possible interpretation of the question, "Why ought I to do what I ought to do?" It might mean "Why should I be prudent?" I take it as obvious that this is senseless. It often happens that people do not care, or say they do not care, what happens to them, or what will be to their own best interest on the whole. Where such an attitude is present appeals to prudence fall on deaf ears. Such people are irrational, at least at the moment. The existence or the rationality of prudence does not depend on such human aberrations. The fact that people do not automatically and invariably consider or act for their own welfare is the very reason why they ought to, and it is what gives point to saying so.

The maxim that "Honesty is the best policy" (and its companion in arms, "Crime doesn't pay"), which has been mentioned along the way, will be worth some attention here. On the whole and in general, honesty is the best policy; and this is a reason, even a good reason, for being honest. Sometimes, indeed, it is the only reason available. It ought to be noted, however, that it is not a *moral* reason. To recommend honesty *as a policy* is not to recommend it morally, or on moral grounds. It is, as should be obvious, to recommend it on prudential grounds. Morality is not a matter of policy, and to be moral is not to adopt a policy. I do not mean that it must be immoral to adopt a policy, even a policy of always acting in accordance with morality. It is possible for someone always to act in accordance with moral rules and principles, so that in fact he never does anything wrong, so far as he can determine this, simply because he regards this as the best policy, the most prudent course. Yet such a person would not be in the full sense moral. For if an occasion should ever arise in which he thinks it would be both advantageous and safe to do something wrong, he is almost certain to do so. This is not just academic. It indicates the importance of inculcating moral motives.

This is one reason more for being clear on the difference between these two types of reasons, prudential and moral. If, for example, your child wants to know why he should not pick the neighbor's flowers, there are two essentially different ways in which you can answer him. You can say, firstly, "Because that would be stealing, and stealing is wrong," or "Because the neighbor does not want you to," or "How would you like it if someone else were to pick your flowers"—or, what comes to the same thing and may be more suitable in the context—"How would you like it if someone else were to destroy your toys?" Or you can say, secondly, "Because I will hit you if you do," "Because you will be punished if you do," or "Because the neighbor will get angry at you." These last are not moral reasons, but prudential reasons. Of course, in advance of any case it is impossible to say which sort of reason will be most effective, and it may be that some combination of both will prove most effective for the immediate purpose. Yet to give only prudential reasons, where one can give moral reasons, is itself immoral. For it is essentially corrupting. It is, in the end, not really to give *reasons*, but only to give *motives*. Essentially the same applies if the child should ask why he should not hit other children. To tell him that the other children will hit him back, or that he will be punished for it, is to give him a motive; to tell him that it is wrong, and that it is wrong because he would not like other children to hit him, and they do not like to be hit either, is to give him a reason. To give only the first, where one can give the second, is itself morally wrong. For it not only does nothing to develop the child's character, it tends to corrupt it.

If, then, a motive is what is wanted when one asks why he should be moral, it is something that often can be given. And if this is what is demanded when one demands a justification of moral principles, such a justification often can be given. Only this would not be a moral justification, and such a reason is not a moral reason.

One final point. It should be evident that the question "Why should I be moral?" is obscure in the asking of it. Analysis can distinguish its different possible meanings. But there is no reason to suppose that anyone actually asking it is aware of the ambiguity. Thus the question continues to be raised. Furthermore, there is no question of getting the questioner to *see* that he ought to do what he ought to do—that he ought to be moral. The problem is to get him to *do* what he ought to do, whether he verbally assents or not. If he does not see it, then he is irrational. But if he does not do it, then he is immoral. The belief that one ought to do something normally functions by itself as a motive for doing it, though in particular cases it may not *prevail*. To ask "Why should I be moral?" is really to ask for some *further* motive, and it may or may not be possible to give one. Yet to ask the question is already a symptom of immorality, since it implies that one is not ready to do what he ought unless there is something further in it for him. And one who asks whether he ought to do this or that, or why he ought to do something or other that it is alleged he ought to do, implies, by the fact of asking, that he is prepared to do what he ought to do, in so far as he can recognize it. He is not asking why he should be moral, but is taking it for granted that he should, and this is a precondition of having a moral problem. If he should go on to ask why he should be moral, this shows that his first question was frivolous. Thus the question with which we have been dealing would have very little relevance in the context of a moral problem.

For virtuous people, therefore, virtue is its own reward— meaning that it needs no reward. For others it is not, and it is here that whips and carrots, rewards and punishments, are required. To suppose, however, that no one ever does anything simply because he believes that it would be morally wrong for him not to, is to live in a dream world. It may not be an idealistic world, but it would not be a realistic one either.

§ 4 §

In my discussion of moral rules and principles (in Chapter V), I argued that moral principles are to be distinguished from moral rules by the fact that the former hold in all circumstances and do not admit of exceptions; that principles are always relevant whereas rules are not; that principles are invariant and do not vary with changes in circumstances or conditions; and by the fact that it is impossible for moral principles to conflict with each other. I tried to show, further-more, how moral principles—and especially the generalization principle and the generalization argument—are involved in the establishment of moral rules, and how, in particular, they can establish different rules in different circumstances. In this connection, I distinguished between fundamental rules, local rules, and neutral norms. Local rules, I maintained, depend on local conditions in a way that fundamental rules do not, and hence are peculiar to, and differ with, different groups and communities—that is to say, different circum-stances. Neutral norms are local rules that are conventional in a way that other rules are not, but both neutral norms and local rules depend on social needs or purposes that are advanced by their general observance and would be frustrated or defeated by their general violation. Hence changes in these needs or purposes or conditions would require changes in these rules, though this does not always take place.

I mention all this now in order to bring out the relevance of this distinction to the problem posed by the diversity and the variety of moral codes and standards, and to the per-plexities to which this has given rise. I have in mind here the theory of ethical relativism, which is often regarded as an in-dex of moral, or scientific, sophistication, and which is perhaps the most popular form of moral skepticism.

Let us distinguish between moral (or cultural) diversity, and ethical (or moral) relativism. The two are distinct, and nothing but confusion can result from identifying them. That their names have so often varied may be a factor in this con-fusion. By cultural diversity (or relativity) I understand the empirically ascertained fact that there are a great many dif-ferent and even conflicting rules and practices prevailing at different times and in different places, so that (what at least appears to be) the same act may be regarded as right in one place and as wrong in another. By ethical relativism I under-stand the theory that moral ideas are all necessarily "relative to" to a particular society, in the sense that they reflect the "standpoint" of some particular society and only "hold for" that society, so that in case of a conflict between these different standards there is no impartial or objective way of deciding between them; any reason that might be given would itself merely reflect the standpoint of the group to which one belongs. Thus on this theory all moral judgments are incomplete unless they specify "the standpoint" from which they are made, and it is a further consequence of it that moral judgments are really expressions of the attitude or characteristic bias of a particular group. On this view, in other words, there is nothing that can correctly be said to *be* right or wrong; it is only a question of what is *called* "right" or "wrong," and by what group it is so called.

That there are varieties of moralities and moral codes is a fact which is not in question. Ethical relativism, however, is not a fact, but a theory which attempts to account for this fact. The fact of moral diversity is of course a main source of this theory, since it provides the data that it tries to explain. But by itself it is not sufficient to give rise to it or to establish it. For this purpose other assumptions are required, and these cannot themselves be established.

This theory arises, in the first place, from a failure to distinguish moral rules, and particular moral judgments, from moral principles. It involves a failure to distinguish the invariant moral principles from the variable conditions that, in accordance with these principles, require or permit a variety of different rules and practices. Though practices and rules may be "relative," it does not follow that principles are. Yet this theory supposes that it does. It should really be obvious that moral principles, and I have in mind here especially the generalization principle and the generalization argument, do not require any uniformity of practices in different cultures. For they do not require any uniformity of practices in different circumstances. What is right in one context or set of circumstances may not be right in another, and differences in social or geographical conditions, or in social or cultural needs, can count as relevant differences in circumstances. Thus what is right in Pomerania need not be right in Polynesia, or among the Dobuans, or in Rome. What is puzzling is that it should ever have been supposed that it should. For this general point, that moral principles are consistent with and allow for a wide variety of rules and practices, has often been made before, and from a variety of "standpoints." It was put in this way, for instance, in 1758, well before the discoveries of modern anthropology:

> Though all men, in all cases, judged rightly what is virtue and right behaviour, there would still prevail a very considerable variety in their moral practices in different ages and countries. The reason is obvious: In different ages and circumstances of the world, the same practices often have not the same connexions, tendencies, and effects. The state of human affairs is perpetually changing, and, in the same period of time, it is very different in different nations. . . . New obligations must arise, and the proprieties of conduct must vary, as new connexions take place, and new customs, laws, and political constitutions are introduced. Many practices, very warrantable and proper under one form of government, or in the first establishment of a community, or amongst people of a particular genius, and where particular regulations and opinions prevail, may be quite wrong in another state of things, or amongst people of other characters and customs.[3]

This point should be fairly clear with respect to local rules, since I have already pointed out that such rules vary with and depend upon conditions and needs that are different at different times and places, and this is in fact the defining feature of such rules. With respect to fundamental rules, however, it may not be so obvious. For there are, it appears, societies in which such rules as the rule against lying are not recog-

---

[3] Richard Price, *A Review of the Principal Questions in Morals*, ed. D. Daiches Raphael (Oxford: The Clarendon Press, 1948), chap. VII, p. 175. Cf. p. 176: "In considering the diversity of sentiments amongst mankind concerning any particular practices, it will be right, amongst other things, not to overlook the difference in the real state of the case, which the differences of times and places make, and how far they alter the relation of such practices to the general principles of morality." See also, for this same general point, Sir W. David Ross, *Foundations of Ethics* (Oxford: The Clarendon Press, 1939), pp. 18-19; Frank Chapman Sharp, *Ethics* (New York: The Century Co., 1928), Chap. XI; Morris R. Cohen, *Reason and Nature* (New York: Harcourt, Brace and Company, 1931), pp. 349, 411-2; and Morris Ginsberg, *Reason and Unreason in Society* (London: Longmans, Green and Company, 1947), pp. 305-7.

nized at all, in which lying is not regarded as wrong; or at least in which the scope of the rule is drastically restricted, so that there are relatively few persons to whom it is thought wrong to lie. But the fact that in some societies it is not wrong, or is not thought wrong, to lie, is not inconsistent with the rule that lying is generally wrong. For the rule does not say that it is always wrong to lie; and under certain conditions, which may prevail in certain societies, the presumption of the rule may be *inoperative*. Where there is a recognized and well-defined class of exceptions to a rule, it is possible to formulate a subsidiary rule stating the conditions under which the fundamental rule does not apply, in which its presumption is inoperative. If the circumstances governed by the subsidiary rule should become general, so that they are no longer exceptional, the subsidiary rule may take precedence. So there may be whole societies, or whole periods of time, where people are governed more by the subsidiary rule than the fundamental rule. Such a set of conditions, as we have seen, would be the "state of nature" so vividly described by Hobbes. Where conditions of mutual suspicion and hostility prevail, so that telling the truth is, in general, likely to place one in a position of considerable disadvantage, there is, in general, no obligation to tell the truth.[4] In such circumstances lying is (or is thought to be) a means of survival, an instrument of self-defense, and in such circumstances the consequences of the general violation of the rule are not what they would be ordinarily. Indeed, in

---

[4] Cf. A. Macbeath, *Experiments in Living* (London: Macmillan & Co. Ltd., 1952), pp. 372-3: "If a man believes, as the Bantu does, that any of his neighbors may be, and that some of them in fact are, endowed with supernatural powers which may be used to do him or his neighbors harm; and if he further believes that giving them information provides them with the means of using those powers, we have a state of affairs in which not mutual trust and confidence but mutual suspicion and fear are likely to flourish. In such circumstances, truth-telling is not likely to be regarded as a virtue except in situations like giving evidence in court, where truth-telling is likely to result in good to others and lying in harm to them." It should be observed that in these matters it is essential to distinguish between explanation and justification. In all such cases, where a certain practice may be explained by a certain peculiar belief, there is always the question whether the belief itself is justified.

such circumstances there is generally no expectation that the truth will be told. What is undesirable, no doubt, is the existence of such a situation, but this is something else again; and of course people in such circumstances could not lie all the time, or to everyone. Now in certain societies and in certain areas, existing even today, people are as close to living in a state of nature (in which the life of man is "solitary, poor, nasty, brutish, and short") as it is possible to come. (Compare conditions in a concentration camp, or in a den of thieves, or "on the waterfront.")

But, in the second place, this theory also arises out of the peculiar and question-begging assumption that if a certain practice prevails in a certain place then it is necessarily right in that place, that if a rule is not *recognized* or *observed* by the members of a certain group then it does not *apply* to or is not *binding* on the members of that group. This assumption is not just peculiar; it leads to contradiction. There is no reason why this assumption must be restricted to a group or a society; if it holds for a group then it would hold for any individual. (Or, if you prefer, one person can constitute himself a society.) On this assumption, one could organize a group of thieves, who, by the mere fact that they like or want to steal, would be justified in stealing. On this assumption the members of "Murder Incorporated" were perfectly justified in murdering whom they pleased, since they had no scruples against it. Indeed, on this view one could justify oneself in doing anything whatsoever merely by refusing to recognize any rule against it or by inculcating a taste for it. I have already pointed out how this is self-contradictory. No one is justified in violating any moral rule, or in violating the rights of another, simply because he wants to or finds it convenient, or simply because he has no scruples against it; and no one would be justified in this simply because he is a member of a group with similar dispositions.

If I were suddenly to hit you on the head, with the jagged edge of a broken bottle, for no reason at all, or "just because I felt like it," this would be immoral, and there is no possibility of justifying such an action (as so described), as distinct from getting away with it. This is a case of wanton assault, of cruelty for the sake of cruelty, and this is always wrong, irrespective of circumstances. After the Indians in the Hudson Bay territory had obtained guns, it is reported, they "used to hunt Eskimos for sport, as we hunt bear or deer . . . When eventually the Eskimos got guns, the Indians left them alone." [5] No doubt hunting Eskimos for sport was, at least for a time, part of the accepted practice of this Indian community; it may even have acquired the status of an institution, into which the young were initiated by elaborate ceremonials. But by no stretch of the imagination does it follow that it was therefore justified, and I have already set forth the principles on which this can be shown. It is one thing to record a practice; it is another to determine its moral standing.

The variety of practices and rules that prevail in different places (or even in any one place) is no greater than the variety of beliefs and of the procedures for arriving at conclusions. There is nothing so fantastic or so unfounded that you cannot find someone to believe it, and there is no line of reasoning so baseless that you cannot find someone to accept it; you may even find a place where it is the practice to do so. It is curious that this has not been thought with any great frequency to justify an epistemological or a logical relativism. This could not be so much as stated without contradiction, for the theory itself could be no more than "relative." But the principle is exactly the same, and if the diversity of beliefs does not establish that logic is "merely relative," then the diversity of morals does not establish that ethics is "merely relative." The fact that a group of people believe something does not make it true, and the fact that a group of people practice something does not make it right.

This is, to be sure, a topic of the greatest complexity, and there is much more to be said about it, though I am not about to say it. I might just add that the observation of different and apparently conflicting codes and practices is a major source of *moral* problems, not just of problems of ethical the-

[5] From an article by Robert Lewis Taylor, *The New Yorker*, vol. XXV, no. 17 (June 18, 1949) (1), p. 30.

ory or moral philosophy. Moral problems are not simply problems of what to do; they are also problems of what to believe. With respect to morality, at any rate, there can be no hard and fast line between theory and practice.

§ 5 §

Ethical relativism, I have been arguing, is shown to be fallacious by the distinction between moral rules and principles. Rules are established or justified by reference to principles, and the same principles can establish different rules in different circumstances and hence for different societies. Hence, though rules and practices may be "relative," and even to some extent what I have called fundamental rules, it does not follow that principles are. But, in this respect, that they are universal in scope, fundamental moral rules are really more like moral principles than they are like other rules—this is part of their definition as fundamental. Hence the sense in which they can be "relative" is quite different from the sense in which other rules are; they can be relative only in the sense that they are not binding under certain types of conditions.

But now how can moral principles themselves be established? On what basis can it be maintained that a moral principle is valid? Perhaps in the end they themselves are "merely relative," and hence, in the end, really arbitrary.

This last suggestion is really impossible. Since moral principles, by definition, transcend the geographical and temporal boundaries of particular societies, and hence all merely local needs and conditions, there is nothing to which they could be "relative," except to morality itself. The fact that in some places, or by some people, a certain principle may not be recognized or accepted is purely irrelevant. So is the fact that there might be someone who does not accept or act in accordance with *any* moral principles. Such a person would be immoral (or perhaps amoral), but this has no more bearing on the validity of moral principles than the existence of fallacious reasoning has on the validity of logical principles. Furthermore, there is no need to deal with purely metaphysical or neurotic or self-seeking doubts. One must have certain moral ideas and convictions, beliefs to the effect that something or other is right and that something or other is wrong, from the start. In fact, all of us do.

As these remarks should indicate, there is a sense in which the demand for a justification of moral principles is a genuine demand, and a sense in which it is not. It makes no sense, for example, to demand a justification for them *all together*, at the same time. This demand is contradictory, if not perverse, and the way in which it is put would effectively preclude any possibility of satisfying it. For to demand this is to demand a moral reason for accepting anything as a moral reason, and this is a self-contradictory demand. It is equivalent to asking "Why should I accept any moral principles at all?" and we have already dealt with this. For the same reasons it makes no sense to demand a justification for any *one* principle where this demand simply amounts to asking "Why should I be moral?" Where this is what is meant by the question "Why should this principle be adopted?" (compare "Why ought I to adopt the generalization principle?"), the question need not detain us. Some relevant standards must be admitted as a basis for argument, and where nothing could count as a justification there is no point in attempting one. In such cases it is the demand itself that requires justification.

None of this, however, need be what is meant by the demand for a justification of moral principles. The question might be simply "What reason is there for accepting such and such a principle as a moral principle?" or "What are the reasons for regarding it as valid or sound?" Such questions as these do make sense and can be satisfactorily and reasonably answered. But to do this we need do no more than review what has already been accomplished.

There are three things to be noted here. In the first place, the procedure that is relevant can be determined from the characterization that has been given of moral principles, which was based on their function and their relation to moral rules. One of the important considerations here is the criterion that moral principles cannot conflict with each other. Nothing is

acceptable as a moral principle that does not meet these qualifications. Or, if it is still to be called a principle, since it is
alleged to be one, it cannot be valid.

In the second place, what is relevant here is not so much a
justification in the sense of a demonstration, or a deduction
from self-evident premises, as a *defense*. This involves the
elimination of misunderstandings, the meeting of difficulties,
and the answering of objections, and this is a procedure I
have in fact followed. But this will vary, depending on the
principle in question, since, as we have seen, some moral
principles can be deduced from others.

Thirdly, the procedure involved is exemplified both (a) in
the arguments that have been given *for* certain principles,
such as the generalization principle, the principle of consequences, the generalization argument, and the categorical imperative; and (b) in the arguments that have been given
against certain alleged others, such as the obverse generalization argument, the obverse of the principle of consequences,
and the principle of utility. Hence the considerations that are
relevant to the justification or defense of moral principles are
to be determined from the arguments already given. This
means that there is no *separate* question about the justification
of moral principles, apart from the justification of this one or
that one. What is relevant to one may not be relevant to another.

Let us briefly review some of the arguments that have been
given. My defense of the generalization principle is contained
mainly in Chapters II and III. There I attempted to clarify
it, to show how it can be applied, to meet various objections
to it, and to show how it is involved in all moral reasoning.
This being so, I cannot think that there is anything else that
is needed. I do not think it impossible that I have failed to
do what I attempted, but if I have not, then any lingering
doubts about the validity of this principle would be unreasonable.

My arguments for the principle of consequences are contained in Chapter IV (section 1) and Chapter V (section 2).
I argued that this principle, like the generalization principle,

is a precondition of moral reasoning, and that once it is properly understood, there could be no reasonable question about it. (Is there anyone who does not regard the consequences of an action as relevant to its morality—not the actual but the foreseeable consequences—and who does not think that if the consequences of a certain act would be undesirable this is a reason for regarding it as wrong? What could be his reason for this?) Thus I attempted mainly to eliminate some possible misunderstandings of it.

With respect to the generalization argument, there is, first, its derivation from the principle of consequences and the generalization principle, which was given in the first section of Chapter IV. I argued there, in effect, that anyone who accepts the generalization principle and the principle of consequences must, in consistency, accept the generalization argument. But this argument, by itself, is not sufficient to justify this principle. There are too many objections and difficulties and anomalous cases that seem to apply especially to it. My main arguments in defense of this principle are contained in Chapters IV, V, and VI. Again, if they are sound, what more is needed?

The categorical imperative has been dealt with so recently that no special mention of it seems required here. At any rate, I can here add nothing to the arguments for it given in Chapters VIII and IX, and also, in view of its connection with the generalization argument (see Chapter IX, section 2), to the arguments presented elsewhere in this book.

From these three (or four) principles all the others I have mentioned can be derived. The principle of justification, for example, follows from the generalization argument and from what has been said about moral rules. The principle that one is never justified in violating a moral rule by the fact that one wants to or would find it convenient, or the principle that one is never justified in violating a moral rule whenever and simply because doing so would be to one's own interest, is also established by the application of the generalization argument.[6]

[6] See *supra*, Chapter V, sec. 5, pp. 121-122; and cf. K. Baier, "The Point of View of Morality," *The Australasian Journal of Philosophy*, vol. XXXII,

What I have called the correlated moral principles, or moral laws, can be established in much the same way. Given that one is never justified in violating a moral rule by the fact that one wants to, then, since doing something simply for the sake of doing so (for its own sake) is (not identical with but) a special case of doing it because one wants to, it follows that one is never justified in doing something that is generally wrong (that is, that violates a moral rule) simply for the sake of doing so. To say that one is never justified in this, of course, is to say that it is always wrong. Thus it is always wrong to kill for the sake of killing, lie for the sake of lying, and so on.

The principle of suffering, which I have expressed in the form "It is always wrong to cause unnecessary suffering" (but which could also be stated in a number of other ways), can also be established in this way. Consider the moral rule that is correlated with this principle, that it is generally wrong to cause others to suffer, or to cause them pain or serious inconvenience or to disappoint their legitimate expectations and plans. This rule can be established both by the generalization argument and the principle of consequences, and it clearly follows from it that any such action requires justification. This, together with the principle that "I want to" is never a justification, will enable us to derive this principle. For any action that *unnecessarily* causes someone to suffer, or causes any of the other things I have mentioned, is unjustifiable. Thus what must be shown is that the act (or its conse-

---

(August 1954), p. 116: "What . . . are the required principles of making exceptions to a moral rule? It has been held that one of the principles is that one must never make an exception in one's own favour. This has been interpreted (and very naturally) as meaning 'Never make an exception to a moral rule when doing so would be in your own interest.' But this cannot be right, for I am at least as justified in killing a man in my own defence as I am in killing one in someone else's. And often it is just as immoral to make an exception when this is in someone else's interest, e.g., my wife's, my son's or my nephew's. In fact, it is quite unimportant in itself in whose favour the exception operates, so long as it was made legitimately, and it is made legitimately in the case of self-defence. The truth contained in this view is simply this, that I must not make exceptions to a moral rule *on the principle* that I will depart from the rule *whenever and simply because* doing so is in my interest or, for that matter, in that of someone else whom I wish to favour."

quence) is unavoidable, or that the consequences of the alternative action would be worse (or at least no better), or that the situation is one that is properly competitive and that the risk involved is one that is unavoidably involved in it. What will count as necessary or unnecessary will of course vary with the circumstances and the nature of the case. But this principle is not therefore insignificant. (Compare Chapter V, section 2, pp. 107-108).

Further arguments for these various subsidiary principles, of course, are provided by their elucidation and their defense against various objections. But apart from this nothing else is needed or even relevant. As I have just said, no separate justification of moral principles can be required, over and above the arguments and the considerations that are particularly relevant to each, once it is understood what is here meant by a moral principle. Furthermore, the justification that has been given is a *moral* justification, not one of some other kind. Nothing else would be appropriate. So none of them can be expected to have any rational force, or even any meaning, for one who has no moral beliefs to start with.

If these arguments are sound, then we have established the rational basis of morality, and nothing more, on this score, is needed.[7]

§ 6 §

There are, as I have admitted, varying moral codes and varying moral beliefs. For there are various customs, traditions, and institutions, just as there are different conditions, needs, and goals. Thus the morality of *some* matters can depend on custom and tradition and even edict. It accordingly makes sense to speak of various moralities, such as Hottentot morality or middle-class morality (though anthropological discussions of these matters too frequently confuse morality with

[7] It is curious that no one would ever think of asking what is the rational basis of prudence. Why is the corresponding question about morality thought significant? No doubt because prudence is already regarded as intrinsically rational, while morality is not. The reason for this can only be a prejudice in favor of the rationality of self-interest.

mores or even manners). But all of this is both allowed for
and accounted for by my concept of local rules and neutral
norms, and none of it can apply to fundamental moral
rules or moral principles.

The great difficulty in morals is not really a matter of
theory. It lies in the resolution of concrete cases. There are
so many decisions it is so difficult to make, so many problems it is so difficult to solve, so many disputes it is so difficult
to settle, that a reflective observer may perhaps be excused for
despairing of objective solutions. The variable factors just
mentioned, no doubt, are partly responsible for this difficulty.
But the main source of it, I am convinced, is the difficulty of
determining with certainty and precision the facts of the
case—what actually happened, just what the circumstances
are, what the consequences will probably be. One might
think that, since these are all empirical matters, they should be
easy to settle and attain agreement on. This is not so, and it
is unwise to think so. Disputes about facts constitute the
major source of the litigation which ties up our courts, and
this is not always because we have a tendency to believe what
we think is in our interest. "Treatises of morality always suppose facts to be ascertained; and not only so, but the intention likewise of the parties to be laid bare." [8] In actual life, as
treatises of morality are actually aware, it is precisely the facts
that are the most difficult to ascertain, and it is comparatively
easy to lay down hypothetical judgments, of the sort, "If the
facts are so and so, then such and such ought to be done."

This being so, it is only to be expected that on problems of
morality, as on problems of law, there is considerable room for
reasonable disagreement. There are some who would explain
this by reference to the varying backgrounds and interests of
the parties. I wish them well, but they cannot be wholly
successful. For this view, when carried to its logical conclusion, is self-defeating. There are as many disagreements in the
social sciences, and about facts, as there are in ethics and morality. It is in the nature of the subject matter that on moral

[8] William Paley, *The Principles of Moral and Political Philosophy* (7th
ed.; London: R. Faulder, 1790), vol. II, bk. VI, chap. VIII, p. 251.

matters reasonable men can, on occasion, reasonably disagree. For the problems are often so complex and difficult, and no man is omniscient. Even if the principles set forth in this book are as clear and as certain as I believe them to be, their application will often be unclear and uncertain. Yet this is no reason for despair or for skepticism. In the reasonable disagreements of reasonable men we may find, so far as we are reasonable, both hope and enlightenment. For it is only in the development of reasonableness, to which this process contributes, that there is any hope for a better world.

BIBLIOGRAPHICAL NOTES

I shall list here some books and articles having special relevance to the basic topic of this book, and to some of the subsidiary topics taken up along the way. This is not a formal bibliography, for which I see no need, nor is this list meant to be exhaustive. Some of the items listed have also been mentioned in the text; others have not; and still other items mentioned in the text receive no further mention here. But the fact of duplication, or the lack of it, should cause no difficulty. If these notes are of use to the reader who wishes to inquire further, they will have served their purpose. They are intended for the serious student, not the general reader; consequently most of these references are to journal articles, not to books, although I have restricted myself to items available in English.

CHAPTER II · THE GENERALIZATION PRINCIPLE

The substance of this chapter, now somewhat modified (along with the first few paragraphs of chapter one), appeared as an article in *Mind*, vol. LXIV (July 1955), pp. 361-75.

HENRY SIDGWICK. Sidgwick discusses the principle of justice (the generalization principle) in the following places in *The Methods of Ethics* (7th ed.; London: Macmillan and Co., Ltd., 1907): Preface to 6th edition, p. xvii; Bk. III, chap. I, sec. 3, pp. 208-10; chap. V, secs. 1 and 2, pp. 266-8; chap. VII, sec. 3, pp. 318-19; chap. XIII, secs. 3 and 4, pp. 379-86; Bk. IV, chap. III, sec. 4, pp. 441-2; chap. V, sec. 3, pp. 485-9. The seventh edition of this important work is a practically unaltered reprint of the sixth (1901), but differs considerably from the others.

A comprehensive work that is a valuable supplement to Sidgwick's is Hastings Rashdall's *The Theory of Good and Evil* (2nd ed.; London: Oxford University Press, 1924, 2 vol.). On the subject of the present chapter, see especially vol. II, bk. II, chap. IV, pp. 107-48 ("Vocation"). See also vol. II, p. 428: "No two cases are exactly alike, but they may be alike in all relevant particulars; or if not alike, the difference can be allowed for in the treatment of the particular case—an allowance which may itself be covered by some more or less definable general principle."

THE GOLDEN RULE. The Golden Rule has received remarkably little philosophical discussion. It is generally mentioned only in passing, as it has been here. Considering its obvious importance, this is unfortunate. Some discussions of more than usual interest are the following: A. T. Cadoux, "The Implications of the Golden Rule," *The International Journal of Ethics*, vol. XXII (April 1912), pp. 272-87. J. O. Hertzler, "On Golden Rules," *The International Journal of Ethics*, vol. XLIV (July 1934), pp. 418-36; this is mainly of historical and sociological interest, and philosophically is not very searching. Much of Hertzler's paper is derived from the article "Golden Rule" by W. A. Spooner in *The Encyclopedia of Religion and Ethics*, ed. by James Hastings (New York: Charles Scribner's Sons, 1914), vol. VI.

There are some searching remarks on the Golden Rule in chap. IV of Richard Whately's *Lessons on Morals* (Cambridge, Mass.; John Bartlett, 1857); and some provocative remarks in L. J. Russell's article, "Ideals and Practice," *Philosophy*, vol. XVII (April 1942), at pp. 109-10.

CHAPTER III · MORAL JUDGMENTS AND MORAL REASONS

MORAL JUDGMENTS AND GENERALITY. On the topic of the generality, or universality, of moral judgments, the following items, not mentioned in the text, may be of interest.

Duncan-Jones, Austin: *Butler's Moral Philosophy* (Harmondsworth: Penguin Books, 1952), pp. 171-4.
Gellner, E. A.: "Ethics and Logic," *Aristotelian Society Proceedings*, vol. LV (1954-55), pp. 157-78.
————: "Morality and *Je Ne Sais Quoi* Concepts," *Analysis*, vol. XVI (April 1956), pp. 97-103.
Hare, R. M.: "Universalisability," *Aristotelian Society Proceedings*, vol. LV (1954-55), pp. 295-312. These last three items should be read together.
Laird, John: *An Enquiry into Moral Notions* (London: George Allen & Unwin Ltd., 1935), pp. 156-9.
Lucas, J. R.: "The Lesbian Rule," *Philosophy*, vol. XXX (July 1955), pp. 195-213. A strange but stimulating paper.

For criticism of the idea of the generality of moral judgments, the following may be consulted, though they are not all of the same quality or pertinence.

Brunton, J. A.: "Egoism and Morality," *The Philosophical Quarterly*, vol. VI (October 1956), pp. 289-303. Comments on the papers by Gellner and Hare.

Durrant, R. G.: "Moral Neutrality and the Analysis of Morality," *The Australasian Journal of Philosophy*, vol. XXXVI (December 1958), pp. 169-88. Comments on the papers by Gellner and Hare, and on the paper by MacIntyre (below); see especially pp. 176-84.

Frankena, William K.: "MacIntyre on Defining Morality," *Philosophy*, vol. XXXIII (April 1958), pp. 158-62.

Hepburn, R. W.: "Vision and Choice in Morality," *Dreams and Self-Knowledge*, Aristotelian Society, Supplementary vol. XXX (1956), pp. 14-31.

MacIntyre, Alasdair: "What Morality is Not," *Philosophy*, vol. XXXII (October 1957), pp. 325-35. Extremely provocative; well-worth reading.

Murdoch, Iris: "Vision and Choice in Morality," *Dreams and Self-Knowledge*, Aristotelian Society, Supplementary vol. XXX (1956), pp. 32-58. See esp. p. 45: ". . . If one is Napoleon one does not think that everyone should do as one does oneself. . . ."

Weller, Gershon: "Universalizability By Me," *The Philosophical Quarterly*, vol. X (April 1960), pp. 167-70.

MORAL REASONING. Out of the mass of material available here, much of it worthless, I shall mention only the four following items, on the grounds of their provocative and original nature.

Brown, D. G.: "Evaluative Inference," *Philosophy*, vol. XXX (July 1955), pp. 214-28.

Foot, Philippa: "Moral Arguments," *Mind*, vol. LXVII (October 1958), pp. 502-13.

Lucas, J. R.: "On Not Worshipping Facts," *The Philosophical Quarterly*, vol. VIII (April 1958), pp. 144-56.

Rawls, John: "Outline of a Decision Procedure for Ethics," *The Philosophical Review*, vol. LX (April 1951), pp. 177-97.

ANALOGY IN MORAL REASONING. Perhaps the most famous example of the moral use of analogy is the one that occurs in Second Samuel 11-12, in which Nathan said to David; "Thou art the man." For an interesting comment on this, see L. Susan Stebbing, *Thinking to Some Purpose* (Harmondsworth: Penguin Books, 1939), pp. 114-16. Of course there are many other sources of comment on this famous passage. See also, Stebbing, *op. cit.*, pp. 50-3, for a brief discussion of the "fallacy of special pleading."

PROBABILITY. On the analogy between moral judgments and judgments of probability, or between the terms "right" and "probable," see the discussion by R. F. Atkinson, entitled " 'Good' and 'Right,' and 'Probable' in *Language, Truth and Logic,*" in *Mind,* vol. LXIV (April 1955), pp. 242-6; in which, among other things, the point is made that questions of probability are at least partly normative and not simply questions of (observable) fact. I alluded to this parallel in a review, in *The Philosophical Review,* vol. LXIII (January 1954), at p. 138.

CHAPTER IV · THE GENERALIZATION
ARGUMENT

Most of the following items have been mentioned in the text, either in the body or in footnotes. They are here listed in the order of their appearance, and they are all required reading on the subject.

> Broad, C. D.: "On the Function of False Hypotheses in Ethics," *The International Journal of Ethics,* vol. XXVI (April 1916), pp. 377-97.
>
> Harrod, R. F.: "Utilitarianism Revised," *Mind,* vol. XLV (April 1936), pp. 137-56, especially pp. 147-55.
>
> Ewing, A. C.: "What Would Happen If Everybody Acted Like Me?" *Philosophy,* vol. XXVIII (January 1953), pp. 16-29.
>
> Harrison, J.: "Utilitarianism, Universalisation, and Our Duty to be Just," *Aristotelian Society Proceedings,* vol. LIII (1952-53), pp. 105-34.
>
> Stout, A. K.: "But Suppose Everyone Did the Same," *The Australasian Journal of Philosophy,* vol. XXXII (May 1954), pp. 1-29.
>
> Baier, Kurt: "The Point of View of Morality," *The Australasian Journal of Philosophy,* vol. XXXII (August 1954), pp. 104-35; especially pp. 110-14, 127-30.
>
> ————: *The Moral Point of View: A Rational Basis of Ethics* (Ithaca: Cornell University Press, 1958), chap. VIII.

Some of the points of this chapter were briefly outlined in a paper in *Mind,* vol. LXIV (July 1955), at pp. 372-5.

CHAPTER V · MORAL RULES
AND PRINCIPLES

The substance of this chapter appeared as an essay, of the same title, in *Essays in Moral Philosophy,* ed. by A. I. Melden (Seattle:

University of Washington Press, 1958), pp. 160-97. For critical discussion, see the review by Kurt Baier, in *The Philosophical Review*, vol. LXIX (July 1960), at pp. 416-7. It was also reviewed by Herbert W. Schneider, in *The Journal of Philosophy*, vol. LVI (August 13, 1959), at p. 708.

RULES AND PRINCIPLES. The following items can all be recommended, on one ground or another. It should be kept in mind, however, that the distinction elaborated in this work is not necessarily the one followed in any of the following discussions. Indeed, in some of them no such distinction seems to be made at all.

Baier, K.: "The Point of View of Morality," *The Australasian Journal of Philosophy*, vol. XXXII (August 1954), pp. 104-35.

E. F. Carritt, *The Theory of Morals* (London: Oxford University Press, 1928), chap. XIII. Sharply critical of the notion of moral rules.

Mabbott, J. D.: "Moral Rules," in *The Proceedings of the British Academy*, vol. XXXIX (London: Oxford University Press, 1953), pp. 97-118; also relevant to Chap. IV, VII, and VIII of the present work. Reviewed by A. C. Ewing in *Philosophy*, vol. XXXI (April 1956), pp. 168-9.

Melden, A. I.: *Rights and Right Conduct* (Oxford: Basil Blackwell, 1959).

Miller, Leonard G.: "Rules and Exceptions," *Ethics*, vol. LXVI (July 1956), pp. 262-70.

Rawls, John: "Two Concepts of Rules," *The Philosophical Review*, vol. LXIV (January 1955), pp. 3-32.

————: "Justice as Fairness," *The Philosophical Review*, vol. LXVII (April 1958), pp. 164-94.

Rees, W. J.: "Moral Rules and the Analysis of 'Ought,'" *The Philosophical Review*, vol. LXII (January 1953), pp. 23-40.

Shwayder, D. S.: "Moral Rules and Moral Maxims," *Ethics*, vol. LXVII (July 1957), pp. 269-85.

See also the symposium, "When is a Principle a Moral Principle?" by P. R. Foot and Jonathan Harrison, in *Belief and Will*, Aristotelian Society, supplementary vol. XXVIII (1954), pp. 95-134.

MORAL CODES. For a useful compilation, now somewhat outdated, see Edgar L. Heermance, *Codes of Ethics* (Burlington, Vt.: Free Press Printing Co., 1924). For an interesting discussion, with further references, see "An Ethical Code for Scientists," by W. Pignan and E. B. Carmichael, *Science*, vol. CXI (1950), pp. 643-7; also *Science*, vol. CXII (1950), p. 656. For further references on this subject, see Harold H. Titus, *Ethics For Today* (2nd ed.; New York: American Book Company, 1954), chap. XIX-XXI.

VERACITY. A useful counterpart to Cabot's *Honesty* (which was cited in the text) is provided by Friedrich Paulsen's *A System of Ethics*, trans. by Frank Thilly (New York: Charles Scribner's Sons, 1899), Bk. III, chap. XI; where an opposite position is taken on the matter of exceptions, and the matter is argued with great force and charm.

CHAPTER VI · THE APPLICATION
OF THE GENERALIZATION
ARGUMENT

All of the items cited in connection with Chapter IV are relevant here. In connection with state of nature situations, see especially the paper by Harrod, pp. 151 ff., and the paper by Harrison, pp. 125-30. One item deserving special mention here is the symposium on "Equality," by Richard Wollheim and Isaiah Berlin, in *Aristotelian Society Proceedings*, vol. LVI (1955-56), pp. 281-326. See also Thomas Fowler, *Progressive Morality: An Essay in Ethics* (London: Macmillan and Co., 1884), pp. 75-80, 116-18, and 146-50. There is an interesting discussion of "Action" by A. I. Melden, in *The Philosophical Review*, vol. LXV (October 1956), pp. 523-41. On punishment, I shall mention only J. D. Mabbott, "Punishment," *Mind*, vol. XLVIII (April 1939), pp. 152-67; and C. W. K. Mundle, "Punishment and Desert," *The Philosophical Quarterly*, vol. IV (July 1954), pp. 216-28.

CHAPTER VII · THE PRINCIPLE OF
UTILITY AND GENERALIZATION

In addition to Paley's, discussed in the text, the classic accounts of this matter are by David Hume and John Austin. See Hume's *Treatise of Human Nature* (1740), ed. by L. A. Selby-Bigge (Oxford: The Clarendon Press, 1888), Bk. III, Pt. II, especially secs. ii-iv, vi-ix; also *An Enquiry Concerning the Principles of Morals* (1751), ed. by L. A. Selby-Bigge (2nd ed.; Oxford: The Clarendon Press, 1902), Appendix iii, "Some Farther Considerations with Regard to Justice," and sec. III, pt. ii, p. 203: "Even in common life we have every moment recourse to the principle of public utility, and ask, *What must become of the world, if such practices prevail? How could society subsist under such disorders?*" For Austin, see *The Province of Jurisprudence Determined* (1832), ed. by H. L. A. Hart (London: Weidenfeld and Nicolson, 1954), lec. ii.

Direct and Indirect Utilitarianism. In addition to the papers by Harrod, Stout, and Harrison, cited in connection with Chapter IV, and the papers by Rawls, cited in connection with Chapter V, the following items, listed in the order of their appearance, are worthy of note.

Laird, John: *An Enquiry into Moral Notions* (London: George Allen & Unwin, Ltd., 1935), chap. XVII, esp. pp. 274-84.

Urmson, J. O.: "The Interpretation of the Moral Philosophy of J. S. Mill," *The Philosophical Quarterly*, vol. III (January 1953), pp. 33-9. Suggestive and valuable.

Mabbott, J. D.: "Interpretations of Mill's 'Utilitarianism,'" *The Philosophical Quarterly*, vol. VI (April 1956), pp. 115-20. Comment on Urmson's paper; very good, and, I think, right.

Smart, J. J. C.: "Extreme and Restricted Utilitarianism," *The Philosophical Quarterly*, vol. VI (October 1956), pp. 344-54. Very suggestive; but, I think, wrong.

Duncan-Jones, Austin: "Utilitarianism and Rules," *The Philosophical* Quarterly, vol. VII (October 1957), pp. 364-7.

John Stuart Mill. In addition to the matter cited in the text, see *The Letters of John Stuart Mill*, ed. by Hugh Elliot (London: Longmans, Green and Co., 1910), vol. II, p. 73: "The duty of truth as a positive duty is . . . to be considered on the ground of whether more good or harm would follow to mankind in general if it were generally disregarded, and not merely whether good or harm would follow in a particular case."

CHAPTERS VIII AND IX · THE CATEGORICAL
IMPERATIVE

The greater part of Chapter VIII appeared as an essay in *The Philosophical Review*, vol. LXIII (October 1954), pp. 577-91.

On Kant's ethics in general, the best commentary I know of is *The Categorical Imperative*, by H. J. Paton (Chicago: The University of Chicago Press, 1948). Not to be overlooked is the valuable analysis of the argument, and the notes to the text, contained in Paton's translation of the *Grundlegung*, entitled *The Moral Law* (London: Hutchinson's University Library, 1948). A work that has just come to hand, and that bids fair to rival Paton's, and is certainly a valuable supplement to it, is Lewis White Beck's *A Commentary on Kant's Critique of Practical Reason* (Chicago: The University of Chicago Press, 1960). Another work of interest, though the issues of the present work are subsidiary in it, is *Practical Reason and Morality*, by A. R. C. Duncan (Edinburgh: Thomas Nelson and Sons, Ltd., 1957); see p. 154: "That Kant did attempt to use his principle as a practical criterion cannot be questioned; his own words and the general consensus of opinion among his critics all point in the same direction. There is also unanimity among his critics that Kant's attempt is unsuccessful in any form." This last statement has all the earmarks of a disguised tautology.

PRINCIPLE OF UNIVERSALITY. I shall cite here a number of valuable or interesting articles. They are all worth reading. The great mass of material on this topic is not.

Beck, Lewis White: "Apodictic Imperatives," *Kant-Studien*, vol. XLIX, no. 1 (1957), pp. 7-24.

Duncan-Jones, Austin: "Kant and Universalisation," *Analysis*, vol. XVI (October 1955), pp. 12-14.

Ebbinghaus, Julius: "Interpretation and Misinterpretation of the Categorical Imperative," *The Philosophical Quarterly*, vol. IV (April 1954), pp. 97-108.

Ewing, A. C.: "The Paradoxes of Kant's Ethics," *Philosophy*, vol. XIII (January 1938), pp. 40-56.

Harrison, Jonathan: "Kant's Examples of the First Formulation of the Categorical Imperative," *The Philosophical Quarterly*, vol. VII (January 1957), pp. 50-62.

————: "The Categorical Imperative," *The Philosophical Quarterly*, vol. VIII (October 1958), pp. 360-4. A reply to Kemp.

Kemp, J.: "Kant's Examples of the Categorical Imperative," *The Philosophical Quarterly*, vol. VIII (January 1958), pp. 63-71.

Kolenda, Konstantin: "Professor Ebbinghaus' Interpretation of the Categorical Imperative," *The Philosophical Quarterly*, vol. V (January 1955), pp. 75-7.

Matson, W. I.: "Kant as Casuist," *The Journal of Philosophy*, vol. LI (December 9, 1954), pp. 855-60.

Paton, H. J.: " 'Kantian Ethics,' " *The Philosophical Quarterly*, vol. II (January 1952), pp. 53-8. A review of Teale's commentary, cited in the text.

————: "An Alleged Right to Lie: A Problem in Kantian Ethics," *Kant-Studien*, vol. XLV (1953-54), pp. 190-203.

————: "The Aim and Structure of Kant's *Grundlegung*," *The Philosophical Quarterly*, vol. VIII (April 1958), pp. 112-30. A review of Duncan's book.

THE PRINCIPLE OF PERSONALITY. I can cite nothing here, in addition to the items already cited, of any value whatsoever. What has been written on the subject consists largely either of panegyrics or naive rejections.

CHAPTER X · THE BASIS OF MORALITY

I shall here mention only some items relating to some of the subsidiary topics dealt with in this chapter. No doubt my highly selective citations will be thought highly arbitrary. They probably are. But what would happen if I were to refer to everything written on these topics?

PRUDENCE. Two items, out of many, worthy of mention are: John Stuart Mill, *On Liberty* (1859), chap. iv; and W. M. Sibley, "The Rational versus the Reasonable," *The Philosophical Review*, vol. LXII (October 1953), pp. 554-60.

DUTIES TO ONESELF. This section has appeared, with only minor differences, in *Ethics*, vol. LXIX (April 1959), pp. 202-5. It has been discussed by Daniel Kading, "Are there Really No Duties to Oneself," *Ethics*, vol. LXX (January 1960), pp. 155-7; and by Warner Wick, "More About Duties to Oneself," *Ibid.*, pp. 158-63. There are some interesting parallels, and some significant differences, between my treatment of this topic and the treatment by Kurt Baier, *The Moral Point of View* (Ithaca: Cornell University Press, 1958), chap. IX.

MORAL MOTIVATION. There is a great mass of material on this, some of it quite valuable. But I shall mention only three items.

Baier, Kurt, *The Moral Point of View*, chap. XI and XII.
Frankena, William K.: "Obligation and Motivation in Recent Moral Philosophy," in *Essays in Moral Philosophy*, ed. by A. I. Melden (Seattle: University of Washington Press, 1958), pp. 40-81.
Prichard, H. A.: "Does Moral Philosophy Rest on a Mistake?" in *Moral Obligation* (Oxford: The Clarendon Press, 1949).

RELATIVISM. This section, now somewhat expanded, first appeared in "Moral Rules and Principles," in *Essays in Moral Philosophy*, ed. by A. I. Melden, pp. 192-7.

THE USE OF MORAL PRINCIPLES. I have used this heading because it seemed best to fit an item that I just had to mention: John Laird, *An Enquiry into Moral Notions* (London: George Allen & Unwin, Ltd., 1935), pp. 159-62.

INDEX

Absolutism: *see* Rigorism
Abuse: neither characteristic of nor peculiar to moral disputes, 323
Act: *see* Action
Acting: way of, different from way of being treated, 286
Action, 77, 79; types of, 136-7; multiple descriptions of, 140-5; no unique description of, 142; how should be described, 145; distinction from intention not always sharp, 247; notion of elastic, 248; ambiguity of term, 249; notion fluid one, 277; importance of intent and circumstances, 278; not morally determinate apart from maxim, 286
Action rights, 313n
Agreement: absence of no refutation of moral opinion, 322
Alexander, Samuel, *quoted*, 15
Altogether inapplicable: defined, 93-4; in connection with categorical imperative, 296; mentioned, 143, 163, 169, 192
Analogy: appeal to, 39-41, 43
Angels: morality does not apply to, 295
Anthropology, 330, 339
A priori, 263n, 271
Argumentum ad populam, 304
Assault, 333

Baier, Kurt, *quoted*, 103-4n, 338n
Baldwin, Hanson W., *quoted*, 174n
"Because statements," 38, 45
Benevolence: not mandatory, 273
Benevolent motive, 290
Bentham, Jeremy, *quoted*, 194n
Bergson, Henri, *quoted*, 283n
Black, Max, *quoted*, 38, 39; *cited*, 123n
Blackmail, 299
Border-line cases: between prudence and morality, 305-6

Bradley, F. H.: famous phrase of, 283n; *quoted*, 287n; *cited*, 251n
Brandt, Richard B., *quoted*, 297
Brentano, Franz, 279
Bribery, 279-82
Broad, C. D., *quoted*, 91-3 *passim*; *cited*, 175n
Brooks, John, *quoted*, 163-4n

Cabot, Dr. Richard C.: on honesty, 125-8
Caird, Edward, *quoted*, 227n
Caligula, 321
Cardozo, Benjamin N., *quoted*, 117-18
Carritt, E. F., *quoted*, 10-11
Carroll, Lewis, *quoted*, 10
Categorical: senses of term, 223-4
Categorical imperative: involves generalization principle, 9, 253; relations to generalization argument, 9-11, 264, 275-6, 295; in conditional form, 224; *a* distinguished from *the*, 226, 230; does not imply rigorism, 227-8, 238; valid, 239; general method of criticisms of, 239-40; typical misunderstanding of, 240-1; not merely negative principle, 241; can be applied directly to actions, 248; relation to consequences, 261, 263-4; apparent counterexample to, 284, 285; not applicable in abstraction from maxims, 288, 293; applicability presupposes a desire, 293; does not presuppose desirability of institutions, 293; does not require that everyone make promises, 294; conditions for application, 295; need not be applied in moral vacuum, 298; mentioned, 95, 140
Categorical imperatives: false cases of, 226, 230
Causal propositions, 38-40, 45
Celibacy, 151

MARCUS GEORGE SINGER

Marcus George Singer is Professor of Philosophy at the University of Wisconsin in Madison, where he has taught since 1952. He is a co-editor of *Introductory Readings in Philosophy* (1960) and a contributor to *Essays in Moral Philosophy*. His articles and reviews have been published in various philosophical journals.